Abigail & John

ALSO BY EDITH B. GELLES

The Letters of Abigaill Levy Franks, 1733–1746

Abigail Adams: A Writing Life

Portia: The World of Abigail Adams

Abigail & John

PORTRAIT OF A MARRIAGE

Edith B. Gelles

WM

WILLIAM MORROW

An Imprint of HarperCollins*Publishers*

HarperCollins books may be purchased for educational, business, or sales promotional use.
For information please write: Special Markets Department, HarperCollins Publishers,
10 East 53rd Street, New York, NY 10022.

FIRST EDITION

Designed by Sunil Manchikanti

Library of Congress Cataloging-in-Publication Data

Gelles, Edith Belle.
   Abigail and John : portrait of a marriage / Edith B. Gelles.—1st ed.
      p. cm.
   Includes bibliographical references.
   ISBN: 978-0-06-135387-1
    1. Adams, John, 1735–1826—Marriage.   2. Adams, Abigail, 1744–1818—Marriage.
3. Presidents—United States—Biography.   4. Presidents' spouses—United States—
Biography.   5. Married people—Massachusetts—Biography.   I. Title.

   E322.G456   2009
   973.4'40922—dc22
   [B]   2008047072

09 10 11 12 13   WBC/RRD   10 9 8 7 6 5 4 3 2 1

For Leila

Contents

Contents

Preface

This is the first double biography of Abigail and John Adams. While biographies of both founders have appeared in recent years, none treats the marriage of the Adamses with the balanced attention that their extraordinary relationship deserves. Biographies of John Adams extol Abigail as his wife, and most biographies of Abigail Adams do the same. Still, no one has written about Abigail and John in tandem; nor, for that matter, has any founding couple received attention in partnership. History has treated the founding of the United States as an exclusive male enterprise. One reason for this is that biographers and historians mostly focus on the political, military, and diplomatic aspects of the era. Scant attention is paid to the social world, where women primarily functioned. This double biography of Abigail and John Adams examines their remarkable marriage in the context of the revolutionary and federal periods by shifting the historical lens to their family.

This is possible because the letters of Abigail Adams, alone among the wives of the founders, have survived, hundreds of them, and Abigail could write. Her letters are artistry. She had the gift of language and she told stories. Her surviving letters are the best record that we have of a woman's experience during the revolutionary era. And John Adams wrote back. John was undoubtedly the greatest literary stylist among the founders. His letters fairly tingle with passion; his personality is revealed with raw insight in a torrent of words that bring life to his world. Between them, and with wit, intelligence, and humor, the world of the founders, the men and the women, comes alive. Only by seeing the

Adamses in tandem, as a couple, can we fully understand John or Abigail Adams and their lives and times.

Abigail and John Adams were married for fifty-four years, a not-uncommon occurrence in the late eighteenth century, when there existed few exit clauses to the bonds of marriage. Couples married for life. The Adamses followed the example set by their own parents and grandparents, aunts and uncles, cousins and friends. Their marriage has been mythologized in American history. Just the mention of Abigail and John calls forth an image of an ideal relationship, one founded upon love, loyalty, friendship, and courage, which it was.

Their union appears modern because it possessed many of the attributes of a successful marriage as we think of it today. It was a love match that endured. It produced a famous son and established a dynasty of great citizens. It overcame adversity intact. Most important, it was a marriage of equals. Abigail's intelligence, wisdom, and strength flourished alongside that of her husband, lending credibility to her more equal status. That happened because of both their characters. Both of them required parity in a life partner. Abigail developed into an erudite woman, because of her own ambitions and talents, but also because John needed a wife he could talk to. John became the leading lawyer, statesman, and diplomat that he did because Abigail, if she didn't always encourage him, never prevented his involvement, whatever the cost to his family.

Still, there should be no misunderstanding that the Adamses did not experience a typical eighteenth-century marriage, for they did. They lived in a culture that survived from the earliest Puritan settlers of Massachusetts. Each of them represented a different strain of that New England background. Abigail Smith's forebears were famous Puritan clerics and later politicians and merchants. John Adams came from the class of yeoman farmers and skilled artisans that populated the early settlements. Both of them grew up in religious communities that left no doubt in their minds about the questions of good and bad or right and wrong. Abigail, more than John, attributed all of her experiences to Providence and therefore accepted adversity as a given in life. John was governed by his compulsion to make a better world rather than to accept what existed. Religion, in the end, was a fundamental force in both their lives.

It was the religion of their New England Puritan forebears, refined into a secular way of life by the end of the eighteenth century, that explains their concept of marriage as well as their patriotism. Fundamental to their behavior was duty, which to them meant service. The purpose of life was to serve, to perform acts of virtue and generosity, to sacrifice for the community and for the improvement of the world.

Their eighteenth-century concept of marriage also required the performance of duty in their "different departments," as Abigail told it, the man in the public world and the woman within the domestic world. Because of the Revolution, Abigail and John had to reassess their traditional marriage; they renegotiated the terms of their covenant. Abigail always believed that John's service to his nation—the performance of his worldly duty, the sacrifice of their years together that both of them made—was synonymous with the success of the Revolution. John never questioned whether that was the case.

So, while the marriage of Abigail and John Adams appears modern in many respects, it can best be understood in the context of their early Massachusetts background, against the world of Puritan New England where they grew up and lived. They represented a transitional era in the history of marriage just as they participated in the revolution that separated America from its colonial past into its modernist present. Abigail Smith Adams and John Adams were unique individuals. They loved each other; they enjoyed each other's company; they relied upon each other even when apart; they trusted each other and were loyal. When asked at the end of their lives what had been the hardest experience of their long years, both separately replied that it was living apart for so many years. For people who believed in sacrifice as a way of life, theirs was the ultimate performance of duty as mandated by their Puritan past.

The Steel and the Magnet

WHEN ABIGAIL SMITH DECIDED TO MARRY JOHN ADAMS IN 1764, she made the most fateful decision of her life. As a young eighteenth-century woman, she knew that marriage was her destiny and her only latitude was the selection of a mate. She needed to choose well. Her parents' opinions carried weight, but they were not conclusive. Her relatives and community might have thoughts, but in the end it would be her own sound judgment and feelings that were the determining factors. She would measure his character and test his affections and hope that her perceptions were accurate. He was educated, appeared honest and sober, was very industrious, and had high ambitions, so finally, after more than three years of courtship, she judged that John had met her standards. He certainly had won her heart.

When John Adams chose to marry Abigail Smith, he made the most fortuitous decision of his life. A twenty-nine-year-old man, he had already made several choices that would shape his future. As the eldest son in his family, he had fulfilled his parents' wishes and graduated from Harvard. However, going against their expectations, he rejected the life of a clergyman and settled instead upon the law as a profession. When he chose Abigail as his life's companion, he took yet another important step. She was attractive, came from a highly respectable family, and had youthful energy. Moreover, her greatest assets would be her steadiness of temperament, her intelligence, and her great sympathy for his ambitions. He believed that his destiny could be fulfilled with Abigail as his companion.

If, as the saying goes, some marriages are made in heaven, the Adams marriage was. They could have hoped, but they could not have known, as their courtship progressed, that this would be the case. Indeed, as the date for their marriage ceremony came closer, both of them became anxious. John postponed the event several times, and Abigail got sick just weeks before their fixed date. Both of them wavered before the commitment that would seal their destinies. Then they took their vows and entered into a marriage bond that has become legendary. But they were not the only ones to express reservations about it.

Rumor has it that when the Reverend William Smith preached the sermon at his daughter Abigail's marriage ceremony on October 25, 1764, he chose for his text "For John came, neither eating bread nor drinking wine, and Ye say 'He hath a Devil.'" Even in the mid-eighteenth century's still-puritanical New England, his topic lacked felicity. Nor did it suggest the optimism or comfort that was generally associated with a wedding, especially the marriage of one's own daughter. Family members and biographers have puzzled over his sermon for more than two centuries. Perhaps he or his wife, Elizabeth, disapproved of their daughter's marriage. He could not have meant to disparage his new son-in-law before family and friends. Maybe, even more likely, he intended to set some record straight within the larger community. Rumors communicate coded information, and clearly, the good reverend was surreptitiously sending a message on that fall day in the parsonage at Weymouth, Massachusetts, when the bright-eyed nineteen-year-old Abigail Smith married twenty-nine-year-old John Adams of neighboring Braintree.

The portrait that survives of Abigail's father, the Reverend William Smith, is a sober picture, in black-and-white hues, a typical image of a New England clergyman. Its most striking features are his eyes, similar to his daughter's, and the furrowed mouth, clamped shut to hide toothless gums. The long visage, framed by a shoulder-length wig, is not unkindly but observant and commanding. The reverend was a strong man, a leader, one accustomed to directing the lives of his parishioners with the fierce determination of a latter-day Puritan. Moreover, this was a man who had experienced a long, satisfying life, marked not only by lengthy hours in the pulpit but also by the prosperity of his family. Significantly, Smith had his portrait painted as a legacy to his children to remind them of their ancestry among the distinguished early Puritan settlers of New England.

For more than fifty years, William Smith had served as the minister of Weymouth's First Congregational Church, preaching two long sermons every Sunday to parishioners who warmed themselves in winter under layers of clothing with containers of hot coals tucked into their wraps or sweated through sum-

mer heat for endless hours on uncomfortable wooden benches. On
Thursdays, he again preached, a
gruelling schedule of delivering
"the word" to a community that, try
as they would, violated regularly the
parson's sound admonitions. Perfection was just too hard, though,
for them, as for their forebears, the
goal of perfect character determined life's purpose.

No portrait survives of Elizabeth Smith, the reverend's wife and
Abigail's mother. Elizabeth's legacy was her maiden name: Quincy.
She was born Elizabeth Norton
Quincy, and her parents' distinguished past represented two different branches of Puritan pedigree,
the religious elect of the Norton
line from her mother and the political elite of her father, John Quincy,

*The Reverend William Smith, father of Abigail
Adams, served for more than fifty years as
minister in Weymouth's First Congregational
Church. Courtesy of the Massachusetts
Historical Society.*

"the Duke of Braintree," the neighboring village to Weymouth.

Life in the small towns in which the Smith and the Adams families resided
was not so different from that of their forebears who had come to the shores of
the Massachusetts Bay Colony in the seventeenth century. Typically they represented a broad range of middle-class yeomen, people who depended upon the
land for their survival. They represented the main streams of developing New
England society, the clergy and the merchants, artisans such as Deacon Adams,
politicians, and farmers. The women and the men worked together to provide
for their large families, their tasks separated by gender. They lived in a dangerous world, made that way not just by the clashing of character and motives
among themselves but also because the physical dangers of disease were en-
demic. So, too, were the larger dangers posed by sometimes brutal nature.
Nearby were the dispossessed of the country, the natives who still lived on the
land that they never knew they had surrendered, now grown into the villages
and towns of the Massachusetts Bay Colony.

Weymouth, the birthplace of Abigail Smith, lies on a little promontory,
protected from the swells and raging waves of the Atlantic Ocean by a small

peninsula, the Hull, and several little islands. It was in this natural seaport that its first settlers—a group of men only, headed by commercial traders who also had funded the Plymouth colony down the coastline—set up their trading venture. Called Wessagussett after the Indian name for the area, this was the second colony, after Plymouth, to have been settled in the Massachusetts Bay area. Unlike Plymouth, however, Wessagusset was founded for commercial purposes in 1622, to trade with the remnants of the local Indian tribes for fur, timber, and fish. This was Weymouth's first incarnation, and it quickly failed because of the indolence and the mercenary motives of its settlers.

A second attempt at settlement, also a commercial venture, included women and children and succeeded temporarily. Renamed Weymouth after the village in England, where most of the immigrants originated, the village had as many as three hundred inhabitants by the time the Puritans arrived at Boston in 1630. But their situation now became precarious; their little colony was nestled between two settlements of a very different nature, Plymouth with its Pilgrim zealots and Boston with its Puritan zealots. Weymouth's heterodox population included papists, as the Puritans referred to followers of the Church of England, Quakers, and even some Catholics. To the colonists on either side of Weymouth, who had risked their lives and livelihoods to emigrate to this barren forest land in order to plant communities as model cities on hills, exemplary cities devoted passionately to heavenly service, such heterodoxy was intolerable. The unwelcome residents of Weymouth were driven out, "warned out" in Puritan parlance, and moved to more hospitable communities in Rhode Island or Connecticut, and the bay area remained theologically "pure," at least for a time.

We know these stories in great part because Charles Francis Adams, grandson of Abigail and John, wrote about the earliest settlers of both Weymouth and Braintree, where his ancestors, Henry Adams among them, planted roots. Moreover, Charles Francis inherited a penchant for storytelling, a talent of his time that provided not only an evening's entertainment but also a sense of history, family history that connected one generation to another. Abigail and John Adams knew these stories, which contributed to their sense of identity as children of New England and bound them forever both in character and spirit to the villages where they grew up.

Charles Francis Adams, for instance, wrote about the legendary Thomas Weston, the merchant promoter of both the Plymouth and Wessagusset "plantations." Motivated by the twin pursuits of adventure and profit, he, too, represented an early-Massachusetts archetype called a Yankee, the kind of man who was independent, industrious, risk-taking, rebellious, ambitious, and materialistic.

Weston and his "merry making" fellows were eventually "warned out" of the area by his neighbors, the Puritans, because of his "lascivious" behavior. They had built a Maypole and, in infidel fashion, danced and drank spirits and cavorted with "fur-clad Indian maidens." The Puritans, both disgusted and threatened by this behavior, banished him and established instead an orderly village along the lines of their own. Notwithstanding this purge, the plantation spirit survived not only in folklore and commerce, but also in one small Church of England parish that continued to function into the mid-eighteenth century when Abigail Smith was born in Weymouth, where her father, the Reverend William Smith, accepted his call to the pulpit of the First Congregational Church, where he served for fifty years.

Just up the coast from Abigail's Weymouth home lay Braintree, the Adamses' homesite. John's ancestor Henry Adams, whose name his progeny would proudly carry on, arrived in 1638 with his wife, Edith, and eight sons from Somersetshire in England. The next-to-youngest of their sons, called Joseph, was the grandfather of John Adams, and he continued the family line in Braintree, but not the family business. Henry Adams, who had been a malster in England, brought this skill to the New World, where it was continued through several generations. The production of malt from barley for household use and in beer couldn't support large families. But Henry's original grant of "forty acres for a family of ten heads" insured their comfortable survival as yeomen farmers.

The land and the occupations remained in the family into the nineteenth century. Over the years, the property was subdivided and expanded many times as fathers bequeathed land to younger sons. It was family tradition that the elder sons received a Harvard education in preparation for entering the clergy, just as was the case with John Adams, who chose instead to become a lawyer. Of John's two brothers, Peter lived on the family farm in Braintree until his death in 1823, as did Elihu, who died of disease as a soldier in the American Revolution. Remarkably, the letters that survive from John Adams's brothers are barely literate.

On both sides, over the long century, the families of Quincy, Smith, Norton, Shepard, Adams, Boylston, and many more proliferated. With each generation the family trees expanded with branches and twigs and new roots planted by marriage until the generations of Abigail and John. There was a vast network of relatives who lived near one another and called themselves aunts, uncles, and cousins. They married into and out of the family until it became common to know Thaxters, Storers, Palmers, and Tuftses as relatives. It was the proximity of this large family network that gave stability and identity to Abigail and John as their generation matured. In the subtle ways that family matters, those relationships provided support and security, even when they launched into the work of fomenting a revolution. The generational and broad kinship connections—Samuel Adams was a second cousin to John, for instance—eased and made common all of their enterprises. Family ties implied loyalty and trust.

But it wasn't only family that mattered. Neighbors were familiar. The Veseys, the Hancocks, the Pratts, and the Nashes had lived in these small villages for generations. They met constantly in the streets; some worked as servants in their households, and others were laborers. Children played and attended school together and exchanged books and toys. They all went to church, some as Anglicans but most as Congregationalists, having inherited the religion of their forebears, who came in the great migrations of the early seventeenth century.

That lingering legacy from the Puritans, transformed now into more liberal Congregational denominations, still resonated in their disciplined code of behavior. Sunday was their day of rest, prayer, and church, where they mingled despite differences in class and gender. No longer was church seating separated by sex; no longer was church attendance mandatory. The law that required regular observance had been abolished, but people attended meeting anyway, not just because of piety but also because of social pressure. Violation of Sabbath rules was unacceptable in that still-religious world where Abigail Smith and John Adams grew up. Besides, church was the place where they could see one another and socialize afterward.

Throughout her youth, Abigail Smith, alongside her mother, Elizabeth, her two sisters, and her one younger brother, sat through sermons, not just because she was the daughter of the minister but also because in that lackluster world of rural Massachusetts, a religious gathering provided entertainment and social life. It was school; it was theater; it was companionship. And at the same time that the young Abigail was listening to yet another long discourse by her distinguished father, not far away, in another meetinghouse in another rural town, the young John Adams was sitting in his church listening to a sermon.

John's observance also was insured by his father's position as a deacon in the church. Although not so elevated a status as minister, it was a role that was revered for its service as well as piety. John Adams Sr. was a farmer and cordwainer, the eighteenth-century's term for shoemaker. A man of great energy, Deacon John, aside from his religious devotion, volunteered for numerous important roles in his community. He became a lieutenant in the local militia, the tax collector, and a selectman for the town of Braintree's governing body.

Young John Adams, too, attended many weekly sermons with his mother and two younger brothers. Susanna Boylston Adams, mother of the deacon's three sons, descended from yet another line in the bay colony's elite circles. Her great-uncle Dr. Zabdiel Boylston had introduced the smallpox vaccine to the British colonies earlier in the eighteenth century, a gigantic stride in medical reform in that age when epidemics of many sorts decimated whole communities. Her marriage to a farmer was always remarked as a comedown from her privileged background. She might have seen it that way as well.

But young John Adams didn't notice; he wanted to be a farmer like his father, and his early life was marked by the pleasures of outdoor living, not by the books that would later become his passion. "I spent my time as idle Children do," he recorded many years later, "in making and flying Kites, in driving hoops, playing marbles, playing Quoits, Wrestling, Swimming, Skaiting." His father became alarmed and pressed John to concentrate more on his studies. "I told [him I did not?] love Books and wished he would lay aside the thoughts of sending me to Colledge," John continued his reminiscence. "What would you do Child? Be a Farmer. A Farmer? Well I will shew you what it is to be a Farmer."

The next day John's father took him along for a day of arduous physical labor cutting thatch. At the end of that long day his father inquired: "Well John are you satisfied with being a Farmer." The work had been hard and "very muddy," but the son responded that he liked it very much. "Ay I don't like it so well; so you shall go to School to day," his father responded.

Grudgingly, the son returned to school, but he didn't like his schoolmaster, whom he considered lazy and ill-tempered. Some time later, John again requested to be released from the drudgery of a school that bored him, and this time, understanding his son's reasons, his father enrolled him in a private school, where the young John resumed his studies with enthusiasm. "To this School I went, where I was kindly treated, and I began to study in Earnest." In little more than a year, Mr. Marsh, his new schoolmaster, pronounced the young man ready to take the entrance exams for Harvard, and despite his great anxiety, John passed with ease to become a member of the Harvard class of 1755.

Another story about John's early home life was telling of the dynamics in the Adams family. His father had returned home from a town meeting one afternoon, bringing with him a destitute young woman who lived on the town dole. He hoped that his wife would take her in as a servant girl. This was not the case, and the hot-tempered Susanna became enraged. "I wont have all the Towns Poor brought here, stark naked, for me to clothe for nothing." Deacon John, in turn, claimed patriarchal authority and "resolutely asserted his Right to govern." The mother scolded; the servants wept; and the young brothers ran away to hide. The elderly John recorded this incident with amusement, recalling the tensions in the Adams household and the characters of both his parents. His memory of a volatile home life was more characteristic of family living than the tranquility that the Reverend William Smith preached as the ideal of marital harmony.

Abigail's early days were spent in a more genteel environment, not only in the parsonage of her parents, but also at Mount Wollaston, the mansion of her Quincy grandparents, and among other relatives. Her uncle Isaac Smith was one of Boston's most prosperous merchants. He and his wife, the former Elizabeth Storer, whose lavish portraits were painted by John Singleton Copley, lived on Boston's thriving Beacon Hill. Abigail's other grandmother, for whom she was named, Abigail Fowle Smith Edwards, possessed a fortune in her own right, and she, too, lived in Boston. On her extended visits to these relatives, Abigail experienced an urban culture that looked to England for its model of social behavior, more so than to its Puritan forebears.

Abigail never attended a public school. Many years later, she explained the reason to her own granddaughter. As a young girl, she suffered from rheumatic fever. In order to protect her from contagious diseases as well as the risks from sitting long hours on benches in a chilly room, they kept her at home. Her parents educated Abigail, which was not uncommon for young women. Her mother was her primary teacher, but her grandmother Quincy, a formidable reader, helped as well. "I shall never forget the maxims of my own grandmother," she reminisced about the "wild and giddy days" of her youth. In addition, she was permitted to browse in her father's considerable library, which included books on theology, of course, but also history and literature.

Rev. Smith had accumulated a collection from which he often made loans to parishioners, especially volumes of the *Spectator,* which was read by eighteenth-century people in the same way that *The New Yorker* is read today. The *Spectator* contained news, poems, and stories, all of which connected the colonial educated class to culture in England. When Parson Smith lent his volumes to his neighbors, he recorded the transaction in his diary, presumably to keep track of their whereabouts: "To Mr. Gay 1 vol. History of ye Reformation . . . To Mr. Shute 1 vol. Of Dr. Watts Sermon . . . To Deb[orah] Badlam 1 vol. Of Spectator." His middle daughter, Abigail, read them as well.

But she also spent hours at home in the parsonage writing. One exercise that she was assigned, probably by her parents, was copying, something John Adams reported that he did, too. As a pedagogical practice, students learned their lessons by copying texts into copybooks. Abigail also regularly wrote personal letters, which was her method of staying in touch with friends. Young women,

Abigail among them, recorded the ordinary and routine events of their daily lives, but they also described the romances they had read, sometimes by candlelight after overwhelming darkness enveloped that rural world in the age before electricity. And they confessed their fantasies to one another, perhaps about travel to foreign countries, more often about their beaux. Abigail also learned rudimentary French, a language she described to her cousin Isaac Smith Jr. as "Sweet, and harmonious," and, she presumed, "pretty much now, what I have heard the Latin formerly was, a universal tongue." As a girl, she was not taught Latin.

John was reading both Latin and Greek literature at Harvard. Much of his interest focused, as well, on mathematics and natural philosophy, as science was called. Later, as an upperclassman, he joined a club where "Poetry or Dramatic Compositions" were recited, and he became a favorite speaker. "It was whispered to me and circulated among others that I had some faculty for public Speaking and that I should make a better Lawyer than Divine." At the same time, he decided that he was unsuited to the life of a clergyman.

Most of his Harvard friends had chosen their professions by the time they graduated. Some, like Moses Hemmenway, became ministers; others, like Samuel Quincy, went into business, often the family business, and a good number went on to study the law. His friend Jonathan Sewall was among the latter. Some of these men, after living so closely together for four years, studying the same subjects, stimulated by the same master tutors in their era—Jonathan Mayhew and John Winthrop—became lifelong friends. Some of them would be allied in the business of making the revolution that they had no idea would be the paramount event of their futures; other friendships would be strained to the point of breaking over that fateful revolution. For John Adams, the richness of the Harvard experience lay in galvanizing not only his intellectual world but his social world as well.

John graduated from Harvard, however, with a dilemma. He had rejected one profession, but his family did not have the resources to support his preparation in another. For the time being, then, he needed to support himself; the one clear option before him was to become a schoolmaster. He accepted a position at Worcester, west of Braintree, a day's journey by horse. He packed up his books and his few other possessions of value and headed into the unknown world of pedagogy. His initial reaction, written to his friend Richard Cranch, was not promising. "The school is indeed a school of affliction, a large number of little runtlings, just capable of lisping A.B.C. and troubling the Master," he complained. "I am certain that the keeping this school any length of Time would make a base weed and ignoble shrub of me." That was his novice reaction to teaching.

Several months later his foul mood had changed, and more comfortable with his students, he observed with great seriousness: "I find by repeated experiment and observation, in my School, that human nature is more easily wrought upon and governed, by promises and incouragement and praise than by punishment, and threatning and Blame." Then, more whimsically, he allowed his imagination to soar: "I sometimes, in my sprightly moments, consider my self, in my great Chair at School, as some Dictator at the head of a commonwealth." He continued his fantasy:

> In this little State I can discover all the great Genius's, all the surprizing actions and revolution of the great World in miniature. I have severall renowned Generalls but 3 feet high, and several deep-projecting Politicians in peticoats. . . . At one Table sits Mr. Insipid foppling and fluttering, spinning his whirligig, or playing with his fingers as gaily and wittily as any frenchified coxcomb brandishes his Cane or rattles his snuff box. At another sitts the polemical Divine, plodding and wrangling in his mind about Adam's fall in which we sinned all as his primmer has it. In short my little school like the great World, is made up of Kings, Politicians, Divines, LLD's, Fops, Buffoons, Fidlers, Sychophants, Fools, Coxcombs, chimney sweepers, and every other Character drawn in History or seen in the World.

Adams had made peace with teaching, and in the diary that he began to keep during those years, he exposed the gentle part of his nature. He expressed fondness for his little scholars, but he did it in his unique style; in a clever little portrait, he imagined their futures as grown-ups.

These qualities of Adams's—his humor, his deep sensitivity to human nature, his empathy, and his brilliant capacity to express it all in language that was at once satirical and eloquent—would later endear him to Abigail when they met as lovers. At present, much of John's composure had to do with his finally resolving his professional dilemma.

In late August 1756 he made his fateful decision. "Yesterday I completed a contract with Mr. Putnam to study Law under his Inspection for two years," he wrote without fanfare. With this abrupt announcement, John Adams began his apprenticeship with Worcester lawyer James Putnam, and he moved into the Putnam house to read law under his mentorship.

Two years later, he moved home to practice law in Braintree. To his enormous dismay, he mishandled his first case by improperly drafting a writ, the legal document required by the court. His first reaction was to blame his mother for encouraging him to take the case. He had wanted to decline it, but by the "cruel Reproaches of my Mother," he took it after all. "I was seduced from that determination, and what is the Consequence? The Writt is defective," he wrote in gloom.

He next concluded that the real culprit of this disaster was Putnam. "Now I feel the Dissadvantages of Putnams Insociability, and neglect of me. Had he given me now and then a few Hints concerning Practice, I should be able to judge better at this Hour than I can now." John had been poorly prepared for courtroom procedure, he whined. "I have Reason to complain of him. But," he wrote, continuing, his descent into self-pity, "it is my Destiny to dig Treasures with my own fingers. No Body will lend me or sell me a Pick axe."

John, nevertheless, dusted off his ego, as he would do many times in the future, and headed into Boston to look for a mentor who would further his mastery of the legal profession. It was his good fortune that the great Jeremiah Gridley, one of Boston's foremost legal minds, recognized John's talents and took him on to read law. Gridley, however, would demand discipline of his new protégé. Pursue the law and not the gain of it, he admonished. Don't socialize, and don't marry too early. "An early marriage will obstruct your improvement . . . and twill involve you in expense." He then sent John off to read Coke's *Institutes of the Laws of England*.

John bound himself to this agreement, but reluctantly because he was twenty-three years old. The pledge to avoid social life entirely, and particularly female companionship, pained him. He was far too extroverted to isolate himself entirely with the law books that Mr. Gridley gave him. Still, he mastered his assigned readings so successfully that Gridley invited him to participate in an elite club of lawyers that met to discuss legal theory. But the command to avoid socializing proved too hard. He managed to fulfill his commitment to Gridley while also keeping company with friends.

In fact, John was under the spell of a different romance when he and Abigail met for the first time in the summer of 1759. His visit to the Weymouth parsonage occurred because he accompanied his good friend Richard Cranch, who was courting Abigail's older sister, Mary. "Polly and Nabby are Wits," he noted dismissively, using the Smith sisters' nicknames. John meant that Abigail and Mary were smart and clever, that they sparkled in conversation. Perhaps he was even intimidated by the young women's erudition. They certainly were interesting and lively. John, however, was currently enamored of Hannah Quincy, a cousin of Abigail's, whom he had met the previous winter.

During that winter, while he was still bound to read law with Jeremiah Gridley, John ardently pursued Hannah. Attractive and flirtatious, she, in turn, was the object of attention from several men, and she was eager to marry in order to escape a difficult stepmother. John was torn between his commitment to Gridley not to marry and competition for the affections of the popular Hannah. Typically, when faced with a tough decision, John fretted and weighed his options. He assessed her character. Hannah was "apparently frank, but really reserved, seemingly pleased, and almost charmed, when she is really laughing with Contempt. Her face and Hart have no Correspondence," he confided to his diary. Still, he went for long walks in the woods with her and recorded at length their conversations, all the while measuring, hesitating, worrying about his future. "What am I doing? Shall I sleep away my whole 70 Years."

Finally, he made his decision. He would propose courtship to Hannah, a step that was tantamount to an engagement. He set the stage carefully, arranging a tryst at her home one evening while her family slept. Then, as they sat alone in her parlor and he cautiously moved their conversation in the direction of his intentions, suddenly "Sewal and Esther broke in upon H. and me." This was his friend Jonathan Sewall and his fiancée Esther Quincy, Hannah's sister. The moment was ruined, and John did not propose.

He later reflected, "Accidents, as we call them, govern a great Part of the World." This conversation "would . . . have terminated in a Courtship, which would have terminated in a Marriage, which Marriage might have depressed me to absolute Poverty and obscurity to the End of my Life." In retrospect, he was relieved. Hannah instead became engaged to Dr. Bela Lincoln, a union that her father had preferred, since John had yet to prove himself in his profession.

Nevertheless, John continued to pine over Hannah for a long time and into the period when Abigail Smith attracted his attention. Moping still, he could not resist comparing them. Hannah was expressive, he confirmed to himself. "Good nature is H's universal Character. She will be a fond, obliging, tender Wife, and a fond indulgent Mother," qualities that he found attractive. "Are fondness and Wit compatible?" he queried, and responded: "P[arson] S[mith']s girls have not this fondness, nor this Tenderness." John judged harshly, but he was blinded by his lingering, though futile, attachment to Hannah.

And Abigail was only fifteen years old. She had no beaux until John Adams appeared on the scene in the summer of 1759. Nor did she record her initial impressions of him. She was living out her romantic fantasy through her sister's courtship with the shy though persistent Richard Cranch. Despite Cranch's stiff and reserved manner, Mary, who was—and would be for her lifetime— Abigail's best friend after John Adams, found his serious demeanor and intelligence attractive. She set Abigail the example by looking beyond the surface qualities to traits that would make him an enduring companion. And John, despite his dismissive judgments about the Smiths, continued to accompany Cranch to the parsonage for many months. In time, Abigail caught his eye. Abigail, in turn, had become interested in this voluble, sometimes arrogant young lawyer who continually reappeared.

She had also heard the gossip about John's former attachment to Hannah, by now married to Dr. Lincoln. As her feelings for Adams intensified, Abigail made her claim to him known to her cousin. When Hannah wrote to inquire why she had failed to respond to her letters, Abigail returned with a stinging reply. "Believe me, it has not been through forgetfulness," she began in language freighted with conventional though disingenuous politeness. She then encoded her message in an enigmatic parable:

> You have, like king Ahasuerus, held forth, though not a golden Scepter, yet one more valuable, the scepter of friendship, if I may so call it. Like Esther, I would draw nigh and touch it. Will you proceed and say, "What wilt thou?" and "What is thy request? it shall be given thee to the half of my heart." Why, no. I think I will not have so dangerous a present.

Her text was the biblical story of Esther, though she scrambled the characters to camouflage her real meaning. Hannah had offered Abigail a "dangerous" scepter, friendship, and Abigail questioned her cousin's motives. She disguised her suspicion by deleting the third person from the tale of Ahasuerus, his wife, Vashti, whom the Persian king had executed before he married the young maiden Esther.

Abigail told the tale of a triad, two women, who were rivals for one man, but she left the space empty where the second woman should have appeared. A religiously educated person would know the true meaning of the story: Once a rival was married (or executed), she could not pursue her former admirer. He was now available to the other.

Abigail wrote this inspired message to the woman who had been the object of John Adams's affections for several years, and whom Abigail still suspected of a lingering flirtation with him. Abigail was coy, but her real meaning was clear to Hannah; there had been a rivalry. Now that Hannah was married, Abigail wrote, her attentions were no longer welcome. Her friendship was now a "dangerous present."

Their romance began to flourish. "Here we are Dick and Jack," John wrote to her inside a message from Richard Cranch to Mary Smith on the last day of 1761. Using fanciful ordinary names, he teased her about "commencing a most loyal subject to young George." The twenty-two-year-old George III had just ascended the throne of England, a topic that was obviously of great interest to them, and John continued his message to Abigail, writing, "Altho my Allegiance has been hitherto inviolate I shall endeavour, all in my power to foment Rebellion." John wrote in jest, but his words would be prophetic in another decade. He was challenging Abigail; he meant that if she were loyal to King George III, he, for argument's sake, would be disloyal. This banter was a test of each other's wit.

Less than a year later, by the fall of 1762, John had completed his apprenticeship with Jeremiah Gridley and was beginning his independent practice of the law from an office at home in Braintree. He was also liberated from his commitment to remain single. His romance with Abigail took root, and he wrote to her, still in a light tone but this time with ardor: "I presume I have good Right to draw upon you for the Kisses as I have given two or three Millions at least, when one has been received, and of Consequence the Account between us is immensely in favour of yours, John Adams." They had moved into serious courtship, which, in that era before central heating, included the practice of bundling, a custom that John highly approved of, according to his diary. With parental approval, a young couple might snuggle under blankets to keep warm.

Some time later he wrote in the language of his profession: "I have taken the best Advice, on the subject of your Billet, and I find you cannot compel me to *pay* unless I refuse Marriage; which I never did, and never will, but on the Contrary am ready to *have you* at any Time." Underscoring both "pay" and "have you," he makes clear that they had gone beyond that stage to talk about marriage.

Before them was the example of Mary Smith and Richard Cranch, who had married that fall. John recorded that after the ceremony, the men, as was the custom, gathered in a separate room to tell bawdy "matrimonial stories." Dr. Tufts, uncle to the bride, began the merriment with the tale of "B. Bicknal's Wife."

She had been "very anxious, she feared, she trembled, she could not go to Bed." Tufts continued his tale: "She put her Hand to the Plow and could not look back, so she mustered up her Spirits, committed her soul to G[od] and her Body to B. Bicknal." In the morning, she could not think "for her Life what it was that had scared her so." There were other stories, John mused in his diary, but he did not record them.

John did not preserve Abigail's letters to him either. Only the romantic disposition of a young woman in love accounts for the survival of a few of John's letters to Abigail. His diary is silent on the subject of romance during his three years of courtship with Abigail. But he did write about his growing success as a lawyer in the Massachusetts Bay area. And he fantasized that if his practice developed sufficiently in two or three years, he might move to Boston. To the privacy of his diary, he confided his aspirations for the distant future: "Before 20 Years," he exhorted himself, "you will raise the fees of the Bar 3 fold." He recorded his vast reading that was not confined to law but also included ancient history, travel and science, in essence, the enthusiasms of a restless and voracious mind. He listed, too, his observations of the exploits and follies of human behavior: "The Character of Aunt Nell exemplified. Mrs. Eunice told us the Catastrophe of two of her Teeth, she broke them out at Table in Company, and to avoid exposing her self, swallowed them."

He was, furthermore, distracted by other factors during the spring and summer of 1761. His father died in May, another deeply affecting event that he skipped in his diary, for John had been close to his father. Also, as a result of the deacon's passing, John inherited considerable property, which meant that along with his growing caseload and prosperity as a lawyer, he was in a position to marry. In addition to the house that was left to him, he received ten acres of adjoining farmland as well as thirty acres of swampland that was not connected to the house. John by this time had become a fairly comfortable man.

He also began to develop a public image as a citizen. He published letters and articles in the Boston newspapers and began a local campaign opposing taverns, railing against dissipation and profligacy. He emerged under the folksy pseudonym of Humphrey Ploughjogger, writing, "Thes fue Lins cums to let you no, that I am very wel at present." He became known within the legal community by traveling the court circuits, which is how lawyers earned their livings.

Courts were convened seasonally in small villages and towns along the Massachusetts Bay coastline. Legal counsels traveled to those communities to serve the litigants, so that sometimes John was on the court circuit for weeks at a time. His absences were a double-edged sword. They meant his law practice prospered, but they separated the lovers. He apologized to Abigail for missing a visit early in 1793: "Cruel for detaining me from so much friendly, social Company, and perhaps blessed to you, or me or both, for keeping me at *my Distance*," he wrote, underscoring a feigned threat. "For every experimental Phylosopher knows, that the steel and the Magnet or the Glass and feather will not fly together with more Celerity, than somebody And somebody, when brought within the striking Distance."

By this time, Abigail was signing herself "Diana," using a fanciful classical name, as young women were wont to do in her time. This Diana, however, alive in Weymouth, was not the chaste virgin goddess of the hunt but eighteen years old and betrothed to a man who was given to huge passions. She saw only his greatness, recognized his genius, and was drawn to his brilliant talk as well as the energy that matched her own eagerness to engage with life. He clearly did have her heart. Still, she was the virgin goddess; she defined that boundary by her chosen name.

Nor can it be said that Abigail and John rushed into matrimony with the discovery of their mutual passion. Many practical factors detained them. Abigail was young. The average marriage age of women was at least twenty-two, though her sister Mary had married at twenty-one. Her parents were reluctant for her to rush into a compact that would seal her destiny. It was a mark of her own will that she overcame their hesitation about an early marriage. By the spring of 1763, the Smiths recognized its inevitability.

There was a vital issue that neither the parents nor the young couple considered an obstacle. When they considered mates in the middle of the eighteenth century, Abigail Smith and John Adams took religious compatibility for granted. Their liberal Congregationalism was part of the bond between them. Belief was like the air that they breathed; it surrounded them as a truth that sustained their lives. At the same time, neither of them was inflexible; their attitudes, especially John's, altered with age. But they retained a moral compass inherited from their Puritan past that governed their aspirations and their behavior.

This is not surprising because Puritanism itself was a system of laws and behavior. No great theological truths emerged in the Puritan colonies. Instead there was at its core a stunning acceptance of truth about human nature. Human behavior was malleable. Therefore, education was imperative. People had to make choices about how to behave, educated choices, and their behavior, in turn, exemplified a virtuous life.

Service was a primary virtue, even when it meant sacrifice. Hard work was a value because too great leisure was indulgent. Giving to others meant creating communities, and no individual could live outside a community, be it the family, the village, or the nation. These ideals, planted early in life, as the Smiths did with Abigail and the Adamses did with John, were in turn translated by them into a word that they commonly used with their own children: *duty*. Duty, in the Puritan sense of virtue and sacrifice, service and love, was the foundation of a good life.

John had decided against becoming a clergyman because he knew that he would be controversial and that he would not easily find a pulpit. He had been accused in Worcester of being a follower of Jonathan Mayhew, which meant that he denied the Trinity, the divinity of Christ. It was not a popular position, and clergy who took this position were shunned. In law, however, his disputatious nature would be an asset.

Abigail considered all of life providential; nothing occurred except by the will of God. Her religion became most extreme in times of crises, when she reverted to the old Calvinism of her forebears. Some adversity she considered as punishment for human sinfulness. John would never go to such extremes, because his religion was more rational. Abigail poured forth her sorrows and depended upon religion for consolation.

Meanwhile she was perplexed by another matter. Abigail had accompanied John to one of his court appearances at Plymouth. Upon returning, she consulted her married friend, Hannah Green, about her conduct on this journey, which had provoked gossip and teasing among her friends. "I could not help laughing at the gaiety of your fancy, in supposing that there was any resemblance between that and Matrimony," Hannah responded enigmatically to Abigail's inquiry. Abigail was apparently naïve about sex. "You ask me whether I do not wish it was well over with you?" Hannah wrote, using the word *it* with the confidence of a married woman. "I know of nothing more irksome than being just at the door of Bliss, and not being in a capacity to enter." She assured Abigail of future "bliss" and signed herself "Caliope," after the muse of poetry, her classical pen name.

In 1764, Boston experienced a smallpox epidemic. Those who could afford to leave town did so. The other option—and a terrifying one—was to submit to a vaccination with live germs. This practice, used with great success in Europe, remained suspect in the colonies because of the fear of contagion. Several colonies, among them Boston, had adopted laws against inoculation. In the midst of an epidemic, however, the law was ignored, and so in the spring of 1764, John Adams decided to go through the ordeal.

This meant postponing the possibility of a spring or summer wedding. The dangerous process of vaccination took four or five weeks and involved an even longer separation for the two lovers. Abigail was devastated, not because of the postponement but because she feared for John's life. Her fears were probably generated by her mother's concerns. Only the reassurances of her uncle, Dr. Cotton Tufts, who had already been inoculated, consoled Abigail. Her mother, however, continued to worry and took the extra precaution of having John's letters from Boston carefully disinfected by smoking before Abigail was allowed to see them.

John wrote regularly to Abigail, his mood light and playful as he described purges, vomits, and the insertion of a thread bearing the disease into a wound in his arm. With nothing better to think about, he mischievously wrote Abigail a catalog of her "faults." She couldn't sing; she blushed at hearing profanity; she was clumsy at cards; and she had a bad habit of reading, writing, and thinking. Returning the tease, Abigail acknowledged that she read her faults "with as much pleasure, as an other person would have read their perfections." There was only one persona, one "character," in which she would ever fear him, she confessed, and that was as a "critick" of her writing.

"I assure you there is another Character, besides that of Critick," he continued their epistolary banter, "in which, if you never did, you always hereafter shall fear me, or I shall know the Reason why."

"But heigh day Mr. Whats your Name," Abigail returned: "For my part, I know not that there is any pleasure in being feard, but if there is, I hope you will be so generous as to fear your Diana that she may at least be made sensible of the pleasure."

Finally, by mid-May they were together again and began the serious plans for a fall wedding and setting up a household in John's Braintree cottage. Abigail would need servants to assist with the multitude of housekeeping chores. John, between rounds of riding the circuit, hired two girls, Rachel March and Judah, who had served in his mother's house.

Before departing for Plymouth, John wrote to Abigail: "Oh my dear Girl, I thank Heaven that another Fortnight will restore you to me," declaring that "my soul and Body have been thrown into Disorder, by your Absence." He continued:

> But you who have always softened and warmed my Heart, shall restore my Benevolence as well as my Health and Tranquility of mind. You shall polish and refine my sentiments of Life and Manners, banish all the unsocial and ill natured Particles in my Composition, and form me to that happy Temper, that can reconcile a quick Discernment with a perfect Candour.

John's expectations were a tall order. But by this time, Abigail had gone to the Boston home of her favored aunt and uncle, Isaac and Elizabeth Storer Smith. Unfortunately she became ill and instead of enjoying this brief time with friends as a kind of last fling, she spent her time in bed under the care of Aunt Elizabeth. By October 13, with her marriage less than two weeks off, Abigail was still in Boston, "confind extremely weak, and . . . low spirited." She recovered and returned to Weymouth, where her belongings were being packed for shipping to Braintree. "The cart you mentioned came yesterday, by which I sent as many things as the horse would draw the rest of my things will be ready for

Monday after you return from Taunton," she wrote to John Adams, adding, "And—then Sir if you please you may take me."

Marriage ceremonies in the eighteenth century were not the elaborate affairs that they became in the nineteenth. They were, in fact, simple by comparison with other social milestones, such as graduation from Harvard, which had become notorious for its hilarity, or election day, at which time local taverns did a brisk business. Marriage had only recently been sacrilized as a religious function, having been earlier performed by magistrates of the law. Now ministers read the contract by which two individuals joined themselves for life, a covenant really, in the Puritan sense of testifying before God to be bound in love and service to each other. Abigail and John took this oath on October 25, 1764, at the parsonage in Weymouth before their families and close friends.

Theirs was an inspired bond. Abigail had described her own covenant with John when she wrote to him:

> There is a tye more binding than Humanity, and stronger than Friendship, which makes us anxious for the happiness and welfare of those to whom it binds us. It makes their Misfortunes, Sorrows, and afflictions, our own. Unite these, and there is a threefold cord—by this cord I am not ashamed to own myself bound, nor do I [believe] that you are wholly free from it.

And she added, "Accept this hasty Scrawl warm from the Heart of Your Sincere Diana."

A Tye More Binding

FOLLOWING THEIR LATE-FALL MARRIAGE, ABIGAIL MOVED TO the house that John had inherited from his father three years earlier. He had not yet lived there because it was considered inappropriate and impractical for a single person to live alone. Until his marriage, John had resided with his widowed mother and younger brother Peter, while his own house was let out to tenants.

The two houses sat catty-cornered to each other, perhaps seventy-five feet apart, separated by a stone fence and a shared well. It was a strange configuration, given the abundance of open space in that rural setting. But the deacon, John Adams's father, had purchased both houses and had lived in harmony for many years with a series of tenants.

This was the home to which John brought Abigail as his new wife, and that she would preside over during the long weeks and years of separation before and during the American Revolution. For two years following their marriage, until Susanna Adams remarried and moved several miles down the road, Abigail lived comfortably next door to her mother-in-law. They lovingly called each other "Mother" and "Daughter."

Many aspects of John's life remained constant. His home, with the exception of his college and teaching years, had always been at the foot of Penn's Hill in this rolling, rich farmland. He had the consistent company of his mother, his brothers, and his Braintree neighbors. The church at Braintree continued to provide a stable community. He had, however, gained a wife and a new status.

For Abigail, everything was new. Not only had she moved away from her

The Adams Birthplaces in Braintree, later called Quincy, Massachusetts. The Adamses moved to the house on the right after their marriage, and Abigail lived there throughout the Revolutionary War. The house on the right was built around 1681, the house on the left sometime during the eighteenth century. Courtesy of the Adams National Historical Park.

lifelong home, she was now the mistress of her own little sphere. While hardly as spacious and elegant as her parents' home, hers was nevertheless accommodating and sufficient for a young couple. If John's mother and brother lived next door, her parents and sisters lived several hours away by horse cart. None of this was a surprise, of course, as she had expected to adjust to a new situation and new neighbors.

Houses, like their occupants, have genealogies, and both Adams houses had pedigrees that went back to the seventeenth century. Both had started as typical structures that were two rooms wide. They were one room deep with a lean-to added later, giving them a saltbox appearance. This meant that both had two-story fronts with one story at the backside and a long rear sloping roof over the lean-to (pronounced "lee-an'-ter" by Abigail and her generation of New Englanders). In order to accommodate his law practice, John had an outside door constructed that led to a front room so that clients could enter without disturbing the family.

During the daytime, family activities occurred mostly in the ground-floor rooms, while the upstairs chambers were used for sleeping. The front room on the north side of the small entry vestibule was the parlor, sometimes called the "best room," reserved primarily for more formal entertaining; it was here that Abigail kept her tea table.

John used this pleasant room for reading in the evenings and mornings, before going into his office. Pulling his Windsor chair before the small fireplace in the cold of winter, he could both read and smoke in peace. A lifelong pipe smoker, John also entertained his friends here in the evening.

Adjacent to the parlor was John's office, with its own entryway. His tall desk stood against one wall. With a flat surface large enough to hold a book or sheet of paper, the desk could still hold the heavy volumes that John began to order from England as soon as his income permitted.

The kitchen was the control center of this multifaceted family enterprise. The largest of the ground-floor rooms, it occupied the space behind the parlor. Its huge fireplace, large enough for several (small) people to stand in, was its main feature, occupying most of one wall. That fireplace defined the room where all the cooking took place, but the kitchen was also a social area. The adults congregated here to work or visit, while children played or learned their lessons. Furnished with a long plank table and a long bench on either side, the colonial kitchen could accommodate a whole family.

John thrived in his newfound domestic life. He marveled to Cranch that "my Squemish Wife keeping the shutters too, have brought me into a vile Habit of dozing in the morning." He claimed that at home he had "leave to lye abed till Eight o Clock, in the morning absolutely, and till 9 upon Condition I shall find it necessary." Abigail, in turn, commented coyly to Mary: "My Good Man is so very fat that I am lean as a [rail] rale," quickly adding, "He is such an Itinerant, to speak . . . that I have but little of his company. He is now at Plymouth, and Next week goes to Taunton."

Within the first year of marriage, their first child was born. "On the 14 day of July of this Year 1765, Mrs. Adams presented me with a Daughter," John recorded with pride. He described, as well, his discomfort in the parlor, as he listened to the sounds coming from the chamber above, where Abigail gave birth. She was attended by a midwife, as was the custom; her mother and at least one sister were present to aid and comfort her.

John had no one to support him during this ordeal. "I was much alone in [the Parlour below] my Office of Evenings and Mornings." Clearly the sounds he heard from above were disturbing. "The Uneasy State of the public Mind, and my own gloomy Apprehensions, turned my Thought to writing," he continued. Childbirth, everyone knew, was hazardous. In order to take his mind off his reflections, he turned his thoughts to other things. "Without any particular Subject to write on, my Mind turned I know not how into a Speculation or rather a Rhapsody which I [later] sent to the Boston Gazette, and was there published without Title or Signature."

So while in an upstairs chamber of their little cottage, Abigail gave birth to their daughter, John below gave birth to his first great essay. To distract himself, he started to write a meditation about the founding of America and its unique historic mission. Eventually the work was published under the title *"A Dissertation on the Canon and Feudal Law,"* and its reception was so laudatory that people speculated the author to be the mature Jeremiah Gridley rather than the thirty-year-old John Adams.

Published serially in the *Boston Gazette*, the essay was a paean to New England's Puritan forebears. It stressed their courage and independence, qualities of character that Adams admired. "The adventurers"—he meant the Puritans—"had utter contempt" for feudal England. "They knew that government was a plain, simple, intelligible thing, founded in nature and reason, and quite comprehensible by common sense." Contemplating the historical differences between the mother country and her colonies, John began to probe the distinctions that would lead to a revolution.

The Puritans, he continued, "created their government not only in church and state" but also in widespread public education. An American "who cannot read and write," he persisted, "is as rare as a comet or an earthquake." If he exaggerated, it was because he judged the extent of public education in the colonies by New England, where schools had been established from the beginning. American freedoms, he argued, derived from three sources: nature, an educated populace, and God. "Liberty cannot be preserved without a general knowledge among the people, who have a right, from the frame of their nature, to knowledge, as their great Creator, who does nothing in vain, has given them understandings and a desire to know."

John observed with pleasure that "this little production had its full Share of praise," but he did not elaborate further about the event that took place in the chamber above. The infant was named Abigail after her mother and great-grandmother and called Nabby, the diminutive form that distinguished her from her mother.

With the birth of their first child, both Abigail and John marked another milestone in their expectations of married life. "Your Diana become a Mamma—can you credit it?" Abigail announced to a friend. She was incredulous at this transformation in her status. "Bless'd with a charming Girl whose pretty Smiles already delight my Heart," she persisted, adding self-consciously, "You my Friend are well acquainted with all the tender feelings of a parent, therefore I need not apologize for the present overflow."

Motherhood added another dimension to her responsibilities, for the management of her little home already involved many tasks that she shared with her servants. She worked alongside the two young women John had hired when they married and, as her family grew, others who joined their "family." Abigail called everyone who lived in her household "family." She had to juggle the roles of manager and co-worker, and it called for a delicate balance between familiarity and distance. She spoke with great feeling about the reception she received from her servants upon returning home after a weeklong visit to her parents: "I could behold joy sparkle in the Eyes of every one of them as I enterd the House, whilst they unaffected express'd it some to me and some to my Babe," she wrote to Mary.

But nothing compensated Abigail for John's absences, which increased along with his growing business. "It seems lonesome here, for My Good Man is at Boston," she complained to her sister. "When my partner is absent and my Babe a sleep, I am still left alone." To John she lamented: "Alass! How many snow banks devide thee and me and my warmest wishes to see thee will not melt one of them."

John's law practice prospered after 1765, and he worked hard to expand his reputation, believing that his future and that of his family depended upon his success. And John was achieving success. He had practiced law for more than five years since his first bungled case and was earning a good reputation. Boston's leading lawyers had noticed him. Jeremiah Gridley, the elder statesman of Boston's bar, invited him to participate in "a private Association, for the study of Law and oratory." Gridley's purpose in founding this group, the Sodality, was to insure the future of Boston's legal establishment once the older generation had retired. John became a charter member in early 1765.

Though on many fronts their first year of marriage had been a good one for the Adamses, during that same year a political dispute emerged in the British colonies that no one at the time found predictable. John observed the early stages of the brewing conflict: "The Year 1765 has been the most remarkable Year of my Life," he wrote. "That enormous Engine, fabricated by the british Parliament, for battering down all the Rights and Liberties of America"—he meant the Stamp Act—"has raised and spread, thro the whole Continent, a Spirit that will be recorded to our Honour, with all future Generations." John's early involvement in the developing dispute was more than political, for the courts had been closed, and his income depended upon the courts. Furthermore, many of the political leaders among the opposition to British policy were among his closest friends. These included his cousin Samuel Adams and James Otis Jr. John was not immune to their powers of persuasion, not because of their affability, for Sam was especially charismatic, but because he already believed much of what they argued.

Like Adams, Otis was a lawyer, though thirteen years his senior and descended from several generations of prosperous Barnstable merchants. He had a brilliant mind and was a dazzling orator. "Otis is extreamly quick and elastic," John recorded after meeting him in 1759. "His Apprehension is as quick as his Temper. He springs, and twitches his Muscles about in thinking." In the following years, however, while he continued to admire Otis's fiery mind and commitment to colonial rights, he became wary of his behavior. The rages and the outbursts that were the early signs of growing instability were already manifest, and it was never certain when Otis would descend into irrational rants. By the early 1770s, Otis was overtaken by madness, but during these years he was a leader, very much admired by Adams.

John observed that his older cousin Sam Adams had the most thorough understanding of liberty as well as a politician's sensitivity to the public temper. He was not educated in the law but "he had the most habitual, radical Love of it, of any of them," John noted. He was "a Man of refined Policy, stedfast Integrity, exquisite Humanity, genteel Erudition, obliging, engaging Manners, real as well as professed Piety, and a universal good Character." John Adams liked his cousin Sam.

So did Abigail, who invited the Boston Adamses to spend a weekend at Braintree. "I have had upon a visit here, from Saturday till tuesday Mr. Samll. Adams and wife, and indeed Sister they are a charming pair." As a young wife, Abigail noted their "tenderest affection towards each other," as well as their "delicacy and good breeding" that appearead genuine. The Adamses, all four, had shared space in the small Braintree cottage for several days, an experience that confirmed their bonds of family and politics. Sam Adams undoubtedly used the opportunity to speak of his radical politics to his younger but clearly receptive cousin. John's radicalism, however, was not a foregone conclusion. Although his study of the law and his experiences in court and among Boston's leading politicians would exert pressure in that direction, he still resisted committing himself to the radical position of James Otis Jr. and his cousin Sam.

THE DETERIORATING RELATIONS BETWEEN THE MOTHER COUNTRY and her colonies had to do with Britain's mounting national debt, due in great part to the costs of past wars in America. That and the maintenance of an army still in the colonies overwhelmed the British government. Grasping for a solution in 1763 King George III appointed a new prime minister, George Grenville, who proposed to solve the debt problem by taxing the colonies.

Many people in the colonies, however, having experienced the "benign neglect" of Parliament for years, perceived the imposition of taxes especially abhorrent. Leaders of the colonial protest argued that the taxes were illegal because the colonies were not represented in Parliament. English legal tradition ensured that a people could not be taxed without their consent. Grenville, in return, argued the case for "virtual representation," a concept that implied that elected representatives in Britain represented all citizens. That included the Americans. In 1764, Parliament passed a series of taxes that were collectively referred to as the sugar tax, because one of the items taxed was molasses coming into the colonies from the West Indies.

The protest in the colonies was immediate. There were riots in Boston. Other colonies petitioned Parliament to repeal the taxes. And they began a boycott that eventually succeeded, as merchants in England, whether or not they supported the colonies, were affected. John Adams was selected to draft the local Braintree resolutions against these taxes, and in 1766 the sugar tax was repealed. But Parliament, under Grenville's influence, passed a new tax. This would be the blow that radicalized many Americans, including John Adams.

The sugar tax had placed a tariff on imports and exports; it was an external tax. This new impost, a stamp tax, was imposed on all paper goods used within the colonies. It prescribed duties on legal documents, such as bonds and deeds for land, on pamphlets, newspapers, leases, contracts, liquor licenses, and even college diplomas. While the revenue would remain in the colonies to supply the army, the tax was hurtful. And it reminded the colonies that Parliament claimed authority over them.

Indeed, John Adams was mobilized by this latest levy, which affected his law practice. Every legal document required a stamp and, consequently, was taxed. He recorded the popular outrage: "The People, even to the lowest Ranks, have become more attentive to their Liberties, more inquisitive about them, and more determined to defend them." He persisted: "Our Presses have groaned, our Pulpits have thundered, our Legislatures have resolved, our Towns have voted, the Crown Officers have everywhere trembled, and all their little Tools and Creatures, been afraid to Speak and ashamed to be seen."

As a conspicuous opponent of the tax, John was appointed, along with his colleague James Otis Jr. and his mentor Jeremiah Gridley, to appear before the governor to petition the reopening of the courts. He had little opportunity to prepare his argument before their appearance but found himself delegated to open their presentation to Governor Francis Bernard. He failed to understand why he had been chosen for this role, but it is clear that within the rebellious legal establishment, John's talents were already highly regarded.

But John did not play a bigger role in the Stamp Act protest. The most dramatic action was in the streets, where people rioted and finally burned in effigy the stamp distributor, Andrew Oliver, and destroyed his home. Adams was uncomfortable about this turn of events. He disapproved of mobs, was suspicious of riots and violence, not because he was an elitist, as some have claimed, but because he feared tyranny from the left as much as from the right. In another thirty years this issue would create a major conflict between him and Thomas Jefferson, who believed that a little rioting and violence now and then was healthy for a democracy.

Meanwhile, with the courts closed, Adams needed something to do. For the first time in their marriage, John remained at home with Abigail for several uninterrupted weeks. The freedom allowed him not just leisure with his family but the opportunity to read and write and, above all, to think: "At home, with my family. Thinking."

These hours of thinking and reading led to another series of newspaper articles, this time under the pseudonym "Clarendon." In them he laid out the colonial position with regard to illegal parliamentary taxes, refuting the anonymous "Pym," whose recent series of letters in the Boston newspapers had defended Parliament's right to tax the colonies. Pym, Adams suspected, was the pseudonym used by Jonathan Sewall, his close friend since their undergraduate days at Harvard. It had been Sewall who, in their courtship days along with his fiancée, Esther Quincy, had burst into the room where John prepared to propose to Hannah Quincy, thus interrupting his mood and changing the course of John's and Abigail's lives. Now, these years later, the two friends engaged in a political rivalry that separated them as well as many other friends and family members over the issue of colonial rights.

At the time Adams and Sewall saw themselves as merely exercising conflicting political agendas, but later the breach between them became larger and more permanent. As a loyalist, Sewall moved to England early in the Revolution. Many years later, when John arrived in London as American minister, the two longtime friends reunited briefly before Sewall, impoverished and broken by circumstances, departed for Canada. The Revolution had created a chasm in this close friendship. For now, Adams's Clarendon essays refuted his friend Sewall's Pym essays in support of the policy of parliamentary taxation. It was a political joust, not yet a war.

The colonial protest worked once again because the boycott of British goods hurt British merchants. The Stamp Act was repealed in February 1766, and John, greatly relieved, resumed his travels on the court circuit. "Since the Stamp Act is repealed," he wrote to his brother-in-law Richard Cranch, "I am at perfect Ease about Politicks. I care not a shilling who is in or out." He would focus on building his law practice and supporting his family, he declared.

Meanwhile, in July Abigail wrote to Mary, "You ask me if I will not come and tarry a Week with you. I have been Scheeming of it this fortnight." The previous year, because the economic downturn caused by the conflicts with Britain had hurt Richard's business repairing clocks and watches, the Cranches had moved to the thriving seaport of Salem, hoping to find better circumstances.

In August the Adamses set out for Salem. Their visit with the Cranches was typical of a family vacation, where easy talk and the pleasures of touring and dining together made the time pass too quickly. They rode by chaise through the streets of Salem, "the most elegant and grand, that I have seen in any of the maritime Towns," John recorded in his diary. They drove the four miles to Marblehead, where the "streets are narrow, and rugged and dirty." They dined and walked in Salem to "Witchcraft Hill," where "famous Persons formerly executed for Witches were buried."

It was either on this trip or on their next visit to the Cranches the following November that Abigail and John had their portraits painted. Why they sat for their portraits is mysterious. Colonial portraiture was confined to a small social class, usually the elite, who could afford the luxury. Perhaps it was the leisure of a vacation that inspired Abigail and John to sit for their portraits. The Salem limner Benjamin Blyth's minor reputation probably derives from his having painted these two famous portraits. Like most colonial artists, he taught himself his craft by copying prints by European artists.

Blyth clearly spent more of his energy, time, and talent painting Abigail's portrait. Her face—its freshness, its intensity, and its intelligence—attracts immediate attention. It is the face of youth, of promise, of high energy, delicately colored except for her strikingly dark eyes. It presents Abigail as she appeared at the age of twenty-one. If the perspective and the proportions are wrong, the viewer adjusts, distracted by the startling personality that emerges from this somewhat awkward portrait. Abigail's strong character appears in the vivid frontal stare of her dark eyes as well as the set of her mouth. She might be ready to speak or to move, and she is certainly taking in her surroundings. Perhaps she is merely intrigued by observing Blyth at work or by their conversation. She is an animated Abigail.

John's portrayal is distinctly inferior to hers. Composed against a green background that lacks subtle shading, it presents John in drab browns and blacks, looking almost boyish, certainly not the man who emerges from his forceful and spirited writing of that same time. His face is round, soft-looking, serene, quite in contrast to the elaborate coif of the curly periwig that was conventional. His features lack expression, and this John is too tame to take seriously as a coming leader of the Revolution.

Bearing their new portraits as souvenirs of their visit to Salem, Abigail and John returned to Braintree and hung them in their parlor, where they remained until the couple's old age.

JOHN'S LAW PRACTICE CONTINUED TO GROW. ABIGAIL'S DOMEStic world expanded with the birth of their second child and first son. He, too, was born in the southeast bedroom above the parlor, and at the request of Abigail's mother, they named him John Quincy to honor his maternal greatgrandfather, who passed away on the same date as his birth, July 11, 1767.

After the repeal of the stamp tax, John returned to his practice, but his escalating success at the bar meant that he was more often away from Abigail and the children. More and more he traveled the circuit or did business in Boston. To lessen their hardship, the Adamses decided to move to Boston in 1768. At least some of John's travel would be alleviated, and they could more often be together. For Abigail it meant being close to Smith relatives as well as the excitement of living in the city, a great contrast to the quiet rural retreat of Braintree. Boston in 1768 was a thriving metropolis of sixteen thousand people.

An assault on all the senses, the city was noisy, busy, and aromatic. Houses were closely built of wood or stone, with the exception of mansions, like that of John's childhood friend John Hancock on Beacon Hill with its spacious grounds overlooking the Boston Common. Boston had hills before they became landfill to extend the city boundaries into the bay, so that wharves of that time later became city streets.

The smells of the ocean were never far, mixing with that of animals and produce, fish and vegetables hawked by children or peddlers, whose other wares supplied the common needs of the city dwellers. Tiny shops—printers, booksellers, barbers, silver- and goldsmiths, cobblers, tailors, bakeries, wigmakers, apothecaries, and many more—dotted the narrow cobblestone streets. Taverns catered to sailors; some women did as well. There were no hospitals, dedicated fire departments, or streetlights—in four more years there would be gaslights— but the city did have public schools and a nearby university. Streets changed names every few blocks, and to compensate for the lack of a reliable numbering system, houses were named. When the Adamses moved to Brattle Square, they identified their location to visitors as the White House. They didn't consider that the name was prophetic.

In December 1768, Abigail gave birth to their third child, a daughter, named

Susanna after John's mother. With three children under the age of four, Abigail focused on child rearing. By now she employed four servants, one a young lad. Within the year, they moved to a different rented house on nearby Cole Lane because the White House, which they rented, was sold. The Adamses were not yet prepared to commit to ownership of property in Boston.

Then, just after her first birthday, baby Susanna died of unknown causes. So painful was this loss that neither parent left a contemporary trace of her death; they grieved privately. While the death of children was common in that era before inoculations and antibiotics, the grief it caused was no less terrible. Abigail, who regarded all earthly experiences as providential, nevertheless suffered a mother's pain. Only in her old age, when her daughter-in-law Louisa Catherine suffered a similar bereavement, did Abigail mention Susanna's death.

John's law practice flourished. He became, as he later wrote, one of the busiest lawyers on the circuit. The young John Adams's dreams had been fulfilled. As an immature lawyer in Braintree he had calculated how to make himself known, how to solicit cases, cultivate influential people who would lead to more business. By 1768, he had built his practice so well that he and Abigail moved to Boston to accommodate his success.

But the law was not John's only activity. He belonged the several "clubbs," so that most evenings when he was in town, he attended either a dinner or a meeting. The Sodality, the group of lawyers who discussed legal theory, survived and increased in size, despite Jeremiah Gridley's death that year. In fact, Abigail was at home with her servants while John attended his Sodality club on the night of March 5, 1770, when the event occurred that one historian has called the "first battle of the Revolutionary War."

To the citizens of Boston, who had observed the buildup of tensions over the previous two years, the Boston Massacre was a disaster waiting to happen. Since 1768, British soldiers had been quartered in Boston "to keep the peace," it was said, but really to prevent smuggling of forbidden items into the city. The local citizenry, including the Adamses, objected to them. Every morning for two years, John complained, they awakened to the sounds of a "spirit stirring drum and Earpiercing fife" as a regiment exercised in front of their house on Brattle Square.

The ubiquitous presence of soldiers in Boston, not only performing their drills but on guard at public venues, became increasingly offensive to the natives. For several evenings in early March 1770, marauding groups of young men taunted the soldiers. On the evening of March 5, a crowd of four hundred gathered, mostly young men, apprentices and laborers, according to reports. It was a chilly night, lit only by a first-quarter moon, reflecting off the foot of icy snow that remained on the ground. A lone British sentry stood guard next to his box at the corner of King Street and Royal Exchange Lane. He greeted several familiar men when a hostile youth approached to hurl an insult. Private Hugh White, the sentry, responded in kind, then quickly found himself surrounded. The angry crowd, carrying clubs and sticks, shouted further abuse, daring him to fire at them. Church bells began to peal, summoning more people into the streets.

A few blocks away, Captain Thomas Preston, the commander of the Twenty-ninth Regiment, struggled with his dilemma. He needed to rescue White. With an equally angry crowd surrounding his barracks, how could he send a rescue mission to the courthouse where Private White had retreated? Every option that he considered had risks. Finally, he called out eight of his largest grenadiers and arranged them by twos, "muskets shouldered with fixed bayonets," and with himself as leader, he marched them through the crowd to the courthouse.

There, lined up with their backs to the building for protection, stood the grenadiers, pelted by jeers—"fire you bastards, fire"—snow, ice, and sticks. One stick struck Private Hugh Montgomery, knocking him "onto his backside." A gun went off. Within a few seconds an entire volley of shots were fired, and the crowd dispersed. Lying there before the courthouse were five bodies, three of them already dead and two more who would die the next day. A few stragglers returned to attend the dead and wounded. Everyone was shocked by what had happened, none more so than Captain Preston. He stood stunned, then gathered his wits and marched his grenadiers, including Private White, back to their barracks. For the remainder of the night, the regiments stood guard to prevent further violence in the city's main squares.

At home with her servants, Abigail heard the church bells tolling, endlessly sounding the alarm that usually meant that a fire was blazing somewhere, a call to the city's volunteer fire department to wake up and battle a conflagration, which in the city could envelop whole districts in a very short time. Only this time the bells spread news of the skirmish. Frightened, she sent a servant to run the few blocks to the site of the chaos. He returned to reassure her that there was no fire. Abigail was more than usually emotional at this time, as she was still in mourning for her baby daughter, Susanna. And she was once more pregnant.

Before long John returned home, alerted by the bells that he, too, believed signaled a fire, only to discover the carnage on his route home. Abigail and John talked about the shooting for the rest of the evening, speculating about its significance not just for the city but, just as ominous, for themselves.

The next morning, as John sat in his office, he received a visitor, the merchant

The Boston Massacre in the famous engraving from 1770 of
Paul Revere that has become emblematic of that historic event,
which helped launch Adams's career as a statesman. Courtesy
of the Massachusetts Historical Society.

James Forrest, who would later leave Boston as a Loyalist. With "tears streaming from his Eyes," John recorded, Forrest had come to beg John to defend Captain Preston, who was in prison. "He wishes for Council, and can get none." Josiah Quincy Jr. and Robert Auchmuty had agreed to serve, but only upon the condition that John Adams would take the lead role. The defense of so unpopular a figure as Preston could spell the end of a professional career.

"I had no hesitation in answering that Council ought to be the very last thing that an accused Person should want in a free Country," John recalled. "Every Lawyer must hold himself responsible not only to his Country, but to the highest and most infallible of all Trybunals for the Part he should Act." The consequence of this agreement—"Forrest offered me a single Guinea as a retaining fee and I readily accepted it"—was that John entered into the most significant case of his legal career.

The trials of the British soldiers were delayed in order to allow tempers to cool. The court decided to separate Captain Preston's trial from that of the soldiers, because he was accused not of murder but rather of giving the order to fire. When his trial finally did take place amidst still-hot tempers in October 1770, John defended the captain in a lengthy speech that was never recorded. By all reports, however, it was erudite and eloquent, and Preston was exonerated.

In the second trial for the six soldiers accused of murder, four were exonerated and two found guilty and branded on their thumbs as punishment. In retrospect, John called these the "most exhausting and fatiguing Causes I ever tried." He had risked his professional career to defend an unpopular cause in a hostile social environment. The strain of this effort cost him long hours of work and loss of sleep. If he felt satisfaction at the successful outcome, he paid the penalty of having exerted himself for a cause that did not, at that time, add luster to his reputation or his purse.

But John's public service was not ended. On the heels of these arduous trials, he was elected to serve as one of Boston's four representatives to the colonial assembly. "At this time I had more Business at the Bar, than any Man in the Province," he recalled. "My health was feeble: I was throwing away as bright prospects [as] any Man ever had before him: and had devoted myself to endless labour and anxiety if not to infamy and to death, and that for nothing, except, what indeed was and ought to be all in all, a sense of duty."

Not a little melodramatic, John continued: "I considered the Step as a devotion of my family to ruin and myself to death, for I could scarce perceive a possibility that I should ever go through the Thorns and leap all the Precipices before me, and escape with my Life." John believed that by accepting this appointment to the legislature he was taking not just a political but a personal risk. The radical faction in Boston had become reckless, and he knew this well from his experience in the two trials. He, nevertheless, accepted the appointment to the colonial council. Then he had to break the news of his new assignment to Abigail.

"That excellent Lady, who has always encouraged me, burst into a flood of Tears," he wrote, "but said she was very sensible of all the Danger to her and to our Children as well as to me, but she thought I had done as I ought." The times were emotional. Living in Boston during that period was unnerving. Groups of hostile men wandered the streets at night, and it could never be predicted when a situation would turn violent. John, himself a member of a radical political group, nevertheless was uncomfortable with the mobs. For one thing, he believed that militant radicals exploited them.

By the next spring, his commitments began to take a toll on John's health. The "Obligation to speak in public almost every day for many hours," to say nothing of the many different loads he carried, had led to pains in his chest and what he called "a complaint in my Lungs." He believed that his symptoms were life-threatening. Both he and Abigail became so concerned about his health that they decided to return to Braintree in April 1771.

Following their return, John undertook a journey to the famous Stafford Springs in Connecticut. For those who could afford its expense in the eighteenth century, bathing in natural mineral springs and drinking the spa water was considered therapeutic. The trip took a week. John recorded these experiences, riding alone by horseback, observing the countryside, and meeting strangers. His journey and ruminations in his diary were for John another form of therapy, a relief from the pace of his recent frenzied exertions.

His colleagues had reacted differently to the stress of these times. James Otis Jr., already predisposed to irrational behavior, became more unbalanced. On the other hand, Sam Adams thrived. But Sam and John were studies in contrast, as John once observed. Sam was not concerned about his career; he was, in fact, a failure in all of his business enterprises. Nor did he weigh the consequences of his ideological commitment on his family, who became impoverished. John observed Sam's irresponsibility but could not admire it.

John returned from his visit to the springs refreshed. In fact, he couldn't wait to get home. He resumed his legal practice, hoping to slow its pace, and began several farming projects. The fences on some of his pastures had deteriorated and needed repair in order to "keep off my Neighbours Creatures, Hogs, Horses, Oxen, Cows and Sheep." He supervised the production of fertilizer: "Take the Soil and Mud, which you cutt up and throw out when you dig Ditches in a Salt Marsh, and put 20 Load of it in a heap. . . . Then to the whole add 20 Loads of Dung, and lay the whole in a Heap." But farming was secondary to his law practice, and he went back to riding the circuit from his home in Braintree.

FOR ABIGAIL, THE RETURN TO BRAINTREE REPRESENTED A homecoming. At the end of April she informed her cousin Isaac Smith Jr. that she wrote

> not from the Noisy Buisy Town, but from my humble Cottage in Braintree . . .
>
> > Where Contemplation p[l]umes her rufled Wings
> > And the free Soul look's down to pitty Kings.

In this letter Abigail signals a new consciousness, a budding awareness of an unfair gender disparity. She hints at dissatisfaction with social conditions, if not with her own life. "From my Infancy I have always felt a great inclination to visit the Mother Country," she wrote. It was a dream she could not fulfill.

> Women you know Sir are considerd as Domestick Beings, and altho they inherit an Eaquel Share of curiosity with the other Sex, yet but few are hardy eno' to venture abroad, and explore the amaizing variety of distant Lands. The Natural tenderness and Delicacy of our Constitutions, added to the many Dangers we are subject too from your Sex, renders it almost imposible for a Single Lady to travel without injury to her character.

Men travel freely, she observed. No great obstacles prevented Isaac's journey. His parents and teachers had encouraged him to pursue this adventure to England and supported his voyage.

Isaac was just her age. He had been her playmate when they were children and her companion as a youth. Later, while he studied Latin texts at Harvard, she married and began raising a family. Now Isaac had sailed to London, while she was constrained by a different destiny. Even married women couldn't travel, she argued. "And those who have a protecter in an Husband, have generally speaking obstacles sufficient to prevent their Roving, and instead of visiting other Countries; are obliged to content themselves with seeing but a very small part of their own."

Abigail expressed a new sensibility, her awareness of something deeply felt that she had not previously articulated. It was, perhaps, a natural consequence of her maturing, the fact that she was no longer a nineteen-year-old, looking forward to marriage, but a twenty-six-year-old wife and mother of three children. Or perhaps it came from her reading. Maybe her discussions with John, which were uncensored and brilliantly wide-ranging, had inspired her. Certainly, it developed from circumstances of the previous five years during which she experienced a heightened emotional life: loneliness when John traveled; grief for the loss of a child; fear during the riots in Boston; and helplessness when John undertook risky cases and his health declined. In a scant half-decade, circumstances transformed her from girl to woman, and with that came a new perspective. For Abigail there was an unfair disparity between the sexes.

Even though women inherited "an Eaquel Share of curiosity with the other Sex," by which she meant that equal intelligence, there were social boundaries that prevented the realization of that curiosity. If there is resentment in Abigail's statement, there is also resignation. A multitude of "obstacles" made it impossible for her to travel. But perhaps she was not just thinking about Isaac. Perhaps, at a level so subconscious that she didn't understand it, there existed in her some resentment of John's freedom to travel. John had merely to pack his books and papers, mount his horse, and depart, leaving her behind to mind the home and family. She could not, however, allow such resentments to come to the surface.

John's peregrinations were a constant in their married life. If Abigail was unwilling to express resentment, her sole but repetitive comment touched on her loneliness. When John traveled the circuit or went to Boston, it was her fate to remain behind, caring for their household; it would become a recurring theme in their future. Wives, however, were not allowed to complain about their lack of freedom. Instead she rationalized her circumstances.

Her letter to Isaac shifted from argument to justification. America is a better country, anyway, she claimed defensively. America lacks the great social inequalities that mark the Old World, she wrote, clearly avoiding the other social disparity that vexed her. And Americans are more religious, she asserted, grasping at a line of reasoning that was both weak and insupportable. To bolster her claim, she wrote that she had recently heard the famed evangelical preacher George Whitefield say so in a sermon.

Unable to let go of her theme, Abigail next expressed interest in the celebrated British feminist and author Catherine Macaulay, whose *History of England* had come to her attention. "I have a great desire to be made acquainted with Mrs. Maccaulays own history," she wrote, requesting information from her cousin. "One of my own Sex so eminent in a tract so uncommon naturally raises my curiosity. . . . I have a curiosity to know her Education, and what first prompted her to engage in a Study never before Exibited to the publick by one of her own Sex and Country, tho now to the honour of both."

Abigail is, in this letter to her cousin, as in her portrait by Benjamin Blyth, earnest, inquisitive, and intelligent, but her note contains traces of resentment. She was anchored to her domestic role despite her curiosity to learn about subjects proscribed to women. That created a paradox, which for now she tolerated. But she was still interested in knowing how Mrs. Macaulay had broken the rules. In the few years following her marriage, she had become more experienced, more confident, more mature than the youthful Abigail who had joined her destiny to that of John Adams in October 1764.

THE ADAMSES REMAINED IN BRAINTREE FOR A YEAR AND A HALF. But more and more of John's practice required his commute to Boston, so in the fall of 1772 he purchased a house in Boston, on Queen Street. He resolved not to meddle "with public Affairs of Town or Province. . . . I will devote myself wholly to my private Business, my Office and my farm," he assured his diary. "I hope to lay a Foundation for better Fortune to my Children, and an happier Life than has fallen to my Share."

Abigail stayed behind in Braintree, where in September she gave birth to Thomas, the last of the Adams children who would survive. John traveled the broad circuit to Plymouth, to Taunton, where he tried nine cases in three days, and to Salem. He marked his thirty-seventh birthday on October 19, 1772, remarking, "What an Atom, an Animalcule I am!—the Remainder of my Days I shall rather decline. . . . My Season for acquiring Knowledge is past." If he prospered, he also acknowledged boredom with his routine.

In late November, Abigail with her children moved into their new home on

Queen Street. They attended church on Sundays, heard Dr. Chauncey sermon-
ize from Paul on "Righteousness, Temperance, and Judgment," and Dr. Coo-
per on sin. Abigail had tea with Mrs. Mayhew and other lady friends. And John
tried to resist politics. He declined to give a public oration memorializing the
Boston Massacre, begging his health as an excuse. But the state of affairs in
Boston politics concerned him.

"My Country is in deep Distress, and has very little Ground of Hope, that
She will soon, if ever get out of it," John wrote to Catherine Macaulay, with
whom he now corresponded. "The System of a mean, and a merciless Administration, is gaining Ground upon our Patriots every Day." His resolve not to
engage in politics was faltering. "I found the old Warmth, Heat, Violence, Acri-
mony, Bitterness, Sharpness of my Temper, and Expression, was not departed."
He struggled continuously to remain aloof from politics while the events around
him attracted him to the fray.

A pleasant social life did, too. He and Abigail dined at the extravagant mansion of his Boylston cousins and with Abigail's uncle and aunt Smith at their
lavish home. "The young Ladies Miss Smith and Miss Lynch entertained us
upon the Spinnet." And that summer John introduced Abigail to a woman with
whom she would form one of the most influential relationships of her life,
Mercy Otis Warren. They stayed at the home of Colonel James Warren and his
formidable wife, when John took Abigail with him to the Plymouth circuit
court.

Older than Abigail by almost a generation, the mother of five sons, wife of
the prosperous gentleman farmer James Warren, daughter of an old Barnstable
merchant family, and sister to the brilliant though unstable James Otis Jr.,
Mercy was already known to Abigail for her erudition and her literary aspirations. If Abigail admired Mercy before she met her, she came away reverent.
She was, in fact, intimidated. But she was also determined to conquer her fear
and establish a friendship with this woman whom her husband so greatly respected.

In one of the most magnificently poetic and revealing letters that Abigail
ever wrote, she began her thanks: "The kind reception I met with at your
House, and the Hospitality with which you entertained me, demands my grate-
full acknowledgment," she began. "By requesting a correspondence you have
kindly given me an opportunity to thank you for the happy Hours I enjoyed
whilst at your house." She continued:

> Thus imbolden'd I venture to stretch my pinions, and tho like the
> timorous Bird I fail in the attempt and tumble to the ground yet

sure the Effort is laudable, nor will I suffer my pride, (which is greatly increased since my more intimate acquaintance with you) to debar me the pleasure, and improvement I promise myself from this correspondence tho I suffer by the comparison.

Remarkable for revealing her struggle to use the proper language, Abigail's letter exudes humility, not just out of proper literary convention, but because of her sincere awe for the learning as well as the social stature of her new acquaintance. In part, Abigail was reaching for the proper tone to express her feelings of admiration but also for the correct phrases to impress this erudite woman. Most unself-consciously, she rose to her best style in the sensuous metaphor of a "timorous Bird." This combination of uncertainty and vivid imagery would mark Abigail's early years of correspondence with Mercy.

John Adams had introduced his wife to the remarkable Mercy because he recognized the curiosity and literary interests they had in common. Smitten, Abigail pursued her friendship independently. Mercy had been tutored in her youth alongside her brilliant and beloved brother, whose mental illness was now breaking the hearts of his family and friends. She was learned in the classics and history and had already begun to write plays. She would soon try to publish her work—under a pseudonym, of course, to hide her female identity—and to do so with the imprimatur of John Adams, whose adulation she reciprocated. In Abigail she recognized a kindred spirit but also a mode of access to John Adams's attention. For Abigail there were different motives. Mercy became not just a friend but a mentor and a model. But first Abigail would have to overcome her timidity.

She did so by finding common ground in their motherhood, asking Mercy for advice about parenting. "I was really so well pleased with your little offspring, that I must beg the favour of you to communicate to me the happy Art of 'rearing the tender thought, teaching the young Idea how to shoot, and pouring fresh instruction o'er the Mind.'" Abigail clearly was using her best imitation of an elevated style to address Mercy, a style that she had practiced in a draft before writing her final copy. It was labored and unnatural.

In signing off, after many paragraphs about the several grounds for her anticipated "improvement," Abigail once more sounded the refrain of deference that established the earliest framework of her relationship with Mercy. "I must beg your pardon for thus detaining you. I have so long neglected my pen that I am conscious I shall make but a poor figure. To your Friendship and candour I commit this," she wrote before finally concluding with the familiar "your obliged Friend & Humble Servant, Abigail Adams."

If at first Abigail felt most comfortable asking Mercy for advice about moth-ering—a ploy to engage the intimidating older woman, certainly, given that her own mother and mother-in-law and sister were handy—the time was not distant when she would shift to another: politics. The conflict between the mother coun-try and her colonies had risen to a dangerous level, as the latest taxes imposed on the colonies became the universal topic of protest. This time it was the tea tax that provided the substance for Abigail's and Mercy's shared outrage.

"The Tea that bainfull weed is arrived," announced Abigail to Mercy in early December 1773. "Great and I hope Effectual opposition has been made to the landing of it," she continued in the event that Mercy had not heard the news. "To the publick papers I must refer you for perticuliars. You will there find that the proceedings of our Citizens have been United, Spirited and firm." By re-porting public events and by expressing her response, Abigail had found a dis-tinctive and comfortable voice with Mercy. "The flame is kindled and like Lightning it catches from Soul to Soul. Great will be the devastation," she cor-rectly predicted, "if not timely quenched or allayed by some more Lenient Mea-sures." The inhibitions that had prevented her natural flow of words disappeared when she was stirred by passion.

Abigail's patriotism was founded on her reasoned sense of justice and injus-tice but also on her emotions. This combination, with its origins in her early religious training as well as more than ten years of association with John Ad-ams, overflowed into heartfelt prose. "Altho the mind is shocked at the Thought of sheding Humane Blood, more Especially the Blood of our countrymen, and a civil War is of all Wars, the most dreadfull, Such is the present Spirit that pre-vails, that if once they are made desperate Many, very Many of our Heroes will spend their lives in the cause," she wrote. Invoking, doubtlessly, both her recent reading of Gordon and Trenchard's essays *Cato's Letters*, and conversations with John, she embedded her grim predictions in the context of her feelings. Finally, she concluded with a bleak but prescient prediction of "heroes" dying "with the Speach of Cato in their Mouths, 'What a pitty it is, that we can dye but once to save our Country.'" Abigail loved to quote others.

Abigail's reaction to the arrival of tea reflected the volatile circumstances that existed in Boston that March of 1774. While John had determined to re-main aloof from politics upon his return to Boston, his resolve quickly evapo-rated. The arrival of a huge shipment of tea in the Boston harbor, in the face of the tax that had been levied by Parliament, had resulted in a boycott. As the beverage of choice throughout the colonies, tea had become the "bainfull weed" of Abigail's description, and Americans had agreed to forgo its consumption in protest against the tax.

Yet there the tea sat in Boston's harbor, and the government and the military were bound to unload it. There could be no accommodation to the inevitable clash. The historic "tea party" occurred on the night of December 16. The next morning John wrote: "Last Night 3 Cargoes of Bohea Tea were emptied into the Sea," and for the first time he exhibited not just approval but exuberance over the behavior of a mob:

> This is the most magnificent Movement of all. There is a Dignity, a
> Majesty, a Sublimity, in this last Effort of the Patriots, that I Greatly
> admire. The People should never rise, without doing something to
> be remembered—something notable And Striking. This Destruc-
> tion of the Tea is so bold, so daring, so firm, intrepid and inflexible,
> and it must have so important Consequences, and so lasting, that I
> can't but consider it as an Epocha in History.

John's prognostication proved correct. Three hundred forty-two chests of tea, worth approximately ten thousand pounds sterling, were floating in the Boston harbor. The destruction of the tea had important consequences in the form of punitive parliamentary legislation.

Among them, the most startling was the closing of the Boston harbor until the tea was paid for, excepting necessary food and fuel. This penalty would cripple Boston's economy. In addition, the governor's powers were increased and the people's legislative authority decreased. A new quartering act gave more power to the military. John wondered, meanwhile, "whether the Destruc-tion of this Tea was Necessary?" And he responded to himself that it was, "ab-solutely and indispensably so." The consequences were indeed far-reaching.

News of the Coercive Acts—or the Intolerable Acts, as they were known—reached America by the summer of 1774. Americans now realized that Britain had no intention of backing down; Parliament was determined to demonstrate its power. While more Americans gained a greater sense of themselves as vic-tims of an oppressive government, others remained loyal to Britain. The colo-nists became more politicized and more polarized. For the Adamses, there was no question. They were American patriots.

Once more his court activity dropped off, and once more John Adams was bereft of professional business. He traveled the circuit, hoping to pick up some cases where there were few. In the summer he ventured as far as Falmouth (now Portland, Maine), where he literally hung around for weeks on end. For com-pany he had other lawyers, but there was just so much conversation they could have. Throughout his life, John wrote when he was bored, and he did so now, but whereas in the past he confided his most private thoughts to his diary, he now had Abigail as confidante. "My Fancy runs about you perpetually," he wrote lovingly to her, soon after leaving Boston. "It is continually with you and in the Neighbourhood of you—frequently takes a Walk with you, and your little prattling, Nabby, Johnny, Charly and Tommy. We walk all together up Penn's Hill, over the Bridge to the Plain, down to the Garden." John's most optimistic fantasies returned them all to Braintree in an idyll of family romance.

He wrote to her every day, sometimes twice in a day, just as he must have spoken to her when they were together, baring his soul, emptying his tormented heart. "I am so idle, that I have not an easy Moment, without my Pen in my Hand," he complained on July 1. "I cant be easy without my Pen in my Hand, yet I know not what to write," he groused on July 5. He described the countryside. He described his companions. He recapitulated sermons. He gossiped. And he reminded Abigail not to repeat his stories. "I write you this Tittle Tatle, my Dear, in Confidence." Mostly, however, he worried about the future.

They could not predict the future. They did not know how the conflict would be resolved. They did not know if there would be further bloodshed or if the situation would remain in a stalemate for some time. They simply did not know how to conduct their lives or how to prepare for whatever was in store. In a particularly low moment, John promised Abigail: "I will not lie down and die in Dispair. If I cannot serve my Children by the Law, I will serve them by Agriculture, by Trade, by some Way, or other. I thank God I have a Head, an Heart and Hands, which if once fully exerted alltogether, will succeed in the World."

Prior to his departure on the northern circuit, patriotic leaders of the thirteen colonies had agreed to convene a conference in Philadelphia for the purpose of coordinating their responses to British policy. John Adams had been elected as one of Massachusetts's four delegates, along with Sam Adams, Robert Treat Paine, a colleague of John's from the bar, and the wealthy merchant Thomas Cushing. John left for the northern circuit knowing that in a few weeks he would make the longer journey to Pennsylvania but wishing to earn some income before setting off. The trip was hardly worth his while, and between complaints about his lack of cases, the Toryism he encountered among the people, and the cramped conditions of travel, he thought long and hard about his future and that of his family.

Within days he had concluded that he would return to farming. "I believe it is Time to think a little about my Family and Farm." And he began to plan. "Let us therefore my dear Partner, from that Affection which we feel for our lovely Babes, apply ourselves by every Way, we can, to the Cultivation of our Farm."

During the spring, prior to his departure for the northern circuit, John had purchased his brother's farm and the house adjacent to his. Having recently married, Peter Adams had moved to the farm of his new wife and was only too happy to sell the property that he had inherited from their father. This purchase more than doubled the size of John's farm in Braintree, and he could no longer manage the property on his own, especially when he was on the circuit, so he worried about it. He wondered about the hay, and if the "mowing and carting" were done. He was concerned that "Sea Weed and Marsh Mud and Sand" were procured to mix with manure for fertilizer. And he counseled Abigail to prepare for hard times.

"I must intreat you, my dear Partner," he wrote, addressing her by the term that they used to describe their shared relationship after nearly ten years of marriage, "in all the joys and Sorrows, Prosperity and Adversity of my Life, to take a Part with me in the Struggle." He didn't prescribe, demand, or order her; he "intreated" her to join her fate with his, knowing what her response would be and yet dignifying her with his petition. And with this he returned to the one alternative where he could envision security for his family: the farm. He asked her "to rouse your whole Attention to the Family, the stock, the Farm, the Dairy. . . . Keep the Hands [their farmhands] attentive to their Business, and [let] the most prudent Measures of every kind be adopted and pursued." Although he did not yet comprehend the dimensions of the role that he would play in future events, he very well knew that Abigail would be his trustworthy partner in them. Between them, the word *partner* was not a euphemism but a definition of their marriage.

Abigail had been seriously ill during the spring and had returned to her parents' home to be cared for. Her health alone would not have been a sufficient motive for the family to return to their Braintree home in early summer 1774. The primary reason was their fear of exposing themselves and their children to the violence that appeared imminent in Boston. British regulars arrived to reinforce the military presence already there. With the closing of the seaport, the economy was at a standstill. The already volatile situation had become more alarming. Besides, the law no longer promised a steady income, particularly as John found it impossible to suppress his politics. Several times when he might have been silent in the company of Tory sympathizers, he spoke up: "Thus you see how foolish I am," he wrote Abigail. "I cannot avoid exposing myself before these high Folk—my Feelings will at Times overcome my Modesty and Reserve—my Prudence, Policy and Discretion." The fact is, he wrote of himself,

> I have a Zeal at my Heart, for my Country and her Friends, which
> I cannot smother or conceal: it will burn out at Times and in Com-
> panies where it ought to be latent in my Breast. This Zeal will
> prove fatal to the Fortune and Felicity of my Family, if it is not
> regulated by a cooler Judgment than mine has hitherto been.

John Adams's zeal for his country, of course, would stifle any ambiguity about
their future.

As his journey to the northern circuit courts began to wind down, his attention turned to his next trip and its mission. "I dread the thought of the Congress's falling short of the Expectations of the Continent," he confessed, "but
especially of the People of this Province." He thought about the distance to be
traveled, about his companions on the trip and the prospect of "seeing more of
the World than I have seen before." And typically, in the face of the historic
event that would engage him over the next months, he began to worry:

> I wander alone, and ponder.—I muse, I mope, I ruminate. . . . the
> Objects before me, are too grand, and multifarious for my
> Comprehension.—We have not Men, fit for the Times. We are
> deficient in Genius, in Education, in Travel, in Fortune—in every
> Thing. I feel unutterable Anxiety.—God grant us Wisdom, and
> Fortitude!

Many thoughts and emotions spun in his head and his heart. But he miscalculated on several fronts. While his fears for sufficient military expertise and resources would prove prescient, his predictions about men and women of genius
and fortitude were incorrect, as he and Abigail would demonstrate. She reassured him: "You cannot be, I know, nor do I wish to see you an inactive Spectator, but if the Sword be drawn"—Abigail too made anxious and prescient
predictions—"I bid adieu to all domestick felicity."

In the meantime, they proceeded with pragmatic determination. He wrote
to her: "I think it will be necessary to make me up, a Couple of Pieces of new
Linnen. I am told, they wash miserably, at N. York, the Jerseys and Philadelphia too in Comparison of Boston, and am advised to carry a great deal of Linnen." John requested several changes of undergarments for his journey to the
First Continental Congress. Abigail would sew them. But she also made him a
light brown silk vest so that he could keep up appearances in Philadelphia.

Separation and the New Covenant

"OH THAT I WAS A SOLDIER!" JOHN WROTE TO ABIGAIL FROM Philadelphia, where the Continental Congress had recently convened in the spring of 1775. "I will be.—I am reading military Books.—Every Body must and will, and shall be a soldier." John was zealous. However, since he had no prior military experience and could not expect a higher rank than lieutenant, he concluded that he would be more effective in the halls of Congress. By 1775, John was widely acknowledged in those halls as a leader of the rebellious faction.

He no longer wavered on the issues of war and independence but had committed himself for the duration. "My Health and Life ought to be hazarded, in the Cause of my Country," he wrote to Abigail, "as well as yours and all my friends." He could foresee that the challenge would be daunting. "The Difficulty and Intricacy of it is prodigious," he wrote further.

> When 50 or 60 Men have a Constitution to form for a great Empire, at the same Time that they have a Country of fifteen hundred Miles extent to fortify, Millions to arm and train, a Naval Power to begin, an extensive Commerce to regulate, numerous Tribes of Indians to negotiate with, a standing Army of Twenty seven Thousand Men to raise, pay, victual and officer, I really shall pity those 50 or 60 Men."

That was John's short list. He was in his element as he never had been, except, perhaps, during his youth when he wanted to become a farmer. Never had

Abigail Smith Adams in a pastel painted in 1766 by the Salem limner, Benjamin Blyth, when she was a young bride and mother. Courtesy of the Massachusetts Historical Society.

John Adams in the companion portrait by Blyth is the earliest image of Adams and fails to capture his dynamic character. Courtesy of the Massachusetts Historical Society.

he experienced such a sense of mission, opportunity, and adventure. He was waging rebellion against the greatest empire of the eighteenth century. He was inspired by the idealism and the optimism that marked the radical wing of revolutionaries at the beginning of the war. Mostly, however, he understood the sense of power that came from executing this rebellion. His spirits had never been higher. He was doing something important, something that made him proud. Altogether this was as capricious an experience as could befall a provincial Boston attorney. He couldn't be a soldier, but he could participate in the planning and execution of the war and think about how to frame and compose a new kind of constitution. He was aware of the historic dimensions of the project in which he engaged with all his passion, intelligence, and belief. He was, in fact, exhilarated.

The practice of law had never exhilarated John Adams. He was fascinated by the study of law, and the opportunity to read law with Jeremiah Gridley and to participate in the Sodality, the monthly meetings to discuss legal theory, had absorbed him. For some time even the practice had engaged him. But to a man of his instincts—his intelligence, passions, energy—the tedium of law had begun to wear thin. The days and weeks of traveling on the circuit, boarding at crowded and inhospitable inns, the routine cases he handled—boundary disputes, family quarrels, business squabbles—portended a life of drudgery. Aside from the Boston Massacre trials, John's practice involved the daily disputes that made up the domestic lives of colonial Americans. He longed for something greater. He wrote drearily on his thirty-seventh birthday in 1772 that more than half his days had run out, and that "the Remainder of my Days I shall rather decline, in Sense, Spirit, and Activity." He complained: "And Yet I have my own and my Childrens Fortunes to make." He hoped, he wrote another time, to provide for his children the foundation for "an happier Life than has fallen to my Share." John had become bored, if not disenchanted, with his life as a lawyer in Massachusetts. He continued its pursuit as his duty to provide for his family.

Now, unforeseen by him and everyone else, he was running a revolution. His spirits were revived, his mind engaged. His duty now became transcendent: to preserve the liberty and civil rights of his countrymen. This duty stimulated his brain; it appealed to his ego; it bolstered his self-confidence. He discovered that the talents that had earned him success as a provincial lawyer—his sagacity and speech—suited him as well in this larger theater. He had arrived somewhat timidly at the First Continental Congress, wondering how he would measure up to the great delegates from the other states. To his satisfaction if not his amazement, he measured up. Now he had joined with them in an undertaking that consumed his attention and his energies in the best of missions. He was liberated from the law. He soon became liberated from most of his family responsibilities, because Abigail, his partner, was a willing consort in this new mission and relieved him of family cares. If not a soldier, John could still be a revolutionary.

SOON AFTER JOHN'S DEPARTURE FOR THE FIRST CONTINENTAL Congress in Philadelphia in the late summer of 1774, Abigail informed him that she had "taken a very great fondness for reading Rollin's ancient History," and she was determined to complete it "in these days of solitude." She referred to an English edition of Charles Rollin's ancient history (one of four editions that John owned), which had become the principal source for learning the classics in America by the late eighteenth century. "I find great pleasure and entertainment from it."

In John's absence, Abigail began this venture as a distraction from her loneliness. The consequence was that she became a profoundly learned woman, an autodidact. Her inspiration came from women she regarded as models, Mercy Otis Warren and Catherine Macaulay. Every letter she received from Mercy demonstrated to her the gap between their educations. Mercy wrote to Abigail in August 1774:

> I hope they will have no uncommon Dificulties to surmount or Hostile Movements to impede them, but if the Locrians should interrupt them, tell him I hope they will beware that no future annals may say they Chose an ambitious Philip for their Leader, who subverted the Noble order of the American Amphyctiones; and Built up a Monarchy on the Ruins of the Happy institution.

Mercy meant she hoped that American democracy wouldn't be subverted. If Abigail failed to notice the ponderousness of Mercy's prose, she admired her erudition. And while she only knew of Mrs. Macaulay by reputation, she was impressed that a woman wrote history. She was also challenged. Rather than retreating to self-pity, Abigail used John's absence as an opportunity to invade his library. She had no suspicion how extensive her opportunity to read would be in the coming years.

John departed from Boston on August 10 alongside fellow delegates Sam Adams, Robert Treat Paine, and Thomas Cushing, who provided their comfortable carriage. They were ceremoniously accompanied for several miles by a train of fifty or sixty men on horseback. Similarly bands of well-wishers greeted their entry into every city along the way: Worcester, New Haven, New York, and Princeton. At New Haven, John wrote: "As We came into the Town all the Bells in Town were sett to ringing, and the People Men, Women and Children, were crouding at the Doors and Windows as if it was to see a Coronation. At Nine O Clock the Cannon were fired, about a Dozen Guns I think."

They met patriots and fellow delegates: Silas Deane and Roger Sherman of Connecticut. Sherman was "between 50 and 60—a solid sensible Man." They met "Mr. Dwight and Mr. Davenport, two of the Tutors," at the college in New Haven. Later "Mr. Burr" came to see them. He meant Aaron Burr, the young lawyer and later legislator. Many of these men would become fellow revolutionaries.

In New York they met Mr. Alexander McDougall, the wealthy merchant who entertained them at his lavish mansion on the shore of the Hudson River. At Prince town, they enjoyed a "Dish of Coffee" with the president of the College of New Jersey (later called Princeton), Dr. John Witherspoon, who was "as high a Son of Liberty as any Man in America." John was impressed by the men he met and awestruck by their cities. New York City's streets were "vastly more regular and elegant than those in Boston and the Houses are more grand as well as neat."

Once they arrived in Philadelphia, the delegates began the hard work of getting to know one another, as individuals and as representatives of separate provinces that had little previous history of cooperation. Their political ties had been with the mother country. The business ahead of them had to do with mounting a unified protest against Britain.

John's days were filled, he wrote to Abigail, from "the Moment I get out of Bed, untill I return to it. Visits, Ceremonies, Company, Business, . . . etc. etc. etc." He had so much to learn, including "the Characters and Tempers, the Principles and Views of fifty Gentlemen total Strangers to me to study, and the Trade, Policy, and whole Interest of a Dozen Provinces to learn when I came here." In addition, there were "Pamphlets, News Papers, and private Letters to read," and his list went on.

Awed by the assemblage of men who congregated in Carpenters' Hall, he observed: "There is in the Congress a Collection of the greatest Men upon this Continent, in Point of Abilities, Virtues and Fortunes." John certainly measured himself against other delegates. He was an obscure New Englander whose reputation would have to be earned. Meanwhile, he prepared for this role by learning about these men with whom he would execute a revolution, by studying their unique characters and their colonies. It was a shrewd move, and doubtless every delegate was doing the same. John's behavior was under scrutiny as well.

Meanwhile, the situation in and around Boston grew more tense. A military government had replaced the provincial government, and the size of the regiments that patrolled the harbor and streets was increased by many thousands of new soldiers. Abigail, who became John's reliable informant from the home front, reported to him that the citizens rebelled by electing their own illicit legislative bodies. "The first of September or the month of September, perhaps may be of as much importance to Great Britan as the Ides of March were to Caeser," she concluded, using her newly acquired knowledge of ancient history. Based upon her reading, Abigail could recognize the historic moment. "Did ever any Kingdom or State regain their Liberty, when once it was invaded without Blood shed?" she wondered. "I cannot think of it without horror."

The weeks passed, and she did not hear from John. She wrote the words that become a trope in their communications for the next decade: "I want much to hear from you." Two weeks later she persisted, "I am very impatient to receive a letter from you," and she delivered a bit of encouragement: "I hear that Mr. Adams [Sam] wrote to his Son and the Speaker [Cushing] to his Lady," offering him an excuse as well, "but perhaps you did not know of the opportunity." Finally by mid-September she complained: "Five Weeks have past and not one line have I received."

Just short of six weeks after his departure, Abigail at last received a letter from John. She described the effect: "It really gave me such a flow of Spirits," she wrote, "that I was not composed eno to sleep till one oclock." Having written her powerful reaction to seeing John's handwriting, giving palpable life to his letter and sensuously responding to his imagined presence, she became nervous about her spontaneous words being read by others. She warned him: "You will burn all these Letters least they should fall from your pocket and thus expose your most affectionate Friend," instructions that John ignored.

Time passed, and factions developed in Carpenters' Hall at Philadelphia, where the delegates of twelve of the thirteen colonies met. Even within the radical faction a spectrum of opinions existed about reconciliation with Britain. Some delegates, such as Sam Adams and Patrick Henry of Virginia, took the most extreme position, arguing for independence, while conservatives such as Pennsylvanian John Dickinson, a Quaker, urged moderation. Some such as Joseph Galloway, then the speaker of Pennsylvania's legislature, would become Tories. There was also the silent, imposing figure of George Washington from Virginia, whose reputation had preceded him. John heard that "Coll. Washington made the most eloquent Speech at the Virginia Convention that ever was made. Says he, 'I will raise 1000 Men, subsist them at my own Expence, and march my self at their Head for the Relief of Boston.'" Legends about Washington already circulated, and these were sweet words indeed to the ears of the Massachusetts contingent.

John considered it his mission to create harmony among the many dissonant voices that clashed within the hall. He proposed compromises not only to create a united front within the colonies but also toward Britain. As the weeks of discussion dragged on, however, his original awe for his colleagues faded.

> This Assembly is like no other that ever existed. Every Man in it is a great Man—an orator, a Critick, a statesman, and there fore every Man upon every Question must shew his oratory, his Criticism and his Political Abilities. . . . I believe if it was moved and seconded that We should come to a Resolution that Three and two make five We should be entertained with Logick and Rhetorick, Law, History, Politicks and Mathematicks, concerning the Subject for two whole Days, and then We should pass the Resolution unanimously in the Affirmative.

If John coped with factions in Philadelphia, Abigail reported similar conflicts at home. Invited to dinner at Colonel Quincy's house, she heard "a little clashing of parties you may be sure," she told John. Mrs. Quincy declared loyalty to the patriots, while her husband argued the Tory case. "Mr. Sam's Wife said she thought it high time for her Husband to turn about, he had not done half so clever since he left her advice." Samuel Quincy left for England, eventually, while his wife remained in Massachusetts.

John expected to be away for two months, but three was more accurate. And he worried about the farm. In his absence, Abigail reported on its conditions: "We are burnt up with the drouth, having had no rain since you left us." She later reported, more whimsically in the spirit of the times:

> The drought has been very severe. My poor Cows will certainly prefer a petition to you, setting forth their Greavences and informing you that they have been deprived of their ancient privilages, whereby they are become great Sufferers, and desiring that they may be restored to them, more espicially as their living by reason of the drought is all taken from them, and their property which they hold else where is all decaying.

Unconsciously, she used the first person singular for her cows, a convention that became her habit. She presented a whimsical face to John, but all was not whimsy in her domestic world.

Mercy best described their dilemma as war grew closer: "Shall I own to you that the Woman and the Mother daily arouse my fears and fill my Heart with anxious Concern for the decision of the Mighty Controversy between Great Britain and the Colonies," she wrote in a typically overloaded sentence to Abigail. "Methinks I see no Less than five sons who must Buckle on the Harness And perhaps fall a sacrifice to the Manes of Liberty Ere she again revives and spreads her Chearful Banner over this part of the Globe." As the mother of five grown sons, she dreaded the fight. If pressed, the defense of colonial liberty would entail a painful price.

Furthermore, as the wives of patriotic leaders, Abigail and Mercy had reason to fear for their personal safety. In their volatile social world, small incendiary issues could ignite huge reprisals. Rising to the occasion in a typical linguistic obfuscation, Mercy remarked that despite the risks involved, "we shall never wish them to do anything for our sakes Repugnant to Honour or Conscience."

John maintained his honor and conscience in Philadelphia, and despite the differences among them and their lack of experience working together, the delegates made huge progress. John chaired the committee that finally drafted a Declaration of Grievances to the King. It was less sweeping than he and many colleagues preferred, but it represented a compromise with the more moderate delegates. Addressed to King George instead of Parliament, which had passed the repressive legislation, the colonists adopted a strategy that was based on tradition. They argued that Parliament did not have the right to pass legislation for the colonies, because their original charters were granted by the king and gave them the right to legislate internal matters.

With this and other achievements, the First Continental Congress concluded its session, and John Adams left Philadelphia at the end of October 1774, feeling weary and triumphant but convinced that war was inevitable. Reports from Boston described military movements. In temper the colonies were united in resistance, though feelings were shy of outright independence. Leaving the city, John became nostalgic. "Took our Departure in a very great Rain, from the happy, the peacefull, the elegant, the hospitable, and polite City of Phyladelphia," he wrote in his diary. "It is not very likely that I shall ever see this Part of the World again." It was one of John's less accurate predictions.

Elated when she heard the news that Congress had disbanded, Abigail took advantage of a safe conveyance to describe her excitement. "I dare not express to you at 300 miles distant how ardently I long for your return," she wrote. "I have some very miserly Wishes; and cannot consent to your spending one hour in Town till at least I have had you 12." Anticipating that he would rush off to Boston for business, she stated her requirements with unguarded affection:

> The Idea plays about my Heart, unnerves my hand whilst I write, awakens all the tender sentiments that years have encreased and matured, and which when with me were every day dispensing to you. The whole collected stock of ten weeks absence knows not how to brook any longer restraint, but will break forth and flow thro my pen. May the like sensations enter thy breast, and (in spite of all the weighty cares of State) Mingle themselves with those I wish to communicate, for in giving them utterance I have felt more sincere pleasure than I have known since the 10 of August.

Once more, Abigail spontaneously described her emotional state but also considered their bleak future. "It looks as tho the curtain was but just drawn and only the first Scene of the infernal plot disclosed and whether the end will be tragical Heaven alone knows."

The delegates' journey from Philadelphia to Boston over the same route that they had taken three months earlier proceeded speedily and without ceremony. They were in a hurry to get home. "My Birthday. I am 39 Years of Age," John recorded tersely on his second day on the road. He was in New Jersey, galloping toward New York. He arrived in Braintree on November 10, 1774.

PRIOR TO CONCLUDING ITS BUSINESS IN LATE OCTOBER, THE Continental Congress had agreed to reconvene the following May, again in Philadelphia. John, not certain of being reappointed as a delegate, busied himself at home with politics and his farm. He also wrote another series of newspaper articles. This time he was inspired by a series of articles, anonymously signed "Massachusettensis," that advocated the Loyalist case. Believing them once more to be the work of his former close friend Jonathan Sewall, John wrote the colonial defense under the title "Novanglus" for New England.

But it was not only John who resorted to his pen during this period of the growing crisis. Abigail did, too, though she wrote in the form most available to her as a woman, the private letter. Her letters maintained her contact with John and others and also allowed her to express opinions, just as John's essays did in the public forum. Because she was natural and spontaneous, rarely making fair copies, she excelled at the letter form. Her artlessness, her capacity to reveal her feelings vividly makes her correspondence the best historical record written by a woman of the entire revolutionary era. But Abigail was not thinking of history or records when she wrote; she was thinking of the crisis that disrupted her world and her family. By contrast, John understood that his compositions were written as history. Their two forms—his the essay and hers the letter—tell two sides of the same story.

Abigail wrote privately to the British historian Catherine Macaulay, in England, knowing her sympathy with the colonies. She began by summarizing events as she observed them.

> Should I attempt to discribe to you the complicated miseries and distresses brought upon us by the late inhumane acts of the British parliment my pen would faill me. Suffice it to say, that we are invaded with fleets and Armies, our commerce not only obstructed, but totally ruined, the courts of Justice shut, many driven out from the Metropolis, thousands reduced to want, or dependant upon the charity of their neighbours for a daily supply of food, all the Horrours of a civil war threatening us on one hand, and the chains of Slavery ready forged for us on the other.

Abigail's catalog of abuses was concise and accurate. This expression of patriotism was her way of entering the political arena, appealing to the sympathy of an influential Britishwoman. She added: "The only alternative which every American thinks of is Liberty or Death."

Warming to her topic, Abigail railed to Mercy against "an Ignorant abandoned Soldiery who are made to believe that their Errant here is to Quell a Lawless Set of Rebels," referring to the British soldiers, who patrolled their roads and streets and harbors. "Who can think of it without the utmost indignation," she wrote, and vowed, "Is it not better to die the last of British freemen than live the first of British Slaves." Patriotic rhetoric was not lost on Abigail, who responded to the same news articles that had inflamed John to write his Novanglus letters. "The die is cast," she quoted to Mercy, and forecast that Britain's collapse would compare with that of Rome.

Abigail's vituperation poured out onto the page. But as she often did with Mercy, she expressed her fears as one woman to another. "Those who have the most to lose"—she meant their loved ones—"have most to fear. The Natural timidity of our sex always seeks for a relief in the encouragement and protection of the other.

> Let these truths . . . be indelibly impressed on our Minds that we cannot be happy without being free, that we cannot be free without being secure in our property, that we cannot be secure in our property if without our consent others may as by right take it away.

Abigail wrote as if she, too, were composing a tract for some gazette that would publish her words. She neither expected nor desired publication; that was not her plan. But she was inspired and needed to record her passions, just as John did, so she wrote letters to friends like Mercy.

Mercy, however, often had a different agenda when she wrote to Abigail. She had begun to write for publication, albeit using a male pseudonym to disguise her identity. She wrote poetry and now had written a play, called *The Group*, in which she satirized the British leaders in Massachusetts. Mercy, further, sought approval from John Adams, who despite the pressure of his obligations wrote discerning and complimentary reviews of the works that she regularly dispatched to him. He also assisted in their publication.

Sometimes, however, he neglected her, and the best recourse to get to him was through Abigail. "If you please," she wrote Abigail, "you may tell a Gentleman of my acquaintance whom I much Esteem"—she praised "Novanglus," before making her point: "Yet I was in hopes Ere this to have heard something particularly from Mr. Adams," and she apologized for her intrusiveness. Mercy recognized the imposition on John's time, but she was eager to publish her work. She chose this circuitous route through Abigail, who understood the difficulty faced by an educated woman of talent.

TENSIONS BETWEEN ENGLAND AND HER COLONIES CONTINUED to move toward confrontation, as patriotic militia groups throughout the colonies gathered for training. In Boston, General Thomas Gage, now governor, felt pressured to quell the nascent rebellion. As spring approached, he decided to surprise the militias. With the utmost secrecy, he planned an action to seize the colonial store of gunpowder at Concord. While his regiments were alerted, preparing for they knew not what, Gage confided his plan to two people, a scout and his wife. Somehow the secret plan leaked, so that William Dawes and Paul Revere could alert the townspeople of Concord and Lexington. The betrayal is now attributed to the American-born Margaret Kemble Gage, the general's wife, who decided to cast her lot with her native land. As a result he banished her to England immediately. Some months later he followed her, but he never forgave her. They lived unhappily ever after. Meanwhile, the British met colonial militiamen first at Lexington and then at Concord; shots were fired; men were killed and wounded on both sides. The war had begun.

By now John Adams had been appointed, along with Sam Adams, Thomas Cushing, Robert Treat Paine, and John Hancock, as delegates to the Second Continental Congress in Philadelphia. Instead of setting off with the others, John detoured to survey the Massachusetts militia at Cambridge and view the battle sites in Lexington and Concord. He found great confusion and distress among the militia. "Artillery, Arms, Cloathing were wanting and a sufficient Supply of Provisions not easily obtained." He added that neither the officers nor the men "wanted Spirits or Resolution." Along the "Scene of Action" he met with inhabitants who described the skirmishes. John decided that "the Die was cast, the Rubicon passed, and . . . if We did not defend ourselves they would kill Us."

On April 26, 1775, John set out for Philadelphia, accompanied by his young servant Joseph Bass, and joined with the rest of the Massachusetts delegation at Hartford. Once more, they were greeted along the way by "a great Number of Gentlemen in Carriages and on horseback, and all the Way their Numbers increased. . . . The same Ardour was continued all the Way to Philadelphia."

The Second Continental Congress convened at the State House (now Independence Hall) in mid-May. This time Georgia sent a delegation, which meant that all thirteen colonies were represented. This full house did not, however, insure unanimity. The same factions that had departed from the first Congress in October returned in May. Some of the delegates favored a confrontation with

Britain, while others demanded further negotiations. This time, however, polarization between the delegates from the northern colonies and those from the southern became more pronounced. While lesser issues such as patterns of trade divided the sections, the issue of southern slavery became the subtle subtext on the convention floor and would continue for the duration of the revolution and afterward. So sensitive was this issue that the delegates avoided it, suppressing the one topic that would become the deal breaker for their unification. It was the elephant in the State House.

To John, then, it was a great relief to inform Abigail at the end of May: "The Congress will support Massachusetts." His satisfaction was palpable. Thirteen states had unanimously—but not without debate—concluded that they would send military aid, and most began immediately to mobilize their militias. That accomplished, the challenges before the Congress were formidable, he explained, but he was optimistic. By now John was widely acknowledged as a leader in Congress.

It was John who recommended General George Washington, who had come to the Congress in uniform, as commander of the American armies. He informed Abigail in glowing terms that "Congress have made the Choice of the modest and virtuous, the amiable, generous and brave George Washington Esqr., to be the General of the American Army." The appointment would take effect immediately, he explained further to Abigail, in order to "cement and secure the Union of these Colonies." The choice of a Virginian was important because it would insure the support of that state—indeed, of the South—for New England. Congress went on to make further appointments to the top ranks of the officer corps, selecting men who would be representative of the states as well as the wealthier classes of men.

The work before Congress was formidable. The delegates gathered every day except Sunday from ten in the morning to five or six in the evening. Early in the mornings, the members met as small committees with specific assignments. In the evenings, various groups went to dinner to discuss strategies or work out differences among themselves. John, serving on many committees, complained endlessly of fatigue, about his severely strained eyesight and the heat. He also wrote cautiously to Abigail about the debates in the Congress. They were bound to secrecy, and besides, he was concerned about the safe conduct of his letters.

All the while an argument continued on the floor of the Congress over the issue of extending a final bid for reconciliation to the king. John was disgusted with this debate, which he saw as taking up valuable time. He fumed and harangued, but ultimately, in the interests of compromise, he conceded and signed a document. One last appeal, the "Olive Branch Petition," was extended to England, where the king summarily rejected it.

Meanwhile, John had earned the enmity of John Dickinson, the author of this petition and a man with whom he had had cordial relations previously. In his nightmare come true, a hastily written and indiscreet letter John wrote to James Warren was intercepted and printed by the Tory press. In it John had referred to Dickinson as a "piddling genious" who gave a "silly Cast to our whole doings." The piddling genious was offended and stopped speaking to John but ultimately fought with the Pennsylvania militia as a colonel. For a short time, John was shunned at Congress, though some, such as the maverick General Charles Lee, applauded him.

WHILE JOHN LABORED IN THE HEAT OF PHILADELPHIA, ABIGAIL passed the early weeks of June in continual fear of an attack. Boston was under siege. The news reported horrible suffering: food shortages, curfews, arrests. There were frequent raids on offshore islands that Abigail related to John, but more alarming was an impending assault. "We now expect our Sea coasts ravaged. Perhaps, the very next Letter I write will inform you that I am driven away from our, yet quiet cottage." John had warned Abigail to flee inland if necessary. Meanwhile, General Gage's failure to move quickly against the rebels after Lexington and Concord puzzled even the British ministry, which sent three new generals to replace him. Rumors of impending battles were rife.

Finally, the British garrison attacked the colonial militias entrenched on Breed's Hill, an engagement that was misnamed the Battle of Bunker Hill. Abigail observed the fighting alongside her eldest son by climbing Penn's Hill near her farm, where, horrified, they watched the deadly fireworks display. "The year 1775 was the eighth year of my age," John Quincy wrote to a friend three quarters of a century later as an elderly statesman. "I saw with my own eyes those fires, and heard Britannia's thunders in the Battle of Bunker's hill and witnessed the tears of my mother and mingled with them my own."

For the duration of the battle, Abigail and her children and servants were witness to sights and sounds of war. "The constant roar of the cannon is so [distre]ssing that we can not Eat, Drink or Sleep," Abigail wrote to John, four hundred miles distant. As she would do in times of distress, she summoned his presence through letters. "The Day; perhaps the decisive Day is come on which the fate of America depends," she wrote, thinking that this battle would seal their destiny, not yet able to imagine that the conflict would go on for eight more years. "My bursting Heart must find vent at my pen. I have just heard that our dear Friend Dr. Warren is no more but fell gloriously fighting for his Country." She referred to Joseph Warren, the thirty-six-year-old patriot who had been their family physician as well as close friend in Boston. Warren's heroic end quickly became symbolic of the revolutionary horror as the romanticized depiction of this scene was portrayed by the painter John Trumbull in his panoramic *Death of Dr. Warren.* The scene was also captured in Abigail's words to John.

> Great is our Loss. He has distinguished himself in every engagement, by his courage and fortitude. . . . The race is not to the swift, nor the battle to the strong—but the God of Israel is he that giveth strength & power unto his people. Trust in him at all times, ye people pour out your hearts before him. God is a refuge for us.

Religion was Abigail's refuge now as in all the hardships of her life. But she poured out her heart to John. "I shall tarry here till tis thought unsafe by my Friends, & then I have secured myself a retreat at your Brothers who has kindly offerd me part of his house." She added: "I cannot compose myself to write any further at present.—I will add more as I hear further." She did add more in a few days but could not accurately account for the battle. Rumors were manifold and she would not trust them, but "the Spirits of the people are very good." She signed herself "Portia."

Portia was the pen name that Abigail assumed to sign her letters during the Revolutionary War. Her classically educated friend Mercy Warren had proposed new epistolary identities for both of them a few months earlier, referring to the "Courage of an Aria or a Portia in a Day of trial like theirs." Their pen names—Mercy signed herself "Marcia"—symbolized their new roles as the wives of heroic statesmen. Portia was the beleaguered wife of the Roman Brutus, who in Shakespeare's version despaired and took her own life. She noted that this unfortunate and unwanted final detail wouldn't have happened if "they Lived in the Days of Christianity." Mercy used her sources selectively. And Abigail became Portia.

Within a week, news of the battle reached Philadelphia in record time. "God Almightys Providence preserve, sustain, and comfort you," John wrote with alarm, his best recourse at a distance a prayer for Abigail. A few days later, he hastily scribbled: "Courage, my dear! We shall be supported in Life, or comforted in Death." He praised the bravery of the Boston militia and noted that Congress was in the process of sending help. Just a few days earlier Generals Washington, Lee, and Schuyler had departed from Philadelphia for Boston. Congress turned its attention to the business at hand, building a unified and national army. Coastal raids continued to plague the citizens of Massachusetts.

An engagement took place at Grape Island, near the Adams home, where British troops attempted to capture coveted grain supplies. Fearing an invasion, Abigail took the precaution of sending John's books inland to be housed at his brother Peter's house.

A difficult issue developed within the family. John's youngest brother, Elihu, wished to enlist in the army, but their mother opposed his plan. He was married with two young children. "Your good Mother is really voilent against it. I cannot persuaid nor reason her into a consent. Neither he nor I dare let her know that he is trying for a place," Abigail informed John. She secured a commission for Elihu by writing, at John's suggestion, to James Warren. All around her, young—and some not so young—men, neighbors as well as relatives, were enlisting. Her own younger brother, William Smith Jr., had just received a captain's commission and was stationed at Cambridge.

Under the circumstances, Abigail carried on with her normal responsibilities as best she could. "I would not have you be distressd about me," she wrote John. "Danger they say makes people valient. Heitherto I have been distress'd, but not dismayed." Her major concerns, she stressed to John, were for her country and "her Sons. I have bled with them, and for them." However, the blockade had made some needed items scarce, so she requested that he purchase and send to her "pins" for herself as well as needles for the local weaver. Many domestic goods were in short supply. "We shall very soon have no coffee nor sugar nor pepper here—but huckle berrys and milk we are not obliged to commerce for." With trade effectively cut off, local production provided the most fundamental necessities.

John did not lose sight of the big picture: "Our Consolation must be this, my dear, that Cities may be rebuilt, and a People reduced to Poverty, may acquire fresh Property: But a Constitution of Government once changed from Freedom, can never be restored. Liberty once lost is lost forever." And he continued to acknowledge Abigail's endeavors: "You are really brave, my dear, you are an Heroine."

Abigail had other problems at home. One of the Adamses' two houses had been allocated for the use of their laborers, a family named Hayden, a father and two sons. The Hayden sons had signed up for the militia—bounties were offered to encourage sign-ups—and old Hayden, who did no work, now occupied the large house by himself, except for a small corner of it that Abigail used as her dairy. As refugees from Boston were desperate for housing, Abigail wanted to offer part of the house to some friends who were now homeless. But she could not persuade Hayden to move or make room for others by using a smaller section of the house.

"I have met with some abuse and very Ill treatment. I want you for my protector and justifier," she wrote to John, knowing the ageless dilemma that strong words from a man were more effective than those from a woman. She explained that their Boston friend George Trott and his family could not "procure a house any where," because of the exodus from Boston. She repeatedly attempted to conciliate Hayden with every kind of compromise, but nothing worked. "He will not [move into the other part of the house] and all the art of Man shall not stir him, even dares me to put any article out of one room into an other."

Meanwhile, Abigail had taken the Trotts into her own crowded house and needed John's legal advice. "I want to know whether his things may be removed into the other part of the house, whether he consents or not?" She ended in a fury. "I feel too angry to make this any thing further than a Letter of Business. I am most sincerely yours," and she signed with her legal name, "Abigail Adams." It would be three more years before Abigail got rid of Hayden by bribing him out. The fate of the poor Trotts is unknown, but they did not remain with Abigail.

John did write to warn Hayden to behave himself, but his priorities were of a much larger scope than domestic disputes. He continued to labor in the business of the Congress, complaining on occasion of the "suffocating Heats of the City, and the wasting, exhausting Debates of the Congress." His respites were his Sunday excursions into the countryside. Sometimes he visited local families, where seeing children reminded him of his own young family and the hardship his absence created for their upbringing. "My poor Children, I fear will loose some Advantages in Point of Education, from my continual Absence from them." And he counseled Abigail to substitute for him. "Truth, Sobriety, Industry should be pe[r]petually inculcated upon them. Pray my dear, let them be taught Geography and the Art of copying as well as drawing Plans of Cities, Provinces, Kingdoms, and Countries—especially of America." John was currently engaged in examining books about military tactics. He translated his own preoccupation into pedagogy for his children, though he added, "But their Honour, Truth, in one Word their Morals, are of most importance. I hope these will be kept pure." In this, John—and Abigail—never changed.

THE SUMMER OF 1775 PASSED WHILE ABIGAIL AND JOHN REmained connected through letters. They exchanged news and gossip in a conversation that was confined to paper. Lapses in time were not so much endured as expected. All the while they developed a manner of communicating that was personal and private. "All the Letters I receive from you seem to be wrote in so much haste, that they scarcely leave room for a social feeling," Abigail scolded John after three months' absence. "I want some sentimental Effusions of the Heart." Tell me that you love me, that you miss me, she pleaded.

> I am sure you are not destitute of them or are they all absorbed in the great publick. Much is due to that I know, but being part of the whole I lay claim to a Larger Share than I have had. You used to be more communicative a Sundays. I always loved a Sabeth days letter, for then you had a greater command of your time—but hush to all complaints.

He, in turn, tried to comply: "It is now almost three Months since I left you, in every Part of which my Anxiety about you and the Children, as well as our Country, has been extreme." Yes, his concern for his family was always with him, he responded, as well as his concern for the nation, but "the Business I have had upon my Mind has been as great and important as can be intrusted to [One] Man."

She requested information, so she could tell stories at home. "There is a degree of Pleasure in being about to tell new's—especially any which so nearly concerns us as all your proceedings do." He couldn't repeat the secret deliberations in Congress, but he did supply her with gossip about other members, good gossip, that wouldn't embarrass him if it fell into unfriendly hands. "Dr. Franklin"—he meant Benjamin—"is a great and good Man." Mr. Biddle was ill. Mr. Mifflin left to enter the military. Knowing her piety, he reported regularly about church attendance and even repeated sermons.

In midsummer, an anxious Abigail wrote with bad news: "Your Brother Elihu lies very dangerously sick with a Dysentery." He had been "very bad for more than a week, his life is despaired of." Against the resistance of his mother, Elihu had entered the army and while in camp had contracted the disease. "Your Mother is with him in great anguish. I hear this morning that he is sensible of his Danger, and calmly resigned to the will of Heaven." One day later Abigail confirmed Elihu's death. "Grief and Sympathy I feel for the looss of your Brother, cut of in the pride of life and the bloom of Manhood!" The casualties of war were mounting among people they cherished. With every report, Abigail was reminded of the dangers to John: "Heaven san[c]tify this affliction to us, and make me properly thankful that it is not my sad lot to mourn the loss of a Husband in the room of a Brother."

Despite the mourning, there was good news, for John was on his way home. Congress took a break in the worst of the summer heat. Everyone needed time out. The press of business had been great. But so were the accomplishments of this small group of dedicated patriots. This Congress created an army, appointed a commander in chief and an officers corps; it began to organize a supply system, issued the first continental money, established a postal system, and discussed a plan of confederation in addition to setting forth various declarations of principles to Americans and the world concerning their mission. Above all, this miscellany of men from divergent backgrounds, holding vastly different opinions, all of which they were compelled to argue over, managed to come together to begin the process of nation building. It was a daunting task. The times were daunting in Philadelphia as well as in Braintree.

John's brief furlough was hardly spent at home in Braintree. He dashed off immediately to report to the provincial government, sitting at Watertown, and he visited the military headquarters at Cambridge, where he conferred with Generals George Washington, Charles Lee, Philip Schuyler, Artemas Ward, and Horatio Gates. General Lee took him to visit the outposts nearest the enemy at Charleston for a frontline view of the military situation. With his eye for amusing detail, John noted that General Lee had brought with him from Virginia his pack of hunting dogs. But John noted that surrounded by his notorious canine entourage, Lee could be easily identified as a target.

In order to spend as much time as possible in his company, Abigail accompanied John to Watertown in late August. There she found her friend Mercy and wives of other delegates who were staying close to their husbands. Abigail had considered accompanying John to Philadelphia several times, but the distance and the length of his sojourns made it impossible for her to make the journey. She was needed at home to care for her children and the household, to say nothing of their farm enterprises. She could, however, spare two days for a visit to Watertown.

In early September John departed for Philadelphia accompanied by Sam Adams. They arrived just before the opening of Congress on September 12. The timing could not have been worse for Abigail.

"Since you left me I have passed thro great distress both of Body and Mind," she wrote to him on September 8. The epidemic that was rife in the military that summer and had taken the life of Elihu Adams in August had spread southward by fall. "You may remember Isaac was unwell when you went from home," she wrote, reminding John of their servant boy's illness. "His Disorder increasd till a voilent Dysentery was the consequence of his complaints." She added, "There was no resting place in the House for his terible Groans." Isaac had lain ill for a week, but appeared to be recovering. "Two days after he was sick, I was seaz'd with the same disorder in a voilent manner," she continued.

Dysentery is a severe intestinal disease that causes extreme abdominal pain.

In the eighteenth century there was no cure, and it was mortal. She had considered sending for John to return home but realized that he would be at risk of contracting the disease himself, so she did not. After three days she recovered, but "the next person in the same week was Suszy," her servant girl. Since Suszy's family lived nearby, she was sent home to recuperate. Meanwhile, "our Little Tommy was the next, and he lies very ill now." Then Patty, the other servant girl, "was seazd." Abigail was distraught. "Our House is an hospital in every part, and what with my own weakness and distress of mind for my family I have been unhappy enough."

The entire neighborhood was afflicted. "So sickly and so Mortal a time the oldest Man does not remember," Abigail wrote, and proceeded to send a catalog of illness and death. "Mrs. Randle has one child that is not expected to live out the night, Mrs. Belcher has an other, Joseph Bracket an other, Deacon Adams has lost one, but is upon the recovery himself. . . . Mr. Wibird lies bad. Major Miller is dangerous. Revd. Mr. Gay is not expected to live." With such widespread misery, there was little hope of getting assistance to care for the ailing in her own home. She feared that her own symptoms would recur, but they did not.

John, meanwhile, was oblivious to the situation at home. He had arrived in Philadelphia and resumed his work in Congress. The first order of business was to persuade the separate states to adopt constitutions. John no longer used the words "colony" or "mother country." He favored independence, which meant that each state needed to convene a representative body to provide for governance. While John was negotiating the establishment of political institutions, Abigail at home coped with a household of dysentery patients. Their struggles could hardly have been more different.

"Tis now two days since I wrote," Abigail reported to John. Three-year-old Tommy was "unwilling any body but Mamma should do for him, and if he was I could not find any body." He appeared to be mending. "His Bowels are better, but was you to look in upon him you would not know him, from a hearty hale corn fed Boy, he is become pale lean and wan." Isaac was slowly recovering, but Patty's condition was worse. Abigail sent a list of medicines that John might procure for her in Philadelphia: a quarter of a pound of nutmegs, an ounce of cloves, two of cinnamon, and one of Indian root. Abigail, like everyone else in the eighteenth century, used herbal medicines, and perhaps also not unique, she was mindful of the cost, so she informed John of the going rates of each. She was also self-conscious about her letter: "Distroy this. Such a doleful tale it contains can give no pleasure to any one," and she included the latest mortality count: eighteen in Mr. Weld's parish. But John valued and saved even her doleful tales.

The debates droned on in Congress. Bored, John scribbled his impressions of his fellow delegates. "Nelson is a fat Man," but he was "lively, for his weight. . . . Rutledge is a very uncouth, and ungracefull Speaker; . . . Sherman's air is the Reverse of Grace; . . . Hogaths Genius could not have invented a Motion more opposite to grace; . . . Mr. Dickinsons Air, Gate, and Action are not much more elegant." John's verbal doodles occupied the hours in between the committee meetings where much of the business took place. If he was disturbed by the snub he received from Dickinson, who had "passed hautily by" on the street, offended by the letter printed in the papers, he denied it. "I shall for the future pass him, in the same manner."

By the end of September, John still had not received Abigail's letters. A note from Mrs. Warren had mentioned that Abigail had been ill but recovered. The reason for the delay was that Abigail sent her letters by way of James Warren in Watertown, as John had advised her to do, and Warren had collected several of hers with some of his own, and their delivery had been postponed by a week.

Finally, on the first of October, John received Abigail's letters and responded: "I feel—I tremble for You. Poor Tommy! . . . You may easily conceive the State of Mind, in which I am, at present.—Uncertain and apprehensive, at first I suddenly thought of setting off, immediately for Braintree, and I have not yet determined otherwise." He continued to express his internal conflict: "Yet the State of public Affairs is so critical, that I am half afraid to leave my Station, Altho my Presence here is of no great Consequence."

John's uncertainties and conflicts, his ambivalence about his commitments, became a classic mark of his ongoing struggles to determine where his duty lay. He was sincerely anguished about Abigail and his family. The dangers at home terrified him. At the same time, even while he acknowledged that his presence might not affect the events unfolding in Congress, he was committed to pursuing a path toward independence that he could foresee so clearly. He was impatient and even alarmed that without him events could take a disastrous turn, caving in to the forces of conservatism that still abounded in the back rooms— and on the floor—of Congress.

Abigail's next letter was hardly more encouraging. "I set myself down to write with a Heart depressed with the Melancholy Scenes arround me," she wrote. "My Letter will be only a Bill of Mortality," and she recounted the numbers of deaths, especially among children. In Weymouth, Dr. Tufts had "betwen 60 and 70" patients. John Thaxter, John's law clerk and tutor of the children, had taken the disease and gone home to be nursed. So, too, had Mr. Tudor, another clerk. Never before had Abigail written so despondently. Never had she been tested so cruelly by circumstances. Never had she been so isolated in times of trial. "So uncertain and so transotory are all the enjoy-ments of Life that were it not for the tender connections which bind us here, would it not be folly to wish for a continuance here?" she asked, not expecting John to respond. "I think I shall never be wedded to the World, and were I to loose about a Dozen of my dearest Connections I should have no further real-ish for Life." Abigail was depressed. "To Bear and Suffer is our portion here." It had been three weeks since John had left home, and she had as yet received no news of him.

Another week passed. Abigail's lament continued: "I set down with a heavy Heart to write to you. I have had no other since you left me. Woe follows Woe, and one affliction treads upon the heal of an other." Her mother had become ill with the disease. Elizabeth Smith, who had come each day to help Abigail with the nursing in her household, was now so ill that there was little hope for her recovery. "The desolation of War is not so distressing as the Havock made by the pestilence," wrote Abigail. "Some poor parents are mourning the loss of 3, 4 & 5 children, and some families are wholly striped of every Member." She had just received word that "Sister Elihu Adams lost her youngest child last night with this disorder." She referred to the widow of John's younger brother.

Abigail spent twelve hours a day at her mother's house, helping her sisters to nurse, and then came home to "the most gastly object my Eyes ever beheld"—Patty—"who is now become such a putrid mass as scarcely to be able for any one to do their Duty towards her." That Patty had survived so long, and would continue for several weeks yet, was probably a consequence of her youth and good constitution. Then came the blow that Abigail dreaded.

"Have pitty upon me, have pitty upon me o! thou my beloved for the Hand of God presseth me soar." Abigail wrote the words as she would have spoken them to John. "How can I tell you (o my bursting Heart) that my Dear Mother has Left me, this day about 5 oclock she left this world for an infinitely better." Her words beg for consolation. "You often Express'd your anxiety for me when you left me before, surrounded with Terrors, but my trouble then was as the small dust in the balance compaird to what I have since endured." Was this cen-sure? John should have been there to comfort her. She tried to imagine his re-sponse: "I know you are a sincere and hearty mourner with me and will pray for me in my affliction."

Indeed, John was a sincere mourner. Her letters were never out of his thoughts, he wrote her. "I should have mounted my Horse this day for Brain-tree," he proposed, "if I had not hopes of hearing further from you in a Day or two." He added that if the news were not better, "I shall certainly come home, for I cannot leave you." The news did not improve, confirmed by a letter from

John Thaxter, who wrote of his respect and pity for "Mrs. Adams." Thaxter affirmed that "one great Distress backed with another as severe has almost unnerved her: but Christian Fortitude cooperating with a firm Dependance of providential Support" had sustained her.

John had made up his mind. Without mentioning the epidemic, without reference to Abigail's difficulties, without suggesting that he might return, John explained his commitment. "From my earliest Entrance into Life," he wrote to Abigail on October 9, and by "Life" he meant his professional life,

> I have been engaged in the public Cause of America: and from first to last I have had upon my Mind, a strong Impression, that Things would be wrought up to their present Crisis. I saw from the Beginning that the Controversy was of such a Nature that it never would be settled, and every day convinces me more and more. This has been the source of all the Disquietude of my Life. It has lain down and rose up with me these twelve Years. . . . And even now, I would chearfully retire from public life forever . . . nay I would chearfully contribute my little Property to obtain Peace and Liberty.—But all these must go and my Life too before I can surrender the Right of my Country to a free Constitution. I dare not consent to it. I should be the most miserable of Mortals ever after, whatever Honours and Emoluments might surround me.

There it was: John's testament that Abigail received a few weeks later, his response to her unspoken plea for him to come home. Neither of them wrote the words that made their exchange explicit. She did not ask him to return. Nor did he state that he would not return. But both of them understood what had transpired. They had renegotiated the foundation of their marriage. Their worlds would be separated for the duration. They would travel parallel paths for the time to come.

But this decision did not diminish their caring for each other. If anything, it intensified their understanding and their empathy. For Abigail's part, it stiffened her resolve to manage without John. On his part, respect and trust for Abigail were confirmed, though not without a measure of guilt. He knew the cost to her of his abandoning active participation in their marriage. She would suffer and struggle and all the while grow in strength to endure and make the decisions she must make to tend to her world—and his—in his absence. He, with her blessings—mostly—would turn his attention to the national struggle.

A few days later he expanded his thoughts: "You and I, my dear, have Reason,

if ever Mortals had, to be thoughtfull—to look beyond the transitory Scene."
Clearly John had been thinking about their relationship.

> Whatever is preparing for Us, let us be prepared to receive. It is
> Time for Us to subdue our Passions of every Kind. The Prospect
> before Us is an Ocean of Uncertainties, in which no Pleasing ob-
> jects appear. We have few Hopes, excepting that of Preserving our
> Honour and our Consciences untainted and a free Constitution to
> our Country. . . . With these I can be happy, in Extream Poverty,
> in humble Insignificance, nay I hope and believe, in Death: with-
> out them I should be miserable, and with a Crown upon my Head,
> Millions in my Coffers, and a gaping, idolizing Multitude at my
> feet.

Abigail wrote no such high-minded statement to justify her misery; she
turned to religion. With the cruel stroke of her mother's death, the death of
Patty at last and five of her "near connections laid in the grave," she could not
overcome her "too selfish sorrow." She realized that a "patient submission is my
duty," and she would strive to obtain it. "Yea tho he slay me I will trust in him
said holy Job," and know that the "lenient hand of time" would alone "blunt the
keen Edg of Sorrow." Again, she returned to her grief over the loss of her
mother.

> Forgive me then, for thus dwelling upon a subject sweet to me, But
> I fear painfull to you. O how I have long'd for your Bosom to pour
> forth my sorrows there, and find a healing Balm, but perhaps that
> has been denied me that I might be led to a higher and a more per-
> manent consolater who had bid us call upon him in the day of
> trouble.

Then, for the first time in weeks, she wrote about public affairs. She had
heard a rumor that Rhode Island had been invaded and burned. She reported
that Sir William Howe had replaced General Gage as commander of British
forces. England's General Burgoyne, another rumor suggested, was headed to
Philadelphia. Rumors, all imprecise or incorrect, were rampant. Finally, she
realized it was midnight and time for her to sleep.

THE MONTHS PASSED AND ABIGAIL'S HEALTH RETURNED. MEAN-
while, the American militias attacked Canada in one of the more ill-conceived
tactical moves of the war. The disastrous mission failed, sending more dismal
news to Philadelphia, where Congress already attempted to manage an inexpe-

rienced and undersupplied military force. They debated how to secure sufficient ammunition under the terms of the embargo. Furthermore, "The delegates of Georgia and S. Caroline were fearful that the landing of troops in their states would signal the freeing of '20,000 Negroes,'" John recorded, noting the recurrent theme that could divide the Congress. This was the temper in Philadelphia, where he was engaged as one of the most forceful negotiators.

The stakes were high. John was appointed to the committee to establish an American navy amid substantial discussion on the floor of Congress about the efficacy of funding ships and sailors. Still, he had time to send Abigail the "medicines" she had asked for. He carefully recorded a receipt for two ounces of "Cinnamon, one ounce of turkey rhubarb, one oz. of Cloves and an ounce of Pink Root." He also ordered a new suit of clothing for himself, made of "nanking," a brownish yellow cotton, and linen.

Recalling the debates when he wrote his autobiography thirty years later, John also observed that his forceful participation in them had the effect of diminishing his popularity. It was the reticent men—he mentioned George Washington, Benjamin Franklin, and Thomas Jefferson—who

> shew that Silence and reserve in public are more Efficacious than Argumentation or Oratory. A public Speaker who inserts himself, or is urged by others into the Conduct of Affairs, by daily Exertions to justify his measures, and answer the Objections of Opponents, makes himself too familiar with the public, and unavoidably makes himself Ennemies.

John, understanding his vulnerability, nevertheless continued to be vocal and passionate in his opinions. It was his temperament to disregard the personal consequences of his candor but also to carry within himself a lingering wound that irritated him when the consequences backfired. It was in his character to be outspoken—considered integrity by some and obnoxiousness by others—and it was a quality that earned him enemies as well as loyal friends.

The most compromising aspect of his commitments, however, was the sympathy he felt for Abigail and his guilt for abandoning her in her time of great need. Instead, John attempted to fulfill his duty to her by employing the next best option to his presence—his voice, resonating in letters. He shifted from his former laconic and reserved correspondence to writing Abigail with heartfelt and expressive prose. His letters to her came as close as he dared to the "sentimental effusions of the heart" that she had once demanded. "Your letters," he wrote, and "indeed every Line from you, gives me inexpressible Pleasure, notwithstanding the melancholly Scenes discribed in most of them of late." And again: "The most agreeable Time that I spend here is in writing to you, and in conversing with you when I am alone." In fact, John began to harbor a fantasy for them: In the event that he were reappointed to Congress, he vowed: "I never will come here again without you, if I can perswade you to come with me."

Abigail acknowledged the new bounty of his letters: "No less than 5 Letters have I received from you," she wrote at the end of October. "Your Letters administer comfort to my wounded Heart. It will sometimes when [off] of my Gaurd swell and exceed the bounds I endeavour to set to it." She still urged him not to be so fearful of the interception of his letters: "I think however you are more apprehensive than you need to be."

With this encouragement to him, she affirmed what they both understood, that their marriage would be conducted by correspondence for some time to come. Neither of them could predict the duration, but they adopted a new method of writing that was closer to a conversation, albeit on paper and with the delays inherent in eighteenth-century postal delivery. They began to "talk" about their separate worlds and their feelings in a way that they had not previously. For Abigail, this was less a shift than for John, who had to free himself of his former constraints. He became more expressive and expansive. And together, they demonstrated in their correspondence the subtle and nuanced dialogue that married people carry on in their speech.

To Abigail and only Abigail, for instance, John wrote about religion in the same language that she used. She wrote to him about God's will operating directly in her life. She reflected about providential care. She, in fact, suggested that recent military setbacks were the consequence of sin and transgressions. She had frequently referred to the dysentery epidemic in those terms. But she went further: "We have done Evil or our Enimies would be at peace with us," she announced to John. "The Sin of Slavery as well as many other is not washed away." Abigail boldly wrote political analysis in religious terms. John used her providential language to explain the "cruel Pestilence. May God almighty put a stop to its Rage, and humble us under the Ravages already made by it." And later he confirmed: "You know that I look upon Religion as the most perfect System, and the most awfull Sanction of Morality." She wrote that "a true patriot must be a religious Man." He, in turn, observed that religion was the foundation of morality.

The ravages of the dysentery epidemic had affected every family deeply. For the Adamses, it provided a settlement of their still-unresolved commitments. Without John's assistance and, perhaps more important, his accustomed emotional support, Abigail had coped on the home front. She had nursed, grieved, and survived depression, calling on other resources, especially religion, to maintain her household and her stability. She had been tried and tempered.

John was profoundly conflicted by the loyalties that he owed in the Puritan sense of duty, torn between responsibility to his family and to the rebellion. Knowing that Abigail would endure without him and suspecting that the rebellion might not, he chose to remain in Philadelphia. His decision established new parameters for their marriage. This was not because Abigail lacked options. While she could not have terminated her marriage legally, she could have become resentful or cold, ending it emotionally. She did not. On the contrary, she understood, and she empathized. She was hurt, but she rallied. She learned that she could manage her life independently within an empathic marriage, and she rose to the challenge.

Many couples faced similar conflicts in the revolutionary caldron. Some tolerated the marital disruption much the way Abigail and John did. Samuel and Elizabeth Adams remained close while living apart. Others resolved it differently. Samuel Quincy left his wife and moved to England. John's younger brother Elihu died, leaving behind a bereaved family. And when Mercy could no longer tolerate James Warren's absence, he returned home to Plymouth.

For Abigail and John Adams the Revolution meant sacrifice. And for both of them the major sacrifice that it required was companionship. They would be apart for they did not know how long, but they agreed to the terms of the sacrifice, which also included Abigail's taking over John's responsibilities to support his family as well as to raise and educate their children. For his part, John sacrificed the opportunity to participate in his family for the duration of time that he saw fit to serve his nation. The covenant, the agreement, was neither written nor spoken, but it was accepted by them both.

Four

A New Code of Laws

AS IT WAS FOR JOHN, INDEPENDENCE WAS ON ABIGAIL'S MIND that spring of 1776. In fact, she wrote to him, after recovering from a bout of "Jaundice, Rhumatism and a most violent cold," the residual effects of dysentery, she thought, to inquire about the status of political alliance. "I wish I knew what mighty things were fabricating," and she asked; "If a form of Government is to be established here what one will be assumed? Will it be left to our assemblies to chuse one? And will not many men have many minds? And shall we not run into Dissentions among ourselves?"

By this time, Abigail was not reticent about politics. She asked the central questions that prevailed in the halls of Congress. From her conversations with John, she knew that many shades of opinion existed among the delegates. Moreover, from reading history and experiencing events around her, she had formulated strong opinions about politics as well as politicians.

A daughter of New England with its Puritan cast of mind, with its suspicions and its skepticism, and from her experiences of the long year past, Abigail had become pessimistic. Her distrust of human behavior became greater even than John's. He believed that with the proper education, people and institutions could be perfected. Abigail's mood was otherwise when she wrote her thoughts to John about what kind of government should be created for the new nation.

Perhaps Abigail's skepticism developed because she had none of the stimulation of laboring in the halls of Congress. There, despite all his grave frustrations and irritations, John was daily motivated by grand ideals and experienced the exhilaration of influence and power. Abigail's daily sensations included fear, fatigue, and grief. John's challenges focused on declaring independence, establishing a government, and executing a war. Hers included coping with invasions, illness, and farmhands. Their immediate worlds, his in Congress, hers in Braintree, had different orbits. So Abigail continued her gloomy late-night reflections about the prospective government: "I am more and more convinced that Man is a dangerous creature," she began,

> and that power whether vested in many or a few is ever grasping, and like the grave cries give, give. The great fish swallow up the small, and he who is most strenuous for the Rights of the people, when vested with power, is as eager after the perogatives of Government.

She continued her late-night "conversation" with John by correspondence, the form in which they now communicated. "You tell me of degrees of perfection to which Human Nature is capable of arriving, and I believe it, but at the same time lament that our admiration should arise from scarcity of the instances." Abigail, since the outbreak of fighting and the danger that hostilities had brought to her neighborhood, and especially since her ordeal in the dysentery epidemic, had developed an independent stance on politics. She observed, for instance, that people had grown accustomed to a lack of formal government since the restraints of Great Britain had been "slakned," and she queried John:

> If we seperate from Brittain, what Code of Laws will be established? How shall we be governed so as to retain our Liberties? Can any government be free which is not administred by general stated Laws? Who shall frame these Laws? Who will give them force and energy? . . . I feel anxious for the fate of our Monarchy or Democracy or what ever is to take place. I soon get lost in a Labyrinth of perplexities.

The labyrinth of perplexities that Abigail surveyed best summarized the vexations of the delegates in Philadelphia. She fully comprehended the complexity of state formation faced by a nation in rebellion, that it was not just ideology that governed people's behavior, but passions and self-interest. Writing at night, after her family slept and the house was quiet, she had the privacy to formulate her thoughts. And once more, she sealed and mailed them to her husband, who wondered about these same issues.

JOHN ADAMS RETURNED HOME AT THE END OF DECEMBER 1775 for a brief visit, arriving in time to spend Christmas Day with his family, a day that was still a solemn holiday in the late eighteenth century, when families gathered in prayer and at church. The following day John departed for Watertown where the General Court, Massachusetts's interim provincial government, met, and he remained there during the next three weeks, traveling home to see his family on Sundays.

This one-month visit developed rather suddenly in early December, driven by two factors. Primarily he was exhausted from his eight months of labor at the Continental Congress. He needed a break from the arduous schedule of committee work, from correspondence for which he had no secretary, and from the long hours of debate that dragged on in the Congress. But also he needed to settle a conflict that had developed. In his absence, the Massachusetts General Court had appointed him chief justice of the state supreme court. The appointment confused him. Was he a delegate to Congress, or was he a state justice? He needed to resolve this dilemma that had, in addition, raised an uncomfortable personal issue.

John had never had a close relationship with his fellow Massachusetts delegate Robert Treat Paine. Early in his career, he and Paine had been adversaries at the bar, not only jousting in numerous cases, including the Boston Massacre trials, but also because Paine was older, richer, more handsome, and more confident. Paine patronized John and John envied Paine. They had reached an accommodation as fellow delegates, however, and treated each other civilly if not cordially. John's appointment as chief justice disrupted the truce between them. Paine, as his senior in years and experience, should have received the honor of primary presiding judge; he was instead appointed as the fourth justice, a lower status, which he turned down. Overwhelmed by resentment, he began a feud with James Warren, John's friend and the president of the Provincial Council, whom he considered responsible for the disparity in the judicial appointments. He also extended his animosity to John. The affront produced a lingering coolness between them.

John, nevertheless, remained perplexed about his dual appointments. His one-month sojourn in Massachusetts was hardly a vacation with his family. He spent most of his time in Watertown, where he reported to the provincial leaders about the accomplishments and challenges before the Philadelphia Congress. He also visited General Washington at his field headquarters in Cambridge, where he and other military leaders discussed supplies and strategies. On the night before his return to Philadelphia he dined with Generals "Washington and [Hora-tio] Gates and their Ladies, and half a Dozen Sachems and Warriours of the french Cocknowaga Tribe." The Indians had come to pay their respects to the generals, and, John recorded, "they were wondrous polite." He continued: "The General introduced me to them as one of the Grand Council Fire at Philadelphia," a rather loose translation of John's office, which greatly impressed the sachems and warriors. They "made me many Bows, and a cordial Reception." John was surprised by the deference and recorded it with pleasure.

Having enjoyed little of his company during this short visit, Abigail was unhappy enough after his departure, expressing dismay to her friend Mercy Otis Warren. "Our Country is as it were a secondary God, and the First and greatest parent," she began her letter, justifying his leaving to herself as much as her friend. "It is to be preferred to Parents, Wives, Children, Friends and all things." Abigail cast her explanation in religious terms, invoking the hierarchy of responsibilities that allowed her to tolerate this decision. John was doing his duty. "These are the considerations which prevail with me to consent to a most painful Seperation."

Abigail's fraught explanation to Mercy also provides insight into the Robert Treat Paine dispute. Petty personal conflicts abounded among the delegates in Congress alongside their colossal political dilemmas. Clearly John told Abigail stories that he had not been able to write safely. Abigail continued: "I was fully convinced he must suffer if he quitted." Concerned about John's reputation be-ing compromised, Abigail consented to his return.

Clearly, John had done the convincing. Whether in reality he worried about his reputation or whether he used this ploy to persuade Abigail, using an argu-ment that she could not resist, is unclear. Both explanations make sense in light of John's character. He was committed to the rebellion, and Congress was mov-ing in the direction of independence, despite the resistance of a few key mem-bers who still hoped for reconciliation with Britain. In his passion for independence he was sure, and he perceived, correctly, that his influence in Congress was pro-found, if not determining. He needed to be there to persuade the few intractable opponents to join the mounting faction in favor of independence. Abigail, who already believed that John with his integrity and brilliance was essential to the survival of the rebellion, was convinced that he must remain in Congress. And so he returned to the fray in late February 1776.

THE MOOD IN CONGRESS IN EARLY 1776 WAS CONTENTIOUS. Many issues remained at stake that had already divided the delegates. For in-stance, nearly a year had passed since Benjamin Franklin introduced his draft plan for an "Articles of Confederation and Perpetual Union," a formal document that would legitimate the union of states. But the issue had been too controversial then and had been tabled. Meanwhile the states, as well as the Continental Congress, were operating, mostly, with extralegal governments. Massachusetts and Pennsylvania had continued with the forms they had used under the British. New Hampshire, on the other hand, had applied to the Congress for direction, while Virginia had moved ahead on its own to write a constitution, sanctioning Thomas Jefferson to compose a preamble that later served him as a model for his declaration.

That season, however, a comet appeared on the horizon, a comet in the form of a little pamphlet, written by an obscure and undistinguished foreigner, that with its exhilarating, patriotic prose provided light and hope to the entire enterprise of the revolutionary mission. *Common Sense* was published in January 1776 in Philadelphia, the product of the talented journalist Thomas Paine, a recent immigrant, who became a champion of the rebellion. The pamphlet produced a sensation that spring and greatly expedited the effort to promote independence.

Paine, an Englishman by birth and education, had met Benjamin Franklin during his time as a colonial agent in London. Franklin gave him letters of introduction to his son-in-law, the journalist Richard Bache, and also to Dr. Benjamin Rush in Philadelphia. With their assistance, Paine became a journalist, producing a number of newspaper articles that honed his skills as a writer. Dr. Rush, in particular, saw a spark of talent in Paine and suggested that he write a pamphlet that explained in clear language the nature of the enmity with Britain.

Paine retired to his desk and wrote. His resulting treatise could be read and understood by ordinary people, not just legal experts and political theorists; it explained the reasons for independence. His arguments were not original, but rather they recapitulated in plain language the reasons that had prevailed in radical circles for a long time. But Paine did more; he based his reasoning on biblical precedent, instead of rehearsing classical precedents and Enlightenment philosophy. He went further still, describing what a future democratic government in America could look like. He proposed a unicameral government, a one-house body that was similar to that already in effect in Pennsylvania and Georgia. *Common Sense* outsold any book previously published in America. Paine claimed that more than 150,000 copies were circulated. More than that, it was reproduced in newspapers and read at public gatherings. *Common Sense* was a public-relations coup that propagandists for generations would envy.

At first John Adams was so impressed by the little book that he sent a copy to Abigail, explaining his hope that it "will soon make the common Faith." Within weeks, however, John became disabused of his first impressions, not just because he was critical of the utopian government it promoted but also because he disapproved of its author. Paine had visited John in Philadelphia and in the course of their conversation offended him by disparaging religion. John recorded that "His Arguments from the old Testament were ridiculous, but whether they proceeded from honest Ignorance or foolish Superstition on the one hand, or from willfull Sophistry and knavish Hypocricy on the other I know not."

Still, what alarmed John most about *Common Sense* was its proposal for a unicameral government that John considered not only unrealistic but lacking in knowledge of history and human nature. In short, he found it dangerously ignorant. In response, he did two things: Recognizing Paine's precarious fortunes, he explored employment opportunities for him. "I felt myself obliged to Paine for the Pains he had taken," John punned, badly, and arranged a clerkship for him in Congress.

More significant, John wrote a rebuttal to the utopian political proposal in *Common Sense*. Despite the superhuman load of congressional work that he carried that spring—he "unquestionably did more business than any other Member," he claimed—he wrote an alternative proposal. Published as *Thoughts on Government*, it was one of the most important essays he wrote. In it he outlined a model for government that was his lifelong ideal.

John's *Thoughts on Government* described a republic, a government composed of three branches that would represent the people. Each branch would have separate powers and would serve as a check on the other branches, but each would function with authority in its sphere. It was based upon John's study of ancient republics but also on his reading of the classical and modern political philosophers. "I had read Harrington, Sydney, Hobbs, Nedham and Lock, but with very little Application to any particular Views: till these Debates in Congress and these Interrogations in public and private, turned my thoughts to those Researches which produced the Thoughts on Government."

He circulated "Thoughts" among members of Congress, and it soon found its way into print. But it was inspired by the danger he perceived in Paine's proposal for a kind of government that he considered no government at all, but anarchy.

Abigail, meanwhile, read *Common Sense* and responded, "Tis highly prized here and carries conviction whereever it is read." She added that she had circulated her copy "as much as it lay in my power, [and] every one assents to the weighty truths it contains." She hoped that it would impress Congress suffi-ciently to vote for independence.

A FEW DAYS LATER, ABIGAIL DECIDED TO CONTRIBUTE HER OWN advice to the ongoing debates in Philadelphia. "I suppose in congress you think of every thing relative to trade and commerce, as well as other things," she wrote, demurring before she forwarded her own recommendations. She pro-posed that Congress place an excise tax on "Spiritous Liquors" that would be equal among all the states. Currently, she pointed out, New England carried a heavier surcharge than others, which damaged their trade.

She had another proposal with regard to the retention of hard currency in America. She suggested barter as a means of exchange for goods in the West Indies. "Would it not be better to carry some commodity of our own produce in exchange? Medicine, Cotton Wool and some other articles we are in great want of." She persisted along this line, describing the inflation that had oc-curred in cotton, wool, flax, coffee, corn, rye, and more items of common use in her household. Having supplanted John as the manager of their household economy, Abigail now felt comfortable writing about tariffs and the export of hard currency to John. She sent as well a list of articles she needed from Philadelphia—items that were scarce in Braintree, such as handkerchiefs and "3 yd. of black Caliminco for shooes and binding for the same." She signed off, requesting John to "be kind enough to burn this Letter. Tis wrote in great haste and a most incorrect Scrawl it is."

Sensing, perhaps, that she was on a roll, Abigail next introduced a topic that the delegates had purposefully avoided. "I have sometimes been ready to think"—she backed into her subject before delivering her blow—"that the pas-sion for Liberty cannot be Eaquelly Strong in the Breasts of those who have been accustomed to deprive their fellow Creatures of theirs." Artfully propos-ing her comment in the conditional form, she then stepped audaciously into the hornet's nest of slavery that the Congress had cautiously avoided in order to maintain unity among the states while engaging in the war for independence.

The one topic that would certainly spell the end of cooperation between southern and northern states was slavery. Abigail, however, reminded John that political expediency contradicted both morality and religion, to say noth-ing of its hypocrisy. "Of this I am certain that it is not founded upon that gener-ous and Christian principal of doing to others as we would that others should do unto us."

Abigail's distress about slavery was not new. She had written to John at the time of the dysentery outbreak that the epidemic had been sent as punishment for the sin of slavery. But even earlier, she had condemned the pervasive system that she saw practiced in her own state. "I wish most sincerely there was not a Slave in the province," she wrote to John when rumors of a slave rebellion circulated during the chaotic days of September 1774. "It allways appeard a most iniquitious Scheme to me—fight ourselfes for what we are daily robbing and plundering from those who have as good a right to freedom as we have." She added: "You know my mind upon this Subject."

He knew her opinion on this subject of slavery, and he also understood her reasoning. Abigail had grown up in a household that owned an African slave. Phoebe had lived in the Smith home just as a series of young women had lived with the Adamses over the years as part of the "family." She had been Abigail's nurse from infancy, and Abigail cared deeply for her. Her affection for Phoebe had translated into sympathy for Africans and revulsion for the institution of slavery. It was that simple. Abigail would always be close to Phoebe, looking after her following her father's death. Removed from the forum of policy making, Abigail used the only access she had to influence affairs in Philadelphia—and powerful access it was—her husband's office. She no longer hesitated to lobby him for causes she felt strongly about.

Abigail had given careful thought to the forum in Philadelphia from which she, as a woman, had been excluded, and there were a number of issues about which she was irritated. Slavery was one, and while she was ruminating on the subject of the paradox of delegates talking and writing about liberty and freedom while all the while excluding some groups from the benefits of their ideological mission, she introduced another delicate subject.

Alone at her kitchen table at night, writing by candlelight as her household slept, Abigail had time to focus her mind, and her thoughts drifted to the forum at Philadelphia and her husband. This was her moment to consider issues that were most important to her, so she initiated another seditious topic. "I long to hear that you have declared an independency," she wrote,

> —and by the way in the new Code of Laws which I suppose it will be necessary for you to make I desire you would Remember the Ladies, and be more generous and favourable to them than your ancestors. Do not put such unlimited power into the hands of the Husbands.

This was an audacious move. Again, as she sat, her thoughts carried her into a territory that was more revolutionary than any American, male or female, had wandered in the course of their rebellious considerations. Slavery was the live specter that the delegates avoided, but the idea of rights of women ran so contrary to anyone's imagination, much less expression in the halls of Congress, that the issue would be considered amusing rather than alarming. But Abigail was serious, very serious.

"Remember all Men would be tyrants if they could," she quoted John the words that he had written in his 1763 unpublished essay "On Man's Lust for Power." Then, recovering her sense of reality, the reality with which she anticipated her claim would be met, she continued with a feigned threat: "If perticuliar care and attention is not paid to the Laidies we are determined to foment a Rebelion, and will not hold ourselves bound by any Laws in which we have no voice, or Representation." She covered her tracks with satire, mocking the same phrases that John and his fellow delegates used in their debates as her method of demonstrating the limitations of their objectives.

Abigail's command to "Remember the Ladies" has resonated for more than two centuries. It is the boldest statement written by an American woman in the eighteenth century, and for much of the nineteenth, as a demand for political rights. It came from the mind—and the soul—of a woman whose life had been transformed over a long decade of rebellion from the model of New England matron, recapitulating her mother's life and that of generations of women before her, into a rebellion of her own. She was earnest. She had access. She made her move on behalf of women in an age when such a demand was no less radical than the states' rebellion against Great Britain. And as radical as her words were, as far out of the context as they were from the mentality of most radicals who fought for American independence, they still were couched in an ethos that reflected the culture of her times.

"That your Sex are Naturally Tyrannincal is a Truth so thoroughly established as to admit of no dispute," she wrote, using language to her husband that she possibly would not have said to him in person. "My pen is always freer than my tongue," she had once written him. "I have wrote many things to you that I suppose I never could have talk'd." But her ideas flowed from the revolutionary rhetoric that surrounded her and had penetrated in a manner that neither of them could have predicted. "Such of you as wish to be happy [will] willingly give up the harsh title of Master for the more tender and endearing one of Friend."

By invoking friendship, she borrowed the language that characterized their epistolary marriage. They—and particularly he—used the address of "my dearest Friend" as their epistolary salute. They were each other's dearest friends. Even to her dearest friend, this letter was daring. Abigail undoubtedly wrote it in a reverie of inspiration that was less premeditated than an outpouring of pent-up passions. She still took the considered next step of sending it. She might have discarded it, but she sent it to John on an impulse that suggested that she realized its message would be acceptable to him.

But she could not have been certain. It expressed rebellion, resentment, truth. John would have to cope. Having written her harshest indictment of his sex, she softened with a suggestion:

> Why then, not put it out of the power of the vicious and the Lawless to use us with cruelty and indignity with impunity. Men of Sense in all Ages abhor those customs which treat us only as the vassals of your Sex. Regard us then as Beings placed by providence under your protection and in immitation of the Supreem Being make use of that power only for our happiness.

Abigail ended her reverie by turning to the religion that expressed her culture; she revisited the notion of hierarchy, in this case gender hierarchy. The new code of laws, she argued, must deny men power to hurt women either physically, materially, or emotionally. It must recognize their human rights. Enlightened men do not abuse women as "vassals" of their sex, she pointed out. They acknowledge a different hierarchy, one that is protective, caring of women. Just as the "Supreem Being" used power over men humanely, so gendered power should be humanely used. She did not argue for political equality. She argued for justice.

She might have gone further, but she did not because it was not in her cultural framework to consider political equality. Few people in her time, even among women, would argue that women could conduct themselves publicly in all the ways that were open to men. Women were considered domestic. However, the most progressive female advocates argued that private virtues were equal in intellectual and social terms to men's realm of activity. Abigail was progressive, but she still pointed out to John that "men of sense," among whom John was her supreme example, understood that women deserved respect as well as just treatment. They were not "vassals"—and here she steered clear of the term "slaves" that was extravagantly used in radical circles to refer to the colonial predicament, favoring the more accurate feudal reference with its hierarchical instead of binary significance.

Abigail did not think beyond separate spheres of activity for men and women, nor did she question the subordination of her gender. But she did argue for women's human rights, among which were the rights of legal protection, material impartiality, personal respect, education, and benevolent treatment as wives and mothers. She would always argue for educational opportunities for women that equaled men's. She considered material equality a given. But she did not demand the vote or representation in government for women. As an eighteenth-century woman, she believed in separate spheres. Her position would alter somewhat over time, when with greater experience of the world, she applauded the opportunity that New Jersey's constitution (inadvertently) permitted some women to vote thirty years later. But in the spring of 1776 she reminded John that half of the rebellious population was female, and that the men in Philadelphia should consider them as partners in constructing the new nation.

Abigail's letter, which at the time had none of the valence of notoriety that it has achieved in the more than two hundred years since she wrote it as a private message to her husband, added to her husband's "perplexities," as well as to his amusement. Her extended monologue, possibly read by him late at night, the time when he, too, achieved some quiet and privacy, confronted him with one more adversary, albeit a friendly one. Worse than Dickinson, worse than Paine, Abigail had presented him with two intractable dilemmas: slavery and women rights. Did this surprise him? Did he believe that Abigail had turned on him? Did he feel the need to put her in her place, reduce her sauciness, as he often referred to her confrontational self? Did he believe that her character had changed in the long decade they had been married?

On the contrary, Abigail displayed the very temperament that had drawn him to her at the beginning of their courtship. His first letter to her teasingly asserted that "she was a good subject of King George." Her ongoing attraction for him was that she was bright, informed, adversarial, and honest. Those were the traits that he first observed and that delighted him. He poked fun at these qualities that he adored. Now, in the spring of 1776, he again played the jester.

"As to your extraordinary Code of Laws, I cannot but laugh," he responded.

> We have been told that our Struggle has loosened the bands of Government every where. That Children and Apprentices were disobedient—that schools and Colledges were grown turbulent—That Indians slighted their Guardians and Negroes grew insolent to their Masters. But your Letter was the first Intimation that another Tribe more numerous and powerfull than all the rest were grown discontented.—This is rather too coarse a compliment but you are so saucy, I won't blot it out.

Joking, of course, belies the seriousness of the underlying message that is the butt of the humor. His remarks did not demean her, as some of his detractors have argued. He had few options. He might have ignored Abigail's letter, thus belittling her comments; he might have angrily abused her ideas, or he might have explained his opposing position. But by making light of Abigail's comments, John instead circumvented the dispute that he could not afford to introduce into his private life while the contests in Congress preoccupied him. But then he continued in a vein that carried more seriousness than humor. "Depend upon it," he began a new paragraph, "We know better than to repeal our Masculine systems." John resurrected the age-old illusion of women's subversive powers over men: "Altho they are in full Force, you know they are little more than Theory. We dare not exert our Power in its full Latitude. We are obliged to go fair, and softly, and in Practice you know We are the subjects. We have only the Name of Masters." John reverted to humor: "And rather than give up this, which would compleatly subject Us to the Despotism of the Peticoat, I hope General Washington, and all our brave Heroes would fight." John's mocking denunciation of male superiority actually repeats an observation that Mercy had written to Abigail a few months previous.

In one of her hyperbolic paragraphs of compliments about an article that John had written, Mercy introduced her cascade of accolades by comparing the genders: "But as our weak and timid sex is only the Echo of the other, and like some pliant peace of clock Work the springs of our souls move slow or more Rapidly," she wrote before making her move into a typically strained expression of praise for John. Mercy's view of her "weak and timid sex," while probably more rhetorical than real, nevertheless recapitulates the current social interpretation of women's place in society, that women were the weaker sex.

Mercy had reason to complain, since she wanted to publish her plays and poetry. Employing an argument similar to John's comment, she, too, acknowledged women's subversive power. "But we have yet one Advantage peculier to ourselves," she observed. "If the Mental Faculties of the Female are not improved it may be Concealed in the Obscure Retreats of the Bed Chamber or the kitchen which she is not often Necessitated to Leave." Mercy took this line of reasoning a step further, noting that when men neglected education, they displayed their ignorance in public. Mercy's point, unlike John's, was that both sexes suffered if deprived of education.

Gender was not on the agenda at the Continental Congress, nor did John intend to put it there. He instead retreated to his and Abigail's private language of humor that had spread from their conversations into their correspondence. "I am sure every good Politician would plot, as long as he would against Despotism, Empire, Monarchy, Aristocracy, Oligarchy, or Ochlocracy," he concluded whimsically and suggested that her letter was part of a plot by the British ministry. "After stirring up Tories, Landjobbers, Trimmers, Bigots,

Canadians, Indians, Negroes, Hanoverians, Hessians, Russians, Irish Roman Catholicks, Scotch Renegadoes"—he summoned all the minorities he could conjure—"at last they have stimulated the [women] to demand new Priviledges and threaten to rebell."

Abigail did not respond immediately to John's impertinence, but she did complain to Mercy. "He is very sausy to me in return for a List of Female Grievances which I transmitted to him," she wrote. "I think I will get you to join me in a petition to Congress." She explained that she had requested that the new code of laws (she meant of course, the Constitution) should include "some Laws in our favour upon just and Liberal principals." And she confessed: "I believe I even threatned fomenting a Rebellion in case we were not considerd, and assured him we should not hold ourselves bound by any Laws in which we had neither a voice, nor representation." She quoted a long passage of John's response to her, that "he cannot but Laugh at My Extrodonary Code of Laws" and the ensuing full paragraph, badly spelled even for Abigail, perhaps written in haste or pique. She concluded: "So I have help'd the Sex abundantly, but I will tell him I have only been making trial of the Disintresstedness of his Virtue, and when weigh'd in the balance have found it wanting." In truth, Abigail was annoyed, and she expressed her irritation to her sympathetic friend Mercy.

Mercy did not respond. At least no response survives among their letters. It could be that at the time she was closer to John's camp than to Abigail's with respect to women's issues. She was writing about the revolution and nation building, and she was not yet ready to point out, as she did in her later history, that she composed her work in a female voice. She was not, nor was John, as progressive on women's issues as Abigail. Abigail had made her plea for women's rights to both of them, and both of them dismissed her case, though in different ways. John used humor, because he didn't care to tackle this particular issue, and Mercy, who lacked humor, dodged the issue completely.

Abigail had the last word. "I can not say that I think you very generous to the Ladies," she chastised John without masking her rebuke as a tease. "For whilst you are proclaiming peace and good will to Men, Emancipating all Nations, you insist upon retaining an absolute power over Wives. But you must remember"—and here she returned to his own early reflections on power—"that Arbitrary power is like most other things which are very hard, very liable to be broken." She concluded: "Notwithstanding all your wise Laws and Maxims we have it in our power not only to free ourselves but to subdue our Masters, and without voilence throw both your natural and legal authority at our feet."

Her pledge of personal autonomy, a form of declaring independence, was more the fantasy of an indignant wife, writing at night about an elusive vision of marriage, than a threat she would fulfill. She, too, succumbed to the fantasy of women's subversive power and joined the rebellious chorus.

ALL THE WHILE, THE MILITARY SITUATION THAT FORMED THE backdrop to the public deliberations in Congress—and the private deliberations between the Adamses—escalated. The British had decided that Boston, which they occupied, was less a prize than New York City, a larger and more important seaport, and one located more strategically. By taking New York, they could separate the states as well as gain a position from which they could move both north and south with greater flexibility.

By mid-March, the evacuation of Boston was under way, and Abigail observed the ships that gathered in the harbor to ferry the vast military might of Britain to a destination that the British kept secret. From the top of Penn's Hill, she and her children watched the spectacle of the largest fleet ever seen in America. They saw seventy or a hundred sails. "They look like a Forrest," she said.

John, meanwhile, had received news of the evacuation, and not yet realizing that it had been peaceful, he wrote, "I shall suffer many severe Pains, on your Account for some Days." He expected news of "Carnage and Desolation" and that Abigail would be in much distress, if not danger. "I believe in my Conscience I feel more here than you do," he wrote, and professed that he could hear the sound of cannon "at four hundred Miles Distance." Thinking about the distance, he mellowed. "Is there no Way for two friendly Souls, to converse together, altho the Bodies are 400 Miles off?—Yes by Letter.—But I want a better Communication. I want to hear you think, or see your Thoughts." John's late-night fantasies ran to the poetic.

Once he was reassured that the evacuation had occurred deliberately and without a battle, the question was its destination. No one could be sure of the British plan. He believed that the fleet had headed toward Canada as a feint and that the real object was New York. John's guess was half-right. The fleet headed toward Halifax to regroup. General Washington, however, guessed New York, and he began to move his forces in that direction. To move his army was no small operation, and he had additional problems. Many of the militiamen had signed up for brief terms that had run their courses, and the soldiers returned home. It was also time for spring planting, which discouraged sign-ups and caused desertions. This was a problem for Congress as well as for General Washington to solve. In May, Washington traveled to Philadelphia to press his case in Congress for lengthening enlistments in the army, as well as many other issues.

The news about the Canadian campaign, begun in the late autumn, was grim. After a disastrous winter operation that ended with the fall of Montreal and a siege of Quebec, the spring battle had been sabotaged by an outbreak of smallpox among the American troops. Death and desertion forced a second chaotic retreat from Canada, delivering a final blow to the hopes of its capture. The bad news reached Congress in May. In addition to making it clear that Canada would never become an ally, it predicted that the war with England would be long and bloody. The one bright spot in the dismal state of affairs was that it promoted the case for independence. Once it was clear that Canada would not be a part of the union, the delegates of the thirteen states could move forward with their discussion about a declaration.

John Adams, meanwhile, believed that independence had effectively been declared earlier, in March, when Congress recommended to the states that they write constitutions. The formation of state governments signified the rejection of the British government, so only the formality remained. But that formality was necessary before Congress could establish relations with other countries. In order to send envoys, to open trade, and eventually to seek aid, financial and military, America needed to declare its independence from Britain.

Therefore, when the flamboyant Richard Henry Lee, delegate from Virginia, introduced a proposal for independence in early June 1776, Adams seconded the motion. Delegates from nine states were prepared to vote affirmatively, but four either resisted or lacked instructions from their state legislatures. The proposal was tabled until July 1, in order for the resistant states to reconsider or to consult with their legislative bodies. Meanwhile, a committee of five members was appointed to draft the declaration. John Adams was appointed to this committee, as were Benjamin Franklin, the elderly sage from Pennsylvania; Roger Sherman of Connecticut, a wise and steady patriot; Robert Livingston of New York, who only lately favored independence; and Thomas Jefferson, at thirty-three the youngest delegate to the Philadelphia Congress.

Trained as a lawyer, polite, diligent, reserved, Jefferson had a reputation as a graceful stylist; he had written both the Virginia Bill of Rights and the preamble to his state constitution. As a figure, Jefferson was lanky and stood out at six foot two, with a cap of reddish hair. John liked Jefferson because he was well read, and they were interested in many of the same topics. However, when Jefferson had objected to the appointment of a fast day in Congress on the grounds of religious diversity, John, a proponent of the fast, had stood to rebuke him. He expected the young man to resent the public upbraiding. Instead, Jefferson took his seat next to John the following day. Their friendship was sealed.

How Jefferson came to write the first draft of the document remains a mystery. Both he and John Adams, the only committee members who left a record of their transactions, did so in the third decade of the nineteenth century, when their memories for small details in the past were unreliable. Remarkably, Jefferson produced this draft in a very few days in mid-June, a staggering accomplishment, given the workload he already carried. In that six-month period, he served on thirty committees, not uncommon among the hardest-working delegates to Congress, but still formidable. Using both of his earlier Virginia documents as templates, as well as the texts produced by other delegates—Lee's motion for independence, for instance—Jefferson, who composed quickly, wrote a first draft that both Adams and Franklin then edited and passed on to Sherman and Livingston. It was ready for presentation to the entire Congress by June 28, and the debates began on July 1.

No congressional records survive to describe the two days of discussion, so little is known about the Declaration's specific rites of passage. Several surviving drafts indicate that many modifications were made to accommodate various factions. And Jefferson's heart sank as delegates recommended change after change to his text.

Just before the vote took place on July 2, however, John Dickinson, the disaffected Pennsylvania Quaker whose Olive Branch Petition had so alienated Adams, rose to make a final plea to postpone the vote. Dickinson argued that the declaration was premature. He delivered a heartfelt message. It was earnest. It was long. And, recorded John, at its conclusion no one stood to respond. Realizing that a defense was required, and in the absence of others, John rose to speak. He talked spontaneously without notes or preparation; his source was his knowledge, experience, and passion, and he talked for more than two hours (some suggested it was four). He rehearsed the history of abuses by Great Britain and the significance of independence for America. Halfway through his presentation, the new delegation from New Jersey arrived, including the Reverend John Witherspoon, who asked that John repeat for them what he had already said, so he began again, reiterating his argument.

So moving and influential was this speech of John Adams's—though it went unrecorded and there is no way of knowing its precise content—that many of the delegates attributed the passage of the Declaration of Independence to his eloquence. Richard Stockton, a delegate from New Jersey, called him "the Atlas of Independence." Others have intoned a variation, "the Colossus of Independence." Many years later, John recorded in his autobiography that he had begun by saying, "This was the first time in my Life that I had ever wished for the Talents and Eloquence of the ancient Orators of Greece and Rome, for I was very sure that none of them ever had before him a question of more Importance to his Country and to the World."

John did not underestimate the significance of this historic moment. Following his speech, and more from others, Congress voted for independence. Dickinson absented himself from the hall during the roll call in order for the Pennsylvania delegation to vote unanimously in the affirmative. Two days later, the Declaration was adopted and signed by the president of the Congress, John Hancock. It was only in August that the final copy, drafted on parchment, was signed by the full body of delegates to the Congress.

Every man who signed this document did so knowing that his signature confirmed his status as a traitor to England. Treason carried the death penalty. The triumph of the battle in Congress, in which John Adams was its most intrepid soldier, provided the inspiration and the momentum to move forward in pursuit of independence both on the battlefield and on the home front. As soon as he received a copy on July 9, General Washington had the Declaration read before his armies to stir their lagging morale, and he had it read again a few weeks later. The Declaration of Independence insured the continuation of the war against Britain. If Thomas Jefferson wrote the script, John Adams gave it a voice.

Five

War and the Way of Duty

JOHN'S HARD WORK IN CONGRESS DID NOT SKIP A BEAT WITH the signing of the Declaration of Independence. He made copies of the document, one of which he sent to Abigail, and continued his labors, focusing now on his new appointment as president of the Board of War and Ordinance, a committee formed by Congress in early June. In this role he served as a "de facto Secretary of War," with responsibility over all aspects of the conduct of war from munitions to appointments to logistics. A more daunting role did not exist, and John occupied that position until his appointment to France in 1777.

At the same time, another, less conspicuous duty preoccupied his quiet moments, few as they were—that of a parent. "The Education of our Children is never out my Mind," he wrote to Abigail, and by education he meant schooling as well as the entire enterprise of shaping the character of his children. "Train them to Virtue, habituate them to industry, activity, and Spirit," he wrote, providing a formula for the conduct of a good life. "Make them consider every Vice, as shamefull and unmanly; fire them with Ambition to be usefull."

John intended his advice to substitute for his presence in his children's lives, because he knew the task of raising children was the joint responsibility of both parents. As an unwritten component of their marriage contract, he had agreed to support a family materially but also to assist in their children's guidance. It was a legacy of Puritan tradition that a father's influence on the instruction of his children was regarded as indispensable. John justified the guilt he felt for his abandonment of this role in the same way that he rationalized his absence from

Abigail. Public service was a higher duty that he owed society. "What will come of this Labour[,] Time will discover. I shall get nothing by it, I believe," he wrote, but "I am sure the Public or Posterity ought to get Something."

With the mention of posterity, John became guilty. "I believe my Children will think I might as well have thought and laboured a little, night and Day for their Benefit." Then he became defensive:

> But I will not bear the Reproaches of my Children. I will tell them, that I studied and laboured to procure a free Constitution of Government for them to solace themselves under, and if they do not prefer this to ample Fortune, to Ease and Elegance, they are not my Children, and I care not what becomes of them. They shall live upon thin Diet, wear mean Cloaths, and work hard with Chearfull Hearts and free Spirits or they may be the Children of the Earth or of no one, for me.

If the words seem harsh, they contained John's heartfelt burden of guilt, defensiveness, and passion. He had weighted one duty against another and wanted to make certain that his children accepted his decision to serve the greater good for their sake. They must inherit his values, he instructed Abigail. They must be taught the meaning of service and duty in order to understand his absence from family life.

He recovered from his fit of pique and reverted to sending Abigail advice for the care of their children. "Cultivate their minds, inspire their little Hearts, raise their wishes." John concluded by asking what each child would like to have as a present. In a harmonious chorus, each child requested a book.

By this time, Abigail and John had developed their "family myth" to explain John's service to the nation. Both believed that without John's presence in Congress, the nation's survival would be in jeopardy. Despite his complaints that he was overburdened and despite his occasional pleas for a delegate to replace him, in his deepest soul, John was unable to let go. He did not trust that any person would successfully take his place. He did not trust that the rebellion would succeed in his absence. In this case, it was not ego but rather distrust of other men. Built into his soul was the sense of responsibility, of duty, of calling, that derived from his being a fourth-generation New Englander. It became the source of his forcefulness, his tenacity, the belief that he was correct. Abigail understood and acquiesced.

John, furthermore, alleviated his guilt by knowing that Abigail was a trustworthy substitute for his presence. He knew that her resilience would preserve the family without his participation. Still, he sent a continuous stream of instructions over the years to reassure himself of having some say in the children's lives. "Education makes a greater difference between man and man, than nature has made between man and brute," he wrote. "The virtues and powers to which men may be trained, by early education and constant discipline, are truly sublime and astonishing." And he reiterated: "If we suffer their minds to grovel and creep in infancy, they will grovel all their lives."

John's instructions were models of pedagogical thoroughness. They were the idealistic standards that he held up for himself. They were the enlightened principles that empowered his ambitions as a public servant. They were the values of a republican father.

From the perspective of the Adams children, the absence of their father from family life resonated in many dimensions. All of them learned to know him as a patriotic hero, who risked his life and sacrificed his presence in the family for the benefit of the country. As the youngest, Tommy hardly knew his father, and the eldest, Nabby, grew up in a household where the model husband was absent. All of the children learned—too well, perhaps—to idealize their absent father and heed his lessons about responsible citizenship. The legacy of a dynastic political family was initiated in the circumstances of the Revolution.

ABIGAIL, MEANWHILE, BEGAN TO TAKE PRIDE IN HER ABILITY to function independently as the head of her household. By the spring of 1776, she wrote John, "I feel a gaieti de Coar to which before I was a stranger." She sparkled: "I think the Sun looks brighter, the Birds sing more melodiously, and Nature puts on a more chearfull countanance." With the British gone from Boston, with the weather turning warm and the prospect of being able to plant crops on her farm and enjoy a safe harvest, she basked in hope that had eluded her for a long time. She counted her blessings. She also had learned many lessons that stiffened her resolve to care for her family independent of John's advice or participation. And she surprised him by making a decision that in its time was risky and courageous. Abigail decided to have herself, all of her children, and her servants inoculated against the smallpox.

Smallpox was the dread disease that produced fear not only among the civilian population but also at the Philadelphia Congress that summer of 1776. News of the devastation in the army earlier in the spring raised the issue of how to protect the armies from the killer disease that appeared as threatening as battle casualties. Washington eventually decided to have his entire force inoculated the following year, a decision that may have preserved the army for the continuance of the war. Meanwhile, John fretted: "Our Misfortunes in Canada, are enough to melt an Heart of Stone. The Small Pox is ten times more terrible than

Britons, Canadians and Indians together. . . . The small Pox! The small Pox! What shall We do with it? I could almost wish that an innoculating Hospital was opened, in every Town in New England."

Abigail had decided what to do about it. Inoculation had been introduced in Boston in 1721 by John's great-uncle Zabdiel Boylston, and John had undergone the procedure himself just prior to his marriage. Yet people feared the practice, because it was innovative and unnatural. The idea of inducing the disease artificially appeared as dangerous as an epidemic. It was not; the induced form was much less lethal. Still, laws were passed in Boston restricting its practice. Despite the precautions that were taken—quarantine of patients in houses and a close observation by doctors who administered the procedure—fear prevailed.

The procedure itself was simple. Patients were assembled in a house and each was inoculated by placing a thread with the infected matter from a sufferer of the disease into a cut, usually in the arm but sometimes in the hand. Within a week, the patient, it was hoped, contracted the disease in a less severe form. It was now clearly recognized by medical professionals that the inoculation worked successfully to prevent contagion. It was still considered a radical course of action. As many as one thousand Bostonians went into "hospitals," houses set up as temporary centers, where a few doctors undertook their care. Abigail with her children and other family members were among the first to participate.

She was so preoccupied with her preparations that she failed to write John before going into Boston. Her aunt and uncle Isaac and Elizabeth Smith had invited Abigail and her family to join them at their large house in the city. Abigail, in turn, invited John Thaxter, the children's tutor, to join her group, which also included a maid, her sister Betsy Smith, and the Cranches. Abigail arranged to take beds and bedding for her entire group as well as food, clothing, and nursing supplies. She even took a milk cow and hay.

John learned about her plan indirectly. "In a Letter from your Uncle Smith, and in another from Mr. Mason which I received by this days Post, I am informed that you were about taking the Small Pox, with all the Children," he wrote. "It is not possible for me to describe, nor for you to conceive my Feelings upon this Occasion," he began his recurrent justification. "Nothing, but the critical State of our Affairs should prevent me from flying to Boston, to your Assistance." Once again, his family was in danger. Once again, he knew he was needed at home. But at the same time, the situation in Philadelphia was perilous. No one could guess General Howe's intentions. The British had landed at Staten Island, while the American army under Washington occupied New York. An attack was imminent, but Howe hesitated. When the battle would begin was anyone's guess.

"I can do no more than wish and pray for your Health, and that of the Children," John informed Abigail. "Never—Never in my whole Life, had I so many Cares upon my Mind at once." Spare no cost, he wrote; borrow from whomever you can, and he would gladly repay with interest. "I shall feel like a Savage to be here, while my whole Family is sick at Boston. But it cannot be avoided. I cannot leave this Place, without more Injury to the public now."

Abigail finally wrote. "I have really had so many cares upon my Hands and Mind," she explained, "that I have not been able to write. I now date from Boston where I yesterday arrived and was with all 4 of our Little ones innoculated for the small pox." She continued that she had "many dissagreable Sensations" about coming herself but had done it for the sake of her children. "I thought [it] my duty," but her fears had vanished as soon as she was inoculated. She would trust to Providence. Furthermore, she was too busy to worry, because the effects of the disease had struck. "The Little folks are very sick then and puke every morning." She thanked him for his concern and requested that he send her some India tea for its medicinal properties.

John sent advice. "The Air is of very great Importance. I dont know your Phisician, but I hope he wont deprive you of Air." He also sought the counsel of Philadelphia's eminent Dr. Benjamin Rush, who forwarded a pamphlet to Abigail's doctors with instructions about how to administer the inoculation. In another ten days, he had calmed down: "It makes me happy to hear that the Spirit of Inocculation prevails so generally," he intoned. "I could wish it, more universal. The small Pox has done Us more harm than the British Armies."

Abigail, in the meanwhile, was having a bad time of it. Some of the inoculations hadn't taken, and she decided on a second round. Johnny seemed to be on course with an ample outbreak of pustules. Nabby, too, was ill. Abigail suffered a milder form of the affliction, which, though she was weakened, allowed her to nurse her sick children. Then it appeared that Nabby had not the mild form of smallpox but something else. The whole process was taking longer than the expected three weeks. In addition to the mounting cost of their stay in Boston—it cost eighteen shillings a week for the doctor as well as a guinea for the inoculation—the farm had been neglected, and Abigail was nervous. "Now I fear it will be 5 weeks before we shall all get through but I must not complain." She described some of their regimen to John: "We are ordered all the Air we can get. . . . We sleep with windows open all Night, and Lay upon the Carpet or Straw Beds, Mattrass or any thing hard, abstain from Spirit, Salt and fats, fruit we Eat, all we can get, and those who like vegetables unseasoned may Eat them, but that is not I." It was an austere regimen.

Nabby finally contracted the disease. Tommy had a third inoculation before breaking out amply. And Charles was very sick. Johnny, fortunately, had recovered sufficiently to help with the other patients as he could. He, for instance, was sent to the post office to collect mail.

Keeping John informed of their progress, Abigail also responded to Dr. Rush's pamphlet, suggesting that the local process was quite similar, "except that they use Mercury here." Unbeknownst to Abigail, indeed to anyone else in her era, mercury can be poisonous. Used as a common treatment for a variety of diseases well into the nineteenth century, it can have effects that are neurologically debilitating, even fatal. Innocently taking the prescribed medication and administering it to her children, Abigail explained: "The common Practice here to an Adult is 20 Grains after innoculation." She took only sixteen grains, because "I don't admire this Mercury at this Season of the Year." Certainly, the use of mercury would explain Abigail's complaint throughout her stay in Boston that she felt "weakened and enfeebled."

Meanwhile, her daughter's inoculation took. "Nabby has enough of the small Pox for all the family beside," Abigail wrote. "She is pretty well coverd, not a spot but what is so soar that she can neither walk sit stand or lay with any comfort." Finally, Charles became very ill, contracting the disease in the natural way, it appears, from having been in the environment of sick people. Alarmed for Charles—he had been delirious for forty-eight hours—Abigail assured John that the doctor cared for him as if he were his own child.

John inquired about her canister of tea that he had sent with Elbridge Gerry. It had cost him an extravagant four pounds. The absentminded Gerry, it turns out, had given it to the wrong Mrs. Adams. Mrs. Samuel Adams was enjoying Abigail's India tea. Not a little embarrassed, Abigail retrieved the remains of the tea for her own use.

When Abigail was not nursing her family and others, she enjoyed the luxury of her aunt's bedroom. "I have possession of my Aunts chamber in which you know is a very conveniant pretty closet with a window, which looks into her flower Garden," she wrote. With her description, she brought John into the room with her. "I have a pretty little desk or cabinet here where I write all my Letters and keep my papers unmollested by any one." She went on to forecast a concept that became a slogan of twentieth-century feminism: "a room of one's own," symbolic of women's grievance more than a century and a half later: "I do not covet my Neighbours Goods, but I should like to be the owner of such conveniances. I always had a fancy for a closet with a window which I could more peculiarly call my own."

In that small room, Abigail read and wrote letters and amused herself without the noise and interference that came with family life. In the crowded world of the eighteenth-century household, privacy was rare. Abigail longed for a retreat where she could experience the freedom to read, write, and think in solitude. At home in Braintree, she waited until late at night, and then, if she was not too tired, she could be alone.

She also experienced great loneliness. "Here I say I have amused myself in reading and thinking of my absent Friend, sometimes with a mixture of paine, sometimes with pleasure, sometimes anticipating a joyfull and happy meeting." Carried on by her reverie, she continued, "I have held you to my Bosom till my whole Soul has dissolved in Tenderness and my pen fallen from my Hand." As if speaking to him, she wrote on: "Forgive this Revere, this Delusion, and since I am debared real [pleasure] suffer me, to enjoy, and indulge In Ideal pleasures." She summoned his presence. "I must leave my pen to recover myself and write in an other strain." Abigail's pen was the best means she had to tell John of her loneliness and her passionate love.

Cheering her on from a distance, John, too, wrote long letters during Abigail's stay in Boston. He never lacked for topics, as the business in Congress was manifold and stirred his imagination to send recommendations for his children's education. "Geography is a Branch of Knowledge, not only very usefull, but absolutely necessary to every person," he began his disquisition on maps and their usage. For page after page he wrote details concerning which maps he was collecting for the war department. His brief list included charts of North and South America, the British and French Dominions, the provinces of Massachusetts Bay and New Hampshire, a general map of the middle colonies, of the counties on the Delaware, of Lakes Erie, Ontario, and Champlain, New France, and so on. In the event that Abigail was interested, he also listed the printers and the publishers of maps that he considered crucial. "You will ask me why I trouble you with all these dry Titles, and Dedications of Maps," he queried, predicting her possible boredom—

> I answer, that I may turn the Attention of the Family to the subject of American Geography—Really there ought not to be a State, a City, a Promontory, a River, an Harbour, an inlett, or a Mountain in all America, but what should be intimately known to every Youth, who has any Pretensions to a liberal Education.

Abigail did not respond to his list, but she pursued his musings on education of youth. "You remark upon the deficiency of Education in your Countrymen." She concurred that "it never . . . was in a worse state." She described the collapse of the Boston education system during the previous few years. "The poorer sort of children are wholly neglected, and left to range the Streets without

Schools, without Buisness, given up to all Evil." Boston's educational system had been renowned for promoting basic literacy, at least, for all children. Its failure was due, no doubt, to the siege and the war.

Abigail had a more universal complaint: "If you complain of neglect of Education in sons," she wrote, and John probably saw what was coming down the path produced by her pen, "what shall I say with regard to daughters, who every day experience the want of it." And to underscore the importance of her lecture, she continued: "With regard to the Education of my own children, I find myself soon out of my depth, and destitute and deficient in every part of Education." Abigail was just warming up.

> I most sincerely wish that some more liberal plan might be laid and executed for the Benefit of the rising Generation, and that our new constitution may be distinguished for Learning and Virtue. [Here Abigail once more made a suggestion for a topic to be included in the Constitution.] If we mean to have Heroes, Statesmen, and Philosophers, we should have learned women. The world perhaps would laugh at me, and accuse me of vanity, But you I know have a mind too enlarged and liberal to disregard the Sentiment.

Her ideas about women's education, she realized, were controversial, but she trusted John to sympathize. If early education were valued, she continued, women must be educated, as they would be the first teachers of their children. "Excuse me my pen has run away with me," she wrote, apologizing for her lecture.

And she was, of course, right in judging John's approval. "Your Sentiments of the Importance of Education in Women, are exactly agreable to my own," he wrote. Behind every great man, he continued, expect there to be a woman of great learning, and he wrote on for paragraphs to list examples from history: Sempronius Gracchus, Gaius Gracchus, the mother-in-law of Scipio, the wife of the great duke who inspired the Portuguese to revolt against Spain. "Indeed," he concluded, history demonstrated many exceptional women. Before signing off, he asked for more gossip. What had happened to Gerry, the absent-minded bearer of the tea to the wrong Mrs. Adams? He had heard a rumor that his colleague was visiting a "mistress."

In fact, there was gossip about Gerry's mistress, and it was related to Abigail's concern about women's education. Elbridge Gerry had gone to Watertown to call on his lady friend, a young woman named Catherine Hunt. She was the daughter of a local shopkeeper, John Hunt, a Harvard graduate. But John Hunt did not think that women should be educated: "Girls knew quite enough," he stated, "if they could make a shirt and a pudding." So all of his daughters remained illiterate.

Gerry, according to the story, later returned to Philadelphia and wrote volumes of love letters to Catherine. She, however, not being able to read them, could never respond. Gerry believed himself rejected and married another woman. Catherine "lived and died at Watertown an old maid," a victim of her father's "system of female education." Clearly there were reasons other than educating children to illustrate the importance of female education.

Meanwhile, Charles recovered, as did Nabby, who had "6 or 7 hundred boils," according to Abigail, who wrote her best estimate to underscore how severely Nabby had suffered. John took the hint. He wrote to console his daughter about the ravages that smallpox would have on her complexion. "Give my love to my little Speckeled Beauty," he wrote, noting that she was like to have a "few pitts." He added lovingly, "She will not look the worse for them. If she does, she will learn to prize looks less, and Ingenuity more." He added some advice. "The best Way to prevent the Pitts from being lasting and conspicuous, is to keep her out of the sun for some time to prevent her from tanning."

By early September, Abigail rejoiced: "This is a Beautifull Morning. I see it with joy, and I hope thankfullness," she wrote. "I came here with all my treasure of children, have passd thro one of the most terible Diseases to which humane Nature is subject, and not one of us is wanting." Upon leaving the city, they had to be "smoaked," a purification process to prevent contagion, should they still carry the disease, and again before entering Braintree, but at last they were home.

THE NEWS FROM THE WAR FRONT WAS BAD. GENERAL HOWE, having delayed sending his 32,000-man army off Staten Island during the long summer months, decided that the time had come to engage the Americans at Brooklyn. Finally, at the end of August, he moved his massive force onto Long Island, attacking the much smaller and inexperienced American troops, who fled before the onslaught. Washington had been outnumbered and outmaneuvered. In a brilliant escape, however, he ferried his remaining army, including cannon, horses, and provisions, under the cover of a foggy night, to Manhattan, where they joined the rest of his forces.

Again Howe hesitated, not following up his victory on Long Island with an immediate pursuit of the Americans onto Manhattan. Again Washington was in a quandary of expectations. Should he abandon New York or stand and fight? His troops were undisciplined; some recruits left as their terms expired, others just left. He attempted to rally morale and discipline both. In the event that he decided to abandon New York, Congress sent orders not to destroy the city.

Finally, in mid-September, Howe struck. Washington, who had been at the northern part of the island, galloped to the scene of the landing to find his militias fleeing. Enraged, he attempted to pull the men together and was only rescued from the approaching British by an aide who grabbed his horse's bridle and led him away from certain disaster. Once again, Washington managed to rescue his remaining army, moving some northward and others south into New Jersey. News of the catastrophic battles of Long Island and New York spread quickly. "In the Course of the week past we have had many reports of Battles at New York," Abigail wrote to John. "But if we should be defeated I think we shall not be conquered." Like the Romans, fired "with Love of their Country and of Liberty," she wrote, "may we learn by Defeat the power of becomeing invicible."

The news of the defeat in New York was met with grief in Philadelphia. Not just grief but recriminations. Some delegates began speaking of replacing Washington with one of his officers. It was hard not to blame the general for decisions that in retrospect—and maybe even with foresight—were disastrous. Time and again, Washington had divided his armies, leaving the two halves more vulnerable than they would have been together. In his defense, he could never be certain where the attacks would come from, and he had covered his bases by separating the forces. Even more to the point, his men were undersupplied and lacked the training of Britain's more disciplined professional armies.

John Adams, while he blamed Washington for some bad decisions, strongly supported him as general for several reasons. He genuinely admired Washington as a man of courage and integrity. Moreover, he believed it would be ruinous to replace him in the middle of the war. Furthermore, no other person of his stature stood out as a replacement, nor would it be reasonable to consider him serving under one of his former subordinates. No, argued John, Congress must continue to support General Washington as leader of the nation's armies. But it would be necessary to supply his armies adequately, to prolong the enlistment of men and allow the general to use military discipline to keep his armies in line, a gesture resisted by politicians who hitherto had feared a standing army more than a militia-based army. That was John's position as well. However, for John as a member of the Board of War and Ordinance, these issues came under his purview. For this reason, he considered his position and his mission in Congress indispensable. But he was weary, and he needed a furlough from his labors.

While Abigail and his children were in Boston, John began to think about taking a break from the heat of summer and the heat of politics. As long as Howe's position was unpredictable, John could not leave, but he began to make preparations, requesting that Abigail send him horses and a man to accompany them to Philadelphia. She made these arrangements from her quarantine at Uncle Isaac Smith's house. Then the battles of New York delayed his return. "I shall wait here untill I see some more decisive Event, in our Favour or against Us," he wrote in early September. But he was pleased with the arrival of horses, for he had not exercised for the eight months that he had been anchored to the floor of Congress and to his desk. On Sundays, the one day of the week reserved for prayer and rest, John rode his new horse with great pleasure. "It is uncertain, when I shall set off, for home," he wrote Abigail.

Meanwhile, the rumor mill did not cease. "The Report of your being dead, has no doubt reach'ed you," Abigail wrote to John a week after her return. "It took its rise among the Tories," she continued, just as a few weeks earlier there had been a report that the Boston water supply had been poisoned. She didn't believe it, but she still requested reassurance.

John, in turn, had a true story to tell. He, in the company of Benjamin Franklin and Edward Rutledge, had just returned from a brief journey to Staten Island. General Howe had requested an interview with some Americans, hinting that he would make an offer to terminate hostilities. The offer did not appear credible to most congressmen, but because some few delegates still hoped for a peaceful reconciliation, they delegated Adams, Franklin, and Rutledge to make the trip. As expected, Howe had nothing new to offer. The best that could be said of the journey, John wrote, was that the ride had been good for his health. But their misadventure also had its lighter side, as related by John.

"At Brunswick," he wrote of the overnight journey, taverns were so full that "but one bed could be procured for Dr. Franklin and me, in a Chamber little larger than the bed." There was one small window in the room, and before retiring John closed it. "Oh! Says Franklin don't shut the Window. We shall be suffocated." John responded that he feared catching cold, to which Franklin responded that they would catch cold if the window was closed. They debated, and John relented. "I had so much curiosity to hear his reasons, that I would run the risque of a cold," he recalled.

> The Doctor then began an harrangue, upon Air and cold and Respiration and Perspiration, with which I was so much amused that I soon fell asleep, and left him and his Philosophy together; but I believe they were equally sound and insensible, within a few minutes

after me, for the last Words I heard were pronounced as if he was more than half asleep.

The incident provoked more than a little discussion between the two statesmen on the subject of colds over the years, and neither man was ever reconciled with the other's view. John felt he had the last word, however, because, he recorded, he had heard that Franklin ultimately died because he sat "for some hours at a Window, with the cool Air blowing upon him."

ABIGAIL'S EXHILARATION UPON RETURNING HOME LASTED FOR a couple of weeks, but in the face of the dismal reports of the battles, the rumors about John's capture or death, and the difficulties of running the household alone, her good spirits waned. "I cannot consent to your tarrying much longer," she finally exploded in a fit of temper. "I know your Health must greatly suffer." But more to the point, perhaps, "whilst you are engaged in the Senate your own domestick affairs require your presence at Home and your wife and children are in Danger of wanting Bread."

Abigail threw down her gauntlet. She warned him that "unless you return what little property you possess will be lost." The house in Boston, she pointed out, "is going to ruin." It had been taken over during the British occupation, and "one of the chambers was used to keep poultry in, an other sea coal, and an other salt." It was a mess. The boat of which he was part owner along with his brother was "lying rotting at the wharf." She had rented their church pew in Boston, but she had to pay the tax for its repair. "I know the weight of publick cares lye so heavey upon you that I have been loth to mention your own private ones," but she, too, was burdened by responsibilities.

A few days later, she was more melancholy than angry. She wrote: "There are paerticuliar times when I feel such an uneasiness, such a restlessness, as neither company, Books, family Cares or any other thing will remove, my Pen is my only pleasure, and writing to you the composure of my mind." She was worried both about the fate of the army after New York and about John's health. If he were to return, what route could he use, now that New York was cut off? Yet an even greater anxiety troubled her: "Your last Letters have been very short. Have you buried, stifled or exhausted all the___" and here Abigail left a blank space. "I wont ask the question you must find out my meaning if you can."

She meant tenderness of heart, emotions, the capacity to feel sympathy or empathy. She was playing with high stakes by suggesting that his sensitivity to her and the family had diminished. She perfectly understood his load of work and wondered if the burden of running this war had changed him in fundamental ways. Her mood was indeed melancholy.

But it was not a mood that lasted. And John responded ardently. "I have not been able to find Time to write you a Line. Altho I cannot write you, so often as I wish, you are never out of my Thoughts. I am repining at my hard Lot, in being torn from you, much oftener than I ought." He apologized for complaining about his "hard Lot" and noted that if this letter fell into the hands of his detractors, they would make a holiday of ridiculing his "Vanity." However, he wrote, "From four O Clock in the Morning untill ten at Night, I have not a single Moment, which I can call my own," and he considered it a "miracle" that he had not become distracted, or depressed or apoplectic or "fallen into a Consumption." And he reassured her that communications between them would not be cut off by the loss of New York.

John did better than that. He asked for and was granted a leave from Congress. He departed from Philadelphia in mid-October and arrived home by early November to be reunited with his family after eight months. He remained in Braintree, setting his affairs in order as much as he could, while still traveling to Boston for meetings with friends and political colleagues. The time passed swiftly.

By the second week of January 1777, he was on the road again, this time traveling with the newly appointed delegate from Massachusetts, James Lovell, who had become a legend among patriots. A former teacher at the Latin School, he was imprisoned by the British for spying in occupied Boston, which he probably did, and was shipped to Nova Scotia. He languished there for a year and a half before he was freed in a prisoner exchange. Soon after his return to Boston, he was elected as a delegate to the Continental Congress, where he remained for the duration of the war, the longest sitting delegate in Philadelphia.

At this time in January 1777, however, he and John were heading not to Philadelphia but to Baltimore. After the New York campaign, Washington had moved his troops to New Jersey and was followed there by Howe, who landed his massive army in Trenton, where they encamped. In a daring campaign, Washington had transported his army across the Delaware River on Christmas Eve, surprising the celebrating Hessian soldiers at Trenton and vanquishing them before successfully retreating back across the river. This was followed by another battle at Princeton, where once more the Americans triumphed. These victories were sadly needed, both militarily and for the morale of the army as well as Congress and the general populace. Washington was somewhat redeemed in the eyes of his detractors, especially those in Congress.

However, the next weeks did not bode well for the Americans. Howe once more feinted, sailing his army briefly up the Delaware, provoking fear that he would invade Philadelphia. He didn't. He returned to New York City, where, it was rumored, he had a comely mistress. Meanwhile, Congress fled to Baltimore for safety. Arriving in the fledgling city, which did not yet have paved streets, in midwinter, most delegates were contemptuous of the conditions; they complained of mud and dirt. John made the best of it. Having just followed a horrifically circuitous route around New York, crossing mountains of eastern Massachusetts and southern New York, riding on difficult trails and in freezing snowstorms, arriving after three weeks of arduous day travel and uncomfortable conditions at night, he found Baltimore at least tolerable. He only complained that the cost of living was too high, because of inflation that in turn was caused by the issuance of paper money. It reminded him that Congress had to stop the flow of this inflating currency and withdraw what was circulating. To that end, the credit of the states had to be supported, and to that end, taxes must be raised. John hit the ground running. He returned to Congress, lobbying for another unpopular but critical issue: taxation.

Abigail, of course, was displeased about his return to Congress. "Many circumstances conspire to make this Seperation more greivious to me than any which has before taken place," she wrote to both John and Mercy. She listed the distance and the difficulty of communication and the many hazards in between. To Mercy alone she confessed: "I had it in my Heart to disswade him from going and I know I could have prevaild," she wrote with confidence. "But our publick affairs at that time wore so gloomy an aspect that I thought if ever his assistance was wanted, it must be at such a time." She continued: "I therefore resignd my self to suffer much anxiety and many Melancholy hours for this year to come." Abigail no longer considered their separation in terms of a few months but rather had resigned herself to a full year.

The situation differed this time. Abigail was pregnant, and both she and John knew it before he departed. When she wrote about the "circumstances" that made "this separation more greivious" to her than others, they understood that she wrote in coded language. "It [is] now a Month and a few days, since I left you," he wrote upon his arrival in Baltimore. "I am anxious to hear how you do. I have in my Mind a Source of Anxiety, which I never had before." John's caution about Abigail's "condition" had to do with discretion. "You know what it is. Cant you convey to me, in Hieroglyphicks, which no other Person can comprehend, Information which will relieve me. Tell me you are as well as can be expected," he wrote, longing for good news. John observed eighteenth-century social conventions that banned the reference to intimate topics, especially those involving sexuality. The mention of pregnancy was considered off bounds, so throughout this period Abigail and John would be restrained by writing indirectly about her condition.

In that vein, Abigail responded. "You make some inquiries which tenderly affect me," she began. "I think upon the whole I have enjoyed as much Health as I ever did in the like situation," and then more sentimentally, "a situation I do not repine at, tis a constant remembrancer of an absent Friend, and excites sensations of tenderness which are better felt than expressed." Having made up her mind to concede to his return to Congress, she also maintained a brave front about her circumstances.

At home in Braintree, Abigail carried on. The barrel of flour that John had sent her had arrived. She rented their house on Queen Street in Boston, but not without some complications. One tenant had contracted to rent the house from her, while another family, having acquired the key from a friend in Boston, had already moved in. Abigail settled this dispute by allowing the rival tenants to sort out their different claims with a lawyer. Her cow died, frozen in the winter ice, and she had to purchase another. Their local Church of England had closed its doors because the minister had preached a sermon that extolled "His Most Gracious Majesty." And Abigail wrote: "I see by the news paper you sent me that Spada is lost. I mourn for him. If you know any thing of His Master pray Let me hear."

Spada was General Charles Lee's dog and his faithful companion. Abigail had made the acquaintance of both Lee and Spada at dinner in Cambridge. She hadn't known what to make of either of them. The general had insisted that she sit down to meet Spada. He then "placed a chair before me into which he orderd Mr. Sparder to mount and present his paw to me for a better acquaintance." Abigail depicted the scene for John these years later. "I could not do otherways than accept it." Now Spada had died, and Lee was held captive by the British. After a couple of weeks, John informed her that Lee was "confined, but otherwise treated well." In time, General Washington arranged an exchange and Lee returned to duty, but not without further incident. He was court-marshaled after the battle of Monmouth and removed from service.

Nothing at this time, however, provoked Abigail's temper more than her younger sister Betsy. Named Elizabeth for her mother and grandmother, she was the youngest of the four Smith children. Betsy lived at home in nearby Weymouth and visited Abigail frequently. In later years, Betsy would become the surrogate mother to Abigail's children and grandchildren during Abigail's many absences from home. At this time, in 1777, she was the "little sister," though she was in her late twenties.

At twenty-seven Betsy was not married. Probably, as the youngest child, she had been designated to care for her widowed father following her mother's death. But also, there appears to have been an unrequited love in her past that left her bereft and suspicious of men. Of the three sisters, Betsy exhibited the most sensitive spirit and the more fragile health. Living for so many years in a household with aging parents, she retreated into literature for experience, which may account for her romantic nature. She described awakening on a snowy winter morning:

> Was anyone Blessed with the descriptive genious of a Thompson, had the sublimity of a Milton, or the ease and perspicuity of the sweet Bard that Painted the Forests of Windsor and made them harmoniously quiver in his Lines, they could not give you an adequate Idea of the Glorious Scene, that this very moment ravishes my Sight and transports my Soul.

At the same time, Betsy carried on a correspondence with John Adams in which he teased her like a little sister, and she in turn joked back. She envied Abigail's good fortune in finding a mate who was intelligent, educated, and appreciative of women who displayed the same qualities. Abigail, she confided to John, had been "highly favored among Women and perculiarly happy in her Lot in sharing the . . . Affection of a Man in whose Breast the Patriotic Virtues glow with unmitigated Fervour."

Now Betsy had won the heart of a man she would marry, and Abigail disapproved of him. John quite innocently inquired after Betsy and asked Abigail to convey his good wishes. She replied: "I cannot do your Message to Betsy since the mortification I endure at the mention of it is so great that I have never changed a word with her upon the subject, altho the preparations are making for house keeping."

Her reasons were never stated. John referred to the Reverend John Shaw, Betsy's intended, as too great a Calvinist. It seems that Shaw, among other things, was too rigid in his religious convictions for Abigail's taste. But further, his prospects as a provider were slim, and he may have had poor health. Whatever the case, Abigail disapproved of him and wrote as much to Betsy.

Wounded, Betsy responded that Abigail's letter had "plunged [her] in the Gall of Bitterness." She composed a little allegory to describe the depth of hurt caused by Abigail's letter, which she opened to find a "shining Weapon" that stabbed "among the veins in my wrist." Betsy struck back. "What thought I, have I done to deserve this fatal Present." This was a mean blow, her allegory concluded, comparing it to "all the direful Events recorded in History."

Unmoved by Betsy's defense, Abigail derided her marriage to Shaw when it took place the following October. "An Idea of 30 years and unmarried is sufficient to make people do very unaccountable things," she wrote, frustrated at losing this contest. As a last strike, Abigail exaggerated Betsy's age. Her comments, which appear unkind these many years later, were meant to be protective of her beloved younger sister, whose choice of mate augured a hard life. John, meanwhile, sent Betsy his blessings from afar and maintained his jovial brotherly attitude toward his now married youngest sister-in-law. The politics of family were to him less exasperating than national politics.

Betsy's courtship and marriage occurred as a backdrop to the major event in Abigail's world, perhaps even as a distraction from her pregnancy, which as it progressed became more difficult. Her distress about her own condition undoubtedly played into her meanness to Betsy. As the weeks and months of her pregnancy advanced, Abigail's initial health and warm feelings became more difficult to sustain. An acquaintance died in childbirth. "Mrs. Howard A Lady for whom I know you had a great respect died yesterday to the inexpressible Grief of her friends," she informed John. "Every thing of this kind naturally shocks a person in similar circumstances." She continued: "How anxious the Heart of a parent who looks round upon a family of young and helpless children and thinks of leaving them to a World full of snares and temptations which they have neither discretion to foresee, nor prudence to avoid."

When she considered the perils of pregnancy, her attention turned to her children and her responsibility to mold their characters. Next she thought about the effect of expressing her fears to John. "I will quit [the] Subject least it should excite painfull Sensations in a Heart that I would not willingly wound." Instead she sent a verbal snapshot. "Coulour and a clumsy figure make their appearance in so much that Master John says, Mar, I never saw any body grow so fat as you do." She further reminded him to burn her letter. "I really think this Letter would make a curious figure if it should fall into the Hands of any person but yourself."

In addition to her physical discomfort, inflation and shortages of food continued to worry her, and pessimistic reports of the military situation discouraged her even more. "Tis four Months wanting 3 days since we parted, every day of the time I have mournd the absence of my Friend, and felt a vacancy in my Heart which nothing, nothing can supply," she lamented. "In vain the Spring Blooms or the Birds sing, their Musick has not its formour melody, not the Spring its usual pleasures. I look round with a melancholy delight and sigh for my absent partner. I fancy I see you worn down with Cares, fatigued with Buisness, and solitary amidst a multitude." More aptly, she described her own circumstances of weariness, busyness, and loneliness.

A few days later she confessed: "I cannot say that I am so well as I have been. The disorder I had in my Eyes has in some measure left them, but communicated itself all over me and turned to the salt rhume which worries me exceedingly, and is very hurtfull in my present situation."

The salt rheum may refer to a rash and itch that can be common in pregnancy and which, though uncomfortable, is not dangerous.

As long as she was bearing unpleasant news to John, she eased into another confession. "A most Horrid plot has been discoverd of a Band of villans counterfeiting the Hampshire currency to a Great amount." She explained that lots of people had been caught with these bills and admitted that she had accepted "about 5 pounds LM of it." She knew John well enough to predict his displeasure. John was furious at her for taking the money and ordered her to return it immediately to its source, which she did and accepted his admonition not to be so gullible in the future. Five pounds had great value; that had been the cost of replacing her frozen cow.

By June, Abigail was very unwell. The hot weather had caused her to "loose my rest a nights," which made the days even more unbearable. "I look forward to the middle of july with more anxiety than I can describe," she wrote, her emotions escalating. "I am cut of from the privilidge which some of the Brute creation enjoy, that of having their mate sit by them with anxious care during all their Solitary confinement." Her low spirits revived as she acknowledged that John, too, experienced difficult times. His frugality, she confirmed, would "astonish your constituents." She pointed out that some local lawyers were earning a fortune, while he had sacrificed his practice.

On the eve of giving birth in early July, she wrote an alarming message: "I sit down to write you this post, and from my present feelings tis the last I shall be able to write for some time," she informed John, adding, "if I should do well." This time she understated her anxieties. "I was last night taken with a shaking fit, and am very apprehensive that a life was lost. As I have no reason to day to think otherways; what may be the consequences to me, Heaven only knows."

Not surprisingly, the circumstances of Abigail's confinement in childbirth are obscure. She did not describe her room, her attendants, the whereabouts of her children, the weather, the smells or sounds of summer. What she did do was summon John into her presence, writing to him though the hours of her labor. She brought him into her chamber by writing about her ordeal, and she closed out the rest of the world but him and herself. "I received a Letter from my Friend," she wrote, "beginning in this manner 'my dearest Friend.'"

That one single expression dwelt upon my mind and playd about
my Heart. . . . It was because my Heart was softned and my mind

enervated by my sufferings, and I wanted the personal and tender
soothings of my dearest Friend. . . . Tis now 48 Hours since I can
say I really enjoyed any Ease. . . . Slow, lingering and troublesome
is the present situation.

She tried to remain sanguine. "The Dr. encourages me to Hope that my apprehensions are groundlesss. . . . tho I cannot say I have had any reason to allter
my mind. . . . I pray Heaven that it may be soon or it seems to me I shall be
worn out."

Then she wrote the most astonishing statement: "I must lay my pen down
this moment, to bear what I cannot fly from—and now I have endured it I reas-
sume my pen." Abigail wrote to John through her labor. In the known annals
of family literature, there is nothing like this, a vivid, candid representation of
childbirth, where a woman describes not her pain but her surrender to pain.
John was not, as in his former children's births, in the room below their bed-
chamber; he was three hundred miles distant in Philadelphia, so Abigail invoked his imaginary attendance to alleviate her suffering.

She continued her epistolary monologue with him, focusing on telling the
mundane. A "prize" had arrived this week at Marblehead—she meant a captured enemy ship—with "400 Hogsheads of rum a board." Inflation had
mounted. The cost of sugar had increased, as had Lamb, which was "1 shilling
per pound." The farm was bountiful this year, despite the cold east winds, and
the corn looked well. She dwelt briefly on the war: She feared for "Tycon[deroga].
Tis reported to day that tis taken." She wondered what Congress had done
lately, concluding with a prayer: "God carry me safely through."

The child, a girl, was stillborn, but Abigail lived. Within a week she wrote
to John: "Join with me my dearest Friend in Gratitude to Heaven, that a life I
know you value, has been spaired . . . altho the dear Infant is numberd with its
ancestors." She confirmed that her apprehensions had been well founded, that
despite the efforts of her friends to encourage her, she had been "perfectly sensible of its discease as I ever before was of its existance." She was aware of her
own danger, and "tho my suffering[s] were great thanks be to Heaven," she had
survived. She understood the "circumstance which put an end to its existance,"
but "in a Letter which may possibly fall into the Hands of some unfealing Ruf-
fian I must omit particuliars." She was satisfied, however, that "it was not owe-
ing to any injury which I had sustaind, nor could any care of mine have
prevented it." She added that she was amazed at her own recovery "after what I
have sufferd"; by the fifth day she was able to sit up to write.

John grieved. News of the stillbirth of their daughter did not reach him until the end of July. "Never in my whole life, was my Heart affected with such Emotions and Sensations, as were this Day occasioned by your Letters," he claimed. He thanked God, who "has preserved to me a Life that is dearer to me than all other Blessings in this World." He wondered how it was possible to feel such grief for an infant that he had never seen. "I feel a Grief and Mortification, that is heightened tho it is not wholly occasioned, by my Sympathy with the Mother."

Abigail recovered and returned to her routine. "I have . . . Health and strength beyond expectation," she claimed, though she was concerned for John's well-being in the heat of the Philadelphia summer. The farm looked good. There had been plenty of rain, so the corn and the grain promised well. The children were healthy, but prices continued to inflate. She had overpaid for scythes and the cost of rum had skyrocketed.

Ironically, Abigail developed an increased sense of purpose and fortitude after her misfortune in childbirth. She turned up the volume on her patriotic rhetoric. Having sacrificed John's companionship, she renewed her focus on the purpose of so great a loss. The only reason she could tolerate for her loneliness was the rationale that John served a noble purpose, which also justified her life. She wrote to Mercy Warren that if she were a man, she would join the militia and fight. She described her indignation about American losses and emphasized the need for leadership on the field of battle. From her current reading of history, she cited Xanthippus, the Greek general, in his wars against the Carthaginians and the Romans as an example of good battlefield command.

Meanwhile, the thermometers measured over one hundred degrees Fahrenheit in Philadelphia and the tempers of John's colleagues rose as well, with many of them leaving for home. John grumbled: "Never was [a] Wretch, more weary of Misery than I am of the Life I lead, condemned to the dullest servitude and Drudgery, seperated from all that I love, and wedded to all that I hate." He wanted to dig potatoes in his own yard.

THEN, IN MID-OCTOBER, CAME THE NEWS OF A GLORIOUS AMERican victory at Saratoga, New York. In a magnificent defeat that vanquished General Burgoyne's army, General Horatio Gates accepted the surrender of more than 5,800 officers and soldiers with their arms and munitions. The true hero of the battle was Benedict Arnold, who had been relieved from his command by Gates, who hated him, but remained anyway to fight. "The troops loved Arnold," writes historian Robert Middlekauff. "Once the bullets began to fly, Arnold decided to insert himself into the battle. He did so brilliantly, riding up and down the line. . . . Arnold in battle was more than a little mad, but it was a derangement that led to success." For the Americans, Saratoga marked the triumph they needed to bolster morale. Historically, Saratoga marked the turning point of the war. It demonstrated that American armies could win on the field against Britain, and it brightened prospects of winning foreign support.

It also made possible John's request to go home for a rest, which he did, leaving Philadelphia in late October 1777. Traveling in the company of his cousin Samuel Adams, he arrived in Braintree in mid-November. At home, he reveled in family life, tramping for weeks over his beloved fields, often with a child or two in tow. From his youth, John had a passionate attachment to his land. As an adult, walking his fields and working alongside his laborers provided his greatest therapy, after time with Abigail. Now John considered remaining at home. He had done his part for the Revolution.

He also observed that lawyers who had remained in practice for the previous four years, some of them his former students, were now earning fortunes. For one thing, the passage of mercantilist legislation in Congress, in which he had taken a part, resulted in many court claims between the states and the national government, as well as numerous private claims. Law was lucrative in Massachusetts. John was aware how much he had personally sacrificed, and so he began to explore returning to his law practice.

Many of the original delegates to Congress had retired and been replaced. Cushing, Paine, and Hancock of Boston had returned home. John also discovered that many of his former clients remained loyal to him. To Abigail's overwhelming joy, he accepted a case that took him to Portsmouth, New Hampshire, in early December 1777. The case, it turned out, was one that over the long run established legal precedents in American maritime law. At the time, it was an interesting and lucrative case for John to try on behalf of the defendant, one that would also permit him to exercise his skill in court once more. It turned out to be the last legal case he ever handled.

While John traveled to Portsmouth, letters to him from Congress arrived in Braintree. Believing them to be important, Abigail opened them. What she read delivered a crushing blow to her hopes for resumed family life. The letters, one from the president of the Continental Congress, another from James Lovell, now the head of the Foreign Affairs Committee, and another from his colleague Elbridge Gerry, announced John's appointment as minister to France and requested that he leave immediately to join Benjamin Franklin and Arthur Lee in Paris. A scandal had developed forcing the recall of the former delegate, Silas Deane. John had been selected as his replacement. The letters emphasized that John's reputation for integrity made it imperative for him to accept this appointment.

Abigail was shocked and devastated. Her immediate response was to write to James Lovell: "Your Letters arrived in the absence of Mr. Adams who is gone as far as Portsmouth, little thinking of your plot against him. O Sir you who are possessd of Sensibility, and a tender Heart, how could you contrive to rob me of all my happiness." She excoriated Lovell as a "family man," as a man who had been imprisoned and separated from his loved ones, as someone who knew the risks he was asking of a friend. "And can I Sir consent to be seperated from him whom my Heart esteems above all earthly things, and for an unlimited time? My life will be one continued scene of anxiety and apprehension, and must I cheerfully comply with the Demand of my Country?"

She knew he must understand or he would never have written. "I know you think I ought, or [would] not have been accessory to the Call." She begged his pardon for writing thus. "It has been a relief to my mind to drop some of my sorrows through my pen."

John received the news while in Portsmouth. By the time he had returned to Braintree, his mind was made up. He would accept the appointment. So was Abigail's. She had determined that she and their four children would accompany him.

The next few days were unhappy ones for both of them. John dissuaded Abigail from her plan. The trip would be too dangerous on several accounts, the same reasons she feared for his going; a winter voyage was hazardous under any circumstances. In addition, there was high risk of John's ship being captured by British naval vessels that patrolled the seas. It had long been known that John Adams's name was high on the list of treasonous rebels for which the punishment was execution. Under those circumstances, along with the fact that there would be no one left to run the farm and other family enterprises, John did not allow Abigail to accompany him. In the end, they decided that John Quincy, then ten years old, should travel with his father. For many reasons this would make sense. John Quincy would benefit from his father's companionship after many years of separation, and he would further benefit from the opportunity to see a foreign country and learn its language. John, in turn, would have a companion.

The next weeks were spent preparing for their journey. Not only were there clothes and personal items to pack but bed, bedding, and provisions for the many weeks at sea. Abigail busied herself with preparation of the food items, while John gathered the reports and books that he would need. The latter included French grammars, which he intended to study on the ocean voyage. They were scheduled to depart from Quincy Bay on the frigate *Boston*, which would call for them in mid-February. Abigail remained at home, while John and John Quincy traveled the short distance to await the arrival of the ship, which was delayed for several days.

On February 13, John visited relatives who lived near their point of departure. "The old Lady, who was an Adams, came out very civilly to invite us in," John reported. Since they had time, they entered and this same "amiable Woman" forecast dire conditions. "Mr. Adams you are going to embark under very threatening Signs," she said, and described the ill omens. "I thought this prophecy of the Sybill, was not very cheering," wrote John in an understatement, nor did he mention the pessimistic prophecy at the time, or take it seriously. "It was only a prelude to a Commedy," he recorded. "It amused me enough to be remembered and that was all." After dinner, John, with John Quincy, Captain Tucker, and Mr. Griffin, a midshipman, walked down to the barge, rowed out to the *Boston*, and went on board at about "five O Clock, tolerably warm and dry."

Abigail, at home and predictably unhappy, consoled herself as best she could. She wrote to her cousin John Thaxter, who had also been John's clerk and their children's tutor. "And now cannot you immagine me," she drew her portrait, "seated by my fire side Bereft of my better Half, and added to that a Limb lopt of to heighten the anguish." She continued:

> In vain have I summoned philosophy, its aid is vain. Come then Religion thy force can alone support the Mind under the severest trials and hardest conflicts humane Nature is subject to. The World may talk of Honour, and the ignorant multitude of profit, but sure I am no Consideration weighd with me, but the belief that the abilities and integrity of Your Friend might be more extensively usefull to his Country in this Department at this perticuliar time, than in any other. I resign my own personal felicity and look for my satifaction in the Consciousness of having discharged my duty to the publick.

In the Adams lexicon, duty was synonymous with patriotism and sacrifice.

Republican Father

MERCY ADVISED ABIGAIL TO EXERCISE THE VIRTUES OF "PA-
tience, Fortitude, Public Spirit, Magnanimity and self Denial." She confessed,
however, that she would not be able to withstand the sacrifice Abigail was making. "I own my weakness and stand Corrected yet Cannot Rise superior to
Those Attachments which sweeten Life and Without which the Dregs of the
Terestial Existence Would not be Worth preserving." Mercy meant that she
could not part with her husband. Abigail did not respond.

Indeed, Abigail wondered who else would sacrifice as she had. "Portia
stands alone," she wrote. And to a sympathetic friend she responded: "I have
sacrificed my own personal happiness and must look for my Satisfaction in
the consciousness of having discharged my duty to the publick. Indulge me
my Friend," she continued her plea, for few people "know the Struggle it has
cost me."

John and John Quincy's struggles began as soon as their little ship, the *Boston*, a twenty-four-gun frigate, departed from the shores of Marblehead, where
John's ancient relative had prophesied an "ominous journey." A fierce north-
easterly storm struck with strong winds and snow; all but the most seasoned
sailors were immediately seasick. After a day the weather improved, as did the
passengers, aided, perhaps, by "a Bottle of a nice French Dram," provided by a
fellow passenger.

Following the storm, Captain Samuel Tucker spied three vessels on the horizon and sailed the *Boston* closer to inspect their provenance. They were Brit-

ish frigates, fast-moving, square-rigged fighting ships, one of which gave chase. After a full day of maneuvering, Captain Tucker managed to outrun the attacking vessel, and the *Boston* continued its journey, carrying on board the two now quite disheveled, though still spirited Adamses, father and son, who believed that they had already received their fill of adventure. Yet one more storm developed after another three days, and this time John regretted that he had taken his young son with him. "It would be fruitless to attempt a Description of what I saw, heard and felt, during these 3 days and nights," John wrote. "The Waves, the Winds, the Ship, her Motions, Rollings, Wringings and Agonies—the Sailors, their Countenances, Language and Behaviour is impossible." Three sailors were struck by lightning; one died an agonizing death a few days later. John had gotten to know one of the victims, a young officer, and wrote to Congress requesting a pension for his widow and children.

"It is a great Satisfaction to me," John recorded after they sailed out of the storm into calm waters, "to recollect, that I was myself perfectly calm during the whole." He noted that "I thought myself in the Way of my Duty, and I did not repent of my Voyage." And he had been proud of Johnny's behavior. "Fully sensible of our Danger," John Quincy, though frightened, assumed a brave front.

The remainder of the journey took on a pleasant routine in calm waters. They proceeded at the rate of "200 Miles in 24 Hours," John recorded. For the next weeks, all the Americans studied their French grammar. John read Molière. He also decided to write his diary in French. *"Acores, Iles sit. Entre L'Afr. Et L'Americ environ a 200 li. O. de Lisbonn."* On occasion the sailors entertained themselves and the passengers with dancing. Always there were social hours of dining and drinking to anticipate.

Finally, they encountered signs of land—birds (*"beaucoup de ces Oiseaux"*) and bits of floating material that informed them that the Spanish coast was in reach. John viewed the sight through his "Glasses," noting with excitement the fine "verdure" and also the snow capped mountains of Galicia. Continuing northward, they headed for the Gironde River, between Nantes and Bordeaux, their destination. At La Rochelle, a pilot came on board to take them up the river, their first contact with the outside world in six weeks.

The pilot also had surprising news. The American diplomats in Paris, Benjamin Franklin, Silas Deane, and Arthur Lee, had just signed a treaty between France and America. Effectively, France had allied with America to support its war for independence and declared war on England. The mission that Congress had dispatched John to help negotiate had already been completed, without him. John, if he was taken aback by this news, did not register this reaction. He was too overwhelmed by the impact of seeing land and arriving on the French coast. "Europe thou great Theatre of Arts, Sciences, Commerce, War, am I at last permitted to visit thy Territories.—May the Design of my Voyage be answered," he wrote.

No ancestor who stepped off the boat from England into the wilderness of the Massachusetts Bay Colony was more struck by the disparity in his new circumstances than John was setting foot in Europe. Nor was any ancestor, who ventured into that wilderness more driven by religious conviction than was Adams, who answered the call of duty to his nation. And no more confounding station existed for a provincial lawyer than the convoluted plots in which he would soon find himself. John Adams had arrived on a stage to play a role he could not have conceived.

First he needed to touch land, to walk, to observe the Old World with his own eyes, to eat, drink, sleep, and talk. Except that here, John Adams, the talker, was frustrated, and no more telling experience could remind him that he was in foreign territory than the loss of language. At first, Dr. Noel, the ship's surgeon, accompanied him as translator in Bordeaux.

After three days of regaining their land legs, they set off once again, traveling overland on a journey of five hundred miles to Paris. On April 8, 1778, John wrote, "We passed the Bridge, last Night over the Seine, and went thro the Louvre. The Streets were crouded with Carriages, with a multitude of Servants in Liveries. For two days, they stayed at a hotel before moving to Passy at the invitation of Benjamin Franklin, John's colleague from the Continental Congress, now the American minister to France.

Franklin lived on an estate called Hôtel de Valentinois as a permanent guest of its owner, M. Le Ray de Chaumont. Located on the heights overlooking Paris and close to the Bois de Boulogne, Franklin's private lodge could easily accommodate the small American mission. The amiable Franklin, with whom John had once debated whether or not it was healthy to leave a window open at night, was already established in French society. He offered to introduce John into that world.

For John's first encounter, Franklin took him to dine at the residence of M. Anne-Robert-Jacques Turgot, the statesman and philosopher and a former finance minister. "It is in vain to Attempt a Description of the Magnificence of the House, Gardens, Library, Furniture, or the Entertainment of the Table," John wrote afterward in astonishment. There were in attendance "twenty of the great People of France," he observed. Other fine dinners followed, as Franklin introduced John into his life as a diplomat: "Dined at Monsr. Brillon's with many Ladies and Gentlemen. Madam Brillon is a Beauty, and a great Mistress of Music, as are her two little Daughters. The Dinner was Luxury as usual," John commented in his diary.

Finally came the invitation to Versailles to meet the Count de Vergennes, the foreign minister with whom the American legation were negotiating. Accompanied by Franklin and Arthur Lee, the other American minister in Paris, John was "politely received.—He hoped I should stay long enough to learn French perfectly," John recorded. While they were being shown through the palace, the king happened to pass by. His Majesty "graciously smiled and passed on."

So it continued for days. John was wined and dined. He walked the boulevards, visited the sights of the city, all the time dazzled by the beauty of the place and the people that he wanted in his deepest soul to dismiss as indulgent and frivolous materialists. But he could not help himself. He marveled at Paris. He admired the manners, the furnishings, and the spectacle of the people.

Sometimes he toured with John Quincy, but the boy was soon enrolled at a nearby boarding school. Franklin had recommended the school where his grandson Benjamin Franklin Bache was also a student. Ironically young Bache, who befriended John Quincy, grew up to become editor of the *Aurora* and one of John's fiercest journalistic critics during his presidency. Later, Abigail, in a stern letter, would reprove Bache as a false friend to her son, when he accused John Quincy of benefiting from nepotism. She never forgave him for his disloyalty. In 1778, however, young Benny and Johnny were school friends.

John Quincy spent his weekdays at school and his weekends with his father at Valentinois. Now approaching eleven years old, already a young man of the world and quite fluent in French, he wrote to his mother soon after his arrival in France that he liked his school "very Well." He gave her an account of his day, which started at 6 A.M. with classes until the 8 A.M. breakfast. Other than breaks for play periods and meals, classes continued throughout the day until eight o'clock bedtime. Clearly, John Quincy was experiencing a cultural upheaval as well.

ABIGAIL RECEIVED THIS LETTER AS WELL AS ONE BY HIS FATHER on the last day of June, the first word that she had from them since their departure in February. She had lived in daily anticipation of letters. She wrote to men who could be of assistance with news, but no official word had come for months to confirm their arrival. Among several of her correspondents were John Thaxter and James Lovell, who finally informed her simultaneously that the *Boston* had landed safely, and that John and John Quincy had joined Franklin in Paris.

John Thaxter had been John's student and later lived with Abigail and her family as the tutor to her children. In early 1778, Thaxter moved to Philadelphia to seek employment as a clerk in Congress. He had responsibility for making copies of the treaties that had arrived from France and therefore had access to information about the delegation in Paris. Abigail considered him a member of her family, and he proved a reliable confidant.

Abigail's second source of information in Philadelphia proved more problematic, not because he was not forthcoming but because in some respects he was too forthcoming. The unconventional James Lovell had traveled with John to Baltimore the previous year, when Congress was in exile for two months. Lovell was as erudite as he was quirky. His fluency with languages—he had been a teacher at the famed Latin School in Boston—made him an indispensable delegate at Congress, where he soon became the chairman of the Committee for Foreign Affairs, effectively the secretary of state. He was a committed patriot and stayed the course of the war at Congress. He was also married. And he flirted with Abigail, albeit in a tame and cryptic eighteenth-century style and at a safe distance by letter.

Abigail was confounded by Lovell. She knew his reputation as a brilliant, eccentric, irreverent, and unpredictable man, all of which made him the more intriguing. She appreciated people of wit, intelligence, and independence. Lovell's letters to her were clever and ambiguous, like puzzles for her to decipher. She continued to correspond with him, because she knew him to be a friend to John, loyal to his country, and a good source of information. His role in the Congress made him a party to developments in France. Besides, this strange exchange with so strange a man provided adventure in an otherwise difficult period.

At first, she wrote to Lovell asking for information. "You cannot wonder at my concern when what I hold dearest on Earth is embarked in the same hazardous enterprise." Lovell responded: "Call me not a Savage, when I inform you that your 'alarms and Distress' have afforded me Delight." He continued:

> If you expect that your Griefs should draw from me only sheer Pity, you must not send them to call upon me in the most elegant Dresses of Sentiment and Language; for if you persist in your present course, be it know to you before hand, that I shall be far more prompt to admire than to compassionate Them.

Ignoring the innuendo, Abigail made another attempt to extract information. She begged forgiveness for "so often troubling" him but wondered what Congress would do in the event that John was taken prisoner.

"Amiable tho unjust Portia!" came the response. Lovell once more transgressed eighteenth-century propriety; the use of her familiar name, even her pen name, implied too great an intimacy. Thaxter, who had lived with Abigail for three years, addressed her as "madam." Lovell ignored convention. "Must I only write to you in the Language of Gazettes?" he queried. "Must I suppress Opinion, Sentiment and just Encomium upon the Gracefullness of a lovely suffering Wife or Mother? It seems I must or be taxed as a Flatterer."

This time Abigail responded to his impudence directly. "I know not whether I ought to reply to your favour," she began, "for indeed Sir I begin to look upon you as a very dangerous Man." She acknowledged that flattery was a "pleasurable Sensation" and a "stimulus to a good Heart," rationalizing her efforts in order to cover up embarrassment on the one hand and still to maintain open channels of communication. She excused herself once more for taking his time but charged boldly ahead, asking for top-secret information: "I have a curiosity to know the contents of Mr. Deans packages," she wrote, "which I could not so conveniently ask for in any other way." Silas Deane had sent private diplomatic correspondence, which she wanted to know about.

The correspondence between Abigail and James Lovell continued in this way for years. They sparred. He wrote outrageously "intimate" (in the tame eighteenth-century sense) missives, while she responded as best she could in this contest of words, because Lovell was an important source of information about John. Also, he made her life just a little bit brighter by allowing her to play, to pretend, to indulge in a little fantasy flirtation—American-style.

MEANWHILE, JOHN OBSERVED SOME OF THE SAME—FRENCH-style. He had discovered that the source of Benjamin Franklin's success as a diplomat—and Franklin had become an enormously successful diplomat—was his social persona. Franklin didn't compete with the French. He couldn't. He recognized that he would be ridiculous, presenting himself as a man of the world in France. So rather than putting on airs that he could never achieve as a sophisticate in dress and taste and manners, Franklin played the aged rustic. Before he arrived in France, Franklin was already famous as a scientist, but he was now in demand as a celebrity guest, because he looked and acted like the American backwoodsman that he was not, and advanced in age, which he was. And his dance card was full. Franklin saw guests from the time he awakened just before noon until he collapsed into his bed in the early-morning hours. John was awed.

At first John tagged along. "The Delights of France are innumerable," he confessed to Abigail. "Stern and hauty Republican as I am, I cannot help loving these People." A few weeks later he wrote: "To tell you the Truth, I admire the Ladies here. Dont be jealous." He meant she shouldn't be suspicious, the eighteenth-century definition of *jealous*. "They are handsome, and very well educated. Their Accomplishments are exceedingly brilliant."

Franklin thrived in this setting. Women, young and not so young, competed for his company. There was Mme Brillon, "beautiful and accomplished," in John's words; Mme Helvetius, widow of the philosopher, Mme Chaumont, and Madam Le Roy. These women and others went to the trouble of acquiring tea sets—a distinctly un-Gallic custom—to accommodate Franklin, who liked tea. Women clamored for his attention at dinner; women hovered over him in the salons; women bussed his cheek. John went along with all of this for a while. He was fond of Franklin. He respected and enjoyed Franklin. He envied Franklin.

John quickly discovered, however, that he was sitting on a hornet's nest. Actually, he sat on two hornet's nests. Nestled into the first nest were two opponents, his fellow ministers, Benjamin Franklin and Arthur Lee. Their feud had begun over the deportment of Silas Deane, their former colleague, whom John had replaced. Lee had accused Deane of financial improprieties, prompting his recall from France. Franklin had defended Deane. The animosity between the two diplomats persisted, and John found himself caught between them. He was determined to remain neutral, writing repeatedly in his diary that he would remain friends with both men and take neither side. It cannot have been easy.

In the other nest was administrative chaos. Throughout their tenure in France, none of the delegates had kept records. So intent were they on their feuding with one another that none of them had organized either the diplomatic papers or their accounts. John Adams was appalled. Granted, the three men, Franklin, Lee, and Deane, had accomplished an amazing feat by crafting the treaties of amity and commerce with France, but their records were in disarray. This mattered because people made claims on the finances of America without there being a trace of where they came from. There were expenses for the diplomats; that was daunting enough. More to the point, there were bills for uniforms and munitions that had been sent to America without receipts. Some of the munitions had been faulty; there was no contract to show for them. John Adams was dismayed. Franklin could have cared less. Lee was sensitive and thin-skinned and wouldn't work in Franklin's quarters, where the papers and records were located. So John set to work, single-handedly, to sort out the mess. He declined most invitations, dined alone, except when Franklin invited guests, and passed his days establishing what order he could among the diplomats' papers.

This was not entirely due to circumstances; in great part it had to do with

Adams's personality. The original motive for his going to France—to replace Silas Deane as one of the three American ministers to negotiate a French treaty—had been accomplished before his arrival. Now he was perplexed about his role. He had no commission. He had no industry. All about him were people who indulged in pleasure as a full-time occupation, which was repugnant to his fundamental character. So he found industry for himself in his self-imposed assignment. And the more he distanced himself from Franklin and the social scene, the more indignant and suspicious and self-righteous he became.

John was not entirely mistaken in his suspicions. There were intrigues everywhere. Franklin retained his grandson William Temple Franklin, a bon vivant like his patron grandparent, on the government payroll as his secretary. When Franklin hired a second secretary, John wondered what other motive he could have than spying on John himself. It was not so outlandish a suspicion, since spying was ubiquitous in that environment.

Given the circumstances and his temperament, the weekends he spent with John Quincy were his greatest pleasure. "Your Son is the Joy of my Heart," he confessed to Abigail. He and the youth explored Paris, attended the theater and opera together, and talked. Not only did John fulfill his parental role by introducing his son to the culture of France, but John Quincy was his close confidant for those fall and winter months of 1778 in Paris. This becomes apparent in the youth's correspondence with his mother and his siblings.

ABIGAIL WAS NOT SO FORTUNATE IN HER EXCHANGES WITH John. Not only were they spare in number, they were brief. In late October, eight months after their departure, a second short note arrived. "How dear to me was the Signature of my Friend this Evening received by the Boston," she wrote. "You could not have sufferd more upon your Voyage than I have felt cut of from all communication with you." And she added in a poetic mixed metaphor: "My Harp has been hung upon the willows, and I have scarcly ever taken my pen to write but the tears have flowed faster than the Ink." In another month, she wrote: "3 very short Letters only have reachd my Hands during 9 months absence." She acknowledged that his letters must have gone astray.

Which, in fact, was the case. He wrote in November that he had received information that "so many of our Letters have been thrown overboard, that I fear you will not have heard so often from me, as both of us wish." He wrote one month later, after another reproach from Abigail:

> You must not expect to hear from me so often as you used: it is impossible. It is impossible for me to write so often. I have so much to

do here, and so much Ceremony to submit to, and so much Company to see, so many Visits to make and receive, that, altho I avoid as many of them as I possibly can with Decency and some People think, more, it is impossible for me to write to you so often as my Inclination would lead me.

John was perennially concerned that his letters would be intercepted and fall into the wrong hands. He therefore censored the information he sent. In fact, so suspicious was he that he discontinued his diary entries in the fall, concerned that they, too, would be subject to spying. While at first his brief notes were affectionate, later he felt he had to curtail even his warmth toward her.

The situation brought out the worst of John's character. He had no occupation that he respected, and by nature he felt useless unless he was engaged emotionally. The role of clerk irked him, as did the dissipation he observed at close quarters. And finally, he was unknown. Since his arrival he had been plagued by the question of whether he was "the famous Adams. Le fameux Adams?—Ah le fameux Adams?" In both France and England, Sam Adams was known as a great American patriot. The French refused to believe that "I was not the famous Adams." Finally, an English newspaper revealed the distinction, and John was no longer bothered with questions. "The consequence was plain," he wrote. He was "some man that nobody had ever heard of before—and therefore a Man of no Consequence—a Cypher," he complained. Clearly, he had spiraled down into a state of self-pity, if not depression.

IN ONE RESPECT, HOWEVER, JOHN PERFORMED CONSCIENtiously. Prior to his departure, Abigail had requested that he send her some items from France that she could sell through her uncle, Cotton Tufts. She had decided to take up commerce in this small way as a means of supplementing their income. For years, Abigail had observed that some people in her area were becoming wealthy by profiting from the wartime economy. She was not alone in her observations. Both Warrens had complained about the mendacity among their neighbors. James Warren wrote to John that while he was still "drudging for a morsel of Bread," others, including "fellows who would have cleaned my shoes five years ago, have amassed fortunes, and are riding in chariots." Mercy wrote the same message in more elaborate language. The formerly affluent Warrens were no longer affluent.

It was in this climate of avarice and materialism, of mounting economic disparities, that Abigail had conceived the idea of supporting her family by engaging in commerce, albeit in a small way. Her objective was survival, not wealth.

Wisely, she did not expect that her commercial enterprises would do more than supplement her income, but that had become imperative. To the people who observed that she did not live in a manner that reflected her husband's high station, she told a story she had read about Queen Elizabeth's minister. When the queen visited him, she remarked about his modest home. He responded: "The House may it please Your Majesty is big enough for the Man, but you have made the Man too big for the House."

Abigail was learning at a school where she was both teacher and student. With the guidance of a few people, she taught herself a new role that she would occupy for the remainder of the time that John served in the public arena. She became the manager of the Adamses' financial enterprises.

Prior to John's entry into public service, the Adams family income derived from two sources—John's law practice, which had vanished, and their farm. Now, she complained, "The Farm remains but the Labour and Rates devour the proffets." In order to attract soldiers, the military offered bounties of five hundred dollars, and consequently, fewer young men remained to work for reasonable wages. Between the inflation and the impossibility of finding workers, Abigail decided to rid herself of this burden by renting the farm. After searching for a couple of months, she found two men, "Brothers newly married," who were perfectly situated to take over the farm management, sharing the bounty "to the halves," which meant that she retained a good part of its produce for her own use. She announced her audacious decision to John, adding with relief that she retained "only one Horse and two Cows with pasturage for my Horse in summer, and Quincy medow for fodder in Winter." The number of people for whom she was responsible was reduced to her children, herself, and two domestics. This meant, however, that she needed to find other means to support the family. "Debts are my abhorrance," she wrote, knowing John would approve.

Her cousin Dr. Cotton Tufts, had "lately sit up in Trade," she explained, and whatever John sent, she could "put into his hands which will serve both him and myself." She meant to sell the items that John sent to her. She reassured John that there was nothing better he could send than "Goods, more especially such articles as I enclose a list of." Her list, the first of many, included items that were in short supply in Massachusetts and that would fetch good prices. In time, Abigail began to place her orders directly with agents in France. Tea was a good item, as was chocolate. Fabrics of various sorts—calico, calimenco, serge denim—flowers, ribbons, and handkerchiefs were good sellers, along with dishes, cups and saucers. Her requests reflected the luxury items that newly wealthy Bostonians coveted to show off their elevated social rank.

Abigail left no account record of her commercial enterprises, so it is not

possible to calculate whether she profited by them. Since she continued this activity for several years, she can't have done badly. Over time she involved
friends in various aspects of her trade. Mercy Warren, for instance, complained
that she could not sell the handkerchiefs that Abigail had left with her because
they were too expensive. Another of her collaborators was the "dangerous
man" in Philadelphia, James Lovell, who took charge of her orders that were
sent on ships that docked in that city. "Yesterday two Cases were brought to my
Chamber," he informed Abigail. They had been damaged by water, so he was
obliged to "pass over every Article separately; for those which are not really
injured were in a warm fermenting moisture." Lovell inspected and rescued the
items that survived the ravages of the sea voyage before repacking and sending
them to Abigail. Her complex commercial enterprise required significant management.

No small part of her preoccupation with finances had to do with her children's education. Nabby was currently enrolled in an academy for young
women in Boston, but she was prepared to send Charles as well. The expense of
having two children at private schools would hurt, but since by the Adamses'
standards education was valued more highly than any other extravagance, Abigail was determined to manage this. She also planned to do it without running
her family into debt. Observing the fortunes that some people acquired, she
became more daring and astute in her enterprises. She would never become
wealthy, but she avoided the dreaded debt.

Given that currency in the fledgling states was so unstable, and would be for
many years, speculation became rampant. One of the great challenges before
Congress, in which John had been actively engaged, had been the attempt to
stabilize currency, a project that was sabotaged on all fronts because the states
were suspicious of centralized control. Some states attempted to control the situation by placing ceilings on the amount of circulating legal tender. Most efforts were vain, and the safest medium, of course, was hard currency.

Abigail could hardly fail to notice that speculators were collecting fortunes.
She realized, too, that investing in currency represented another opportunity to
support her family. John approved. Following his advice, in June 1777, she informed him, "I propose to send in to the continental Loan office a hundred
pound LM." Like him, she speculated on the credit of the provisional government, and while it was a gamble, it was also a patriotic investment.

Both Adamses agreed to risk their small resources betting on the success of
the Revolution. Abigail further informed John, "Your sister Adams took up a
Note to the amount of a hundred & 27 pounds," perhaps thinking that this
made her own speculative enterprise appear small. The whole family, she de-

scribed, was involved in the business of speculating through exchanging notes or taking up bonds or purchasing property.

The expansion of their landed property was another venture of which John highly approved. He had purchased his brother Peter's neighboring farm just a few years previous. After the death of his brother Elihu from dysentery in the early months of the war, his widow offered a portion of their property to Abigail. The "28 acres of wood land" was for sale with its bounty of walnut as well as other wood and was "prized at forty shillings per acre which by looking into his deed of it, I find to be the same he gave for it." Abigail expressed a reservation about the distance of the property from her own house, and she waited for John's confirmation before making the purchase. In this case, both the seller and the purchaser were women, though only Elihu's widow, could legally own property as a single woman. Abigail made the purchase in John's name.

The longer Abigail was apart from John and the more distance that separated them, the more daring Abigail became as the source of family income and manager of their finances. While it was not a position she had bargained for, it was one at which she became competent. In the coming years she continued to sell items that she imported from France, invest her money in speculative funds, and purchase property, all in the interest of maintaining Adams solvency, which she pretty much did. In the future she made good calls and bad calls and some calls—such as her land purchases in Vermont—that sent John into fits of apoplexy. The Adamses didn't become rich, but that was not Abigail's ambition. Her aim was to maintain the family, to feed, clothe, and educate her children without going into debt. She found that a satisfying goal.

BY THE END OF OCTOBER 1778, CONGRESS DECIDED TO ECONO-mize by reducing the size of its delegation in France to one man, Franklin. The news didn't reach France until February 1779. The reduction made perfect sense to John, given that his days were miserably spent doing clerical work, while the rest of the delegation feuded. The decree, however, made no mention of his position. He was neither recalled nor reassigned. In that situation, he decided to reassign himself to home, and with dispatch made plans to return. Learning that the ship *Alliance* would sail from Nantes in March, he quickly took his diplomatic leave, where appropriate, and departed for Nantes with John Quincy, elated at the prospect of an early homecoming.

It was not to be. The *Alliance* was delayed elsewhere and then redeployed. Instead, John was advised to leave from Lorient on the *Sensible,* a French frigate that would carry the newly appointed French minister, the Chevalier de La Luzerne, and his party to Philadelphia. His departure was scheduled for June.

"This is a cruel Disappointment," wrote John, not one who cared to cool his heels for four months. Like travelers in any period who have found their careful plans upset by unforeseen delays, John moped and complained and tried to occupy himself and his son. They passed the time sightseeing. John tutored John Quincy, translating "Cicero's First Phillippic Against Cataline" into English and later a French text into English. They dined with the ship's captain and with John Paul Jones, whose naval vessel had docked nearby.

He hated the leisure time. He inspected himself in his mirror, observing "my Eye, my Forehead, my Brow, my Cheeks, my Lips," and what he saw didn't please him. "By my Physical Constitution, I am but an ordinary Man. The Times alone have destined me to Fame," he groused, "and even these have not been able to give me, much." Boredom spiraled into self-pity. Still another time, he focused his thoughts on Franklin: "He has the most affectionate and insinuating Way of Charming the Woman or the Man that he fixes on. It is the most silly and ridiculous Way imaginable . . . but it succeeds, to admiration, fullsome and sickish as it is."

Finally, La Luzerne and his party came on board, and a fresh wind soon took them on their westward way. A few days out, John recorded, "The Chevalier de la Luzern and M. Marbois are in rapture with my Son. They get him to teach them the Language." He found the three of them one day in his stateroom, the chevalier lounging on a pillow and Marbois, his secretary, stretched out on a cot, as was John Quincy, reading aloud Blackstones's *Common Law*, "my Son correcting the Pronunciation of every Word, and Syllable and Letter." Marbois and La Luzerne were delighted with the boy; "We must have John" for a teacher. Adams was very pleased with "my little son."

They arrived home in the first week of August. Abigail had not seen her husband or son for eighteen months. For a full week, John remained at home in Braintree, reacquainting himself with Nabby, his fourteen-year-old daughter, Charles, who was nine, and little Tommy, who was now six and hardly knew his father. The Adamses were reunited, but not for long. John was soon elected to represent Braintree in the convention that would draft a new state constitution. He accepted the position and spent some of the next few months at Cambridge, where the convention met.

At first the convention appointed a committee, including John Adams, to draft the document. This committee then appointed a subcommittee, including John Adams, to do the work, and finally the subcommittee appointed John Adams to write the constitution. It had been years since John had written or studied constitutional law, so he assigned himself the work of reexamining the literature. Then he set about drafting the instrument. Reviewing the Declaration of Rights, written by George Mason for the Virginia Constitution, a template then used by Thomas Jefferson in writing the Declaration of Independence, John wrote a declaration of citizen's rights. Then he wrote the full text.

With minor revisions by the subcommittee, the committee, and then the entire convention, John's document was adopted in 1780. This constitution for the Commonwealth of Massachusetts, written by John Adams in the fall of 1779, remains in force today, the oldest state constitution still in effect. If Abigail and the children regretted that John was so quickly drawn back into public life, it couldn't have been a great surprise. It was, after all, his duty to serve and theirs to support his service.

John's constitution for the commonwealth—Massachusetts chose to use this term rather than *state*—created a government that he had sketched in its fundamentals earlier in his *Thoughts on Government*, his response to Thomas Paine's *Common Sense*. Its opening line drew upon his earlier political plan. "In the government of the Commonwealth of Massachusetts the legislative, executive and judicial power shall be placed in separate departments to the end that it might be a government of laws, and not of men." He further established a two-house legislature, with an upper house, which was more exclusive, and a lower house, to which every town would elect a representative. In the senate, the upper house, membership was based upon property ownership of at least three hundred pounds' value, whereas in the lower house, where membership was based upon population, a member had only to own the value of one hundred pounds property. Voting, limited to males over the age of twenty-one, was also restricted by property value, though it was not so high that most men couldn't qualify.

Most controversial was the veto power allowed to the executive, a governor "who must be of the Christian religion and possessed of a freehold of the value of one thousand pounds." The term of office for the governor, like that of the legislators, was one year. The members of the independent judiciary were appointed for life. The constitution encouraged education, providing for the continuance of Harvard College because education at all levels provides advantages and opportunities for citizens. It declared, further, that education, as well as good government, "tended to the honor of God as well as the United States of America."

The most radical Massachusetts revolutionaries, such as Elbridge Gerry and even the Warrens, considered it a conservative constitution. But John Adams had been consistent in his politics. He was suspicious of popular government. He feared mobs. He believed that people who owned property had a vested interest in the operation of good government. He observed that people were not born equal but should be equally treated by their government, have equal opportunities and equal justice. He hated tyranny, but he had observed too much of human indifference in the course of his law career. His experience as a delegate to the Continental Congress and as a diplomat in France confirmed his beliefs about human behavior. People operate in their own self-interest. The law was needed to restrain human passion as well as to permit it. He wrote a constitution that restricted participation in government, but he also limited the power of governors and legislators with term limits. John Adams's constitution for the Commonwealth of Massachusetts became a template for the Constitution of the United States when it was written in 1787.

Meanwhile, John's fortunes had changed. The Philadelphia Congress, which had not defined his situation when it had reduced the French delegation just a few months earlier, now reached consensus on a new mission for him. In October, while John labored away on his Massachusetts Constitution, Congress appointed him as the sole minister plenipotentiary to negotiate a peace treaty with England.

While the war had gone badly for America during the previous two years, when the British won battle after battle, it was also widely understood that it had become too costly for England. Ministries came and went, collapsing under the burden of a war that now appeared not worth more effort. Now with France's entrance into the war on the side of America, and Spain's support of France, the military equation had changed. There was hope in Congress that Britain would be open to a settlement. Among congressmen, the almost unanimous choice to serve as minister to negotiate peace was John Adams, by a vote of twelve states to one. Pennsylvania remained loyal to Benjamin Franklin.

JOHN ADAMS RECEIVED THE NEWS OF THIS ASSIGNMENT IN OCtober 1779 as did Abigail. So once again John immediately accepted the mission to France, this time to meet with the English minister. Once again, Abigail was determined to accompany him. And once again, her decision was vetoed. He argued that the voyage would be too awful for a woman and small children, meaning Tommy. He would take John Quincy, however, and this time, Charles. John Quincy was less enthusiastic, having crossed the ocean twice, but he was persuaded, and Charles was excited by the prospect of adventure. In November, before John had passed significant time at home with his family, he set off for France, with two young boys as companions.

Cosseted among the valuable artifacts on display at the Adams National Historic Site in Quincy is a locket, a small oval frame perhaps an inch and a half

Charles Adams, the middle son, in his mid-twenties, painted by an unknown artist sometime during the 1790s. He was a favorite wherever he traveled, though he died tragically at the age of thirty-three. Courtesy of the Massachusetts Historical Society.

Thomas Adams at twenty-three, the youngest of the Adams children, who grew up hardly knowing his father. Painted sometime during the 1790s. Courtesy of the Massachusetts Historical Society.

long, concealing a fine line drawing of a woman sitting on a rocky shoreline looking out to sea and a departing ship. This locket, it is claimed, was given to Abigail by John at the time of his departure for France. Even if the attribution is inaccurate, the sentiment is true. In her first letter to John, after his departure on November 13, 1779, Abigail wrote: "My habitation, how disconsolate it looks! My table I set down to it but cannot swallow my food." She wished to see him again, and knowing that the ship, the *Sensible*, had not yet departed Boston, she considered going to town, "tho my Heart would suffer over again the cruel torture of Seperation." She did not. "My dear sons I can not think of them without a tear, little do they know the feelings of a Mothers Heart!"

John, meanwhile, had gone on board the *Sensible*, where his small party gathered for this journey. In addition to John Quincy and Charles, it included John Thaxter, who would serve as John's private secretary; Francis Dana, a young lawyer from Boston, appointed by Congress as secretary to the American delegation; and two servants. "Charles is much pleased with the Novelty of the Scaene," John informed Abigail. Small wonder, since they had been saluted as they rowed out to their ship by the seamen on neighboring vessels as well as their own. The *Sensible* was rigged, and its 350 sailors stood ready for departure. On November 15 they sailed out of the Boston harbor. One day later John informed Abigail that both children were seasick.

The voyage proceeded smoothly at first. The winds were good; they outran two British privateers and made progress. Then, following a storm that John described as mild, compared with those encountered on his previous trip to France, he noticed that the ship's pump was working. The vessel was taking on water, but the situation seemed to be under control. As the days passed, it appeared that two pumps were working. In a very short time, the two pumps were working around the clock, and all hands on board, including the officers and passengers, had to take turns manning them. The work was fatiguing. The situation was dangerous. So dangerous, in fact, that the captain changed course, heading for the closest land.

The *Sensible*, it turned out, "was an old Frigate, and her Planks and timbers were so decayed" that a violent storm or gale "would have torn her to pieces." They reached land at El Ferrol, the westernmost edge of Spain's coast, on December 7, just three weeks after leaving Boston. As they entered the harbor, John noted "two large mountains, one sharp and steep, the other large and broad," harbingers of what lay ahead.

Grateful that the ship had made it to land, John was still dismayed that the land lay more than one thousand miles from Paris, his destination. Even before landing, he had begun to ponder his alternatives. They could wait for the *Sensible* to be repaired, but it was now clear that even if the ship were ever to be seaworthy again, it would be many weeks before that would happen. The alternative was to travel by land to Paris, an arduous journey over mountainous terrain where the roads were primitive and the accommodations no better. There were no horses to make the trip; they would have to use mules.

In the end, John hired mules and carriages, called *calashes*, that were balanced on two wheels and were similar to New England's conveyances of fifty years earlier. In other words, they were not sturdy or comfortable. But that's what they had. John hired guides and provisions, and they set out on their way, an entourage that John Thaxter described as a retinue of "Don Quixots, Sancha Pancas and Squires in Abundance." His good mood lasted, perhaps, until sundown, when they stopped at their first "inn." "We entered into the Kitchen, where was no floor but the ground, and no Carpet but Straw trodden into mire, by Men, Hogs, Horses, and Mules." These conditions might have been tolerable; however, there was no chimney to serve as exhaust for the fire, built upon a mound in the middle of the kitchen. "The Smoke filled every part of the Kitchen, Stable, and all other Part[s] of the House . . . so that it was very difficult to see or breath." Their "room," actually a kind of loft that was shared with a "fatting

Hog," was covered with straw, upon which they lay the bedding that they carried with them. "Nevertheless amidst all these Horrors," John recorded in his diary, "I slept better than I have done before since my Arrival in Spain."

For three weeks they traveled under these and worse conditions. The weather grew harsh; it snowed and it froze. Everyone got colds. John quickly gave up riding in the uncomfortable *calash* with the boys, preferring to ride a mule that he purchased along the way. They traveled at the rate of twenty miles a day, on a good day, before they reached their destination of Bilbao. He had traveled for twenty-five years, John complained, "but I never experienced any Thing like this Journey. Every Individual Person in Company has a great Cold. We go along barking, and sneezing and coughing, as if We were fitter for an Hospital than for Travellers, on the Road."

Hardly resting, the weary little party departed five days later, trekking into France. Once more, having shed their Spanish conveyances for horses and carriages, they trudged over mountains and valleys until they reached Bayonne. From there, another three days of travel took them to Bordeaux, where they rested. Finally, following the same route that John and John Quincy had taken two years before, they completed the more-than-thousand-mile overland journey, sick, exhausted, and relieved. John arranged for accommodations at the Hôtel de Valois on the rue de Richelieu. Altogether, the trip from Boston to Paris had taken three months.

THIS TIME ABIGAIL DID NOT EXPECT TO HEAR FROM HER ITINerant family members for many months. Nor was she aware of the extent of their wanderings. She occupied herself in the business of her little world of Braintree. In her spare time, which was extended now that she had reduced the size of her family and farm enterprises, she concentrated on maintaining her financial solvency. She also spent hours perusing the shelves of John's library and reading. By this means she entertained and educated herself, and also found a distraction from her everyday routine as well as the loneliness that pervaded her solitary family life at the little cottage in Braintree. Still she had her worries.

Chief of which, of course, was concern for her husband's whereabouts and circumstances. Then there was the war and its progress. If anything, the sacrifices she had made in this revolution intensified her patriotism. "Our present situation is very dissagreable, it is Alarming," she admitted to John after a series of military defeats, but she expected it to change. She lamented her lonely situation, describing herself as a nun; this condition was open-ended. Fundamentally, religion provided her greatest consolation, her belief that all of life's circumstances were providential. Her continuing correspondence with James

Lovell provided one form of diversion. Several objectives coalesced in that exchange.

Within days of John's departure, Abigail wrote to Lovell in Philadelphia, renewing their correspondence, which had been disrupted during John's return. She wanted to keep the lines of communication open. Still, she needed to tread a careful course, friendly to maintain contact and distant so as not to encourage his impertinence. Lovell behaved himself in his first few notes that accompanied the newspapers he sent to her.

She responded that she was grateful, but there was more he could do. While John had been in the Congress, she explained, he had sent her the Congress's weekly journals. She wondered if he could send her these privileged reports. "I dare venture to say this only to you, since a hint of this kind would restrain many Gentlemens pens possessd of less liberal sentiments," she wrote flattering him. When she finally got to her point, she asked for information about the exchange rates on currency. She wanted data for her investments that appeared in the congressional reports. She had heard, she admitted, that the rate in Philadelphia was "25 for one" when "thirty has been given here." She wanted to insure herself the best return. Lovell was in a position to help her.

"You may always give me the go by, when I ask an improper Question and I shall take no umbrage," Abigail continued, and she added a "but." The "but" was followed by a query about John's account to Congress for his expenses. This meant that during the time that he was home, between August and November, while he had written the Massachusetts constitution and much else, John had not followed up on his expense account from his previous trip and left that chore to Abigail. Lovell was her important intermediary with Congress.

"You will see, lovely Woman," Lovell's impertinent reply began, "that we shall have more post Advantages of Communication than we have had for some time back." He meant that Congress had established a regular postal route between Philadelphia and Boston, running "twice in every week," but he couldn't resist presenting this irrelevant information without teasing her. "I would only tell you that I regard, esteem, and respect you and will certainly write to you *as often as I possibly can.*" The language and the phrases were perfectly proper, but the tone and the manner in which he juxtaposed these thoughts were suggestive. Without body language—the raised eyebrow or the wink—Lovell continued to convey boyish impudence.

He described how hard he was working, and that he was worried about his health; then he added, because he wanted "to preserve some Remnant of a good Constitution" for behavior that "Church Parsons" might consider sinful. Not skipping a beat, he turned to politics. "Our Affairs are unpleasant in many

Views, but not ruined. Every Patriot ought to be *allarmed* and then all will be safe." In a fashion very typical of him, he said the situation was not bad and yet it was not good. America was surviving, but not united.

Lovell, despite his flippancy and ambiguity, tried to explain himself to Abigail. He was a man of deep feeling who disguised his emotions within irreverent and impious prose. He would never be a straight man, someone who believed in clarifying his meanings; they came in an undercurrent of hidden ideas and feelings, a message delivered with double meaning. As a tease and a flirt, he was seldom able to convey the depth of his sentiments, out of either fear or the shame of being found out.

And so it was in his next package to Abigail, one that included several newspapers, that he suddenly interrupted his topic to write: "How do you do, Lovely Portia, these very cold Days? Mistake me not willfully; I said *Days*." He went on: "I suspect I shall covet to be in the Arms of Portia"—and here he ended his page, to continue on the backside—" 's Friend and Admirer—the Wife of my Bosom." He meant, of course, his own wife. He intended to shock her. Abigail got the point.

She responded in kind. "I must I will call you—wicked Man. I told you that I had discovered in your character, a similitude to that of Sterns and Yorick, but I never was before tempted to add that of Shandy." Yorick was a character in *Tristram Shandy*, a current popular novel, a witty and misunderstood country parson, often taken to be author Laurence Sterne himself. But Yorick, both Abigail and Lovell recognized, was also the jester in *Hamlet*. "From your own Authority I quote him as a wicked creature—What demon prompted you to carry the character through." She demanded that he explain why he had adopted the irreverent pose of jester.

Abigail had read much of Sterne, she continued, the *Sermons*, *A Sentimental Journey*, his *Journal to Eliza*, "but I never read Shandy and I never will." She, the pious New England matron, chided Lovell, the impious former schoolteacher, on the subject of morality in fiction—and in life.

In the midst of the American Revolution, these two American patriots, both of them sacrificing enormously for their country, both of them lonely, both of them tired of the hard work of being revolutionaries in a war that they could not predict would be successful, escaped from the drudgery of an uncertain cause by playing with language, he the flirt and she the coy but prim damsel.

Abigail considered Lovell a friend. Only because she cared for him, only because she understood that he was a man of "exquisite Sensibility" and generosity, of "universal philanthropy," did she remove her conventional polite discourse to confront him. She chided him seriously, too, because she feared the consequences of his letters to her being intercepted. "What a figure would some passages of a Letter Dated Janry. 6th and an other of Janry. 13th have made in a publick Newspaper?" And she added, "For a Senator too?" He would not be chastened.

AS THESE EXCHANGES OCCURRED, NEITHER ABIGAIL NOR LOVELL imagined the plight of John Adams and his small party of "Quixotic" travelers, making their way over the Pyrenees to Paris, where they arrived on February 9, 1780. Anxious to begin his mission, John enrolled the boys at school the following day—the same school at Passy that John Quincy had previously attended—and went to work. He wrote almost daily reports to Congress in a legendary series of letters that detailed his efforts to jump-start peace negotiations. He diligently explained, in his first letter, that the morning after his arrival in Paris, "Mr. Dana and my self went out to Passy and spent the day with His Excellency Dr. Franklin, who did Us the honour the next day to accompany Us to Versailles." There the Americans waited upon their French counterparts, and, reported John:

> I never heard the French Ministry so frank, explicit and decided, as each of these were, in the Course of this Conversation, in their declarations to pursue the war with vigour and afford effectual Aid to the United States. I learned with great Satisfaction, that they are sending under Convoy Cloathing and Arms for fifteen thousand Men to America; That seventeen Ships of the Line are already gone to the West Indies under Monsieur De Guichen, and that five or six more at least are to follow in Addition to ten or twelve they have already there.

Best of all, John continued:

> I asked Permission of the Comte De Vergennes to write to him, on the Subject of my Mission, to which he chearfully and politely agreed. I have accordingly written to his Excellency and shall forward Copies of my Letter and of his Answer as soon as it may be safe to do so.

Herewith John's troubles began. In the next few days, he wrote to the Count de Vergennes, explaining his peace mission and asking permission of the French prime minister to reveal his assignment to initiate peace talks with the British. Under the terms of the American alliance with France that had been negotiated prior to his first trip to France, both countries had agreed not to make overtures to Britain without consulting each other. Vergennes's response was the opening volley in a contest that John would eventually lose. *"Non,"* replied the canny French diplomat; it would be prudent to wait.

Not a patient man when it came to pursuing his objectives, John was frustrated. He had come to Paris to initiate peace negotiations. It was his duty and his obligation to Congress to persist. He continued writing not just to Congress on a daily basis but to Vergennes in an effort to move him by reasoning about the critical nature of his mission. John had mistakenly understood Vergennes's initial friendliness and openness to mean that he could write freely to the Frenchman and that he would receive in return open and honest replies. This, as the shrewd tactician Franklin well knew, was not the way diplomacy worked, and certainly not the way the French operated. Not only was it a matter of personality, but there were myriad texts and subtexts that went into the complicated diplomacy of French support for the American cause, complexities that involved the French treaty with Spain, but further, and disregarded by most Americans, maneuverings that involved Austria, Prussia, and Russia. To Vergennes, the issue of peace was immensely sensitive, far from the straightforward overture by America to Britain that John expected.

Nor did John Adams register that another aspect of his candid style irritated his French counterpart. Born of New England, if not American pride, John considered that France and America operated on an equal basis in their partnership. The Frenchman understood the situation differently. From Vergennes's perspective, the Americans were clients, suppliants, inferior in status to the great European nation that had come to its aid, not because of generosity or charity but for its own purposes. Vergennes's intention was always to enhance the status of France over England. The defeat of England was the primary French objective and the independence of America merely a secondary issue. Benjamin Franklin understood this. While John badgered Vergennes about opening negotiations for peace, Franklin better understood the French *mentalité*. His posture of patience and deference toward the French ministry worked to the advantage of America more successfully than what one diplomatic historian has termed the "shirtsleeve diplomacy," of John Adams, meaning "undisguisedly telling the world where one stands in frank and open language and letting the world take it or leave it." The canny French diplomat found Adams's blunt style exasperating and crude.

Negotiations, further, were contingent on the military situation in America. By this time, much of the attention had shifted to the southern states; the British had taken Savannah in 1778. The English believed that Loyalists in the South would help them to disconnect that region from the union, causing the American rebellion to collapse. From Georgia, the British forces, aided by the navy and reinforced by Indians and Loyalists, moved into South Carolina. A series of bloody attacks and counterattacks raged on the frontiers. Charleston fell to the British in May 1780, and in Camden, South Carolina, in August 1780, General Horatio Gates suffered the most stunning American defeat of the war. The militia fled like sheep, it was reported. The military events of 1780 did not bode well for the Americans.

At the same time, the cost of continuing this war was draining Britain's ministries and the treasury. Clearly, the war would not soon end. Despite their reversals, the Americans were unwilling to give up. To the British, their victories were too costly. These were the conditions that gave the hapless Americans hope that Britain might be open to consider peace negotiations, but only on their terms of complete independence for America.

While the war raged in America, John Adams, at considerable inconvenience and difficulty, had hastened to Paris to begin to negotiate for peace that wasn't happening, and it wasn't happening, as far as he was concerned, because of French duplicity. Vergennes, for his part, became fed up with Adams, who, he believed, had overstepped his rank and could not be trusted. He approached Franklin to notify Congress that he, Vergennes, would no longer deal with Adams; he would meet only with Franklin as the American minister to France.

Franklin, without informing John, explained the situation to Congress, including in his dispatch copies of the correspondence between Adams and Vergennes. He further repeated the French minister's demand that John's commission be revoked. The communications between Paris and Philadelphia took months. It took more months for Congress to deliberate, and when they did, it was not to revoke John's commission but rather to expand the delegation and thus diminish John's effectiveness. It would be many months before all of this became clear to John.

Meanwhile, discouraged by the situation in France and frustrated with letter writing as his sole occupation, John began to consider a concrete occupation for himself. Not waiting to hear from Congress, he made a decision. He removed his sons from the boarding school where they had been happily enrolled, hired carriages, and began a northward journey to the Netherlands with the intention of seeking loans for America among government officials and private bankers of the Low Countries, where his talents and his style would be better accepted. He arrived at Amsterdam and began the rounds of talks that eventually supported the remainder of the American war effort.

Seven

Diplomacy at Home and Abroad

JOHN UNDERTOOK THIS JOURNEY TO THE NETHERLANDS TO look for Dutch support. It was a fishing expedition. At the beginning of the American war, the seven United Provinces of the Netherlands—often called Holland after the wealthiest province—had joined England in a treaty of mutual defense. An attack upon one would be considered an attack upon the other. In fact, these two great Protestant maritime empires had been allies for centuries in opposition to France and Spain, two rivals for global empires, both Catholic countries. Because of the alliance between them, France had hesitated to attack English shipping upon entering into its pact with America; Vergennes had not wished to alienate the Netherlands with its navy and great wealth.

Still, several attributes had softened the Dutch position toward the American colonies. Historically, the Netherlands had rebelled against and won its independence from Spain, which promoted sympathy for other states that sought autonomy. Politically it was a republic and favored popular government. And economically, the Dutch bankers saw in America the opportunity for greater riches. They were, in fact, already benefiting from their illicit trade in arms to the rebellious colonies.

On the other hand, the war was not going well for John's country in the summer of 1780, as he with his two sons and a servant headed for Amsterdam. The Americans had won no major battles since Saratoga two years before, when the British campaign to cut off New England from the rest of the country had failed. British forces, having abandoned Philadelphia, were now concentrated in the

South, where two devastating American losses took place. The first occurred in Charleston, South Carolina, where after a long siege, more than three thousand militiamen were taken prisoner. Then General Horatio Gates suffered an overwhelming defeat at Camden, where more than two thousand of his soldiers either were killed or ran away in panic. In further bad news that fall, Benedict Arnold's betrayal of secrets to the British was discovered, and Arnold went over to the Tory side.

The information that traveled across the ocean to the American diplomats in Paris, and now Amsterdam, failed to boost their lagging spirits or increase their options. Their best hope was still that the cost of this war had worn down its advocates in Parliament. The British treasury was hemorrhaging; support for the war was as well. John Adams had nothing to lose by turning his sights on the Dutch. So, against the advice of Franklin and without his country's commission, he entered the fray. His critics believed he was tilting at windmills. A quarter-century later, before the end of his life, he considered his Dutch negotiations among his greatest patriotic contributions.

That's ahead of the story. Further, it was an outcome that John could not have foretold as he arrived in Amsterdam at the beginning of his self-appointed mission. He had taken the opportunity of the two-week journey to introduce his young sons to that part of the world, northern France and the Low Countries, an excursion that each appreciated differently. John Quincy and Charles, liberated from school, saw their time in the countryside and small cities— Mons, Brussels, Antwerp, and Rotterdam—as a vacation. John, ever the farmer at heart, observed the variety and methods of cultivation. In contrast to their previous journey from El Ferrol to Paris, they traveled in style if not luxury.

Soon after arriving in Amsterdam in mid-August, John enrolled his sons in the famous Latin School and began his round of visits among the city's famed bankers, who had made their little country an early commercial power. With energy and determination, John traveled the financial circuit from Amsterdam, to The Hague, to Leyden and Rotterdam. A few bankers would see him; others could not spare him their time. Of those who granted him a meeting, some were friendly, but none would consider loans.

Worse still, John's efforts to be received in government circles met with cold rejection. He had no official title and no commission. At both the national and provincial levels, his efforts to meet with government officials were turned down. His days, weeks, and then months passed in fruitless rounds of visits.

Meanwhile, a problem had surfaced in the boys' school. Classes were conducted in Dutch, and neither boy spoke the language. Consequently, John Quincy had been placed in an elementary-level class, where he was miserable.

Charles, more complaisant by temperament, tolerated his situation. John Quincy expressed his outrage, politely at first, but with increasing impatience as time passed, until his escalating expressions of unhappiness were finally censured as insubordination.

"La Desobeissance et L'impertinence de Monsieur votre Fils aine," wrote M. Verheyk, the rector, referring to John Quincy's mutinous behavior, had led to an impasse, and he informed John that his son was discharged. "Je vous prie donc Monsieur d'avoir la bonte de le retirer d'ici." John immediately withdrew both sons from the school. Amsterdam, it turned out, was going to be a difficult residence for all the Adamses.

John Quincy, now thirteen, and Charles at ten were more worldly than most American adults. Both boys now spoke French; John Quincy, older and more experienced, was completely fluent. Charles could understand and carry on conversations after just six months in a French school. But they were still boys and they still needed attention that John lovingly—though firmly—provided.

Given John's situation, his sons provided his best consolation. They toured together sites of historical and cultural interest. "This morning Pappa brother Charles and I went to see the city," wrote John Quincy. "We saw the statue of Erasmus, he is in the Grande Place." A few days later they took a boat trip to Delft and Rotterdam. John reported to Abigail that Charles "is a delightful little fellow. I love him too much." John Quincy attended a commencement where the orations "set his Ambition all afire."

By December, John informed Abigail that he had sent the boys to Leyden to begin their studies at the university. "It is perhaps as learned an University as any in Europe," he confirmed. He boasted to their mother: "One of these Boys is the Sublime, and the other the Beautifull."

ONCE AGAIN ABIGAIL RECEIVED VERY LITTLE NEWS OF HER FAMily abroad. "How long is the space since I heard from my dear absent Friends?" she wrote in November 1780, having no idea at all that they had resettled in Amsterdam. She quoted Rousseau that "one of the greatest evils of absence" is failure to know "the actual state of those we love." Absence is a torment, she emphasized, because "we can only enjoy the past Moment, for the present is not yet arrived." She meant that letters only explained that which was already long past. She expected that when next she saw her sons, they would be of an age "to place them at the Seats of Learning and Science." They would no longer live with her. "I long to embrace them." She considered herself like Penelope awaiting her Ulysses and just as uninformed.

Abigail advised them from a distance. "As you are separated from me I must endeavour to supply my absence" with letters, she lamented and apologized. "O My dear children, when shall I hold you to my Bosom again?" She worried that the attention Charles received would make him arrogant. "Praise is a Dangerous Sweet unless properly tempered," she warned. "If you ever feel your Little Bosom swell with pride and begin to think yourself better than others; you will then become less worthy." No Puritan preacher could have put it better.

Nor did John Quincy escape her admonitions across the wide ocean. "I hope my dear Boy that the universal neatness and Cleanliness, of the people where you reside, will cure you of all your slovenly tricks." She recommended that he read history, because it would teach him about the evils of the world and that his own country was best suited to make people "Bold, hardy and intrepid." She feared that her son would be seduced by the luxuries and extravagance of Europe. It was her intention and her task to teach him that America was better suited for a valuable life. Her lessons were distilled into succinct messages that she could post and mail to Europe. She added, as well, a plethora of religious injunctions.

Abigail's world was full. No longer did she spend long hours in an agony of loneliness. No longer did she feel incompetent or unable to cope with circumstances. No longer did she survive "like a nun," bereft of company. She had periods of anxiety, she longed for the reunion of her family, she did on occasion despair of the life she wished she had, but mostly Abigail accepted her circumstances. Religion was a primary support; it provided spiritual as well as rational assistance. But so was the myth that had grown and developed since John's first days in public service.

Abigail now believed even more firmly that the American Revolution would founder without John's active participation. His individual genius, proven by years of service, was necessary to the success of the mission. And more than ever, it was his duty as a citizen and a uniquely talented man to sacrifice his personal comfort for the greater cause of American freedom. "Those who Envy him, his situation see not with my Eyes, nor feel with my Heart," she wrote to her friend Mercy Otis Warren, adding, "Perhaps I feel and fear too much."

It was her duty to encourage his participation and to pick up the slack at home. She was now capable of exercising her power, because she understood her place in the community and because she was committed to the principle of sacrifice for an important cause. Perhaps this is one reason that John wrote to her so infrequently in the course of the next two years. He had shifted family responsibilities to her and did not want to hear about them. He was doing his part by taking care of the two older sons. He needed to focus the remainder of his attention on his diplomatic work.

In fact, the correspondence between them during the period while he lived in Amsterdam takes on a different valence. John wrote infrequently. Abigail wrote to him primarily about her business matters, about local and national politics; she gossiped about friends and about their children. She expressed love and longing for him and the children, but she no longer dwelled in that sphere. Instead, her most sentient and animated letters of this period were mailed to Philadelphia; indeed, they were inscribed to James Lovell.

Several reasons accounted for this. One was that Philadelphia was accessible while Europe hardly was. The turnaround time for letters to Pennsylvania was weeks, not months. The other was that Lovell responded; his letters to her were always amiable. He was a very busy man who took the time from his many cares to pay attention to Abigail and to render her many services. Lovell was a friend.

At the forefront of Abigail's daily routines were the occupations that kept her family solvent, primarily her investments and mercantile ventures. Taxes had risen hugely as Massachusetts carried its part of the war burden. "The Quarterly tax for the state and continent amounts to 7 hundred pounds Lawfull, my part," she informed John in the summer after his departure. Speculation in currency, as well as in state and national bonds, provided her one method to raise money.

At the same time, she continued to purchase land. "I have some prospect of making a purchase of the House and land, belonging formerly to Natell. Belcher who died this winter," she informed John. "I have been trying to agree with the Heir." She explained how inflated the currency had become. "He asked the moderate price of 20 thousand Dollors when exchange was at 30, it is now 60 and he doubles his demand." Abigail did not ask for John's advice or his permission. She informed him about her negotiations, knowing that he entrusted their affairs to her oversight. Although she mentioned this property once more, she apparently did not acquire it.

In the next few years, though, Abigail did make several successful land purchases and one very bad one. While John was still abroad, she wrote that she had purchased a wooded lot at the foot of the hill "that had belonged to the Estate of your uncle [Ebenezer] Adams," which had been sold by his heirs. She purchased it, she explained, because "I felt loth it should go to any person who could not pass to it, but through land of yours." In all it amounted to seven acres and had cost her "2 hundred dollors." John was elated: "Your Purchase of Land," he wrote, "gives me more Pleasure than you are aware." He supposed it "to be that fine Grove which I have loved and admired from my Cradle. If it is, I would not part with it, for Gold." His satisfaction with her fairly jumped off the page on which he wrote. "Pray don't let a Single Tree be cutt upon that Spot. I expect, very soon, to be a private Man, and to have no other Resource for my Family but my farm." During his many years in public service, John dreamed about returning home to farm. As he traveled about Europe, he noted methods of farming. Fertilizer was a favorite topic.

Abigail dreamed about retirement in Vermont, which accounted for her one lapse in judgment. "I have a desire to become a purchaser in the State of Vermont," she informed John. "I may possibly run you in debt a hundred dollors for that purpose." Land was available at bargain rates in Vermont, she had learned. "I know you would like it, so shall venture the first opportunity a hundred and 20 or 30 dollors will Buy a thousand acres." An acquaintance, a Colonel Davis of Worcester, had been granted a charter for a township. He made a sales pitch to Abigail, and she purchased the land. Ironically, John was named as the original proprietor. Abigail had studied the information, made the decision, and taken the risk, but as a woman, she could not possess land in her own name.

John was displeased. "Don't meddle any more with Vermont," he growled from The Hague after learning about it. To his friend James Warren, he was more explicit: "God willing, I will not go to Vermont. I must be within the scent of the sea." The next year, after learning that the land deal had fallen through, to their disadvantage, he brutally scolded Abigail:

> I am afraid that all the Money you have laid out in Vermont Lands is lost. You can ill afford it, I assure you. You are destined to be poor in your old Age, and therefore the more perfectly you reconcile your self to the Thought of it the better. Your Children have no Resource but in their own Labour. They will have this Advantage, they may labour a little for themselves, more than their Father could ever do, without betraying Trusts which it was his duty to Accept.

John was in one of his snits, a moment of despair and self-pity. Abigail with her mistaken venture in Vermont became the target of his unhappiness.

Abigail's small business ventures proved more reliable. Whereas she had once depended upon John to send her merchandise to sell, she now corresponded directly with the agents in Europe. Joseph Gardoqui and Sons in Bilbao and Jean de Neufville and Son in Amsterdam sent their shipments and invoices to Abigail for items such as damask tablecloths, pins, bed ticking, teacups and saucers, and wineglasses. Abigail's inventory reflected the tastes of the newly rich in Boston. And it was Lovell, very often, who received her

European orders, sorted them if there had been damage at sea, and forwarded them to Braintree, where Abigail conducted her business.

JOHN'S FORTUNES, MEANWHILE, IMPROVED IN ONE RESPECT. Congress had finally appointed him minister to the Netherlands, replacing Henry Laurens, who had been captured at sea and was now imprisoned in the Tower of London. In the interim, John had not been inactive. He had made a discovery during his many months of futile encounters with bankers and government officials. The Dutch, he concluded, were ignorant about his country and the nature of the war for independence. He decided that he could be most effective as a propagandist for his country, educating the Dutch about America. He turned into a one-man public relations team, writing articles for the media and reports to be delivered to influential people. He had his *Thoughts on Government* translated into Dutch and published. He sent to Abigail for copies of the Massachusetts Constitution to be published in Holland. All this activity did take its toll on Adams; his health suffered in the damp climate. Nevertheless, he carried on his work.

In the summer of 1781, Vergennes invited John back to Paris, to discuss a possible opportunity for peace. That trip proved to be—as John anticipated—a fool's errand. His reservations were validated when he learned that he would be addressed as a "British subject." John denounced the label. "I am not a British subject," he replied. "I renounced that character many years ago forever. I should rather be a fugitive in China or Malabar than ever re-assume that character." But Vergennes had another trick or two up his sleeve, involving mediation by the Russian emperor and empress that John quickly rejected as being equivalent to a truce. This, he announced, "would leave our trade more embarrassed, our union more precarious, and our liberties at a greater hazard, than they can be in a continuance of the war." And he returned to Amsterdam.

An opportunity had developed with John Quincy over the course of a few months. Francis Dana, the legation's secretary, who had remained in France after they moved to the Netherlands, received an appointment from Congress to represent his country at the Russian court. He needed a secretary who could speak better French than he. After making several futile attempts to find a man to fill that position, he turned to John Adams and requested the assistance of John Quincy, now fourteen years old, as his companion to Saint Petersburg. John's initial response was negative, but after some cajoling and more thought, he saw the prospects that it presented his elder son. Not only would he see more of the world and gain experience, he now could serve his country as few young men of his age could. John Quincy was willing to go, so John, with mixed emotions, bid farewell to his son in August 1781. The young man set out on the thousand-mile journey through northern Europe that would take seven weeks.

Charles's story, too, caused John heartache of a different kind. Charles, whose health was delicate, had been ill in the spring and remained weak. More to the point, Charles became homesick, and with John Quincy gone to Russia, he pleaded with his father to allow him to return home to Braintree. "My dear Charles will go home," he wrote to Abigail in early July in a letter that she received after she had already learned of Charles's departure. "Put him to school and keep him steady.—He is a delightful Child, but has too exquisite sensibility for Europe." Writing later, John explained more fully:

> My second son, after the departure of his brother, found himself so much alone, that he grew uneasy, and importuned me so tenderly to let him return to America to his mother, that I consented to that, and thus deprived myself of the greatest pleasure I had in life, the society of my children.

Charles's journey home took an ironic turn.

John had placed his son in the care of a friend, Major William Jackson. Other friends traveled on the same ship: Benjamin Waterhouse, a young physician who had been studying in the Netherlands, now retuning to Boston to practice medicine, as well as the artist John Trumbull. Their ship, the *South Carolina*, departed from Texel on August 12 under the command of Alexander Gillon. When a storm developed, Gillon steered his ship off course and entirely around the British Isles. Three weeks later, he was forced to land in order to take on more supplies. They landed in La Coruña, Spain. Charles's journey had come full circle from his arrival two years ago on the Spanish coast.

At this point, Major Jackson, who had been quarreling with Gillon about his decision, became fed up and left the ship with Charles, as did Trumbull. Waterhouse remained on the *South Carolina*. Few vessels were scheduled to leave from that area at that time of year, so once more Charles, along with Major Jackson and Trumbull, made the trip to Bilbao, this time by boat—another arduous passage that took twenty-one days—in order to get transportation to America. There they boarded the vessel *Cicero*, whose destination was Beverly, just north of Boston. They did not arrive until mid-January, almost six months after their departure. In the interim, Abigail became frantic with worry, having received no information on her son's whereabouts.

With no news in December, Abigail wrote to John, "Ah! How great has my anxiety been, what have I not sufferd since I heard my dear Charles was on Board and no intelligence to be procured of the vessel for 4 months after she saild." She cursed Gillon and she cursed the weather. John, meanwhile, had been informed that Charles sailed from Bilbao with Jackson and Trumbull. Abigail with her woes turned to her friend Lovell: "I have been Sick confined to my chamber with a slow fever. I have been unhappy through anxiety for my dear Boy, and still am apprehensive of our terrible coast should he come upon it, besides the tormenting cruisers infest our Bay with impuinity and take every thing."

The exact date of Charles's arrival at home is unknown, but by the end of January Abigail acknowledged "the safe arrival of my dear Charles, an event which has relieved me from many anxieties and filld my Heart with gratitude to that gracious Being who protected him from the perils of the deep . . . and has restored him to his Native land." Uncharacteristically, she boasted about her son. "The fond Mother would tell you that you may find in him the same solid sober discreet Qualities that he carried abroad." Abigail's relief knew no boundaries. Her typical reticence about her children's talents disappeared before her sense of joy at having Charles safely home.

Still, her resolve weakened by worry, she complained to John. It had been a year since she had received a letter from him, she wrote in late September. "You flatter me with a pleasing Illusion that if ever you see you Native land again you will not quit it," she rebuked him a month later. "I can have little faith in the promise." A few months after that, she declared to John that the Adamses had done their share, and it was time to consider resuming private life. "Two years my dearest Friend have passd away since you left your Native land. Will you not return e'er the close of an other year?"

ABIGAIL WAS NOT AWARE, HOWEVER, THAT JOHN HAD BECOME seriously ill. John had never cared for the climate of the Netherlands. He complained mightily about the "pestilential vapours" and the "stagnant waters" of a country that was situated almost entirely on waterways. His symptoms became more alarming soon after his children left him in August. Having returned from his arduous diplomatic mission to Paris to face a multitude of concerns about his country, where the military situation appeared bleak as ever with the defeat of American armies in the South, and struggling against odds to gain recognition and funding in the Netherlands, he was taxed to the limit. In addition, he received the not entirely unwelcome news that he had been demoted from the post of sole minister to negotiate peace to one of five. Congress, bowing to heavy pressure from the French foreign minister, added Benjamin Franklin, John Jay, the minister to Spain, Henry Laurens, still in the Tower, and Thomas Jefferson to its delegation. While John welcomed the expansion, he also felt the blow to his integrity. In September, he fell ill. "Soon after my Return from Paris, I was seized with a Fever, of which, as the Weather Was and had long been uncommonly warm, I took little notice, but it increased very slowly, and regularly, untill it was found to be a nervous Fever, of a dangerous kind, bordering upon putrid."

Like many illnesses of the eighteenth century that are described as "fevers," this one is difficult to diagnose. Adams himself described it as a "nervous Fever." "This is the first Time, I have been able to write you, since my Sickness," he wrote to Abigail in early October 1781. He continued, describing a fever that became so acute that he had lost consciousness for many days—"for five or six days I was lost, and so insensible to the Operations of the Physicians and surgeons, as to have lost the memory of them." His friends had ministered to him and summoned excellent physicians "whose Skill and faithfull Attention with the Blessing of Heaven, have saved my Life."

John didn't dwell on this life-threatening illness with Abigail or with any of the other friends to whom he described his symptoms. Probably he had contracted malaria, or perhaps typhus. Either is a candidate for the symptoms he described, as is the fetid climate that produced the circumstances for malaria to flourish. He did say that the administration of Peruvian bark—quinine— accounted for his recovery, that and the "Blessing of Heaven." But he worried "I shall not be able to re-establish my Health in this Country." At "half a hundred Years old," he worried that he "cannot expect to fare very well amidst such cold damps and putrid Steams as arise from the immense quantities of dead Water that surround it." In fact, John Adams would live to the age of ninety-six, his continuous grim prognostications to the contrary.

Abigail began to press more insistently for John to return. She described her "constant anxiety and solicitude for your Health," although he had written that he was gaining strength through exercise and good care. "I have been in daily expectation," Abigail wrote, "that Letters would arrive from you requesting leave to resign your employments: and return again to your Native Land." She continued that she was "sick, sick of a world in which selfishness predominates, sick of counsels unstable as the wind." She wished "most sincerely" to reunite with him in the "sequestered Life, the shades of Virmont."

JOHN WASN'T MOVED, BECAUSE BY THIS TIME SOME HEARTENING news had arrived from the military front. The British commander in the South, General Cornwallis, had surrendered his entire army of more than seven thousand soldiers to Generals Washington and Greene at Yorktown in southeastern Virginia. This victory represented a complete turn in American fortunes, which had not experienced a major success since Saratoga. A naval blockade by the French, who had lately arrived on the coast, in addition to the redeployment of much of the northern army to the South, completely surrounded the British force. General Cornwallis had no alternative. At last the Americans had a victory that changed the nature of the war. While John suspected that the British would continue to fight for some time, his situation in the Netherlands shifted in favor of the Americans. The Dutch, for this and other reasons, had become amenable to his approach. And, John suspected, the British would be forced to the peace table.

By spring, when Abigail urged John to come home, his world had turned around. "Your humble Servant has lately grown much into Fashion in this Country. Nobody scarcely of so much importance, as Mynheer Adams," he announced with unusual good cheer. "Every City, and Province rings with De Heer Adams." He expected at long last to be acknowledged by the government. He could not yet predict what England would do, but the political and diplomatic situation had shifted due to Yorktown, due to changes in the British ministry, and, no doubt, due to his efforts. And he promised her vaguely: "Oh When shall I see my dearest Friend.—All in good Time. My dear blue Hills, ye are the most sublime object in my Imagination." John was, in fact, euphoric: "At your reverend Foot, will I spend my old Age, if any, in a calm philosophical Retrospect upon the turbulent scaenes of Politicks and War. I shall recollect Amsterdam, Leyden and the Hague with more Emotion than Philadelphia or Paris."

He did not mention Vermont.

BY THE SPRING OF 1782, IT WAS CLEAR THAT JOHN'S EFFORTS IN the Netherlands had paid off abundantly. He reveled in his success. Under these conditions as well as the uncertainty about peace negotiations, he refused to commit to leaving Europe. He foresaw that his best times were ahead. "A Child was never more weary of a Whistle, than I am of Embassies," he wrote to Abigail. But he added: "The Embassy here however has done great Things. It has not merely tempted a natural Rival, and an imbittered, inveterate, hereditary Ennemy, to assist a little against G[reat] B[rittain] but it has torn from her Bosom, a constant faithfull Friend and Ally of an hundred Years duration."

John could not leave at the moment when his fortunes—and those of his country—had turned. At the same time, he was lonely and concerned about John Quincy, who by now had spent almost two years in Saint Petersburg. He wrote to his son, suggesting that the time had come for him to return to The Hague. "I want you with me. Mr. Thaxter will probably leave me soon, and I shall be alone. I want you to pursue your studies too at Leyden." He suggested that a boat would be the best conveyance, and that he should return as quickly as possible.

John's letter did not reach Saint Petersburg until late summer, by which time it was not prudent for John Quincy to come by boat. He would, however, in response to his father's summons, return as quickly as arrangements could be made. His remarkable trip began in October, when he set out on his voyage, which would take six months. After a treacherous journey to Stockholm, made so by the arrival of early snow and freezing temperatures, he remained in that city for six weeks. For another two weeks he was marooned in a small Swedish village. If, for John Quincy, the traveling was unpleasant—and this was a young man accustomed to difficult travel—it was also an opportunity to see more of the world. "Sweeden is the country in Europe which pleases me the most," he wrote to Abigail. "That is; of those I have seen. Because their manners resemble more those of my own County, than any I have seen." The people were friendly to strangers, he explained. His travels continued through Denmark and then several German states. At almost every point, bad weather prolonged his journey. Finally in late April he arrived at The Hague.

"My Son is with me in good health," John later reported to Abigail; adding with pleasure, "He is grown a Man in Understanding as well as Stature. "I shall take him with me to Paris, and Shall make much of his Company." At the same time, John informed Abigail that he could not yet determine his plans for return. "I hope Soon to be informed of the orders of Congress. If they accept my Resignation, I may come home in October. If not, I know not what will become of me."

ABIGAIL BEGAN TO NEGOTIATE WITH JOHN. HE HAD BEEN ABROAD for three years; she had performed her role, and his, as they had agreed, but they had been separated long enough, she opined. "I cannot say, but that I was disappointed when I found that your return to your native land was a still distant Idea." A different kind of worry disturbed her, she hinted in several different ways. Were his affections diminished? "I think your Situation cannot be so dissagreable as I feared it was," she wrote. She had kept her spirits alive by hoping, and now hope was no longer sufficient. She expressed her loneliness in the best way she knew, by borrowing from the religious language of her ancestors:

> Desire and Sorrow were denounced upon our Sex; as a punishment
> for the trangression of Eve. I have sometimes thought that we are
> formed to experience more exquisite Sensations than is the Lot of

your Sex. More tender and susceptible by Nature of those impression[s] which create happiness or misiry, we Suffer and enjoy in a higher degree.

Even more dejectedly, she continued: "I never wonderd at the philosopher who thanked the Gods that he was created a Man rather than a Woman." This was a low point for Abigail. Nor was she done with her portion of a dialogue that could not take place, because he would not respond to her anguish.

> Surely my dear Friend fleeting as time is I cannot reconcile myself to the Idea of living in this cruel State of Seperation for [4?] or even three years to come. Eight years have already past, since you could call yourself an Inhabitant of this State. I shall assume the Signature of Penelope, for my dear Ulysses has already been a wanderer from me near half the term of years that, that Hero was encountering Neptune, Calipso, the Circes and Syrens.

She shifted her metaphor from the religious forebears to the poet. She begged him to return in every medium she could summon.

> In the poetical Language of Penelope I shall address you

> Oh! Haste to me! A Little longer Stay
> Will ev'ry grace, each fancy'd charm decay
> Increasing cares, and times resistless rage
> Will waste my bloom, and wither it to age.

Then she shifted again to a different argument. "You will ask me I suppose what is become of my patriotick virtue? It is that which most ardently calls for your return." He could serve his nation at home, she argued. Her poignant letter continued for many paragraphs along that line. "Adieu my dear Friend," she concluded. "I cheer my Heart with the distant prospect. All that I can hope for at present, is to hear of your welfare which of all things lies nearest to the Heart of Your ever affectionate," and she signed herself "Portia."

John was not insensitive to her plight. "The Letter of the 10, I read over and over without End—and ardently long to be at the blue Hills, there to pass the Remainder of my feeble days," he wrote, but then continued to describe his return to health, his prospects at The Hague, and his changed mood. In fact, John was in good humor. He spent his days wining and dining as a courtier among "Princesses and Princes, Lords and Ladies of various Nations," now that his credentials as the American minister had been accepted. The Netherlands had recognized the independence of the United States and would now offer the assistance he had sought for his country for more than two years. John had gone from being a nuisance to becoming a celebrity. And he loved it.

"When shall I go home?" he asked. "If a Peace should be made, you would soon see me," he responded enigmatically. He would remain to see this process completed. John reveled in his success. He could not restrain himself from an overflow of self-congratulations. Of course, he knew that he was writing to his most devoted and loyal admirer, albeit one who had just written to him of her misery, but he could not withhold the pleasure he felt with his own circumstances. "You will see, the American Cause has had a signal Tryumph in this Country. If this had been the only Action of my Life, it would have been a Life well spent," he assured her.

Abigail was overcome with pride and pleasure when the news of John's triumphs reached her. Benjamin Waterhouse—the same Dr. Waterhouse who elected to remain aboard the *South Carolina* with Captain Gillon when Major Jackson abandoned that ship with Charles in La Coruña—had finally arrived home after more than a year of misadventures due to Gillon's ineptitude. He visited Abigail and extolled John's efforts. With this firsthand information— "the sweetest of all praise is that which is given to those we love best"—Abigail again launched into an argument for John's return. "But will you can you think of remaining abroad? Should a peace take place I could not forgive you half a years longer absence. O there are hours, days and weeks when I would not paint to you all my feelings—for I would not make you more unhappy."

Then, having said she wouldn't, she did.

> I would not wander from room to room without a Heart and Soul at Home or feel myself deserted, unprotected, unassisted, uncounseld.—I begin to think there is a moral evil in this Seperation, for when we pledged ourselves to each other did not the holy ceremony close with, "What God has joined Let no Man put asunder." Can it be a voluntary seperation? I feel that it is not.

Abigail by now introduced her heavy artillery. He was violating their marriage vows. This separation was evil. In reality, she had not for two years past been "unprotected, unassisted and uncounseld." Deserted, perhaps, but, if anything, she had functioned with extraordinary independence during John's absence. By casting herself as a helpless and needy woman, she appealed to his sense of responsibility to her and the family. Abigail was conducting her own hard-line diplomatic negotiation with John about the status of their marriage.

But even as she begged him to return, she began to reconsider that which had been so many times discounted by both of them—that it was her duty to travel to Europe to care for John. At the same time that she urged him to return, she sent out tentative hints to assess his reaction to the idea of her coming abroad. Following Benjamin Waterhouse's visit to her in the summer, she wrote to John that their common friend had suggested her going. "He wished me exceedingly to go to you. He was sure it was necessary to your happiness and he could see no prospect of a peace." She added: "Had my dear Friend been half as earnest . . . that I should go to him, he would have prevaild over my aversion to the Sea." Perhaps her ambivalence related to her daughter's situation.

Nabby, left behind while her two younger brothers accompanied their father, had longed to go with them. No doubt she wanted to join both brothers and their father on the second trip as well. Her disappointment at being rejected for the adventure of European travel on the basis of her sex rankled. "Our daughter thinks of nothing else but making a voyage to her pappa," Abigail informed John. In fact, by midsummer 1782, Nabby wrote to John for permission to travel to the Netherlands, a petition that Abigail reinforced. "What think you of your daughters comeing to keep House for you? She proposes it." John's note of rejection to his daughter was worded gently. He described the dangers and the discomfort of sea travel. Instead he sent her a present: a book.

WHEN JOHN DENIED ABIGAIL'S PLEA THAT HE RETURN IN THE early summer of 1782, because of peace negotiations, he described a process that was already under way. While King George remained adamant against declaring peace without military victory, Parliament reacted differently. The prime minister sent an envoy, Richard Oswald, to France to explore with Franklin the possibility of coming to an agreement. Encouraged by his conversation with Franklin, Oswald had returned to Paris in the summer of 1782 with a parliamentary mandate to negotiate the terms of peace. He began talks with Franklin and John Jay, another member of the American delegation, who had traveled to Paris from Spain.

Meanwhile, John Adams worked furiously to conclude his negotiations with Dutch bankers for their huge loan to America. Finally, in October, he packed his papers to head for Paris. Henry Laurens, freed from prison at the Tower of London on bail supplied by his friend Richard Oswald, would follow in November. Thomas Jefferson had begged off his presence on the committee because of commitments at home. Thus, the heavy work of the American delegation was conducted initially by John Jay and Benjamin Franklin but, by the late fall of 1782, included Adams and finally, in the last month, Henry Laurens. The groundwork of two years' hard negotiation by the American diplomats had at last paid off. The peace process took root.

*Benjamin West never completed his painting, sketched in 1783, of the signing of the
Treaty of Paris that ended the Revolutionary War, reportedly because the British envoy
refused to sit. Here are (left to right) John Jay, Adams, Franklin, Henry Laurens, and
William Temple Franklin, secretary to the delegation. Courtesy of the Henry Francis
DuPont Winterthur Museum.*

In contrast to his previous experiences in Paris, John was now recognized as
a triumphant diplomat because of his achievements in the Netherlands. His reception at the peace conference contrasted hugely with his previous treatment
in France. Vergennes was positively cordial, inviting Adams to dine and seating
him at a place of honor next to his wife, urging him to eat more and tempting
him with fine wines. He was at last "the famous Adams."

At first reluctant to call on Franklin, with whom his relations had become
decidedly frosty, John was prevailed upon by John Jay to visit "the old con-
jurer," as he called him. They, too, overcame the bad feelings of the past and
worked as colleagues once more at the business of crafting a peace that achieved
for America the best possible conditions. The elderly Franklin, no less sharp as
a diplomat for all the physical distress he now suffered, shifted his long-held
position of deference to France by placing French demands in the background
at these negotiations. The Americans worked together more effectively than

ever, resulting in a treaty that became as good (and better) than most had hoped for.

On November 30, 1782, the preliminary Treaty of Paris was signed, first by Richard Oswald, representing the king, and then by the delegates, "John Adams, B. Franklin, John Jay and Henry Laurens," in alphabetical order, for the United States of America. The treaty was a brief ten articles; the first stated that "His Britannic Majesty acknowledges these United States," followed by a list of thirteen states, "to be free sovereign and Independent States." The articles that followed fixed the boundaries on the north quite close to their present situation, on the west at the Mississippi (not the Appalachians, as was proposed during the negotiations), and at thirty-two degrees in the south, a major victory for a fledgling nation. The rights to fishing in the northeast were guaranteed, in a great feat of diplomatic success on John's part, as were reparations on both sides. Any lands taken after the signing would be returned. There were other issues, some of which would become problematic, but peace was achieved with each side mostly satisfied, marking this treaty as a major accomplishment.

To celebrate their signing, Adams reported in his diary, "We all went out to Passy to dine with Dr. Franklin." He added, "Thus far has proceeded this great Affair. The Unravelling of the Plott, has been to me, the most affecting and astonishing Part of the whole Piece." When he used the word *affecting*, he meant "emotional." After eight years of war, its conclusion appeared to have happened miraculously fast, but it was years in the making. The definitive Treaty of Paris was signed the following September after the governments of both nations gave final approval to its contents. The celebrations in America began as soon as news of the preliminary treaty was received. John Adams comfortably remained in Paris. The city where he had suffered his great humiliation now became the center of his great triumph.

IN BOSTON, ABIGAIL ATTENDED A CHURCH SERVICE WHERE THE treaty was commemorated. The Reverend Mr. Clark delivered a sermon that summarized the events of the Revolution. "How did my heart dilate with pleasure when as each event was particularized," Abigail reported to John,

> I could trace my Friend as a Principal in them; could say, it was he, who was one of the first in joinning the Band of Patriots; who formed our first National Counsel. It was he; who tho happy in his domestick attachments; left his wife, his Children; then but Infants; even surrounded with the Horrours of war; terified and distresst,

the Week after the memorable 17th. of April, Left them, to the protection of that providence which has never forsaken them.

She continued, taking pride in their participation. "These are not the mere eu-
logiums of conjugal affection; but certain facts, and solid truths. My anxieties,
my distresses, at every period; bear witness to them."

Meanwhile, she had resumed negotiations with John about his homecoming. Now that the peace was concluded, a new matter had revived their debate.
Congress would appoint a minister to Great Britain, a diplomat to represent
American interests in the former mother country. John Adams was the likely
candidate. Still, many issues claimed attention in Congress, such as disband-
ing the armies and compensating the soldiers, so John waited. He consulted
with the American diplomats Laurens, Jay, and Franklin in a continuous
round of social events. "Went to Versailles to pay my respects to the King and
Royal family," he noted on the first of the new year. Many issues remained to
be resolved among the parties to the treaties, so John was not bored. He was,
rather, enjoying himself. He then began a campaign to urge Abigail to come to
Paris.

Abigail, on the other hand, saw the future differently. "If my dear friend you
will promise to come home, take the farm into your own hands and improve it,
let me turn dairy woman in getting our living this way." She no longer mentioned her Vermont retreat, but her romantic vision instead included herself as
a dairymaid. Their imaginations were taking them in different directions. She
envisioned a simple agrarian life; he fancied the high life of Paris. "If it were
only an Affair of myself and my Family," he wrote, "I would not accept a Commission if sent. But I consider it a public Point of Honour."

She wrote more forcefully. "Permit me, my Dearest friend to renew that
Companionship—my heart sighs for it—I cannot O! I cannot be reconcild to
living as I have done for 8 years past." And more strongly still: "Who is there
left that will sacrifice as others have done? Portia I think stands alone, alone
alass! in more senses than one." The note of sarcasm is clear.

But to no avail. The negotiations between the Adamses over the status of
their marriage continued. John awaited his appointment from a beleaguered
Congress, while Abigail languished in Braintree. She continued her occupations, receiving goods sent to her from Europe and selling them for profit at
home; speculating in currency whenever possible, socializing in her little community. "I cannot bear to go into publick assemblies," she wrote, referring to
the great receptions and balls that once more took place in Boston. "If I cannot

go by your side, and be introduced as your companion, I will not go at all," she continued her argument to persuade him to return.

John persisted, at first providing a rich inducement: "Come to me with your daughter," he wrote, hoping to tempt her by including Nabby. More weeks passed, and he wavered: "I am determined not to wait," he declared, "but to come home," adding a safe condition, "provided it does not arrive in a reasonable Time." Months passed: "Here I am, out of all Patience," he wrote. "Not a Word from America. . . . The total Idleness, the perpetual Uncertainty . . . is the most insipid and at the Same Time disgusting and provoking Situation imaginable."

Still he remained in Europe, becoming bored and then angry, lashing out at the world that wouldn't behave by his rules: "You know your Man. He will never be a Slave. He will never cringe. He will never accommodate his Principles, Sentiments to keep a Place, or to get a Place, no nor to please his Daughter, or his wife." Then, repentant after his tirade, he followed with reassurance : "I wonder if any body but you would believe me Sincere if I were to Say how much I love you, and wish to be with you never to be Seperated more?"

By the fall of 1783, their positions could not have been farther apart. "If Congress should think proper to make you an other appointment, beg you not to accept it," she pleaded. Almost simultaneously John wrote: "My life is Sweetened with the Hope of embracing you in Europe. Pray embark as soon as prudent." It was her turn to lash out at John: "I know not whether I shall believe myself how well you Love me, unless I can prevail upon you to return in the Spring," she wrote, out of tolerance with his ambivalence.

For as much as she protested, her last efforts to persuade John predicted her capitulation. Having played her strongest cards, Abigail weakened and confessed a different reason for her reluctance to travel. The fears she expressed were no longer of of seas and storms but rather about the status she would occupy. Abigail felt timid about going abroad in a public position.

> I think if you were abroad in a private Character . . . I should not hesitate so much at comeing to you. But a mere American as I am, unacquainted with the Etiquette of courts, taught to say the thing I mean, and to wear my Heart in my countantance, I am sure I should make an awkward figure. And then it would mortify my pride if I should be thought to disgrace you.

By coming to grips with her apprehensions, she admitted to herself as well as John the underlying issue that prevented her from making the European

*Abigail Adams Smith, called Nabby, the
only daughter of Abigail and John Adams,
was married to William Stephens Smith in
London after a fairytale romance. Painted
sometime during the 1790s. Courtesy of the
Massachusetts Historical Society.*

journey. She didn't know how to behave in the social circles where John
now traveled. She didn't want to embarrass him.

BUT ANOTHER FACTOR HAD
preoccupied her for the past two years
that together with the conflict over
John's return prompted her to travel
to Europe with her daughter. Nabby
had a suitor. Abigail had first introduced the topic to John soon after the
preliminary peace treaty was signed
in Paris. "We have in the little circle
an other gentleman who has opend an
office in Town, for about nine months
past, and boarded in our Cranch
family," she wrote. "His Father you
knew—His Name is Tyler, he studied
law upon his comeing out of colledge
with Mr Dana." Abigail continued to
describe background and character—
not just to relate idle information to her absent husband but to advance a delicate agenda. "I am not acquainted with any young gentleman whose attainments
in literature are equal to his," she persisted, "who judges with greater accuracy
or discovers a more Delicate and refined taste." She moved from fact to analysis, and now to judgment: "I have frequently looked upon him with the Idea
that you would have taken much pleasure in such a pupil." Finally, Abigail rose
to her purpose: "I wish I was as well assured that you would be equally pleased
with him in an other character, for such I apprehend are his distant hopes."
Royall Tyler was courting Nabby Adams.

Abigail's concerns were not unfounded, for she knew her husband well. Neither had she underestimated the reverberations from Paris. "I dont like the
Subject at all. My Child is too young for such Thoughts. . . . I Should have
thought you had seen enough to be more upon your Guard." John continued
his salvo for five paragraphs before concluding: "This is too Serious a Subject,
to equivocate about. I don't like this method of Courting Mothers. There is
something too fantastical and affected in all this Business for me." Having finished with Abigail, he added, "This is all between you and me."

What inspired this outburst was not just John's shock at discovering that his only daughter had a suitor. Royall Tyler's reputation was suspect, and Abigail's letter had reported, in the most diplomatic of terms, the stories that she had heard. It was rumored that Tyler had led a dissolute life while an undergraduate at Harvard. Having inherited a "pretty patrimony," he had "dissipated two or 3 years of his Life and too much of his fortune," owing, Abigail generously allowed, to his "possessing a sprightly fancy, a warm imagination and an agreeable person." This exchange between Abigail and John provides the opening chapter to the tale that complicated their dialogue for the two years before Abigail decided to travel to Europe.

Royall Tyler, as Abigail wrote to John, had arrived in Braintree early in 1782 and opened a law practice. He boarded with Mary and Richard Cranch, sister and brother-in-law of Abigail and parents of two teenage daughters, Lucy and Betsy. Tyler, rather than pursuing a Cranch daughter, turned his attentions to their sixteen-year-old cousin, Nabby Adams. If his visits to the Adams home were initiated with intent to borrow books from John's library, they were continued because Abigail, the mother, and young Abigail together found his company delightful. He was literate and literary, a well-born lawyer with charm and good looks. Further, he seemed smitten with young Abigail, who by all reports was a quiet, reserved, serious, and cerebral young woman.

Abigail described their daughter to John, reporting, "Indeed my dear sir you would be proud of her," and continued:

> She has a Statliness in her manners which some misconstrue into pride and haughtyness—but which rather results from a too great reserve; she wants more affability, but she has prudence & Discretion beyond her years. She is in her person tall large and Majestick, mammas partiality allows her to be a good figure—her sensibility is not yet sufficiently a wakend to give her Manners that pleasing softness which attracts whilst it is attracted. Her Manners rather forbid all kinds of Intimacy; and awe whilst they command.

She concluded: "Indeed she is not like her Mamma. Had not her Mamma at her age too much sensibility to be *very prudent*." She meant, of course, that at sixteen, Nabby's age, Abigail had met John Adams. Still, her (perhaps) too accurate description of her daughter, both seen from the viewpoint of other people and mitigated by a mother's bias, was intended to explain the young woman to a father who had been absent while his child matured.

Nor is it clear what precise rumors were circulated or how much Abigail knew about Tyler's past. His allies suggest that he was mischievous; more seriously, it is reported that he fathered a child by a housemaid at Harvard. He was rusticated (exiled) for a prank that inadvertently offended a professor. By his own admission, he recklessly spent much of his inheritance; by Abigail's admission, he neglected his studies. Nor was he, it seems, repentant. Tyler was an incorrigible iconoclast, a character of man—his values aside— that appealed to Abigail Adams.

Both young Abigail and Abigail the mother were chastened by John's response, which continued in a barrage of letters from France. With time, as is the case with time, John became calmer, more rational, and eventually even resigned to the inevitability of romance. Yet the slow course of his letters across the Atlantic could not keep pace with events at home. While John conceded to the situation, his daughter took his admonitions seriously and broke off her relationship with Tyler. Abigail reported to her husband that Nabby, responding to his disapproval, had gone to stay in Boston for the winter of 1783. Tyler, who remained in Braintree, kept his nose to the grindstone, built his law practice, and generated no unseemly talk. When young Abigail returned from Boston in the spring, however, the romance resumed. Tyler, meanwhile, had excited rumors by purchasing and beginning to renovate the Borland property, a grand albeit neglected homestead in Braintree.

Abigail the mother had become doubly conflicted. She liked Tyler very much for all the qualities that she had described to John, but she feared the reality of the rumors. Further, while she was struggling with her own future, she did not trust her judgment well enough to encourage the romance. She even began to use the issue of her daughter's courtship to leverage her position with John. "I wish most sincerely wish you was at Home to judge for yourself. I shall never feel safe or happy untill you are."

In the end, John triumphed. By the winter of 1783–84, Abigail decided that the two problems—her separation from John and her daughter's romance— could best be resolved by taking Nabby with her to Europe. "In consequence of your last letters," she wrote, responding to his request that she come as soon as possible, "I shall immediately set about putting all our affairs in such a train as that I may be able to leave them in the spring." Once she made this decision, events moved quickly. She needed to put their family accounts in order. She wanted to bid on a farm that John liked, because it appeared that wealthy foreigners were buying up property, driving up prices. Further, she wrote that she intended to make another investment in state notes. Her financial advisor, her uncle Dr. Tufts, proposed to do the same.

As she prepared to leave for Europe, she monitored her investments, though she carefully explained to John the details of how she would accomplish the complicated transaction. But it was her own good eye for investments that fundamentally had maintained the family without debt so far, and she did not intend to miss an opportunity for a profit even as she prepared to leave home. "Forgive me if I sometimes use the singular instead of the plural," she wrote, conscious as she referred to *their* financial dealings as *hers*. "Alass, I have been too much necessitated to it," she continued, getting in one last reproach.

She asked Uncle Isaac Smith to find her a "suitable vessel" for travel. The important issue of her youngest sons' education was resolved by sending them to board with her sister Elizabeth Shaw, whose husband ran an academy for boys. Her house, she put into the care of Phoebe, "to whom my Father gave freedom, by his Will, and the income of a hundred a year during her Life." Phoebe, her parents' slave, had been Abigail's childhood nurse. "A fortnight ago," Abigail wrote, "she took unto her self a Husband in the person of Mr. Abdee whom you know." Their marriage had been celebrated in Abigail's home. Phoebe was pleased with the trust of staying in the Adams house, and "I have no doubt of their care and faithfullness, and prefer them to any other family." Having discharged as many responsibilities as she could, Abigail was prepared to leave Braintree.

Meanwhile, John, sensitive to his daughter's conflict between her suitor and her family, wrote to Abigail that she might marry her daughter and leave the couple behind, if they chose. The young couple, probably reflecting the decision of a dutiful daughter, agreed to part, though they pledged faith to each other. Tyler, meanwhile, possibly to console himself for the separation, wrote to John for permission to marry his daughter.

The last letter that Abigail wrote to John in April, to apprise him of her departure on the *Active,* spoke of her sorrow at leaving friends: "I derive a pleasure from the regret of others," she wrote, "a pleasure which perhaps I might never have experienced if I had not been called to quit my Country." She meant that people tend only to express affection when a person is departing. She mentioned "the blessing and regret of the poor and the needy, who bewail my going away," people whom she had cared for over the years who didn't know that they would ever see her again. And she continued to describe apprehensions that she gendered feminine.

"I am embarking on Board a vessel without any Male Friend . . . a stranger to the capt. and every person on Board, a situation which I once thought nothing would tempt me to undertake." Suppressing her personal reservations, she had once more surrendered to John's ambitions. By joining him in Europe, she would again liberate him to pursue politics in the international sphere, rather than retiring to private practice and domestic life. Her capitulation was posited on her determination to live within her understanding of their marriage contract. "And now I have adjusted all my affairs and determined upon comeing out," she wrote to tell John that she was prepared to travel. "I summon all my resolution that I may behave with fortitude upon the occasion. . . . My thoughts are fixed, my latest wish depend On thee Guide, Guardian, Husband, Lover, Friend."

In June 1784, mother and daughter departed for the long journey to Europe, leaving behind a bereft suitor. More sadly for Royall Tyler, John Adams's letter of assent to the marriage arrived after the sailing.

In the Midst of the World in Solitude

PRIOR TO BOARDING THE SHIP THAT WOULD TRANSPORT THEM to Europe, Abigail and her daughter stayed one night in Boston. That evening she received a surprise visitor. Thomas Jefferson appeared. Recently appointed to the joint mission to negotiate commercial treaties with Adams and Franklin, he had attempted to reach Boston "in hopes of having the pleasure of attending Mrs. Adams to Paris and lessoning some of the difficulties to which she may be exposed," he informed John. But he had been delayed by meetings in Philadelphia and New York and arrived in Boston "to find her engaged for her passage and to sail tomorrow." As the ship was fully booked, Jefferson remained behind, but he wrote to reassure John that she goes "in a good ship, well accommodated as merchant ships generally are."

Without Thomas Jefferson, Abigail and her daughter, accompanied by two servants, Esther Field and John Briesler, sailed from Boston on June 20, 1784, on the merchant ship *Active*. Immediately upon departure, she recorded, "the Capt. sent word to all the Ladies to put on their Sea clothes and prepare for sickness. We had only time to follow his directions before we found ourselves all sick."

For the next ten days Abigail was miserable, and since both of her servants were as sick as herself, the person to whom she could turn for assistance was Job Field, a seaman whom she had known as a Braintree neighbor. Job sat near her, ministering as best he could, even taking off her shoes. Her typical modesty had disappeared: "The decency and decorum of the most delicate female must in some measure yield to the necessities of nature," she later wrote to her sister Mary, "and if you have no female capable of rendering you the least assistance, you will feel grateful to any one who will feel for you, and relieve or compassionate your sufferings." She also admitted that she could not "conceive any inducement sufficient to carry a Lady upon the ocean, but that of going to a Good Husband."

The *Active* was well outfitted for a merchant ship, but it was certainly not commodious; sea travel in the late eighteenth century had not changed greatly from the time the Adams forebears had traveled to Massachusetts Bay in the early seventeenth century. Commanded by Captain Lyde, who later became a family friend, the ship was a mere 125 feet in length. A conventional ship with three masts and three decks, it carried a cargo of oil and potash that gave off a repulsive odor, which contributed to discomfort along with the rough waters.

Abigail, her daughter, and Esther occupied a compartment that was eight feet square, and had three bunks and a small iron-grated window, which provided no fresh air. The only breeze came from leaving open the door to the larger compartment where the men passengers slept. This area also served as the living space for passengers, where they ate, read, wrote, played games, and talked—when they felt well enough to leave their bunks. The voyage would take precisely thirty days before reaching the English shore, thirty days that marked not only time and distance, but the beginnings of a transforming experience.

When Abigail had recovered sufficiently, she went up on the deck to enjoy the breeze. "A fine wind and a pleasant day," she recorded with relief. "Our sea sickness has left us in a great measure." She hemmed a handkerchief. Feeling like herself again, she became aware of the squalid conditions on the ship. "Very little attention is paid on Board this ship to that first of virtues Cleanliness." Since the ship's crew ignored the unsavory conditions, she recruited her servants and several hands to clean her "abode" with "scrapers, mops, brushes, infusions of vinegar, etc." Further, she boasted, "Once I found I might reign mistress on board without any offence, I soon exerted my authority." Abigail took command of the galley, where conditions appalled her: "If our cook was but tolerable clean I could relish my food," she wrote. But meals came in "higgledy-piggledy, with a leg of pork all bristly; a quarter of an hour later a pudding . . . and when dinner is nearly completed a plate of potatoes." She cleaned the milk pail and made puddings. "I think the price we paid entitled us to better accommodations," she complained.

As the hours at sea passed, Abigail's mood improved. The ship sailed at seven knots per hour, approximately one hundred miles each day. There were times when Abigail observed the tranquility of the ocean. "I went last evening upon deck," she wrote, "to view that phenomenon of Nature, a blazing ocean . . . resembling our fire-flies in a dark night." She added, "I never view the ocean without being filled with ideas of the sublime."

Land was sighted on July 18. The view was exhilarating. "You will hardly wonder . . . at the joy we felt this day in seeing the cliffs of Dover, Dover castle and town." To reach land, however, represented a wholly different story. A pilot came on board near Dover, and the captain decided that the passengers should embark for the shore aboard his little boat. The pilots did not disclose that the surf ran as high as six feet, that the little boat "about as large as a Charlestown ferry-boat" would battle waves for a distance "about twice as far as from Boston to Charlestown."

The passengers were lowered into the listing boat. So stormy was the sea that the women, wrapped up in oil coats, were each held fast by a man who braced himself against the side of the boat. "We set off from the vessel, now mounting upon the top of a wave high as a steeple, and then so low that the boat was not to be seen." When they reached shore, so great was their anxiety that rather than wait for the waves to carry them farther up onto the land, the passengers scrambled out of the boat "as fast as possible, sinking every step into the land, and looking like a parcel of Naiads, just rising from the sea."

Abigail had landed in England. Fortunately an inn was located nearby, where the travelers engaged rooms and changed to dry clothing. In the four days from the time land was first sighted to the time she landed at Deal, Abigail had slept but four hours and was suffering from a "violent sick headache." Despite the ordeal and her fatigue, she again passed a sleepless night at the inn.

The next morning at five o'clock, the passengers from the *Active* set off by post chaise on the first leg of the journey to London. Abigail began to register the novelty of her experiences by comparing them with what she knew from home. She was fascinated by inns and their dining rooms; she had never stayed at an inn before, nor had she dined at a public house or restaurant, for in New England she always stayed with family or friends. She was struck by the whole process of service.

> A well dressed hostess steps forward, making a lady-like appearance, and wishes your commands; if you desire a chamber, the chambermaid attends; you request dinner, say in half an hour; the bill of fare is directly brought; you mark what you wish to have, and suppose it is to be a variety of fish, fowl, and meat, all of which we had, up to eight different dishes besides vegetables.

Ordinary experiences appeared unusual in a foreign land.

The feast completed, the party proceeded toward London, where a different adventure lay in store. The notorious Blackheath, the forest respite of robbers and brigands, had to be negotiated before dark. As Abigail's coach entered the forest, it was stopped and the Americans were warned, "A robbery, a robbery!" even then by daylight. "We were not a little alarmed," Abigail recorded, "and everyone was concealing his money." She observed the whole incident: "The robber was pursued and taken in about two miles and we saw the poor wretch, ghostly and horrible, brought along on foot." She sympathized, "He looked like a youth of twenty only, attempted to lift his hat, and looked despair. You can form some idea of my feelings when they told him: Ay, you have but a short time; the assize sets next month; and then my lad, you swing." Theft in England was still punishable by death. "Though every robber may deserve death," Abigail wrote, "yet to exult over the wretched is what our country is not accustomed to. Long may it be free from such villanies, and long may it preserve a commiseration for the wretched." The process of comparison that became a regular theme in Abigail's reports of her foreign travels had begun. It was her way of registering difference.

At eight o'clock that evening the travelers arrived in London and "set down at Low's Hotel in Covent Garden, the court side of town." Neither John nor John Quincy was present to greet Abigail. Communications between them had so greatly lagged that they were unclear about her plans. John had earlier dispatched his son to London, but after waiting more than a month, John Quincy became puzzled when a ship arrived from Boston without his mother and sister. By mid-June he wrote his father in The Hague that he still did not know if "the ladies have decided to come over this season or not." John had advised his son "not to wait any longer in London for the Ladies," so John Quincy had returned to The Hague, where he served as his father's secretary.

For ten days Abigail visited and was entertained, toured the sights of London, shopped, dined, and waited. During those ten days, John Quincy hastened from The Hague to London. Abigail, meanwhile, did not know whether John might come as well. Despite the excitement of being a tourist, seeing her family ranked uppermost in her thoughts. On July 30, perhaps having calculated the travel time from the continent, she "determined on tarrying at home, in hopes of seeing my son or his pappa." She was writing a letter to her sister when a servant "runs puffing in to announce, 'Young Mr. Adams is come.' 'Where is he?' 'we all cry out. 'In the other house, madam; he stopped to get his hair dressed.'"

Abigail reported the excitement of the moment. "Impatient enough I was; yet, when he entered . . . I drew back, not really believing my eyes, till he cried out, 'O momma and my dear sister!'" Abigail registered the shock of seeing a grown son in place of the boy who had left home nearly six years ago. "Nothing but the eyes at first sight appeared what he once was."

Abigail had last seen John Quincy when he was twelve years old. "I think you do not approve the word 'feeling,'" she wrote Mary Cranch, "but I know not what to substitute in lieu, or even to describe mine." Abigail was groping for the language to express her emotions in an age that lacked an adequate vocabulary. John Quincy was equally stirred and wrote to his father, "I will not attempt to describe my feelings at meetings two persons so dear to me after so long an absence. I will only say it was completely happy."

Meanwhile, Thomas Jefferson had arrived in Paris, so John, who had maintained the American diplomatic presence in France, decided to meet his family in London. He wrote urgently to Abigail on August 1, "My dearest Friend . . . I have changed my plan . . . stay where you are, and amuse yourself, by Seeing what you can, untill you See me. I will be with you in Eight Days at farthest, and sooner, if possible." To John Quincy he sent instructions to prepare for the journey; he must purchase a coach and hire drivers, and not overlooking the details, he added, "Purchase Johnsons Lives of the Poets which will amuse us on the road." John considered crossing the channel by balloon, just then becoming popular, but instead he made the conventional journey by coach.

John arrived in London on August 7, 1784. Returning to her hotel from an excursion at noon that day, Nabby noticed a hat on the table with two books in it. "Everything around appeared altered, without my knowing in what particular." She sensed a change. Learning that her father had indeed arrived, Nabby moved quickly. "Up I flew, and to his chamber, where he was lying down, he raised himself upon my knocking softly at the door, and received me with all the tenderness of an affectionate parent after so long an absence." Nabby, too, was at a loss for words to express her emotions. "Sure I am I never felt more agitation of spirit in my life; it will not due to describe."

Neither Abigail nor John recorded their reunion, drawing a curtain over this one moving event of their lives. John, who was assiduous in maintaining his diary, merely wrote on August 7, "Arrived at the Adelphi Buildings and met my wife and Daughter after a separation of four years and an half. Indeed after a separation of ten years excepting a few visits." He soon wrote to his uncle, "I think myself one of the happiest men in the World."

The next day, August 8, the reunited members of the Adams family embarked on the journey to Paris.

"YOU INQUIRE OF ME HOW DO I LIKE PARIS?" ABIGAIL RESPONDED to her niece soon after her arrival. "I am no judge for I have not seen it yet. One

The Adamses' Paris home was located in Auteuil, on the outskirts of the city near the Bois de Boulogne, in part so that John could enjoy daily walks in the country. Courtesy of the Massachusetts Historical Society.

thing I know is that I have smelt it." While she intended her sarcasm to be taken literally, reflecting the reality of conditions in late-eighteenth-century Paris, she also expressed antipathy to a scene that she could not understand or yet appreciate. Proud, prim, and provincial, Abigail confronted a culture that violated her values of industry, frugality, and sobriety. She passed judgment on Paris with her still-fresh New England opinions. Almost everything she saw bore witness to a hedonistic life that merited her disapproval. She was a spectator in France and never a Francophile. To her friend Mercy Otis Warren at home in Plymouth, she described herself as "in the midst of the world in solitude."

John had already rented their house at Auteuil, which in 1785 was a small village about four miles southwest of Paris. John had chosen this suburban residence for several reasons. Always conscious of his health, he could exercise daily in the nearby Bois de Boulogne. It would be convenient as well to Benjamin Franklin, the least mobile of the American ministers, who lived in neighboring Passy, where much of the Americans' business was conducted. Primarily the choice of the Auteuil house was dictated by economy; Paris was expensive and American ministers' salaries were meager. At times John had negotiated loans from bankers in the Netherlands merely to sustain Franklin and himself. A theme in Abigail's lament for the years to come, the restrictive penury in which she conducted her household, contributed mightily to her discomfort in France. She had always lived modestly and frugally and was shocked at the elevation in the standard of living required of her as a minister's wife.

For one thing, compared with her cottage at Braintree, the Hôtel de Rouault, as their rented home was called, after the name of its owner, was colossal. "Upon occasion, forty beds may be made in it," she wrote her sister Mary. The first floor contained the public rooms, "the saloon, as it is called, the apartment where we receive company. This room is very elegant, and about a third larger than General Warren's hall," comparing it with Massachusetts's finest. The family chambers on the second floor were tastefully furnished and so pleased her that she described them meticulously in her letters. "The windows of all the apartments in the house, or rather glass doors, reach from top to the bottom . . . and give one a full extensive view of the gardens." Her sewing room was "about ten or twelve feet large . . . and panelled with looking glasses; a red and white India patch, with pretty boarders encompasses it; low backed stuffed chairs with garlands of flowers; a beautiful sofa is placed in a kind of alcove." Abigail wrote on, describing room after room. So large, in fact, was the house that she claimed never to have entered some of its chambers. The spaciousness and the grandeur astonished her.

However, the house and its five acres of garden had been neglected for years. She wrote to her niece "with twenty thousand livres of expense in repairs and furniture, the house would be elegant." She lamented that "the stairs which you commonly have to ascend to get into the family apartments are so dirty that I have been obliged to hold up my clothes, as though I was passing through a cow yard." In addition, she correctly anticipated that the house would be "exceedingly cold in winter." John had rented this poorly maintained establishment prior to the family's arrival, and it would be the family seat until Congress acted on his appointment to Great Britain.

Further, she coped with rules of domestic service that required enormous accommodation on her part. She could not define the performance of their duties, so that no one of her eight "specialists" would "lift a finger to perform the work of another." She was frustrated and concluded they were all a "pack of lazy wretches." The sole feature of the Auteuil establishment that rated her uncritical approval was its garden, and the only servant she indulged was her gardener. The house was a curiosity and a burden, but the garden provided pleasure.

But none of these problems could account for Abigail's discomfort with French culture. The real issue was that the prospect of speaking intimidated her. "I have been but little abroad," she early confessed to her sister. "As I cannot speak the language, I think I should make an awkward figure." To Mercy she wrote: "It is customary in this country for strangers to make the first visit [but] Not speaking the language lays one under embarrassment for to visit a Lady merely to bow to her is painful."

Because of her self-consciousness, Abigail at first limited her visits to English-speaking acquaintances; but she also studied French. Under the tutelage of her husband and son, both of whom were fluent speakers, she undertook a rigorous regime of study. John recommended to her, as he had previously to his sons, reading the classics of French literature and attending the theater. Abigail began by reading Racine, Voltaire, Corneille, and Crébillon. "I took my dictionary and applied myself to reading a play a day," she wrote her niece. In time she reported to Royall Tyler that she understood French much better than she could speak it.

To her relief, she was not required to attend court functions, since John's rank as minister did not carry that privilege for his wife. Only wives of ambassadors were invited into the highest orders of French society. Her attendance at diplomatic affairs, however, was required, and she began to learn the protocols. "Conversation is never general, as with us, [and] when company quit the table they fall into tete-a-tete or two and two when the conversation is in low voice, and a stranger, unacquainted with the customs of the country would think that everybody had private business to transact."

Puzzled by strange customs, Abigail reacted defensively. John, after his many years in Europe, had become a fixture in diplomatic circles, where he now participated with fluency and ease. If at first he, too, had been stiff and uncomfortable, he had learned the etiquette of social life and adjusted both as a guest and a host. Now it was Abigail's turn. Social life in Paris gave her a picture of the roles she would occupy in years to come. But Paris provided a hard initiation because of her awkwardness with the language.

In time, Abigail's judgments softened, and she admitted that she no longer looked "with so much amazement when I see a Lady rapturously put her arms around a gentleman and salute him first upon one cheek and then upon the other. I consider it a thing of mere course."

Despite her best effort to be open-minded, Abigail gossiped breathlessly about Madame Helvétius, whom she met at the Passy residence of Benjamin Franklin. Madame "entered the room with a careless, Jaunty air; upon seeing ladies who were strangers to her, she bawled out 'Ah! mon Dieu, where is

Franklin? Why did you not tell me there were ladies here? How I look!'" Abigail recounted this to her sister, continuing, "Her hair was frizzled; over it she had a small straw hat with a dirty gauze half-handkerchief round it, and a bit of dirtier gauze, than ever my maids wore was bowed behind."

Fascinated but disapproving, Abigail related that when Franklin entered, "she ran forward to him, caught him by the hand . . . then gave him a double kiss, one upon each cheek and another upon his forehead." Furthermore, at dinner, Madame Helvétius, placed between Franklin and Adams, "carried on the chief of the conversation"—shocking to Abigail—"frequently locking her hand into the doctors and sometimes spreading her arms upon the backs of both gentlemen's chairs"—even more shocking to a polite New England matron. Shy and excluded from much of the French conversation, Abigail confessed she was "highly disgusted and never wisht for an acquaintance with any ladies of this cast."

Eccentric even by French standards, Madame Helvétius was the sixty-year-old widow of the French philosopher. She was highly educated, cosmopolitan, and disregarded appearances. "After dinner," Abigail continued, "she threw herself upon a settee where she showed more than her feet." Nor did Abigail's indignation diminish when "her little dog wet the floor and she wiped it up with her chemise."

Of the people she met, one man became her special friend. She described Thomas Jefferson to her sister as "one of the choice ones of the earth." After her family, Jefferson was the one person with whom she felt most comfortable. He had arrived just prior to Abigail and had taken a house on the Cul de sac Taitbout, near the opera house, a convenient and choice location in Paris. He enrolled his young daughter Patsy, who had accompanied him, in a convent school where several other Protestant girls were educated. Alone in Paris except for his servant James Hemings, and his secretary, David Humphreys, Jefferson happily adopted the Adamses as his family-away-from home. Equally happy with Jefferson, all of the Adamses adopted him.

John had known Jefferson since the two men had insured that America declared its independence, Jefferson by writing the document, Adams by arguing its passage through Congress. Now, nearly a decade later, they were reunited on the commission to negotiate commercial treaties with European nations. The two worked diligently together, meeting often at Franklin's residence in Passy. Their effort proved ineffective in the long run, but it strengthened their friendship.

The Adamses—all of them—loved Jefferson. He frequently rode out from Paris for dinner or for an afternoon of amiable conversation. On occasion

Abigail, her daughter, or John Quincy accompanied Jefferson to concerts or the theater or to visit the attractions of Paris. Relations between the Adamses and Benjamin Franklin, on the other hand, remained polite and restrained. Abigail wrote respectfully of him, but not with fondness. "I dined with the Dr. on Monday," she wrote John Thaxter, adding that Franklin has "always been very gracious and sociable with me."

Nabby, who accompanied her mother to social events, reacted more generously. Certainly she felt less on trial when she went into company. Her youth was an advantage; there were fewer expectations of her. Further, she received compliments on her beauty and manners from John Quincy's friends, who clearly must have been disappointed to learn that she was pledged to a man at home in Boston.

When she was comfortable, Abigail, the mother, enjoyed society. Among her French acquaintances, she especially liked the Marquise de Lafayette. Dutifully calling upon the wife of the Revolutionary War hero, she was pleasantly surprised. "She is a very agreeable lady," wrote Abigail to Mary.

> [She] met me at the door, and with the freedom of an old acquaintance, and the rapture peculiar to the ladies of this nation caught me by the hand and gave me a salute upon each cheek, most heartily rejoiced to see me. You would have supposed I had been some long absent friend whom she dearly loved.

Madame Lafayette's graciousness alone set Abigail at ease, but more important, Abigail reported, she spoke English "tolerably" well. Therefore, when an American lady observed to Abigail of the marquise, "Good heaven! how awfully she is dressed," Abigail retorted that "the Lady's rank sets her above the formalities of dress."

Madame Lafayette invited the Adamses and Thomas Jefferson to join her party at Notre Dame to celebrate the birth of the dauphin. On that occasion the streets were so congested with traffic that the police had to guide their carriage through the crowds. Jefferson suggested that more people were in the streets of Paris that day than populated the state of Massachusetts. The ceremony was extravagant, and the dress elaborate. The Abigails were impressed. Madame Lafayette, however, commented that for a religious event it was too noisy, bustling, and ostentatious. But young Abigail astutely explained the importance of the ceremony: "If the man who has the whole kingdom at his disposal is not respected, and thought of as next to their god, he will not sustain his power."

Another favorite of Abigail's was the Swedish ambassador Baron de Staël. "He lives in a grand hotel, and his suite of apartments, his furniture and his table are the most elegant of any thing I have seen." For the first time, Abigail dined upon gold plate at a table so burnished that it "shown with regal splendor." The opulence reinforced Abigail's resentment of Congress. John's income could not match their expenses. "I have become steward and book-keeper, determined to know with accuracy what our expenses are," Abigail wrote. The results so distressed her that she considered leaving Europe. She noted that John Jay had returned home "because he could not support his family here with the whole salary." John, however, was determined to stay. Typically, Abigail worried about the practical matters of sustaining family life, while John focused on public service.

Rather than blame John for his determination to remain abroad, Abigail directed her resentment at Congress, which had again voted to reduce ministerial salaries. Of this "penny wise and pound foolish" policy she wrote, "For that nation which degrades their own ministers by obliging them to live in narrow circumstances, cannot be expected to be held in high estimation themselves." She also denounced Congress for not sufficiently appreciating John:

> Yet I cannot but think it hard that a gentleman who has devoted so great a part of his life to the service of the public, who has been the means in great measure of procuring such extensive territories to his country, who saved their fisheries and who is still laboring to procure them further advantages should find it necessary so cautiously to calculate his pence, to fear overrunning them.

The theme of identifying John with America's success had sustained her through many years of hardship during the war. Once again it served her well. She did not blame John for choosing this destiny for her family. Rather, she joined forces with him as his advocate. Familiar and consistent also was John's high-minded concentration upon the public good and his dependence upon Abigail to make ends meet. This she did effectively though begrudgingly.

Despite all her complaints, one area of life was magnificent. The Adamses were reunited. After nearly five years of complete separation or, as John more accurately pointed out, ten years with a few brief visits, the fact was that Abigail and John had not only sustained their marriage, they carried on in the most natural way. To people of a later century, their uncomplicated, complete acceptance of each other—changed as both of them were—seems improbable. After more than two centuries of scrutiny, no "issues" have surfaced to indicate that either of them regarded the phenomenal hiatus—for one full year, for instance, Abigail received no letters from John—as more than an interruption of their partnership and their passion for each other. They came together and they moved on.

Perhaps, simply, this was not exceptional in the eighteenth century, since it was impossible to terminate a marriage except in some few biblically sanctioned circumstances. Perhaps their religion mandated their behavior. Perhaps eighteenth-century couples maintained their relationship perfunctorily without requiring emotional engagement. Or perhaps they succeeded in disguising the rift that had developed from probing later generations. None of these seem a likely explanation. Indeed, despite a ten-year hiatus during which their experiences could not have been more different, they reunited with all the warm affection and compatibility that marked their courtship and early marriage. Theirs was, indeed, even in their own era, an exceptional marriage. It was, simply, blessed by love, tolerance, and generosity.

The only reflection from either of their pens on the subject of their resumed marriage came from Abigail. She informed her uncle without a great deal of effusiveness that John

> profeses himself so much happier for having his family with him that I feel amply gratified in having ventured across the ocean. He is determined that nothing but the inevitable stroke of death shall in the future separate him from one part of it; so that I know not what climates I may yet have to visit.

THE FULL STORY OF FAMILY LIFE AT AUTEUIL CREATES A PICture of domestic contentment. On a typical day, Abigail would rise "not quite so early as I used to when I provided the turkeys and geese we used to feast upon, but as soon as my fire is made and my room cleaned." She then awakened her daughter and knocked at the door of her son "who always opens it with his book in his hand. By that time we are all assembled to Breakfast." Breakfast completed, John retired to his reading or writing and she to her household chores—directing her staff or sewing, "for I still darn stockings." John Quincy translated Horace and Tacitus in preparation for college, while his sister, struggling with her French, translated Fénelon's *Télémaçhe*. "In this manner we proceed till near 12 o'clock when Mr. A takes his cain and hat for his forenoon walk which is commonly four miles. This he completes by 2." At noon, the ladies "repair to the toilete" where they dressed and were coiffed—"at 2 we all meet together and dine. In the afternoon we go from one room to another sometimes chat with my son or make him read to me. Emilia (her daughter's pen name) in the same manner works reads or plays with her brother which they can do together in a game of romps very well."

Abigail described the texture of daily life in order to explain her life in

France to her family and friends but, more than that, to draw a closely detailed picture for herself. By writing, she accounted for the unbelievable turn her fortunes had taken since the anxious, lonely, difficult times of recent years. Recording her experiences made them concrete, because they were so far beyond the context and predictability of her Braintree life. "The afternoon here is very short," she continued,

> and tea very soon summons us all together. As soon as that is removed the table is covered with mathematical instruments and books and you hear nothing till 9 o'clock but of theorems and problems, bisecting and dissecting tangents and sequences which Mr. A is teaching to his son; after which we are often called upon to relieve their brains by a game of whist. At 10 we all retire to rest.

Again and again Abigail drew this picture of domestic harmony, of evenings with "Mr. A in his easy-chair upon one side of the table, reading Plato's Laws; Mrs. A upon the other, reading Mr. St. John's 'Letters'; Abby setting upon the left hand in a low chair, in a pensive posture . . . John Quincy entering from his own room." While she did not explicitly reveal the details of her resumed marriage and family life, she admitted: "I have pleasures and I have entertainments, but they are not what the beau monde would esteem such."

The lives of the "beau monde" scandalized her. Sexual promiscuity violated her every standard of morality and propriety. She returned to the theme continuously in letters home, at first with astonishment, and later, when she realized its pervasiveness, with the conviction that decadence was rooted in French society and marked the distinction between the Old World and New. She asserted that "there are some practices which neither time nor custom will ever make me a convert to. If I thought they would I would fly the country and its inhabitants as a pestelence walketh in darkness and a plague that waisteth at noon." Biblical injunctions supported her vocabulary in times of heightened emotion.

Adopting her most high-minded tone for her erudite friend Mercy, she wrote: "What Idea my dear Madam can you form of the Manners of a Nation one city of which furnishes (Blush o my sex when I name it) 52,000 unmarried females so lost to a Sense of Honour and Shame . . . to commit iniquity with impunity." She continued, more sympathetically, "Thousands of these miserable wretches perish, annually with Disease and Poverty; whilst the most sacred of institutions is prostituted to unite titles and estates." Abigail could cope with servants and language; she could adapt to living with strange manners once they made sense to her, but she was fundamentally appalled by the pervasiveness of promiscuity "from the footstool to the thrown."

Moreover, Abigail was shocked to observe that promiscuity existed within the ranks of the clergy as well. She speculated that many of the foundlings whom she heard singing so beautifully in the churches were the offspring of clergymen. She reported to Mercy that only in the family of Mr. Grand, "a Protestant," did she observe "decorum and decency of manners, a conjugal and family affection."

For the first time in her life, Abigail discovered how it felt to be socially marginal, in great part because France was a Catholic country. The immensity, the art and architecture, of the churches impressed her, but she described them as literally and figuratively cold. She disapproved of social conduct on the Sabbath, a day of prayer and rest at home. "We have no days with us, or rather in our Country by which I can give you an Idea of the Sabbath here, except Commencement and Election," which she considered the extreme form of decadence in New England. Abigail's indictments were confined to the institutions and the ritual of religion. Never did she criticize theology, nor did she ever proclaim spiritual superiority. The distance between America and France was to be measured not only in terms of miles but in cultures, new compared with old, and morals—virtuous and profoundly decadent.

If marriage, religion, and social relationships in France were permeated with licentiousness, tainted by vice, according to Abigail's New England standards, she did make allowances in the theater. Her aesthetic sensibilities accounted for the distinction. Behavior that threatened her family values earned her contempt, but she also developed a new taste for the arts, and she learned to appreciate the beauty of theatrical dance.

"The first dance which I saw upon the stage shocked me," Abigail wrote to her sister Mary in February of 1784. "The dresses and the beauty of the performers were enchanting; but no sooner did the dance commence than I felt my delicacy wounded and I was ashamed to be seen to look at them." Her reaction revealed as much about herself as the dance. "Girls dressed in the thinnest silk and gauze, with their petticoats short, springing two feet from the floor, poising themselves in the air with their feet flying and as perfectly showing their garters and drawers as though no petticoat had been worn, was a sight altogether new to me." For as much as she was shocked and embarrassed, Abigail could not contain her admiration for the beauty and the accomplishment of the technique. "Their motions are as light as air, and as quick as lightning. . . . They balance themselves to astonishment. No description can equal the reality." Something about ballet had captured her imagination, and she responded with a newly learned tolerance.

FOR JOHN QUINCY, THE MONTHS AT AUTEUIL PROVIDED THE OPportunity to experience family life in a way that he had not during all the years

John Quincy Adams as a young man, painted in 1795 in England by John Singleton Copley. Courtesy of the Museum of Fine Arts, Boston.

of his adolescence. A precocious youth, he had developed intellectually and socially, but he lacked an intimate acquaintance with his mother and siblings. The Revolution, his father's role in it, and the family's decision to send him abroad—all had deprived him of a normal youth.

John Quincy had been well cared for during the six years of his travels. John Adams had not only attended to his son's needs and secured him the kind of education that he considered best for a young man, but he had enjoyed his son's company. As a father he became friend as well as counselor to his son. There were months and years for John when John Quincy was his best friend in Europe and his best source of camaraderie. They had toured together, attended the theater together, read together Latin and Greek texts that John Quincy studied. Further, John confided in his son during the times of his great troubles in France and the Netherlands.

John Quincy in many ways was spared his youth; he became a man without a typical experience of the years between childhood and manhood. He became John Adams's best pupil. When Abigail wrote to her sister Elizabeth that her son possessed exceptional talents for a young man of his age, she did not exaggerate. John Quincy, the prodigy, exceeded his parents' highest expectations as an eighteen-year-old. Given his natural brilliance, he had taken to books and learning with a discipline that matched his father's. He had traveled broadly, but not in the ordinary tracks of a tourist; he had traveled among diplomats and nobility. He had manners and polish and, now, good looks. He had been loved by his father and liked by most of the men and women who met him. Jefferson, who had no son, was smitten with John Quincy and spent much time in his company during their year together in Paris. But all of this came at a cost to the young man.

John Quincy had best learned the message that had become myth in his family lexicon of values, the lesson of duty. Underlying all of his endeavors, all of his striving to fulfill his parents' and other people's requirements of him, was the principle of doing his duty, the religiously based mandate of sacrificing personal happiness for the good of the community. He had seen up close—and heard repeatedly—that his father had sacrificed by giving up his career and his best years to serve as a patriot, and his mother sacrificed family life for the same purpose. He saw how others did the same: Franklin, Jay, Dana, and the Warrens, and all his close acquaintances at home. John Quincy knew that sacrifice of personal happiness to perform one's duty was a natural force in life.

And if observing this phenomenon, as reenacted in the revolutionary crucible, was not enough, his father's continuous preaching, admonitions, and complaints about his own life reinforced the message in bold print. John Quincy was too good a student to have missed the point. He had learned that his own feelings, his own happiness, were secondary to the performance of his duty in the short run as well as the future. His success in this mission was achieved at the cost of suppressing his feelings. He felt things deeply, because he was a sensitive young man, but he also learned to keep his emotions hidden, sometimes even from himself.

His diary for these years comprises a record of his adventures, all noted with precision and detail. Unlike his father's youthful diary, John Quincy did not examine his soul and his spirit; he rarely explored his emotional temperament. In a rare lapse of control, however, when the news of his father's appointment came in late April 1785, John Quincy wrote: "I believe that he will promote the Interests of the United States, as much as any man; but I fear his Duty will induce him to make exertion which may be detrimental to his Health." He then continued:

> Were I now to go with him, probably my immediate Satisfaction might be greater than it will be in returning to America. After having been travelling for these seven years, almost all over Europe, and having been in the world and among Company for three: to return and spend one or two years in the Pale of College, subjected

to all the rules, which I have so long been freed from; then to
plunge into the Dry and tedious study of the law; for three years. . . .
it is really a Prospect some what discouraging.

John Quincy did not want to return home to college. He wanted to live in
England with his mother and father and sister. He then reasoned himself out of
this impulse.

John Quincy had learned to conquer his feelings and follow his reason. He
suppressed indulgence of immediate gratification in favor of conforming to the
family mandate to do the right thing. In the short term, it meant that he would
not remain with his family in Europe but return home to prepare for his future.
In the future it meant that his relations with other people would appear stiff and
cool, unsentimental, or, in the case of women, unromantic. It meant that he
would decide to enter politics, like his father, to correct the ills of the world and
that, again like his father, he would have his greatest triumph not during his
presidency, which, like his father's, would be undermined by the malice in
politics; for John Quincy it was during his last years as a representative in the
people's branch of government. That, too, would be his greatest source of satisfaction.

The few months at Auteuil had compensated him in some small measure for
his years of discipline and, at times, isolation. He rediscovered family life, especially a relationship with his sister, just two years his senior. John Quincy and
Nabby became close friends, attending theater and exploring Paris together.

From the time of his mother's arrival in Europe, John Quincy's future had
become a prime topic of their discussions. Abigail viewed European universities
as training grounds for decadence; she wrote her sister Mary, "I am convinced it
will be much for his advantage to spend one year at Harvard."

John Quincy was accepted at Harvard, and his tuition was waived in recognition of his father's patriotic service. Abigail confronted the conflicting feelings of satisfaction—to her, America was "the theater for a young fellow who
has any ambition to distinguish himself in knowledge and literature"—and
sadness at the prospect of another separation. When the time came for him to
embark for Boston in May, Abigail was glad that she too would be leaving
within a few days for England. "You can hardly form an idea of how much I
miss my son," she wrote after he had gone. Once again she faced a separation
that pained her. Abigail's brief acquaintance with John Quincy during the ten
months at Auteuil proved to be the most extended time they would have together. And John Quincy, no less lonely, sailed for the homeland to which he
was a stranger.

When the time came to leave France, Abigail did so gladly, though she professed some regrets. John's commission from Congress, appointing him minister plenipotentiary to the English court, was sent in February, though it did not arrive until late April. Within weeks the Adamses departed. Among her sorrows about leaving, Abigail wrote that she would miss some people: Mr. Jefferson, the Lafayettes, some of her servants. She would miss her garden, which in spring was just coming into bloom. She even expressed a strange ambivalence about leaving Paris. "This day was in Paris for the last time—I took my leave without tears—yet the thot that I might never visit it again gave me some pain for it is in a way a dying leave when we quit a place with that Idea." The knowledge of its being a "dying leave" finally endeared Paris to her.

Abigail, furthermore, contemplated England with apprehension. John's office was bound to encounter hostility as well as "more company and more expense." However, she acknowledged that she had fewer expectations and greater confidence now that she had lived in a foreign land. "I have seen many of the beauties and some of the deformities of this Old World," she wrote. "I have been more than ever convinced that there is no summit of virtue and no depth of vice which human nature is not capable of rising to." Like John Adams, she was prepared to do battle for virtue in a world where they both knew that vice was a continuous threat.

At the Court of St. James's

THE ADAMSES ARRIVED IN LONDON AT THE END OF THE HIGH social season in May 1785, when the city was so crowded that they had difficulty finding a hotel. Finally they settled into rooms at the Bath Hotel, Westminster, Piccadilly, that were "too public and too noisy for pleasure." Abigail, however, was "glad to get into lodging at the moderate price of a guinea per day for two rooms and two chambers." In addition to the usual activity of the season that marked the departure of high society for their country homes, crowds had come to the city to attend the birthday celebration for the king and a festival of Handel's music at Westminster Abbey.

Despite their fatigue from the arduous weeklong journey from Paris, they immediately plunged into official business. In contrast to her arrival in France, where she had responded peevishly, Abigail became once more her naturally animated self. No small part of her transformed attitude resulted from her command of language, and many times over she expressed her relief at being able to communicate with people. The simple process of directing the servants who carried her luggage or assisted with her unpacking returned a level of control over her circumstances. She used the metaphor of a poor man who kept a dog with whom he shared his meager portion of food. Asked why he kept the dog, when it was so difficult to live himself, he replied, "Why whom should I have to love me then?" Abigail added, "You can never feel the force of this replie unless you were to go into a foreign Country, without being able to understand the language," and concluded, "I could not have believed if I had not experienced it."

John, who never ceased his efforts to take command of circumstances, had no sooner deposited his hat in his rooms than he made immediate contact with Lord Carmarthen, the British foreign minister, to announce his arrival and request an interview. Lord Carmarthen responded early the next morning, generously proposing several alternative hours that day for their meeting. John chose to visit with the foreign minister at his home in the early afternoon. He did not realize at the time that he had already committed a breach of protocol by requesting that meeting. The custom in England, as he later informed Thomas Jefferson in Paris, unlike in France and Holland, was for the foreign minister to make the first call. John was not displeased with this first small gaffe, however, because it saved the minister "the embarrassment" of making the first awkward visit.

This first difficult step, the meeting between himself as the newly appointed minister from a former colony and the parliamentary head of state, was cordial. "His Lordship said that on Wednesday next after the Levee, I should be presented to his Majesty in his Closett, and there deliver my Letter of Credence." This would be a private meeting in the king's personal apartment with just the three of them present. And this time there would be no room for breaches of etiquette. The king's master of ceremonies, Sir Clement Cottrell Dormer, called upon John to explain the protocols of meeting with the king.

The day came. Properly dressed in court attire, a formal suit of dark hues, shoes buffed, wearing a sword at his side, John walked through the palace apartments, accompanied by Lord Carmarthen. "When we arrived at the antechamber, the *oeil de boeuf* of St James's, the master of the ceremonies met me and attended me," John wrote to Secretary Jay in a lengthy letter. "You may be sure that I was the focus of all eyes," he continued, describing the room "very full of ministers of state, lords, and bishops, and all sorts of courtiers." In a short time, he was summoned. "I went with his Lordship through the levee room into the King's closet. The door was shut, and I was left with His Majesty and the secretary of state alone."

As he had been tutored, John made three bows to the king, the first upon entering the door, the next in the middle of the room, and the last before King George III. "I then addressed myself to his Majesty in the following words:— "Sir,—The United States of America have appointed me their minister plenipotentiary to your Majesty, and have directed me to deliver to your Majesty this letter which contains the evidence of it." A few more formal statements followed, including wishes for Their Majesties' good health and for amicable relations between the two nations. Then he spoke more personally:

I think myself more fortunate than all my fellow-Citizens, in having the distinguished Honour to be the first to Stand in your Majesty's Royal Presence, in a diplomatic Character; and I shall esteem myself the happiest of Men, if I can be instrumental in recommending my Country more and more to your Majesty's Royal Benevolence, and of restoring an entire esteem, confidence and affection, or, in better Words, "the old good Nature and the old good Humour" between People who, thou separated by an ocean, and under different Governments, have the same Language, a similar Religion and kindred Blood. I beg your Majesty's Permission to add, that, although I have some time before been intrusted by my country, it was never in my whole Life, in a manner so agreeable to myself.

At stake in this speech was not only John's personal success as a diplomat in a most delicate position, but the standing of his country in a most awkward circumstance. That he was nervous is evident not only from the imposing role he performed but from his description of the effect it had on the England's monarch.

The King listened to every word I said with dignity . . . but with an apparent Emotion. Whether it was the Nature of the Interview, or whether it was my visible Agitation, for I felt more than I did or could express, that touched him, I cannot say. But he was much affected, and answered me with more tremor, than I had spoken with.

King George III had faced this momentous, perhaps humbling meeting with as much foreboding as John did with enthusiasm. The king had opposed peace without victory but had been persuaded by his ministers. He had no desire to meet John Adams as the minister of his former colony or, moreover, as the minister of a nation equal in status to all other nations. But Adams's speech had moved him, and he responded:

Sir,—The Circumstances of this Audience are so extraordinary, the language you have now held is so extremely proper, and the Feelings you have discovered, so justly adapted to the occasion that I must say that I not only receive with Pleasure, the Assurances of the friendly Dispositions of the United States, but that I am very glad the Choice has fallen upon you to be their Minister.

Both men were gracious and both were on their good behavior. Diplomatic etiquette had demanded that they speak the words of friendship and amity, and both did so with eloquence. George III went on to mention that by pursuing the war, he had done the "duty which I owed to my people." He candidly remarked that he had been the last to consent to separation, but now recognized that it was inevitable. And "I say now, that I would be first to meet the Friendship of the United States as an independent Power."

A few more formalities passed between the two men, and then, to John's surprise, the king "put on an air of Familiarity," and laughingly said, "There is an opinion among some people that you are not the most attached of all your countrymen to the manners of France." John wondered: Was this a trap? Or a tease? But he met the challenge by responding: "I must avow to your Majesty, I have no Attachment but to my own Country." The king replied, "as quick as lightning, 'an honest man will not have any other.'" After a few more words of light conversation, the historic moment concluded. The king of England had accepted the diplomatic commission from the United States, recognizing the country as an independent nation. John realistically concluded his report to Congress by noting, "We can infer nothing from all this concerning the success of my mission." He cautioned—himself foremost—"patience is the only remedy."

WHILE JOHN PLUNGED INTO HIS CEREMONIAL LIFE AS A DIPLO-mat, Abigail began to search for a suitable residence. For several weeks she looked and could find nothing that would meet their standards "under £ 50 or £ 60," until she came upon a house on the corner of Brook and Duke streets on Grosvenor Square. It was a short distance from Hyde Park, which, she explained to her sister Mary, "resembled Boston Common, (tho) much larger and more beautiful," and where she could make excursions either by foot or carriage. The house, Nabby informed John Quincy, was a "discrete house," one that was both suitable for family life and "such as you would not blush to see the foreign minister in."

Although Abigail protested that she was much too republican to be impressed by titles, she noted that the neighborhood could claim some distinction. Lord North was a neighbor, though she pointed out that at Grosvenor Square they still lived "opposite to him." Lord Carmarthen, the British foreign minister, lived "about five houses from us." Abigail, whose responsibilities so far were less in the realm of ceremony and more in the practical world, complained about the expense of their exalted lifestyle: "The wages of servants, horse-hire, house rent and provisions are much dearer here than in France." Congress, rather than provide for their increased expenses, had reduced John's salary, just as they had for Thomas Jefferson, who had been appointed to replace Benjamin Franklin as the American envoy in Paris. Jefferson complained about congressional penury as well. He wrote to the Adamses to inquire how they managed their expenses without going into debt.

From the time of their arrival, the Adamses were overwhelmed with visitors—social calls, expatriate Americans, war widows, and foreign ministers. Abigail took time from her busy schedule to attend a performance of Handel's *Messiah* in the great hall of Westminster Abbey. "Though a guinea a ticket" (by habit, she regularly recorded her expenses), she declared to Mary, she had never experienced more satisfaction. When the "Hallelujah Chorus" was performed, she wrote,

> the whole assembly rose and all the Musicians, every person uncovered [removed their hats]. Only conceive six hundred voices and instruments perfectly cording in one word and one sound! I could scarcly believe myself an inhabitant of Earth. I was one continued shudder from the beginning to the end of the performance.

Clearly, London would have its compensations for Abigail, though her mandatory attendance at court was a mixed blessing.

While John had welcomed his presentation to the king and queen as a milestone in history, Abigail had reservations about her appearance at court. John's ceremonies had been private. Abigail and her daughter would be presented to the royal family at one of their "levees," a weekly "drawing room," where they greeted less distinguished visitors. Abigail, if she dreaded the ceremony, considered it her duty. She worried about court etiquette, for which she, like John, had been tutored. The fact that she would have to curtsey to royalty rankled. Besides, special court dress was prescribed, and "what renders it exceeding expensive is, that you cannot go twice the same season in the same dress." Abigail ordered her dressmaker "to let my dress be elegant, but plain as I could possibly appear, with decency," thus preserving her republican image. She was, however, pleased with her dress; it was made of white lutestring, a glossy silk fabric, and was

> covered and full trimed with white Crape festoond with lilick ribbon and mock point lace, over a hoop of enormous extent; there is only a narrow train of about 3 yard length to the gown waist . . . ruffel cuffs for married Ladies, thrible lace ruffels, a very dress cap with long lace lappets two white plumes and a blond lace handkerchief.

For the occasion, John had purchased her "two pearl pins for her hair, earring and necklace of the same kind." Certainly Abigail had neither possessed nor worn such extravagant attire. She practiced walking in her new dress to be assured of carrying it gracefully, and aside from complaining about the cost of costuming for official functions, her overall reaction bespoke not only pleasure but pride. "This is my rigging," she concluded, somewhat embarrassed.

After arriving at St. James's she and Nabby were led through several chambers to the drawing room. "We were placed in a circle . . . which was very full, I believe two hundred persons present," she wrote. The king and queen accompanied by the princesses entered the room and began greeting each person individually. The King "goes round to the right; the Queen and Princesses to the left." For four hours, Abigail and her daughter stood, waiting their turns to greet the royal family. "Only think of the task!" she wrote, considering the royal family.

The king approached her first. "The lord in waiting introduced 'Mrs. Adams' upon which I drew off my right-hand glove, and his majesty saluted my left cheek; then asked me if I had taken a walk today." Noting the irony, she wrote, "I could have told his Majesty that I had been all the morning prepareing to wait upon him, but I replied, no Sire. Why don't you love walking? says he. I answered that I was rather indolent in that respect. He then Bow'd and past on." Despite this stylized social exchange, Abigail liked King George III.

They waited another two hours until Queen Charlotte and the princesses made their way around the circle: "The Queen was evidentally embarrassed when I was presented to her. I had dissagreeable feelings too." She, however, said, "Mrs. Adams have you got into your House?" and again a few formal comments passed between the ladies. Abigail found the princesses sympathetic, but Queen Charlotte was "not well shaped or handsome." Abigail would never be fond of Charlotte. "As to the ladies of the Court, rank and title may compensate for want of personal charm; but they are in general, very plain ill-shaped and ugly. But," Abigail warned her sister, "Don't you tell any body that I say so." Relieved that the ordeal had ended, she added, "Congratulate me, my dear sister, it is over."

The snubs she experienced from upper-class English people accounted for much of Abigail's distaste for social events. "I know I am looked down upon with a sovereign pride, and a smile of royalty is bestowed as a mighty boon. As such, however, I cannot receive it. I know it is due my country and I consider myself as complimenting the power before which I appear as much as I am complimented by being noticed by it."

Abigail was appalled by the extent to which aristocratic power and wealth rested upon the labors of a poverty-ridden populace, and she observed that both the government and religion were complicit in the perpetuation of injustices that accounted for crime and vice. "When I reflect upon the thousands who are starving and the millions who are loaded with taxes to support this pomp and show," she wrote, "I look to my happier country with an enthusiastic warmth."

She was especially concerned about the plight of poor women. "In Europe all the lower class women perform the most servile labour and work as hard without door as the men," she wrote to her aunt. Some Americans in Europe, she observed, affected aristocratic identity, imitating their dress and manners. Alarmed by this tendency, Abigail warned against such indulgence. "The foolish idea in which some of our youth are educated, of being born gentlemen, is the most ridiculous in the world for a country like ours," she complained. "I have very different ideas of the wealth of my countrymen from what I had when I left." She was convinced that Americans could best preserve their institutions by developing a purely American culture, by which she meant that of New England.

JOHN'S PRIMARY OBJECTIVE AS THE AMERICAN MINISTER WAS to normalize relations between Great Britain and her former colonies. His country was a fragile newcomer among the independent nations of the world, and England was still a major European power with a grudge against her states that had rebelled. His mission would not be easy. He was expected on the one hand to insure that both nations honored the terms of the peace treaty of 1783, on the face of it a simple goal, but in reality it was vexed by complications. Second, he was charged to negotiate commercial relations between the two recent enemies.

Aware of his country's fragile position, John intended not to criticize British customs but to work within them. If he had to attend the king's drawing room on a weekly basis, he did so because ceremony was required of all diplomats. If he was snubbed, that was not new to him, as he had experienced worse from Vergennes and been ignored for several years at The Hague. John's work was defined narrowly and specifically.

He first sensed the resistance he would encounter once the formalities of his recognition were concluded. After his first diplomatic interview with Lord Carmarthen in mid-June, he presented his agenda in person to the prime minister and then again in writing, asking for British compliance with specific articles of the peace treaty that had been violated. Several forts in the Northwest Territory had not been abandoned, for instance. Lord Carmarthen did not respond.

"Although I have been received here, and continue to be treated, with all the distinction which is due to the rank and title you have given me," John reported to John Jay, "there is, nevertheless, a reserve, which convinces me that we shall have no treaty of commerce until this nation is made to feel the necessity of it." The government of Great Britain was ignoring him.

The fact was—as Abigail acknowledged—Britain perceived no reason to fulfill any treaty obligations, because those in power didn't expect the United States to continue as a nation. And for good cause. The states could not unite on the critical issues required for survival. There was no uniform currency. There were riots in some cities, such as Boston, indicating the inability of the government to suppress internal problems. Further, as Lord Carmarthen pointed out to Adams, some Americans failed to pay their debts to English creditors. Individual states, such as Massachusetts, furthermore, had established trade barriers against British commerce. Finally, John learned that some states no longer bothered to send delegates to Congress, which hampered that body's ability to act." From the British point of view, it was sheer hubris—if not comedy—for the American minister to send demands to the British government.

As the summer wore on, there was no response to John's list of conditions. "The popular pulse seems to beat high against America," and if they could afford it, "they would soon force the ministry into a war against us." It was the court, meaning the king, that appeared to be the "principle barrier against a war, and the best disposed towards us." Whatever optimism John had at the beginning of his time in England—and realist that he was, it was low—was quickly dissipating. He made the rounds of ceremonial visits. By the end of the summer, he had all but given up hope of a response from the foreign minister of Britain.

He did, however, hope to negotiate commercial treaties with other countries. A treaty with Prussia had been in the works for some time, as were talks with the ministers from Portugal, Denmark, and the Barbary States. Adams stayed in close touch with Thomas Jefferson, whose difficulties in Paris were similar. The French government faced an economic crisis that, left to ferment, would lead to the French Revolution. Besides, Vergennes had died, and he, despite the obstacles he placed on John's peace mission, had been America's best ally in France.

Adams and Jefferson communicated during the long winter, in a joint effort to promote commerce in Europe, where commercial agreements punished American trade. England and France both had navigation acts that restricted shipping. In the Mediterranean, the Barbary pirates captured American ships, imprisoning or enslaving their seamen. These tactics, corrupt and inhumane, were the work of poor nations extracting payment for hostages. Finally, Adams suggested that Jefferson visit London so they could communicate personally. Jefferson arrived in London in mid-March 1786.

Thomas Jefferson's presentation to King George III occurred early in the visit and reinforced what both he and Adams had come to understand about their stations. The king turned his back on both Adams and Jefferson, and he did this in full view of other courtiers and ministers. Whether it was because Jefferson had written the Declaration of Independence with its detailed list of indictments against the king or because the political climate between England and America had declined since John's presentation, the king, by snubbing the Americans, clearly delivered his message.

Nevertheless, during Jefferson's visit, the two American diplomats successfully concluded a treaty with Prussia, carried on negotiations with the Portuguese minister (though a treaty was never signed because of domestic disruptions in that country), and decided to send emissaries to Morocco and Algiers to negotiate with those countries. Then the two friends set off on a garden tour, Jefferson carrying Thomas Whately's *Observations of Modern Gardening* and Adams in search of historic houses. They made an interesting pair, the tall, red-haired, refined Virginian and the shorter, stocky, blunt John Adams.

The two Americans roamed at leisure, continuing their rambling conversation on topics that interested them. Their brief shared history in Congress provided the foundation of a friendship that grew stronger in Paris. They had in common their fierce dedication to their country and belief in the democratic process. Currently they were joined in the common project of establishing parity in diplomatic relations with countries that disdained America as an insignificant nation. But just as the one man set out to explore gardens while the other was drawn to houses, there were differences in temperament between them.

Adams, the secular Puritan, had developed a deeply pragmatic view of life, while Jefferson, the idealist, lived in a world of abstractions. Adams was convinced of the human conflict between moral or corrupt behavior. He knew that the outcome of this struggle was contingent on circumstance and timing. He could face his own and others' shortcomings, but he did not forgive bad behavior. Rather he understood it. The same was true of politics. History was the story of people navigating through the shoals of self-interest. Because they would not or could not steer their courses without creating chaos, governments existed.

Jefferson, the idealist, did not acknowledge this disordered nature of human character. To him the world was abstractly uncomplicated and basically benevolent. Jefferson's archetypal individual was more benign, requiring the least amount of intervention by political institutions. His was an Enlightenment view of a world grown more perfect with time. Jefferson was less concerned about going into debt, because he trusted in some unpredictable future resolution. In the conflict between his ideal of an abstracted beautiful life and the affordable real life, he believed that his indulgence in beauty and sentiment would somehow work out. He overlooked the constraints of a budget in the same way that he managed to disregard the stain of slavery, by anticipating the best of all possible worlds.

The pragmatic Adamses—both Abigail and John—lived in terror of debt and in horror of allowing history to take its course. Their religious system, integral to their worldview, convinced them otherwise. The friendship between Jefferson and the Adamses was predicated more upon respect, fascination, and tolerance than upon similarities.

Within that friendship, Abigail was central, and her affection was reciprocated. Only a week after her arrival in London, Abigail wrote to Jefferson, describing her pleasure upon hearing the *Messiah* and that "I most sincerely wisht for your presence as your favorite passion would have received the highest gratification." Her letter recapitulated a conversation between them, one that included family news, cultural criticism, and politics. And one last thing: She included her appraisal of John's new personal secretary, William Stephens Smith, appointed by Congress at the same time that John received his appointment, and who had also recently arrived in London. "Mr Smith," she allowed, "appears to be a Modest worthy Man, if I may judge from so short an acquaintance. I think we shall have much pleasure in our connection with him." Little did Abigail know that she was describing her future son-in-law.

Nabby's romance with Royall Tyler had cooled. In fact, Tyler had disappeared from view after the Abigails' departure for Europe. For more than a year, he did not write to any of them, including Nabby. They did write to him, long letters from Abigail the mother and a steady stream from the benighted fiancée. From the Adamses' point of view, Tyler's actions were most peculiar, an indication that perhaps he had reverted to his former behavior. Then news came that Tyler had moved to Boston, where he resided in a boardinghouse kept by Elizabeth Hunt Palmer, who was the niece by marriage of Abigail's sister Mary Cranch. What transpired with Tyler was long a matter of speculation; but now it has come to light as a scandal.

Friends in Boston informed Nabby that Tyler had pridefully showed around letters that Nabby had written to him. Furthermore, he had failed to deliver letters to friends that she sent under cover to him, keeping and reading them himself. With this disclosure, young Abigail acted. She spoke with her parents, confessed her distress with Tyler, and expressed her doubts about his "strickt honour." John, characteristically, declared that he would rather see both himself and his daughter in their graves than united with Tyler. Following this conversation, if John's rant may be called such, Nabby returned Tyler's miniature and other mementoes and requested that he return her gifts and letters to her uncle Dr. Cotton Tufts. In the early fall of 1785 young Abigail terminated her engagement. The family at home was informed.

With this announcement, and the ensuing outpouring of relief from relatives and friends, more elements of the picture began to fall into place. "My dear neice has acted with a spirit worthy of her parents," wrote Mary Cranch. "We have been for a long time very anxious for her—Happiness." "Such *neglect* to such *affection* and to *such a person* was what I could not silently nor patiently see," wrote Elizabeth Shaw. Clearly, the folks at home had been talking among themselves and concluded that Tyler's behavior warranted suspicion.

Friends and family disclosed that in the months after the Adamses' departure Tyler had "showed about" John's letter of assent to his suit, as well as the many letters he had received from Nabby. Pressed by friends to explain this behavior, he responded that he was so proud of them that he wished to show them publicly. He had boasted that he had "never wrote her" but that Nabby had repeatedly written to him. In all, the picture that emerged from Tyler's behavior confirmed the family's initial assessment of his character.

At this point, while family and friends expressed relief, Tyler shifted tactics. He first denied that the engagement had terminated; then he announced that he would travel to London to set the affair straight, and finally he began a campaign of letter writing. He wrote to Abigail. He wrote to John. And he wrote to his erstwhile fiancée—all to no avail. The Adamses, reinforced by the news they heard, stood firm in opposition to Tyler.

Eventually Tyler sank into a depression that conceded his defeat. At the same time, he constructed his own theory to explain his rejection; the family, all the relatives, he claimed, had mounted a conspiracy against him. They had written lies about him to the Adamses, and behind the campaign was Mary Cranch, who was punishing him for having overlooked her daughters in favor of her niece.

In fact, after Nabby broke off with Tyler, he moved back into the Palmer household, where he fathered a child by his landlady, Elizabeth Hunt Palmer, the wife of Joseph Pearse Palmer and mother of six other children. She was also a niece by marriage of Mary Cranch's. Joseph's inability to support his growing family during the postwar recession resulted in his wife's taking in boarders, while he traveled to New Hampshire for work. Apparently the lonely wife and the lonely fiancé consoled each other, for in the allotted time Sophia Palmer was born.

"We live in an age of discovery," Mary Cranch gossiped to Abigail, her message typically coded: "One of our acquaintance has discover'd that a full grown, fine child may be produc'd in less than five months as well as in nine." Joseph Palmer had returned from New Hampshire five months before his wife gave birth. And Tyler's history with the Adams family concluded.

Later Royall Tyler went on to write a play that was produced on the stage, the first play written by an American playwright and performed in public. He married a Palmer daughter (not his own) and moved to New Hampshire, where he became chief justice of the state supreme court.

Meanwhile, in London, a handsome and gallant replacement for Tyler had appeared on the scene: William Stephens Smith, John's newly appointed secretary. The Adamses were at first wary of Smith, because John had wanted to select his own secretary, but after meeting him, all were impressed. He was highly recommended, having risen through the military ranks to become an aide to General Washington at the end of the war. He came from a respectable Long Island family and had attended Princeton. He had good looks, manners, and charm, excellent qualities in a diplomat post. And quickly, he took an interest in his boss's daughter.

As part of his mission, Smith escorted Abigail, the mother, and Abigail, the daughter, to the many social events. He was constantly present among the family as John's secretary, performing the clerical tasks that John required as well as accompanying him to meetings. In effect, Smith filled John Quincy's role in the family. Then, surprisingly, in August, just two months into his work, he asked for a brief leave to travel to Prussia to observe a military review. John, thinking the trip would be brief, assented to his going for a few weeks, especially since business was slow during the heat of summer. Smith then disappeared for more than three months.

In October, Abigail explained to John Quincy that his father was "overwhelmd with writing," since Smith had not yet returned. Nabby substituted as her father's secretary. Smith eventually turned up in Paris, where Thomas Jefferson met him and was smitten. "I congratulate you on Colo. Smith," and especially upon "the extreme worth of his character, which was so interesting." Smith, it turns out, had reconnected with a friend from revolutionary days, a South American named Francisco Miranda. This man, some twenty years later, would lead a revolutionary expedition to liberate Venezuela from Spain, with unfortunate consequences for the Smith and Adams families. Whether the two former soldiers met by accident or by a prior plan is not clear, but for the next few months they toured leisurely through Europe as far as Berlin and back. The Adamses were puzzled by Smith's absence.

When Smith returned, though he was unsure about the kind of reception he would receive at Grosvenor Square, he discovered that his charm was still able to win over all of the Adamses. They received him warmly. In his absence, Nabby had broken off her engagement with Tyler, so Smith was not only restored to his office as secretary to the legation but also accepted as a suitor. Abigail and John were relieved to be rid of Tyler and were so sensitive to their daughter's feelings that they failed to read anything into Smith's strange three-month disappearance. Over the long run, this trait of irresponsible behavior would be as enduring as his charm. None of the Adamses was capable of acknowledging what they observed at the time.

Even Abigail employed an atypical vocabulary when she described Smith to her relatives. She noted his valor, his good looks, his integrity and courage. In contrast, the values that Abigail encouraged, even demanded, within her family related to education, service, industry, and frugality. Certainly, these were John's values as well. The marriage, nevertheless, took place in June 1786, pressed on by the impatience of Smith and his agreeable bride.

On the eve of her daughter's marriage to Smith, Abigail Adams experienced a strange premonition that she recorded for her sister. "Some evil Spright sent Mr. T. to visit me in a dream. I really have felt for him." One of the few dreams that Abigail Adams recorded, it had disturbed her. Although she submitted to circumstances that were no longer in her control, her most unconscious self—accepting that dreams are a manifestation of the potent subconscious—protested against the impending marriage. Her own intuition, her initial inclination to care for Tyler, persisted. "I wish the Gentleman well," she wrote of Tyler. "He has good qualities, indeed he has but he ever was his own enemy."

Following their marriage, the newlywed Smiths moved into their own home on Wimpole Street, and Abigail, especially, felt the loss of her daughter's companionship. This was, in fact, the first time since her early marriage that she lived without any of her children. She would turn forty-two in the fall and John fifty-two. To her sister Elizabeth, she acknowledged: "I do not wonder now as I formerly did that people who have no children substitute cats, dogs, birds, etc." John, too, felt at loose ends, having little to do beyond the performance of ceremonial duties. He did continue to correspond with Jefferson about the Barbary pirates.

The two men differed in their perspectives about how America should confront that situation. Jefferson, the idealist, argued that piracy and hostage taking

represented crimes against America; he favored war. Adams, the realist, contended that his government, indebted on every front, was incapable of resisting,
much less waging war, even in its own best interests. He preferred to negotiate.
Since the pirates would not cooperate, however, John favored paying tribute to
purchase commercial lanes on the Mediterranean. In the end, Congress adopted
Adams's approach to bargain for shipping rights.

THE SUMMER AFTER THE SMITHS MOVED OUT, ABIGAIL AND JOHN
made several excursions outside of London. For their first modest journeys,
John took Abigail to see country houses that he had seen previously. Then, in
the fall of 1786, Abigail accompanied John to Holland, because she wanted to
see the country where her "partner and fellow-travellor had exhibited some of
his most important actions and rendered to his country lasting blessings." The
purpose of the trip was to attend a ceremony at the Prussian embassy in Amsterdam, where John signed the commercial treaty with Prussia that he and
Jefferson had negotiated. Abigail liked Holland because it reminded her of her
own country, but also because people spoke to her in English. Predictably, she
appreciated the Dutch values of industry, cleanliness, friendliness, and piety.

One evening they dined in Harlem and sent their servant John Briesler
ahead of them to return by boat, "and he had very carefully locked the carriage," and taken the key with him. When the Adamses emerged from dinner,
they found their coach locked and themselves with no key. A locksmith was
sent for, but he could not budge the lock, so Abigail suggested that someone
climb in through a window. "O that was impossible!" everyone claimed. However, after she insisted, they found a ladder and "the difficulty was surmounted!"
Abigail noted that men never listen to women's good advice.

Their return trip was fierce. Two boats ahead of them were lost, crossing the
Channel, and only two people survived. "Such a storm has not been known in a
long time," Nabby informed her brother.

Back in London, Abigail and John were excluded from English society. "Of
civility, cold and formal, such as only the English know how in perfection to
make offensive, there was enough," wrote C. F. Adams of his grandparents'
position in English society. John continued to attend mandatory diplomatic
functions, as did Abigail. Accompanied again by her daughter, she went to an
anniversary celebration of the coronation. "This is such a ridiculous ceremony
that I always feel provoked when I am present," wrote Nabby to John Quincy.
"I like the King better than the Queen," she continued, "at least he dissembles
better. She is a haughty, proud imperious Dame."

Early in 1786 the family again attended the celebration of the queen's birthday at a reception at St. James's Palace. The crowds were so great for the occasion that they had to abandon their carriage to walk across the park. Further, they waited for hours to be greeted by royalty, and the king asked Miss Adams the same question: "Do you get out much in this weather?"

Among the Adamses' acquaintances in London were the American painters John Singleton Copley, Benjamin West, John Trumbull, and Mather Brown. The entire family—John, Abigail, and young Abigail—were so impressed by Brown's artistry that they sat for portraits. "A very tasty picture I assure you, whether a likeness or not," wrote young Abigail of her own picture. "He had taken the best likeness I have seen of *pappa*," she commented, "and a good likeness of Mamma too." They visited Trumbull's atelier, where Abigail was so moved by the painting of the *The Death of General Warren at the Battle of Bunker Hill* that "my whole frame contracted, my blood shivered, and I felt a faintness at my heart." The group of artists became frequent guests at the Adamses' dinner table. They were especially pleased at Benjamin West's recent good fortune. At a sale of old pictures he purchased a marred and disfigured painting, which after he cleaned it turned out to be Titian's *Death of Actaeon*. For two hundred guineas he took home a painting for which he was later offered one thousand guineas.

Most poignant and dramatic of their social encounters, not only in personal terms but also emblematic of the tragedy of revolution, was John's meeting with his old friend since their days at Harvard, Jonathan Sewall. They had been not only students together but afterward young lawyers and young gallants. It had been Sewall who, with his fiancée Esther Quincy, had burst into the room as John was about to propose to Hannah Quincy and thus fatefully terminated that relationship. It had been Sewall whose newspaper article, signed "Pym," had inspired John to respond as "Clarendon." It had been Sewall who one afternoon in 1774 had tried to persuade John to change his politics, arguing that he was choosing the losing side in a revolution.

Sewall had returned to England as a Tory in 1775, and misfortune plagued him the remainder of his life. Now, in September 1788, he had moved from Bristol to London en route to Halifax, where his son had since migrated. He was John's age but appeared old from heartache and anger.

Both men recorded the warmth of their reunion at Sewall's London lodgings. John noted that as soon as he learned of Sewall's arrival in London, he drove to his residence, "laying aside all etiquette to make him a visit. Upon seeing each other, "both of us, forgetting that we had ever been enemies, embraced each other as cordially as ever." The two men talked for hours "in a most delightful freedom, upon a multitude of subjects." Sewall wrote his version of their meeting to a friend: "When Mr. Adams came in, he took my hand in both of his, and with a hearty squeeze, accosted me in these words—*how do you do my dear old friend!*" Adams had pleaded with Sewall to come home with him for dinner, but Sewall, who had isolated himself from company for years, declined.

Theirs was a bittersweet reunion. They had served on opposite sides in the revolution that had turned against Sewall's prophecy, and he had suffered greatly. Perhaps that explains his blunt judgment of John's success. John was unqualified "by nature or education to shine in the Courts of Europe," he asserted, although acknowledging John's brilliance. However, Adams could neither "dance, drink, game, flatter, promise, dress, swear with the gentlemen, and small talk & flirt with the Ladys." He concluded, "He has none of the essential *Arts* or *ornaments* which constitute a Courtier." John, for his part, accurately diagnosed Sewall's death a few years later as caused by a broken heart.

Sometime after Nabby's marriage, Thomas Jefferson wrote to Abigail that he had sent for his younger daughter, Mary, called Polly, to join him and his older daughter in Paris. She would sail for England from Virginia in late June 1787, accompanied by a maid. He asked Abigail to look after the child until he could come for her, an opportunity that Abigail welcomed.

Polly arrived after five weeks at sea, lonely and frightened, looking "rough as a little sailor," Abigail announced to Jefferson. She was reluctant to warm up to Abigail, even with the offer to attend Sadler's Wells. "She is indeed a fine child," Abigail affirmed, and took Polly shopping to purchase her some new outfits. She also advised Jefferson that the fourteen-year-old Sally Hemings, sent to accompany Polly, "is quite a child," one who the ship's captain "is of the opinion will be of so little Service that he had better carry her back with him." Abigail added that the slave girl "seems fond" of Polly and appears "good Natured."

Within a few days, Abigail, who longed for her own children, and Polly, who longed for a parent, formed a loving bond. Then Jefferson wrote to say that because of business, he was detained in Paris, and that he was sending instead a servant, named Adrien Petit, to fetch Polly. Distressed for two reasons, Abigail responded: "If I had thought you would so soon have Sent for your dear little Girl I should . . . have kept her arrival here from you a secret for I am really loth to part with her." Aside from her affection for Polly, Abigail was displeased with Jefferson for sending a servant instead of coming himself. She described the child's unhappiness:

> Last evening upon petit's arrival, [she] was thrown into all her former distresses, and bursting into Tears, told me it would be as

hard to leave me, as it was her Aunt Epps. . . . She will not quit me a moment least She should be carried away, nor can I scarcely prevail upon her to see petit. . . . She depended on your comeing for her . . . and told me this morning, that as she had left all her Friends in virginia to come over the ocean to see you, she did think you would have taken the pains to have come here for her, & not have sent a man whom she cannot understand. I express her own words.

Abigail quoted Polly, but the words conveyed her own disapproval as well; she continued:

I have expostulated with "my little girl," for so she chooses I should call her, upon the difficulty you had to leave home . . . and upon the kindness of petit . . . but forcing her into a carriage against her will and sending her from me almost in a frenzy as now will be the case, indeed I have not the heart to do it . . . I have given her my word that petit will stay until I shall hear again from you.

For as much as Abigail was displeased with Jefferson, she was upset because the visit of Polly Jefferson had filled a void left by her own children; she harbored a fantasy that the child could stay with her for a time.

Jefferson, unmoved by the sentiments or the rebuke, explained his interpretation of the situation, "that your goodness had so attached her to you that her separation would be difficult." He added that, given her choice, Polly "would stay till you cease to be kind to her and that madam, is a term which I cannot wait." He reasoned "her distress will be in the moment of parting."

Polly returned with Petit to Paris. The next fall, Jefferson wrote to acknowledge that Polly had received Abigail's letter, which sent her into "such a flutter of joy that she could scarcely open it." He added, "She is in a convent where she is perfectly happy." For the three weeks of Polly Jefferson's visit, Abigail entertained the little girl, who, despite her loneliness and fear, was plucky and wise beyond her years. For good reason, they became friends.

That same spring of 1787, Nabby gave birth to a son, and Abigail and John became grandparents for the first time. "I am a *Grandmamma*!" Abigail announced to her niece Lucy Cranch. "My Grandson be sure is a fine Boy, & I already feel as fond of him as if he was my own son, nay I can hardly persuade myself that he is not." The christening took place at Grosvenor Square because in England infants were not taken into the church for this ceremony. Their friend Dr. Richard Price conducted the service. "About a dozen of our Friends together upon the occasion. we supped & drank the young Heroes Health." To her sister Mary she confided, "You will rejoice with me that an event which as a parent so nearly concernd me, is happily over." Abigail was greatly relieved that her daughter and grandson had survived the perils of childbirth in good health.

She extolled the birthing practices in Britain, noting that the nurse "washes the little master with cold water from the day of his Birth, & is exceedingly attentive to Cleanliness." At the same time, she informed her sister that her son-in-law was about to embark on a four-month journey to Portugal, dispatched by John to conduct negotiations. Her daughter was "unhappy enough," Abigail informed Mary, because she feared that her life would recapitulate her mother's long marital separations.

In fact, however painful their decade-long separation had been, Abigail and John were making up for lost time. In France and now in England, their marriage had resumed its original warmth and commitment. John claimed never to have been happier, and Abigail wrote that his health had never been better. The Adamses clearly enjoyed each other's company and thrived when together. He had introduced her to the amazing world of diplomacy, and she embraced her new roles. Together they savored travel and the arts, as well as the people they encountered. Their loving relationship in middle age had mellowed into understanding and deep devotion to each other's well-being. And they shared a sense of obligation to several great responsibilities in life: to bring up their children to become industrious and useful adults and to serve their nation.

The news from their nation, however, had not been good. That most gloomy of John's informants, James Warren, after protesting that the situation at home was "so novel and so extraordinary" that he "dared not describe it," described it. He complained that hard currency was drained by the spending spree of the newly rich "on baubles," by which he meant imported luxury goods. He grumbled that the local commerce was ruined, and farming and manufactured goods couldn't be sustained. Debts were not paid or taxes collected. Because of "a total Change in principles and Manners," he argued, the economy had collapsed. He further accused Adams of failing to understand the troubles at home, a charge that John would often hear in the next years: that he had been abroad too long to comprehend conditions in America. Warren was pessimistic.

Adams viewed the situation differently. Realist that he was, he had anticipated that the end of the war would bring difficulties, but he considered this a period of adjustment, one in which the new nation was recovering from a revolution both military and social. "It is easier to tear down than build up," he reminded Warren. He did not underestimate the problems, but he believed that they were surmountable just as the war had succeeded against odds. Strangely enough, the skeptical John Adams was optimistic about America's future. "I wish everything may be so Conducted as to restore Order and submission to Government; but I fear it will be some time first," he concluded.

Both men were right. Many people, not just Warren, confirmed the serious conditions at home. Adams, however, had distance, and he also had invested himself too greatly in the Revolution to allow for its failure. He would not yield to the bad news. From his vantage point in London—and before in France— where he had observed poverty and despair repeated through successive generations of most people, he believed that America possessed advantages of land and resources that would lead to prosperity. But he also foresaw a need for change that would alter the structure to achieve better policies at home. He wanted to participate in the coming transformation. Meanwhile, his mission in Britain was compromised, partly because of the situation at home, but also because of Britain's punitive strategy that caused a stalemate in his efforts to negotiate treaties.

In early 1787 he submitted his resignation to Congress. Writing to John Jay, he explained that after one more year, at the termination of his three-year appointment, he wanted to return home. Not only did he write a formal resignation, but fearing that it would not be taken seriously, he wrote to friends to confirm that he would no longer remain abroad. He asked to be relieved of his posts, not just in England but in the Netherlands and as commissioner for the Barbary States. He begged Jay: "I now write to you this private letter to entreat you, as a friend, to promote in every way in your power, an arrangement as early as possible by which I may be permitted to return with decorum." He had been abroad for nearly ten years; he had concluded treaties with the Low Countries; he had been part of the peace negotiations; he had negotiated with the Barbary States; and more. He wanted to return respectably, but if Congress would not recall him, he would return anyway. He was done with his diplomatic posts abroad. After almost a decade, it was time to return to America.

Ten

Looking Homeward

"YOUR FATHER IS MUCH ENGAGED IN A WORK THAT MAY PROVE of no Small utility to our Country," Abigail wrote to John Quincy in late 1786. "It is an investigation into the different Forms of Government, both ancient and modern, Monarchical Aristocratic Democratical and Republican, pointing out their happiness or misery in proportion to their different balances." Abigail captured the essence of the new project that had occupied John for some months and would continue to do so for the remainder of their time in England. He had begun to write *A Defence of the Constitutions of Government of the United States of America,* the first of a multivolume work that contained the subtitle *Against the Attack of M. Turgot, in His Letter to Dr. Price, Dated the Twenty-Second Day of March, 1778.* John wrote in haste, hoping to affect from afar the political debates taking place at home.

The genesis of this work was both simple and complex. He had long planned to set forth his understanding of the best type of government for the new nation, based upon his lifetime of reading and thinking about political institutions. The impetus came from the reports that continued to arrive from his friends, describing alarming events at the time. The insurrections, the crises of debt, commerce, and governance, had provoked an argument about how best to confront these dilemmas. The debate was fueled by the writings of a radical French reformer, the Baron Anne-Robert Turgot. Like his friend Benjamin Franklin, Turgot proposed a one-house legislative and executive body combined, a unicameral government, as the most direct form of democracy. Turgot's famous letter represented to Adams the essence of his dispute with the radical wing of philosophers that he needed to repudiate. Most unsettling to him, however, were the events at home that he felt required his contribution. These were complex.

Recently, an incident in Massachusetts confirmed that factions had arisen to contest the power of government. In the western part of the state an uprising of farmers, called Shays's Rebellion after its organizer Daniel Shays, had provided the alarm. A crowd of two thousand farmers had closed their courthouses to protest taxes that had impoverished or bankrupted them. Throughout the state, large numbers of people sided with the Shaysites, arguing that the government did not have the right to tax them. They had just fought in a revolution to prevent a government from unfair taxation. Opposing the rebellion was the party of order, those who believed in granting the government the power it needed to maintain stability and harmony. The two political factions had taken form soon after the Revolution ended.

Abigail, as soon as she learned about Shays's Rebellion, was indignant, writing to Thomas Jefferson that "Ignorant, wrestless, desperadoes, without conscience or principals, have led a deluded multitude to follow their standard, under pretence of greivances which have no existance but in their immaginations." This was strong language, even for Abigail.

John, on the other hand, was not terribly disturbed. "Don't be alarmed at the late Turbulence in New England," he wrote to Jefferson. "The Massachusetts Assembly had, in its Zeal to get the better of their Debt, laid on a Tax, rather heavier than the People could bear," he explained, " but all will be well, and this Commotion will terminate in additional Strength to Government." He believed that people exaggerated the threat. Jefferson, true to form, responded to Abigail, "I like a little rebellion now and then. It is like a storm in the Atmosphere." The storm, however, was symptomatic of a dysfunction. Even John had to admit this after repeated alarms from his informants at home. Within this climate, he decided to write the *Defence*.

For most of his adult life, John Adams had reflected upon political theory and especially the question of what constitutes the best type of government. He had engaged in the dialogues that preceded the drafting of a constitution for the Continental Congress. In *Common Sense,* Thomas Paine had proposed a unicameral legislature that inspired John to write his *Thoughts on Government,* proposing instead a government of three branches. He had written the constitution for the commonwealth of Massachusetts, based upon three separate branches. Now, symbolically in response to Turgot, he began a larger study of constitutions, but it was not only Turgot that motivated him. A climate of political change had developed at home, and he wanted to influence the debate.

Central to Adams's argument in the *Defence* was his case for balanced government. Three branches, each strong in its own right, would safeguard against
dominance by one branch. Moreover, John was concerned about balance of
representation in the legislature, recommending two houses that would restrain
each other. A further belief that informed his thinking was the (perhaps) naïve
assumption that political parties would not develop. John actually thought that
in a balanced system, opposition would disappear. John's primary arguments in
the *Defence* focused on balancing government in three branches that would stabilize one another by performing separate functions and by balancing representation in a two-house legislature. He wrote this at the time when the Articles of
Confederation of the United States had created a weak central government, focused in one branch, the Continental Congress, which had no power to compel
the states to act. Power resided in the states, despite the fact that they were still
jealous of their own prerogatives, fearful of a national government, and competitive with one another.

John believed initially that he was addressing his advice to the states. It
turned out otherwise, as a convention called to revise the Articles in 1787
drafted instead an entirely new constitution for the national government. That
government remarkably resembled John's proposals in the *Defence,* especially
volume 1, which he concluded in time for delegates to the Philadelphia convention to become familiar with it. Certainly his ideas drew on a body of political
theory and debates that circulated among his contemporaries. But his three volumes were unique in addressing the pressing ideologies of his era, grounding
them in classical as well as modern philosophy, and in providing concrete examples both from history and the present.

Because he worked quickly and because his style under ordinary circumstances contained many digressions, the *Defense* was not an easy book to read,
and its detractors were copious for that and other reasons. If its cluttered and
disorganized style made it difficult for people to read, its content and its scope
were a tour de force. Some theorists still consider it America's best if not its only
contribution to political philosophy. In its day, it received accolades from some
of John's contemporaries. Jefferson wrote to congratulate him. "I have read
your book with infinite satisfaction and improvement. It will do great good in
America."

There were, as well, harsh critics, mainly because of two controversial ideas.
While John argued that the government belonged equally to all the people, he
made the case that not all people are equal. There exists, he asserted, a "natural
aristocracy." His nemesis, Turgot, had maintained that all citizens are equal,
but John asked:

> Are the citizens to be all of the same age, sex, size, strength, stat-
> ure, activity, courage, hardiness, industry, patience, ingenuity, wealth,
> knowledge, fame, wit, temperance, constancy, and wisdom? Was
> there, or will there ever be, a nation, whose individuals were all
> equal, in natural and acquired qualities, in virtues, talents, and
> riches?

He responded to his own question: "The answer of all of mankind must be
in the negative." This "natural order," he maintained, derived not through he-
redity. "We cannot presume that a man is good or bad, merely because his
father was one or the other." It comes into being because of industry, birth,
wealth, stature, genius, luck, a host of advantages, and

> it forms a body of men which contains the greatest collection of
> virtues and abilities in a free government, is the brightest ornament
> and glory of the nation, and may always be made the greatest bless-
> ing of society, if it be judiciously managed in the constitution. But
> if this be not done, it is always the most dangerous; nay, it may be
> added, it never fails to be the destruction of the commonwealth.

He believed that if left to rule alone in a one-house legislature, this talented
minority would become tyrannical. The remedy to a potential imbalance of
power was a second house of the legislature, which would represent the "masses"
of citizens, who would prevent the rise of abusive power in the other house. But
the "masses" could not be trusted alone either; they, too, could descend into
tyranny if left unchecked. Two houses would prevent each other from gaining
excess power. Effectively, John argued for the same two-house legislature that
the Constitutional Convention of 1787 created, but he justified it for different
reasons.

The compromises that the men in Philadelphia achieved had more to do with
balancing power between the small states and the large, the South and the
North, the slave states and the free. John worried about different excesses,
those among social classes. His term "natural aristocracy" was used by his opponents to paint him as an advocate of conservative European values, which he
was not. America, his detractors asserted, was unique in having no social
classes, and they believed that none would develop. James Madison, a rising
star in the political arena, told Jefferson that there was nothing new in the *Defence,* and that men of taste would find much to criticize.

Likewise, John's proposal for a strong executive, a "monarchical element,"
he most unfortunately called it, evoked the same response for the same reason.

He chose language that some at home interpreted as tainted by his affection for European institutions. John advocated a strong executive to balance legislative power, as well as to mediate between the two legislative bodies in times of conflict. Again, his language was misinterpreted to suggest that he recommended a king. His detractors argued that he had been away too long, and the contagion of Old World political traditions had affected him. He was accused of being antidemocratic.

In fact, John's political views had been remarkably consistent. He wrote within the framework of his Puritan New England past, an ethos that he inherited. His early suspicions about human nature, demonstrated by his continuous berating of his own weaknesses, suffuses his early diary. He dreaded his own impulses—ambition, jealousy, covetousness, indolence—because they represented the human condition that he struggled to overcome.

Just as he yearned for balance in his own soul, he created a blueprint for balance in the body politic. People created governments to secure collective order for the discord caused by their disordered natures. The old Puritan notions of covenant and duty were modernized in the *Defence*. They became a prescription for balancing governance of the nation, reflecting the balance he struggled to achieve within himself.

His detractors failed to see the balance, either in the prescription for government he set forth in the *Defence* or in his character. In both cases, his bold ideas were too often expressed in the wrong language or too plain language. To Adams the political theorist, this mattered less than it did to Adams the politician. As a theorist, he received criticism; this was troublesome to a man of sensitive yet pugnacious character, but not damaging. As a politician he was subjected to subterfuge and disloyalty. His best support, both as a theorist and as a politician, was Abigail.

WHILE JOHN WROTE THE *DEFENCE*, HE ENCOURAGED ABIGAIL to travel without him. Not long after her daughter's marriage, she had been afflicted with one of her mysterious illnesses. Initially she diagnosed her malady as rheumatism, but her English doctor suggested that she was suffering from a "Billious complaint." For therapy, Dr. Jeffries suggested that she visit Bath, the health spa and resort, where she could take the waters and rest. John declined to accompany her, she informed John Quincy, because the printers were waiting for his book, but he urged Abigail to go, accompanied by her daughter and son-in-law.

From Bath, she wrote to John, worried about leaving him alone. It was a measure of their lifelong consideration of each other that they consistently expressed concern about each other's well-being. She gave the spa mixed reviews: The town, she observed, was a resort "not only for the infirm, but for the gay, the indolent, the curious, the gambler, the fortune-hunter and even the girl from the country who came *out of wonteness*. It is one constant scene of disippation and gambling." By now accustomed to European social life, she was less appalled than amused. "Tho I sometimes like to mix in the gay world," Abigail confessed to her sister Mary, "I have much reason to be grateful to my parents that my early education gave me not an habitual taste for what is termed fashionable life."

She described her schedule to John: "We have been to 3 Balls one concert one play, two private parties, to the publik walk . . . and a Ball tomorrow Evening." And she concluded that "having visited Bath once I am satisfied as you have no fancy for that which makes it so delightful to most people. I do not wonder that you preferred building up Republics and establishing governments."

John took time from republic building to write to Abigail, reassuring her that he was well. "Dont be solicitous about me. I shall do very well—if I am cold in the night, and an additional quantity of Bed Cloaths will not answer the purpose of warming, I will take a Virgin to bed with me. Ay a Virgin—What? Oh Awful! What do [she] read?"

He teased her, just as he had teased her during their courtship years:

> Dont be Surprized—Do you know what a Virgin is? Mr. Bridget brought me acquainted with it this Morning. It is a Stone Bottle, Such as you buy with Spruce Beer and Spa Water, filled with Boiling Water, covered over and wrapped up in flannel and laid at a Mans Feet in Bed.—An Old Man you see may comfort himself with Such a Virgin . . . and not give the least Jealousy even to his Wife, the smallest grief to his Children or any Scandal to the World.

Abigail's frail health persisted in the summer of 1787, so partly by prescription of her doctor and partly out of curiosity, she and John set out on an extended trip through Devon. Since Colonel Smith had been dispatched to Portugal to conduct some diplomatic business, Nabby with her infant son accompanied her parents.

The party traveled by coach, drawn by four horses, in easy stages, resting frequently for meals, lodging at quaint and comfortable inns in small villages. They paused at Winchester to see the great cathedral. Abigail discovered that the first earl of Winchester, who signed the Magna Carta, had been her own maternal ancestor. Her curiosity piqued, she wrote to her sister Mary, recalling that as a child she had seen a genealogical chart in the home of her Grandmother Quincy bearing the name of Saer de Quincy, Earl of Winchester. She wondered if it still survived. "Can it be wondered at that I should wish to trace an ancestor amongst the signers of Magna Charta?"

Southampton, Abigail discovered, was a "bathing place." She wrote, "I tried the experiment," and she was thrilled. She recommended swimming, noting that "it would be delightful in our warm weather . . . if such conveniences were erected in Boston, Braintree, and Weymouth." She meant the complicated contraptions that had become popular in Europe in which women could undress, change into swimming attire, and then be transported in seclusion into the water. She described her swim outfit as an "oil-cloth cap, a flannel gown, and socks for the feet."

She wrote to Elizabeth that the visit to Devonshire was "like a garden and the cultivation scarcely admits any other improvement." However, she continued:

> I wish I could say as much for the inhabitants, but whilst one part
> of the people, the noble and wealthy, fare sumptiously every day,
> poverty, hunger, and nakedness is the lot and portion of the needy
> peasantry. . . . The most industrious of them are stinted to 6 pence
> per day feeding themselves from that pittance. Youth and age feel
> the extremes of misery. Their cottages and miserable huts astonished me.

Living in France and England had provided Abigail a larger perspective for evaluating her own country. "When I reflect upon the advantages which the people possess in America . . . the ease with which property is obtained, the plenty which is so equally distributed, the personal liberty and security of life and property, I feel grateful to heaven who marked out my Lot in that Happy Land."

Abigail's already passionate American patriotism was inflated by her observations, and conditions in England and France reaffirmed her social consciousness and her politics. America, she wrote, was exceptional.

News from home arrived from a variety of sources. John Quincy now lived with the Shaws in Haverhill, joining his two younger brothers, who already lived with Aunt Elizabeth Shaw and her husband, the Reverend John Shaw. Shaw became "preceptor" to all three of the boys, and Elizabeth had reassured Abigail that she took the same good care of them "that I think you would." She wrote that "Thomas is a very good child," and he "does not want for fondling over because you are absent." Charles had been accepted at Harvard. John Quincy prepared to enter Harvard as an upper-division student, which required that he learn more mathematics. That he did and entered the following year, rooming with his cousin Billy Cranch, son of Mary and Richard.

Mary visited John Quincy at Harvard and reported that "He Was well and quite a gallant among the Ladies," surprising news because everyone complained that John Quincy was studying too hard and neglecting both his health and his appearance. Probably he spruced up for a visit from his aunt. "Cousin Tom is a great favorite," Mary continued. "We cannot be thankful enough my dear Sister that our children are such as they are. Cousin Charles is a lovely creature. He is so amiable and so attentive that he will be beloved wherever he sets his Foot."

Sometimes painful news arrived from home. Two of Abigail's aunts, Elizabeth Smith and Lucy Tufts, died while she was abroad, as did her father's only brother, Isaac Smith. Abigail grieved the losses. "I loved her like a parent," she wrote of Aunt Elizabeth Smith. Most distressing, however, was news that her brother, William, had died. Younger than herself, he had long been the family black sheep, abandoning his wife and children before the Revolution and disappearing from their lives for long periods. William Smith was described as an alcoholic, and from the few remaining accounts, his life was irregular.

When William died of jaundice in September 1787, his sisters informed Abigail. Elizabeth Shaw reflected on the irony that baffled them: "The same air *we* breathed, the same cradle rocked us to rest—and the same parental arms folded us to their fond bosoms." They could not explain what had gone wrong in William's life. Rather than condemn the lost brother, the family wrote compassionately of Smith's misfortunes, mingling sympathy with hope for his redemption.

In contrast, Abigail responded with high emotions to the glowing reports of the Harvard Commencement of 1787, for John Quincy graduated at the top of his class and consequently had been selected to read an oration at the ceremony. Expressing her keen disappointment at missing yet another milestone in her son's life, she wrote on the day of the graduation, "I give you joy of the day as I presume it is commencement with you at Cambridge, and as it is about 4 o'clock in the afternoon, I imagine you have passed thru your performance."

The political situation at home came to life through the family letters, especially difficulties in their state. Both Mary and Elizabeth informed Abigail about Shays's Rebellion, and both criticized the "deluded farmers." Because the state representatives hadn't been paid for three years, Mary's husband, Richard, who had served loyally, resigned his position to take up his old craft of watchmaking. In the lives of all of the family members, politics were personal.

Abigail, in return, wrote about the conditions abroad, including John's mission. Because of their secret nature, she added: "You will consider some parts of my politics as confidential," which meant John told her sensitive stories. And even though she thrived on politics, she sensed that these topics were an inappropriate topic for a woman. To Uncle Tufts she explained, "Excuse my being so busy in *politics* but I am so connected with them that I cannot avoid being much interested." And to John Quincy she finally expressed exasperation: "Begone Politicks! I hate you, did not I say I would not speak of you."

Dr. Cotton Tufts, Abigail's uncle and the local physician, was the caretaker of their financial interests. Abigail had given him power of attorney to pay their taxes, oversee their investments, and conduct business, which had proved no small assignment. Knowing the Adamses' interest in acquiring property, Tufts kept an eye out for possibilities as they arose. Abigail alerted him to the potential of the Borland house, which Royall Tyler had purchased. If it should come on the market, she advised Tufts, "Mr A would wish to purchase it." By that she meant that *she* would wish to purchase it. Most often when she deferred to John, it was a formality based on custom. The primary consultations about family finances took place between Abigail and her uncle Tufts.

Meanwhile, negotiations for their return dragged on, but Abigail was making plans. She wrote to Mercy, "I long my dear Madam to return to my native land. My little cottage encompassed by my friends has more charms for me than the drawing rooms at St. James." Mary Cranch on the other hand realized that after living in mansions, "You never can live in that house when you return. It is not large enough for you." Abigail did not need to be persuaded by her relatives, and already through the agency of her uncle Tufts negotiated the purchase of a larger home in Braintree.

By the beginning of 1788, Abigail wrote her uncle that they had arranged passage "to come with Capt. Callahan," but confided that the prospect of another sea journey didn't appeal: "I could wish that I had not the ocean to encounter." Still, her plans could be disrupted, because Congress had not yet issued formal recalls to John from his posts, a necessary protocol before they could depart. John served as minister not just in England but also in Holland. "He has asked Congress to write letters of recall" but received in return only a "leave of absence."

In early March, John went to Holland to officially conclude his mission, but there he found a surprise. Abigail had told Thomas Jefferson of John's trip, and Jefferson hastened to Holland to prevail upon John to negotiate one last loan. "This delay is very painful to me and you must blame yourself for it altogether," John complained to Abigail, perhaps not seriously. He stayed for three weeks in

Amsterdam, writing triumphantly at the end that the loan had been successfully concluded: "Remember, it is all your own intrigue," he groused. "I suppose you will boast of it as a great public service." An unrepentant Abigail returned: "I rejoice in the idea of your having met again [with Jefferson] before you leave Europe."

In John's absence, Abigail began to close their household on Grosvenor Square. She complained that the packing was a "much more laborious piece of business than I had imagined and takes much more time." Finally, at the end of March she declared the job done and told John that she had gone back to the Bath Hotel, where they had stayed three years earlier. "I came here to this hotel last Monday evening that the beds and furniture might be sent on board and the house given up." Unlike her departure from Paris, she expressed no loss or disappointment, because they were going home.

News had arrived from New York that the Constitution had been ratified by seven states and that two more were imminent; New Hampshire was sitting as was New York. The new Constitution, she informed John, would be in effect at the beginning of the New Year. "My dear friend," she wrote "I think we shall return to our country at a very important period and with more pleasing prospects opening for her than the turbulent scenes which Massachusettes not long since presented. May wisdom govern her course and justice direct her operation." And she signed off, "Adieu and believe me ever yours."

Together, the Adamses departed from England on Sunday, April 20, 1788, on board the merchant ship *Lucretia,* closing a chapter in their history with some satisfaction and facing their next with heartfelt curiosity and guarded feelings of hope.

The Most Insignificant Office

THE ADAMSES' HOMECOMING TO BOSTON "AFTER A VERY TE-dious passage of eight weeks and two days" contrasted mightily with their exhausting journey. Governor John Hancock had arranged for a heroes' welcome. In a classic understatement Abigail later informed their daughter that they met with a "gracious reception." A discharge of cannon from the fortress at Castle Island had marked the passage of their ship into the harbor, and huzzas from the crowd of thousands that lined the streets of Boston along their carriage route to the governor's mansion greeted them. Weary and overwhelmed, they slipped away as quickly and quietly as they could to Braintree, where they lodged with the Cranches for a few days before moving into their new home, which had been purchased while they were in London.

For days and weeks, old friends and relatives dropped by to greet them. Their three sons, John Quincy, Charles, and Thomas, came to Braintree, and, excepting their daughter, who had returned with her husband and child to his home on Long Island to live, the Adams family was reunited. The Shaws, Elizabeth, her husband, John, and their children, arrived from Haverhill. Every hour was filled by visits from neighbors, who congratulated their now famous local residents, "His Excellency, the Ambassador and his Lady." It was more than a month before either of them had the time to register their reactions to being home by writing to Nabby.

Abigail described her dismay with the house. After the spacious abodes that

Peacefield. "You cannot live in your old house," Abigail's sister Mary informed her. It would be too small and too inappropriate after their years abroad. John named their new home, built in 1731, Peacefield, but often he referred to it as Monticito ("little hill"), as opposed to Jefferson's Monticello ("little mountain"). Courtesy of the Adams National Historical Park.

they had lived in both in Paris and in London, the new dwelling seemed more like a "wren's house," with ceilings so low that Colonel Smith would need to take care not to bump his head. Further, "the Garden was a wilderness & the House a mere Barrack." They had already plunged into repairs. "Your Pappa," she continued, "is Employd in Building Stone wall and Diging ditches." She had become more "reconciled to the spot than I was at first, but we must build in the Spring an other kitchen a dairy room & a Library." Her servants were ill, but John had already engaged "ten laboring men in a day." The Adamses did not have time to properly adjust to their new situation but rather immediately set to work in their former pattern of living in Braintree, John on his farmland and Abigail fixing up their house.

People had changed, none more than Richard Cranch, who appeared, to have aged more than ten years. Cousin Lucy, a girl when Abigail departed, was engaged to marry. "Mr Wibird like most old Batchelors is become nearly useless and fears his own Shadow." John, after not seeing his youngest sons, Charles and Thomas, for nearly a decade or John Quincy for three years, reported that each had grown into adulthood. The latter, now studying law with an attorney in Newburyport, pleased him greatly: "There is not a youth of his age whose reputation is higher for abilities, or whose character is fairer in point of morals or conduct," John boasted to Nabby. "The youngest is as fine a youth as either of the three, if a spice of fun in his composition should not lead him astray," he wrote of Thomas, just matriculated at Harvard, whom he had last seen at the age of six. "Charles wins the heart, as usual," he wrote, "and is the most of a gentleman of them all." John was clearly pleased.

Since Colonel Smith, Nabby's husband, was part of the family, John offered an assessment about his future as well. No longer a soldier or diplomat, Smith had his future to consider, and for the same reasons that he advised all of his sons to follow in his footsteps, John recommended law to his son-in-law. "In my opinion, [the law] is the most independent place on earth." He meant that lawyers did not have to work for other people.

John worried about his children's future. And for good reason. He had returned to a state and a community where many people struggled with the financial crises that afflicted the new nation. The economy had been very good for a few enterprising people, but it had impoverished many of his formerly affluent or even comfortable friends. Among them were the Cranches. So, too, the fortunes of the Warrens had declined. With his own future uncertain and his income invested in his farms, John could not ensure the providence of his family by means other than advice, and that troubled him. He had sacrificed his best years of earning to service of his country and did not have the capacity to provide for his children's future, so he recommended that they follow the route he had deserted.

For the first time in her life, Nabby lived a great distance from her parents' home, a situation that they all lamented. She and Colonel Smith had received nearly the same gala reception in New York that Abigail and John had in Boston. The Continental Congress sat in New York, which made that city the political center of the nation, and undoubtedly as a show of respect for the senior Adamses, the Smiths were fêted by Governor and Mrs. Clinton ("Mrs. Clinton is not a showy, but a kind, friendly woman") and General and Mrs. Knox ("Her size is enormous; I am frightened when I look at her"). Nabby reported that "every body is looking forward to the establishment of the new Constitution" but that she foresaw difficulties in its acceptance that would have dire consequences for the continued union of states. "There are very few who have not personal aggrandizement in View," Nabby wrote, echoing the familiar skepticism of both her parents, "and there are so many little causes intermingled with the really important, that I begin to think that disinterestedness is a word not to be found in the modern vocabulary." At the same time, she mentioned that among many respected persons, it was suggested that John Adams "must come and be President next year."

JOHN WAS NOT UNMINDFUL OF THE RUMORS THAT WERE CIRCU-lating about his role in the new government. He believed it unlikely that any person other than General Washington would be tapped for the presidency. Another rumor suggested that he might become governor of Massachusetts, the place currently occupied by John Hancock. Prior to his arrival home, John had been elected as a Massachusetts delegate to the Continental Congress, a position that he considered beneath his stature and that he never filled. In response to Nabby's comment about the presidency, then, he wrote: "You may be anxious, too, to know what is to become of me." At his age, he continued—he was now fifty-three—"this ought not to be a question; but it is." He lamented "in strict confidence" that after all of his years abroad, he had "got quite out of circulation." Other men, who had remained in the public purview, were being considered for the only posts he would accept. The options he envisioned were "private life at home, or to go again abroad. The latter is the worst of the two." He concluded, whimsically, that he could not see himself as an agent in the East Indies or Surinam.

It was too soon after his arrival home, however, for John or anyone else to predict his future. For the time being he was content to immerse himself in farming enterprises, mending fences, collecting manure, purchasing cows for a planned dairy, and imbibing the air and the atmosphere of his beloved blue hills at Braintree. In a sense, he had become a stranger to the place he cared for most. His soul required that his body reengage with the land and the people, and he left plans for the future in suspension.

Eleven states had ratified the new constitution by mid-August. Nabby's location in New York allowed her to observe and comment presciently about the increasing political tempers in the capital city. Most problematic, she wrote to her mother, was the rise of "party cabals." It had become "a matter of party, *totally*," she complained. She had dined in a large company of senators, she wrote, and "had you been present, you would have trembled for your country, to have *seen* and *heard* and *observed*, the men who compose its rulers. They were different from the patriots of the past. "To what a state this country is approaching, I don't know; time only can determine."

Nabby also informed her father that her husband had decided against the profession of law. "At the bar there are so many persons already established," and who were already well known, that it would be too difficult for him to make his mark in the field. Besides, Colonel Smith was breathing the heady air of high office and high intrigue that circulated in New York. His sights were set on elevated stations. A new government was forming, and he planned to benefit from his contacts among the ranks of the founders. His wife, on the other hand, in true Adams form, wrote to her brother John Quincy that already she was tired of "the subject of Federal or antefederal." Her observation of the intrigues in the capital convinced her that "it is a most important and critical era in the fate of our Country."

Summer passed into fall, and the politics of forming a new government remained central to the discussions among the Adams family and friends. "The happiness of our family seems ever to have been so interwoven with the Politicks of our Country as to be in a great degree dependent upon them," Nabby wrote to John Quincy at the end of September. Everyone expected John to hold office in the new government. The talk now was that he would become vice president or perhaps chief justice. Still perplexed about his future, John thought about returning to law practice, should a government position be offered to him that he didn't want.

Meanwhile, the transition from the authority of the current government to the new constitutional administration was in process. The change meant that the existing single-house legislature, the Continental Congress, would be transformed into two houses, a Senate and a House of Representatives. Fall elections were taking place in the states, and the results were coming in. Caleb Strong and Tristram Dalton were elected to the Senate from Massachusetts; Pennsylvania elected Robert Morris and William Maclay. Nabby, sounding more like an Adams than ever, described to John Quincy her observation of the electoral process: "If you can be of service to me in promoting my views, I will give you my assistance in yours." She added that fear more than approval controlled the entire apparatus of voting. Contrary to the best hopes of many of the founders, including John Adams, political factions had developed and there was great infighting.

Tensions between the groups who had approved or disapproved of the new Constitution, the Federalists and the Anti-Federalists, lingered into the election campaigns for Congress and further into the newly devised system of electioneering for the executive branch. The electoral college, as established by the Constitution, would stand between the voters and the presidential candidates. Each state would devise its own system of assigning electors, who in turn would vote for two candidates, the majority winner of the two becoming the president, and the second person, the vice president. The system was new, and it was unwieldy for many reasons, one being that a tie could reasonably develop for the presidency. The tensions, even the animosities that surfaced that fall as the new government was being created, did not surprise the Adamses. John stayed put in Braintree and expended his energy on his farm. Abigail, whose health had not improved with her return home, decided that she must travel to New York State, where Nabby gave birth that November to her second child, a son, named John Adams Smith. John had chosen not to accompany her to New York to meet his namesake, because he worried that his presence in the capital would be interpreted as campaigning for political office. As Nabby had remarked, among the Adamses, politics was interwoven with family life.

But what made this journey especially difficult for Abigail was that she missed being with John. "I think every Seperation more painfull as I increase in Years," she wrote to him. John's letters to her in return expressed affection in a way that they never had before. "I am my dearest Friend, yours forever," he signed his first note to her. "I am with the tenderest Affection yours," another time, and "Yours with the tenderest Affection." In John's eighteenth-century lexicon, this was uncensored passion. The word *love* was not employed by them to describe their feelings for each other. But *affection* connoted emotions as opposed to reason, and together with *tender,* it expressed the most delicate of emotions, gentle and soft emotions combined with longing, even sexual ardor. The Adamses profoundly missed each other, now that they once again had grown accustomed to companionship. Her need and her duty to be with her daughter at the time of her giving birth was the only reason Abigail could countenance this separation.

She found the Smith residence at Jamaica on Long Island too rural. "This place is much more retired than Braintree," she informed John. Furthermore, it had been a hotbed of Tory sympathy during the war and "some are so still." She also learned more about the political shenanigans taking place in the capital from Colonel Smith, who attended his "club" once each week in New York City, where he rubbed elbows with Alexander Hamilton. Smith reported that Hamilton showed him a letter from James Madison, affirming that Virginia would cast its vice presidential ballot for Adams. Behind the scenes, it would become apparent much later that Hamilton had campaigned against Adams, and only when it appeared possible that Governor Clinton of New York, a man he sincerely hated, might win that office did he shift his influence to Adams. Too late, though, for Clinton's candidacy severely cut into Adams's electoral margin. New York, it was clear, was abuzz with politicking.

John, meanwhile, at home in Braintree, resisted every effort of Mary Cranch to entertain him in Abigail's absence. He remained content to sit by his fire with books and papers spread out around him. For Thanksgiving, he turned down her invitation in order to dine with his mother and brother, explaining "he was sure it would be the last that his kind Parent would ever keep with him." Mary also spilled the beans to Abigail: "I call'd upon Mr. Adams yesterday," she wrote, "and found him looking with great pleasure upon 15 head of young Heifers which he had just purchas'd." He was determined to run a dairy farm, despite the fact that their financial situation and future residence were uncertain.

BY APRIL, THE NEW CONGRESS HAD ASSEMBLED A QUORUM IN New York and begun to count the electoral votes. Predictably, General Washington was unanimously elected president, but John just squeaked through to receive a plurality of votes for the vice presidency. Disappointing as this was to him, he accepted the position and within a few days departed for New York. He did not learn until much later how Hamilton's intrigues had affected the voting. Hamilton did not have a personal grievance with Adams—yet—but he did fear

George Washington took the oath as first president on the portico of the newly renovated Federal Hall in New York City, as shown in this painting from 1790 by Amos Doolittle. Crowds attended the inauguration, establishing the precedent for this ceremony as a public event. Courtesy of the Library of Congress.

him as a powerful rival for leadership of the Federalist party. Not until it became clear that his maneuverings would backfire did Hamilton shift his support back to Adams.

Nevertheless, along the entire route from Boston to New York, John was celebrated. Happily arrived in New York City, he wrote that the House of Representatives had voted to keep their proceedings open to the public, which reassured him that democracy was functioning. The Senate still met behind closed doors, just as it did during the Revolution. These gestures were among the first of multitudes of decisions that the new Congress would have to make in the years to come, establishing the traditions by which it would operate. It was also an omen of some of John's upcoming difficulties.

Abigail had not accompanied John to New York, partly because she had just returned from her arduous round trip and partly because she had so many responsibilities at home. They had agreed that she would join him later.

In a simple ceremony on April 21 at the new Federal Building in New York, John was presented to the Senate as its new president and as vice president of the United States. He then took his seat under a canopy of red damask at the head of the large room that was the Senate chamber. Situated on the second floor of the building, the room measured forty by thirty feet and was two stories in height. The building had recently been renovated to accommodate the new government, but formerly it had been New York's city hall. When the Continental Congress named the city as the nation's temporary capital, the city fathers hired Pierre L'Enfant, a young architect much admired by George Washington, to draw up plans for the renovation. It became the grandest building in the city.

The renovations were, to borrow a word, "revolutionary." Done in the new Federal style, the hall boasted an exterior three stories tall, topped by the original cupola that, unfortunately, did not match the elegance of its new façade. Most striking about the new building were the two stories of columns that culminated in a pediment "on which a large eagle, surrounded with a glory, appears bursting from a cloud, and carrying thirteen arrows, and the arms of the United States." Beneath this pediment and extending out from the Senate chamber on the second floor was the balcony where George Washington would soon take his oath of office. The chamber within had been refurbished as elegantly as the exterior with pilasters and wainscoting, a richly decorative carpet, and "curtains of crimson damask." Twenty-two desks were arranged in a semicircle around John's presidential chair, which was slightly elevated. A larger, though equally elegant House of Representatives chamber occupied much of the ground floor of the building, which was located at the intersection of Wall and Broad streets.

New York was, according to the census of 1790, the nation's largest city with a population of about 33,000 people. Its business center existed primarily south of Wall Street, although venturesome and enterprising people were flooding into Greenwich Village and New Haarlem to the north. Across the East River, Brooklyn was still a summer resort for those who could afford to escape the heat of the city. It was a helter-skelter city in many respects and unique among the cities of America. Its population was more heterogeneous; it streets, many of which had been mere mud alleys but a half-century earlier, were arranged in no particular order, a relic that survives into the present. It was crowded as no other city at the time, being an island between two great rivers, the mighty Hudson and the East River, which provided commercial waterways to the north and the west for trade from the bustling harbors. Its panoply of streets were covered with cobblestone, and to either side were buildings reminiscent of the city's Dutch past, buildings made of brick to resist the continual risk of fire, covered with the stepped roofs of Holland, sitting so close together that they appeared sometimes to be leaning against one another. Buildings often housed businesses on the ground floor and were occupied as residences above. New York, at the end of the eighteenth century, could boast fire departments, public schools, and the King's College, later Columbia University. It was a metropolis, and its pride was its new Federal Building.

Twenty-two senators attended the simple ceremony at which John Adams took his seat as the new president of the upper body of Congress. Two states, North Carolina and Rhode Island, had not yet ratified the Constitution and would not send representatives until the following year. And it was during his first day in attendance at the Senate that John Adams delivered his inaugural address. Abigail, seeing it reprinted in the Boston newspapers, found it "courtly and masterly in stile." It was "exactly what it ought to be, neither giving too little, or too much." She was his loyal critic. John's words were appropriately chosen.

He acknowledged his emotion upon seeing "so many of those characters, of whose virtuous exertions I have so often been a witness," noting that their examples had so often inspired him and their friendships had supported him. He praised George Washington as one "whose portrait I shall not presume to draw." Then, after a few more paragraphs of praise for the senators, the representatives, and the president, he turned to his duties.

John reassured his audience that he realized that in his role as presiding officer he should not interfere in their deliberations, but he acknowledged: "Not wholly without experience in public assemblies, I have been more accustomed to take a share in their debates, than to preside in their deliberations." He promised them, however, that "It shall be my constant endeavor to behave toward every member of this most honorable body with all that consideration, delicacy and decorum, which becomes the dignity of his station and character." John knew himself well.

"The eyes of the world are upon you," he said, paraphrasing John Winthrop, alluding to the awesomeness of their mission as analogous to that of their Puritan forebears. The nation expects from these bodies "prosperity, order, justice, peace, and liberty." In a brief five words, John precisely defined the purpose of government. And he concluded with a blessing: "May God Almighty's providence assist you to answer their expectations."

If John got off to an impressive start with his elegant address, the next days, weeks, and months were more difficult. Precedents were being established for the functioning of the Senate and at such a basic level that it is, these years later, hard to regard some of these issues as more than trivial. But they were not to these founders. They were of vital concern for the correct operation of government and were hotly deliberated. The first question introduced into the new Senate was the matter of how to deliver messages to the House of Representatives. Fortunately, there was little disagreement over the method of sending them by way of the secretary of the Senate. Should he bow upon entering the chamber? Should he bow once or twice? Here was a question of principle, and after deliberation it was decided that in a republic, the bow was an inappropriate sign of aristocratic deference.

The next issue, which appears innocuous, was not to the participants. It related to greeting the new president. John fretted greatly over this issue, and his response got him off to a bad start in the government. President Washington was soon to a deliver his first address to the Congress. John would introduce him. How to perform this role? Should the congressmen sit or stand when the chief executive entered the room? When he read his address? And of great import: How should he be addressed? Here, indeed, was a conundrum, and it occupied many hours of acrimonious debate. At first, John appointed a Senate committee to decide, and that committee came back with the recommendation: "His Highness the President of the United States." The House would have none of that exalted tone and returned with the simple, if "republican" recommendation: "President of the United States." At this point John Adams entered the debate, performing one of the greatest blunders of his political career. "Mr. Adams, the Vice President, (this being the second day after his installation as President of the Senate)," recorded William Maclay, the outspoken, even curmudgeonly senator from western Pennsylvania, in the only written documentation of the Senate's early years, "addressed the Senate in favor of titles."

Indeed, John Adams did argue for imposing titles not just for the president and vice president but for all elected officials, and perhaps some appointed officials.

From this misstep he has had little historical recovery; it branded him a royalist, an elitist, and a European-style aristocrat. John hardly meant to stir up this hornet's nest; nor did he exactly wish to promote elitism. Two things especially inspired his (minority) opinion. He had just returned from Europe, where titles were a matter of course and set magistrates apart from their constituencies. Every government, to his knowledge, used titles. If America was to function as an equal among nations, if Americans were to be respected by other nations, it should observe this practice. It was that simple.

Titles would help to insure the country's survival by symbolizing the authority of those people in power. Titles would bring respect to government. This was John's reasoning. He also, of course, had already the reputation as a monarchist, and so his proposal to call the chief executive "His Excellency" only served to reinforce it. It was, in fact, the butt of some humor. Behind his back, his enemies referred to him as "His Rotundity."

John's transgressions went further. He had not controlled his impulse to enter the debate. He had, in fact, not only interfered with the discussion, he had lectured the lawmakers. From that time, almost anything he said had its detractors. Maclay recorded with malicious delight: "A solemn silence ensued. God forgive me, for it was involuntary, but the profane muscles of my face were in tune for laughter." Nor was the hilarity of it lost on others; Oliver Ellsworth observed: "Wherever the Senate is to be, there, sir, you must be at the head of them," and added that his title elsewhere was of no concern.

John's awkwardness in this, his first political office in the new government, perplexed his allies and delighted his enemies. Clearly, he felt overwhelmed by the protocols of a position he would later refer to as "the most insignificant office that ever the Invention of Man contrived or his Imagination conceived." For one thing, he was accustomed to participating in the debate and he was frustrated by exclusion when issues of interest and importance arose. More than this, however, he seems not to have been aware of the ludicrous figure he cut. In an effort to act in a role for which he had no rehearsal, he did a caricature of himself that fulfilled the expectations of his detractors. From his earliest youth, he had sketched the figure of a successful man as dignified. Now that he appeared in that role, rather than as a pugilist in the trenches of congressional debate, now that his passions were under lock and key, and he needed to present himself as a mere figurehead, he became not just anxious but overwrought. Perhaps it was his hurt, because of the small majority that had elected him to office. Perhaps he was trying too hard to be likeable and in the process made himself ridiculous. Or perhaps he was just being honest before a crowd of mostly disingenuous politicians.

George Washington had dignity. The pageantry that marked his arrival in New York City on April 23 matched his reputation. A decorative barge ferried him across the river from New Jersey after an eight-day journey. Crowds, hundreds and thousands of citizens, had heaped tribute in every city, town, and village along his route, forcing him in some instances to leave his carriage and mount a noble steed, thus showing off his horsemanship and his stature, and reinforcing his image as the man whom the framers of the Constitution had in mind when establishing the executive office in article 2. One week later, on the thirtieth, he took the oath of office as first president of the United States of America, the title Congress had agreed upon.

The inauguration itself was a simple ceremony. Both houses of Congress assembled in the Senate chamber before the president arrived, escorted by three senators. The president sat, and John Adams arose to say that it was time to take the oath of office. So agitated was Adams that he forgot most of his little speech. He then bowed, and the "President was conducted out of the middle window into the gallery," where the oath of office was administered in front of the citizenry. Another custom was established by this ceremony. The oath of office would be taken publicly. The crowd cheered, the president bowed to them, and the crowd cheered again. Then, led by President Washington, Congress filed back into the Senate chamber, where they sat while the president delivered his inaugural address.

Fisher Ames, a new representative from Massachusetts, described his elation with the inauguration ceremony and address. "It was a touching scene, and quite solemn kind. His aspect, grave, almost to sadness; his modesty, actually shaking," he wrote, "produced emotions of the most affection kind upon the members." The day concluded with brilliant fireworks and feasting late into the evening.

Overshadowed by the president and lonely in New York, John nevertheless rose to the occasion and reported to Abigail: "Yesterday the President was Sworn, amidst the Acclamations of the People." He added that "the President has received me with great Cordiality, of affection and confidence." Washington was a gentleman. "Every Thing has gone very agreeably," he wrote, adding, "His Lady is expected this Month."

Two weeks later, after several more bruisings in the Senate, however, John wrote differently to Abigail: "I have taken an House, and now wish you to come on, as soon as possible." He told her that Charles and perhaps Thomas should come with her. He had given her no hint of his troubles, but certainly she must have read into this surprising demand a hint that all was not perfectly well with John in his new office. The next day he changed his mind about disrupting

Thomas's life: "If you I think it best, leave Thomas at College, but I pray you to come on with Charles, as soon as possible." Later he wrote, "I have as many difficulties here, as you can have; public and private." John needed Abigail. She would be there in three weeks, she responded. More than that, he wanted his whole family around him. He invited "Col Smith and his Family and Furniture into the House with us." Fortunately, the home that John had rented, called Richmond Hill, was a large, stately house and could accommodate the Adamses, including Charles and Abigail's niece Louisa, as well as the Smiths and a fleet of servants.

RICHMOND HILL WAS LOCATED ON A BLUFF OVERLOOKING THE Hudson River, about a mile north of the city. He had chosen the spot because the city air didn't agree with either him or Abigail but also because it was the right price. The salary for the vice president, which Congress had yet to establish, would be a mere five thousand dollars, from which he had to pay his living expenses. The president's salary, which Washington refused to accept just as he had received no salary for commanding the armies during the Revolution, would be $25,000. Adams absorbed this disparity in the same way that he took all slights to his dignity, and now his pocketbook, by grumbling that it was his lot in life to suffer.

Once settled into her new surroundings, Abigail was happy. She loved the house and its location. "Richmond Hill was situated upon the North River [as the Hudson was called] which communicated with Albany," she wrote to Mary.

The house commanded "a most extensive prospect, on the one side we have a view of the city & of Long Island, the River in Front, Jersy and adjasant Country on the other side." She described the house, room by room, drawing a verbal floor plan for Mary. She further reported that her son Charles's behavior was changed. "C. will not go into any company but such as his Father or col Smith introduces him to. He appears steady and sedate & I hope will continue so—Time and example will prevail over youthfull folly I trust." Clearly, Charles was involved in some incident at Harvard that had alarmed his parents. Now that he was settled among them, they could monitor his activities. In fact, John, still unaware of the machinations that had nearly cost him the vice presidency, had arranged for Charles to study law with one of New York City's top legal minds: Alexander Hamilton.

Having departed from Braintree so suddenly and without regard to a number of family situations, Abigail carefully approached a sensitive topic for Mary: "I know very well that a small Farm must afford you a scanty support and that you are a sufferer from being obliged to receive pay in paper [money]." In a gesture of family loyalty, she offered to pay their debts. Suspecting correctly that Mary, from pride and knowing also that the Adamses were not wealthy, would turn her down, she preempted her sister's protest: "This I consider my self at full liberty to do," she wrote. "Do not talk of obligations. Reverse the matter & then ask yourself if you would not do as much for me?" Duty to one's family was an obligation, perhaps greater, in Abigail's lexicon of values, than duty to the nation. Abigail worried about Mary. And she had another worry:

"I have a favour to request of all my near and intimate Friend's." She worried that in her elevated position, she would cease to behave as an equal among her relatives and friends. She acknowledged that high status had the potential to inflate vanity. Sensitive to the fact that she could not always scrutinize her own behavior, she asked her friends to be sincere with their observations. She wrote this to Mary; she wanted reassurance that her behavior toward those closest to her—to her sisters, who labored to maintain a basic standard of living, to John's brother Peter, a farmer like his father and their close friends—remained consistent. She knew that their circumstances appeared grand. Abigail sought to maintain her local identity in her exalted station.

Indeed, she moved in exalted circles. She had first met President Washington a decade earlier at his encampment in Cambridge, and she was smitten. She was fond of him again, when they met in New York. He asked her if she approved of the "simple manners" in America after having resided in Europe. Everyone, it seems, believed that Abigail—and John, of course—had been spoiled by their diplomatic experiences abroad. Perhaps it was embedded in a peculiar American "inferiority complex," the comparison of domestic ordinariness with the perceived extraordinariness of other nations. Abigail responded to the president that she believed Americans loved their luxuries and mannerisms every bit as much as Europeans. She disapproved of the tendency among the Americans to emulate European extravagance and style. In contrast, she reported to her sister, "Our August President is a singular example of modesty and diffidence. he has a dignity which forbids Familiarity mixed with an easy affability which creates Love and Reverence." Abigail captured Washington's cool dignity.

And she immediately warmed to Martha Washington, who became a friend during the few years when, together, they set the social style of the new government. Nor was this a small issue during the first presidential administration. Even the Senate got involved in the question of how many open houses and dinners the president should schedule each week and who should be invited. As everyone knew, the boundary between social and political events was blurred. How the first wives set the style was important to the perception of the government at home and abroad. Abigail quickly judged that Martha was not pretentious. Like her husband, Abigail ascertained, "Mrs. Washington is one of those unassuming Characters which Create Love & Esteem." Her deportment was "unaffected," her face "pleasant." She gave Martha high marks: "I found myself much more deeply impressed than I ever did before their Majesties of Britain."

One consequence of the Adamses' new status was that many acquaintances expected that they could benefit from John's office. Numerous petitions arrived from their friends, requesting patronage. A number of those requests were addressed to Abigail, even before she had left Braintree. Among them was a letter from her problematic former correspondent James Lovell, written in his typically elliptical style. "I could say twenty Things to you which I would not *dare* to trouble your Husband with," he wrote in paragraph three of nonsensical prattling, and went on to heap contempt upon the number of people whom he knew would "ask for patronage." Typically ironic, he mentioned his candidacy for a position at the port of Boston. Within a barrage of language, he asked her to intercede for him with the vice president. Abigail responded: "Tho' you love a labyrinth you always give a clue," she began, indicating that she had deciphered his code that she would pass on his request. John answered Lovell, as he did all his former acquaintances who petitioned him, that he could not exercise his authority to get patronage positions for them.

Most confounding, and in the long run, one that would have the most consequences for a friendship, was the letter that John received from Mercy Otis Warren, requesting his patronage for her husband and son. In her own way, Mercy, too, wrote in an elliptical style, not so much in an effort to be playful, as did Lovell, but rather because she pressed her case by excoriating the same political partisanship that her letter exhibited. Mercy's plea was that of a sadly embittered patriot. She described the circumstances that had reduced her family to the fringes of party intrigues in Massachusetts: "Gen Warren has unfortunately been the butt of party malice headed by a man (I know you very justly and heartily despise)"—she meant Governor John Hancock.

In fact, James and Mercy Otis Warren had become opponents of the new Constitution. They ranked along with others of John's former Massachusetts colleagues, including Sam Adams and Elbridge Gerry, as Anti-Federalists, fearing strong central government. John Adams had lost patience with the Warrens' political sympathies and ceased to regard them as political allies.

Mercy failed to acknowledge these differences and relied instead upon their former friendship. She went further. She suggested that John had survived the political partisanship that had destroyed her husband's career: "You, my Dear sir, have successfully surmounted all; you have baffled the intrigues of your foes; have reached the acme of applause, and are placed in a situation to do eminent service to your country, to establish your family and to assist most *essentially* your friends." Her husband, on the other hand, had been injured by "enemies," by "intrigues," and by "prejudice." She continued: "And though none of my Family are soliciting, at least I am persuaded you will not forget them at a time when you have it so much in your power to oblige without injustice to yourself, your Family, or your Country." She implied that because of his good luck in surviving political intrigues, he owed assistance to those less fortunate. It could not have been an easy letter for Mercy to write.

John's response could not have gone down well. He saw the disparity in their situations differently. He warmly acknowledged their longtime friendship: "There was no necessity of any apology for writing to me," he affirmed. "There has never been on my part any failure of friendship to Mr. Warren or yourself." However, he wrote, "You are very much mistaken in your opinion of my situation. I have neither reached the acme of applause nor am I in a situation to establish my Family or assist my Friends." He then described the criticism of Mr. Warren that he had heard from "all quarters" since his return to America. He had listened to many reports, and it had become apparent that Warren "did countenance measures that appear to me, as they did to those Friends, extremely pernicious."

John was clearly angry with the Warrens for what he considered their political defection. He regarded their opposition to the Constitution as hostile to the success of the Revolution, just as they regarded Adams's belief in a strong central government as a betrayal of the Revolution. And he was baffled by Mercy's disingenuousness in seeking office for her family in the government they opposed. So with typical bluntness, he wrote: "You are pleased to say, Madam, that you are sure of our Patronage for certain purposes. In the first place, I have no patronage, in the next, neither your children nor my own would be sure of it if I had it." John's response was harsh, but he could not exercise restraint when impassioned. And the Warrens' position as opponents of government stirred his passions. The repercussions of this exchange would not be felt for several years, but Mercy would settle this score in her own way.

The Warrens were not the only people to fear the strength of the new government. Many of those who supported it, and even some who participated in it, were suspicious of power, and no branch of the new government was scrutinized more closely than the executive branch. His stature as commander in chief of the Revolution and his stoic behavior in office shielded George Washington from the strain that existed between the branches. Significantly, he submitted his schedule of public appearances to the Senate for their approval. He came himself to seek "advice and consent" of his first diplomatic venture, a treaty with the Indians of the Southwest. When he suffered a rebuff, he suppressed his irritation and changed his pattern of dealing with Congress. Washington survived the potential tensions between the branches because his reputation made him invincible, but also because he exercised great powers of judgment and wisdom in his dealings with the parties.

John Adams, however, continued to experience the fallout from the tensions between the branches, as well as fractiousness between the parties. In an innocuous effort to craft a polite response to the president's inaugural address, for instance, he used the word *gracious*. A full debate ensued in the Senate over the use of this word, and it was dropped from the final reply that the Senate sent to the president. Some senators believed that the word implied too much deference on the part of the Senate to the executive branch. John was the object, then, by inference of yet another accusation of elitism. Unlike the president, he was sheltered by neither his reputation nor his office.

With time, John learned how to function in his new role. He learned to confine himself to presiding over the chamber and breaking tie votes when necessary. It was a measure of his unflagging sense of duty that he readjusted to this role that ran counter to his character. That he did it, despite the amount of self-control it required, was a measure of his determination to make the new government work. His ideology supported him as well. The new government must rise above parties; by setting the example in his office, perhaps he could expedite the process of unifying the government. So much needed to be done to set this new administration on a sound course that he focused his energies on the challenges and suppressed the little irritants that bruised him. And it's likely that he knew that, if well executed, the vice presidency might be a stepping-stone to higher office.

IN THAT FIRST SESSION OF CONGRESS, WHICH LASTED THROUGH the summer, the executive branch was augmented. No provisions had been established in the Constitution to provide for officials below the top ranks. Major cabinet offices were created and filled by President Washington, who appointed his secretaries with an eye toward representing different states and parties. Not surprising, Alexander Hamilton headed the treasury. Thomas Jefferson, who had not yet returned from France, was appointed to the Office of Foreign Affairs (renamed the State Department), and General Henry Knox continued in his position at the head of the War Department, which he had chaired in the earlier government. The judiciary branch was also shaped, with John Jay of New York serving as the first chief justice in a six-man Supreme Court. Among his other accomplishments of this first challenge to his office, Washington, after Congress recessed in September, visited New England. Having toured the South prior to his inauguration, he traveled through the northern states, symbolizing by his presence that his office represented all sections of the nation.

While other delegates of Congress returned home during the recess between September and January 1790, when the second session would meet, the Adamses remained at their residence in New York. They could not afford the cost of travel and avoided another disruption of their family life. John, however, traveled briefly to Massachusetts, where he proudly joined the president during the celebrations in his home state. When Congress resumed in January, the big battles began over the issues of Hamilton's financial plan for the new nation. At the same time and because of the range of difference between the emerging parties, animosities sharpened, none more so than that between Hamilton and his former ally in support of the Constitution, James Madison.

The major concerns had to do with the tariff and funding the debt. The two issues consolidated the opposition between parties and spilled over into every other topic that was debated, including the location of the capital and foreign policy. Contentiousness was further inflamed because of the French Revolution, which had begun in July. The tariff pitted the manufacturing and financial interests of the cities against the agricultural interests of the rural communities. Hamilton's funding plan was favored by supporters of a strong central government and opposed by the states-rights faction. Finally, the French Revolution divided those who backed France from those who wanted to maintain good relations with England.

The Federalists were Hamilton's supporters and favored a strong central government that would enhance the manufacturing and money interests of the cities, and they favored trade with the English colonies, especially the West Indies, where much of the nation's wealth in trade came from. Madison became suspicious of the same strong government that he had been most instrumental in creating, because as a southerner, he rejected most of the Hamilton program, which strengthened the reach of the national government over the states.

Not only did the two men become fierce adversaries, they became emblematic of developing party rancor. Both, born in the early 1750s, were younger than the revolutionary leaders. Hamilton had been the closest aide to the commander in chief for four years during the war, and the two men had bonded easily. Washington, who had no son, and Hamilton, who had been abandoned in childhood by his father, trusted each other. And Washington, who had trimmed his visibility in Congress during the first session, was content to allow Hamilton to put his face on the administration's plan for financing the new government.

Madison, who was considered the theorist, the man whose ideas about government most effectively shaped the powers that the new government possessed, also grew to fear that power. He further allied with his fellow Virginian Thomas Jefferson, whose enthusiasms for the French Revolution, for states' rights, and for agricultural interests were most in line with his own. The brilliant, gallant, charming, ambitious Alexander Hamilton and the brilliant, shy, almost reclusive, but equally ambitious James Madison were the two faces of the new political parties, the Federalists and the Republicans.

John Adams, who believed that he could rise above party disputes, nevertheless would be drawn into the fray. His disavowal of party preferences was in some cases vacant hope and in other cases made him vulnerable to the machinations of both parties. Political parties, not anticipated, not written into the Constitution, inevitably arose to influence every aspect of government. This sealed Adams's fate not only during the Washington administrations, both of them, but would in good measure sabotage his years in high office and cause the failure of his own administration to win a second term. As much a politician as any of them, Adams was opinionated, combative, and ambitious. Nevertheless, as vice president he suppressed his opinions, his passions, and his ambitions to the role of presiding officer with an occasional opportunity to break tie votes. And President Washington, once he figured out that it was not in his best political interest to ally with Adams, ceased to consult him. They met mostly at the social functions that both were obliged to attend.

Abigail was preoccupied with social obligations. "I have never before been in a situation in which morning noon & afternoon I have been half as much exposed to company," she wrote Mary, describing her days. Clearly, Old World social customs served as models for the new government. "I have proposed to fix a Levey day soon. I have waited for mrs. Washington to begin and she has fix'd on every fryday 8 oclock."

Abigail attended her first levee at the Washington residence, accompanied by Nabby and Charles. Several of the president's aides met them at the door to escort them across the crowded room, where they "respectfully curtsied" to Mrs. Washington. The same aides then conducted the Adams party to seats, where after some time the president approached them "with grace dignity and ease, that leaves Royal George far behind them." The entertainment included "ice creems & Lemonade" during the heat of summer, and in the winter coffee and tea cake were served.

Of course, these gatherings had more than social value. They provided an informal environment in which important business was incidentally accomplished. Politicians could meet and chat in an informal setting. Most important, the president, along with his wife, personified the United States of America before the many communities that attended these events, including his administration, diplomats from foreign states, businessmen, and the local elite. It was one place where women could be present among the men who governed or supported the government. Their presence smoothed social encounters, whether by charmingly engaging men in idle chatter or participating in political talk. In that sense, all social life was merely an extension of political life.

Abigail presided over the Adamses' levees on Thursday evenings. But in addition, she arranged dinner parties for smaller groups, "in the first place all the Senators who had Ladies & families, then the remaining Senators." Next, she began with the members of the House, "and tho we have a room in which we dine 24 persons at a Time, I shall not get through them all, together with the public Ministers for a month to come." Her great dilemma was finding competent servants. "I cannot find a cook in the whole city but what will get drunk." She depended upon Briesler, their majordomo, who had gone with her to France and England, to run her household. "I can no more do without mr Brisler, than a coach could go without wheels or Horses to draw it." The servant dilemma would plague her, too, for as long as John served in high office. "I can get Hands, but what are hands without a Head," she wrote, cursing her situation.

A partisan press had developed that jumped at every opportunity to publicly embarrass the government. Abigail told Mary about the scurrilous articles that appeared on a regular basis and that would only become more damaging in the future. "The News writers will fib—to answer particular purposes," she wrote. In one case, an article described the president's appearance at an event, resplendently wearing "the Eagal most richly set with diamonds at his Button." Yet, she pointed out, the president had been ill at the time and not even present for the event described. Her tribulations with the too "free press" had only begun, and she was wary of them.

In all of her letters to her sisters or absent family members, Abigail discussed the political situation. "I have reason to think," she wrote to Mary in the early fall of 1789, "that Congress will fund the Debt." She meant the controversial part of Hamilton's economic plan that provided for strengthening the government by assuming the state debts at face value and paying for it through an excise tax. The downside for her personally was that the Compromise of 1790 traded the funding of the debt for the location of the new capital city. "I fear they will Remove from this place," she wrote. "Should they go to Philadelphia I do not know how I could possibly live through the voilent Heats." In fact, they did go to Philadelphia.

In exchange for agreeing to funding of the debt, Congress, when it reconvened for its second session in 1790, voted to locate the new capital on the banks of the Potomac on land donated by Virginia. In the interim, the capital would move to Philadelphia for ten years while the new city was under construction. The North, the South, and Pennsylvania, in the short run, would benefit from this compromise. Abigail would not. She loved New York, because of her home at Richmond Hill and because her children lived in her household. Furthermore, she was tired of moving and indeed had much to fear from the climate of Philadelphia. Nevertheless, the deal was done, and she would move. After eighteen months in New York, John found them a home, again located on the outskirts of Philadelphia, called Bush Hill.

Abigail's spirits sank with the prospect of moving again. John's service to the country was costing her great anguish, not just emotionally, but her health suffered as well. She experienced bouts of rheumatism that caused her body to ache all over. In her case, the rheumatism caused fevers as well as severe headaches. She was weary of continuing public service that drained the pleasure from her daily life. She confessed her dejection to Mary: "I feel low spirited and Heartless. I am going amongst an other new set of company to form new acquaintances, to make and receive a hundred ceremonious visits, not one of ten from which I shall derive any pleasure or satisfaction."

While she dreaded the move, she consented to go. She might have resisted, but there is no evidence that she did. She agreed to accompany John because of her loyalty, not loyalty to the nation necessarily—Abigail's patriotic sacrifice had already been tested for too many years—but loyalty to John Adams. It was her duty to be at his side.

However, John Adams could not have been unmindful of her declining health and spirits. How he justified the strain he placed on her by his ambition for public service is more the question. His preceding her to Philadelphia to find a home for them indicates some sensitivity on his part. He, furthermore, took a house outside the city to allay her worries about the heat and noxious "airs" of Philadelphia.

After many years of suffering guilt because of the burden he placed on his family, John was no stranger to that tension. He had created his own myth about the eminent importance of public service that required sacrifices by all of his family members. He had given his best years to his country, and they must live with the same set of values that mandated his rectitude. He never ceased to see his service in other than sacrificial terms. Further, his dedication represented purer virtue, because he received so little acknowledgment. Men like Washington and Franklin, he observed, were regarded as heroes, with praise heaped upon them. Adams, on the other hand, served without public reward. But in Abigail's eyes he was a hero. She shared with him not only his suffering but his view of himself as a martyr. In a sense, their perspective was accurate.

The rest of the Adams family conducted their lives in the shadows of this overarching commitment by their parents to public service. John Quincy had gone into private practice as a lawyer in Boston, living and working out of his parents' house on Court Street. He, true to the Adams spirit, suffered as well. He suffered from lack of business. He suffered from the failure of his first case, reminiscent of his father's first losing case. He suffered because he was frustrated in his pursuit of women, a cause that his parents devoutly warned him against until he was suitably established to support a family. Actually, Abigail did try to promote his alliance with the wealthy Nancy Quincy, but before John Quincy made his move, Nancy married another man.

Charles diligently studied for the law in New York, and his behavior was satisfactory to his parents, even a source of pride, until he became enamored of Sally Smith, Nabby's sister-in-law. Then both Abigail and John discouraged him, pleading with him to wait until he, too, established his practice and could afford a family. Just as John Adams did not propose to Abigail until his law practice thrived, they did not believe that their sons could afford premature marriages.

Thomas had graduated from Harvard without his parents' attendance to hear him deliver an oration, but Mary Cranch loyally substituted for their presence and provided the grand celebration afterward. Thomas's health continued to be a source of concern to Abigail; he had inherited her rheumatism. He joined his parents in New York after graduation and moved with them to Philadelphia, where he, too, began law studies. Abigail wondered if he wouldn't be better off in business, but John's recommendation of law for all his sons prevailed.

Except in one notable case. William Smith, Nabby's husband, had refused to take up the law and was still, these years later, not settled on a productive way of earning a living. When Abigail wrote to Mary that there were "other things I have upon my mind and spirits which I cannot communicate by letter," she probably referred to Smith and his prospects. By this time the Adamses suspected that Smith was not the responsible person that they had at first believed. He gave all appearances of a dandy, a man of good looks, charm, given to boasting about his connections to people of power, but with little direction. He clearly lacked the Adams industriousness. Smith was looking for quick profits, and to the Adamses' dismay, soon after they left New York for Philadelphia, he departed for England, seeking business connections and leaving Nabby alone in New York with their three small children. Confirming their worst fears about him, Smith returned after a few months and asked John to recommend him as the American minister to St. James's, John's former position, which was still not filled. That did not go down well with the recent minister, and he let it be known to his son-in-law—in gentle terms for Nabby's sake.

Family life was not uncomplicated. Nor was Abigail's arrival at Bush Hill. She informed Mary right away about the misnomer. "There remains neither bush nor shrub upon it, and very few trees." Still, it was beautiful, but not "grand and sublime," as had been Richmond Hill. "The Schuylkill is no more like the Hudson, than I to Hercules," she observed wryly. Her furniture had arrived before her, but otherwise there were many inconveniences: "I suppose no fire had been kindled for several years," she wrote, implying that the house was cold, so cold that they had spent their first night at an inn. Once moved in, they began unpacking boxes and beds, but "the cold damp rooms, the new paint, etc, proved almost too much for me." Then Thomas was laid up with a bout of rheumatism, and most of her servants became ill as well. Abigail gave Louisa an emetic, and Polly was twice bled and blistered "on her side." Polly had not been out of her bed since. Abigail, who relied on the most advanced eighteenth-century medical practice, was a great fan of purging and bleeding her patients. Her remedies for others were no worse than she prescribed for herself.

Congress reconvened, with John presiding over the Senate, and continued the still-acrimonious debates about Hamilton's policies, the tariff, and foreign policy. By this time, parties were heatedly aligning either for or against the French Revolution. France had many partisans in this country who saw in its revolution a recapitulation of the American Revolution, in which the people had displaced a despotic monarchy. Despite news of the bloodbath in France, and later the horrific news of the beheading of the king and queen, which the newspapers embellished in graphic detail, people still cheered the Revolution. Men and women both wore the tricolor ribbon, and French flags were displayed from windows throughout Philadelphia.

John Adams was appalled. He observed no similarities in the revolutions. France had no history of democracy. Monarchy and aristocracy would ultimately be replaced by another monarchy and another aristocracy. John did what was natural to him in circumstances where he wanted to speak out and influence opinions. He began a series of articles that appeared weekly in John Fenno's sympathetic *Gazette of the United States*. He threw himself wholeheartedly and unguardedly into the frenzied debate about France. Throughout the articles, which would be collected into a book called *Discourses on Davila*, Adams posited his argument for titles, which he knew would only draw fire from his enemies. But he was determined. "I have run the gauntlet too long among libels, halters, axes, daggers, cannonballs and pistol bullit, in the Service of this people, to be at this age afraid of their injustice," he wrote to his friend John Tudor.

Davila's argument for the use of titles, stemming from man's "passion for distinction," made the case for people of all ranks. He quoted Adam Smith, who suggested that the "horror of poverty" lay not in hunger but in "obscurity." Poor people suffer the indignity of being ignored. "To be wholly overlooked, and to know it, are intolerable." And if poor people cannot look to themselves, then they must look up to another person, whom they consider a hero. Their identification with heroes provided meaning in life. In a complicated set of discourses, John argued that all men, from the highest to the lowest ranks, depend upon titles to give meaning to their existence.

As night follows day, the outcry of "monarchist" proceeded. So strong was the reaction to *Davila* that Fenno eventually discontinued printing the articles, so John published the book. Why, aside from his certainty in his own beliefs, did Adams want to stir this fray? Few people who hoped for a political future would be either so foolhardy or so bold as to express unpopular opinions so candidly. But John, who always lamented the criticism of his ideas, continually risked his reputation and wrote on topics that would backfire on him. Aside from whether he was right—and most contemporary theorists would question whether the most fundament human need is for recognition—John committed another political misstep. Why he risked his political prospects is a conundrum that perhaps may best be answered by his recent discovery that Hamilton had meddled in his election to the vice presidency. He was further frustrated by his inability to engage in the debate of Congress. And he was so revolted by the scheming and small-mindedness of politicians that he wanted to tell them something fundamental about themselves.

In May 1791, Abigail headed home to Braintree after an absence of two years. She stopped in New York to visit the Smiths before continuing her journey through Connecticut, where she became ill. John referred to her disease as the "ague," but it is not possible these centuries later to diagnose the symptoms. "I have been so weakned and debilitated as to be unable to walk alone, and my Nerves so affected as to oblige me to Seclude myself from all company except my most intimate connexions," she wrote to Martha Washington after she got home.

THE SUMMER, OF COURSE, PASSED TOO QUICKLY, BUT IT WAS time enough for Abigail to recover her health and John his spirits. They had decided to give up Bush Hill as their Philadelphia residence. The house was too cold and too far from the city. Instead they rented a small brick house in the middle of the city, where they kept only a few servants, Briesler and a cook among them. Abigail returned to Philadelphia and her social rounds, pleased with some of her newfound friends.

John returned to yet another political tempest. In the spring of 1791, Thomas Paine, author of *Common Sense*, had published in England another small tract, called *Rights of Man*, that justified the French Revolution. A copy of this pamphlet reached an American publisher that fall. It also came into the hands of Thomas Jefferson, who wrote a note to the publisher, extolling the work and mentioning as well that he was pleased to read a refutation of the "political heresies which had of late sprung up among us." Unbeknownst to Jefferson—as he later claimed to President Washington—the letter was published as the preface to the Paine volume. The phrase "political heresies" was then picked up in the Republican press throughout the country. Everyone understood the code. Jefferson was attacking Adams for his *Discourses on Davila*, adding fuel to the accusations that Adams was a monarchist.

Adams felt betrayed. While he and Jefferson had had little contact since the latter had returned from France to become the secretary of state, they also had not quarreled. Adams considered Jefferson his friend, based on the many years of working together, especially in Europe. Jefferson, during his years as secretary of state, had focused his animosity on Hamilton, whose person and policies he detested. He colluded closely with Madison to undermine the president's economic policies, and together they were cheerleaders for the French Revolution. If anything, Jefferson considered Adams benign, perhaps a little mad, but he knew the vice president to be honest and above party influence. He probably did not intend his mean words to be publicized. But the cat was out of the bag, and John felt injured.

He thought about responding in anger but for once reconsidered and did not. His son did, however. John Quincy, who in Paris had spent many a fine hour in Jefferson's company, attending theater and opera and discussing many topics of common interest, defended his father in a series of newspaper articles, published under the pen name of "Publicola." They were a scathing refutation of the heresy indictment. "I have always understood, sir," wrote John Quincy, "that the citizens of these States were possessed of a full and entire freedom of opinion upon all subjects civil as well as religious; they have not yet established any infallible criterion of *orthodoxy*, either in church or state."

His argument repeated the claim that debate and opposition were components of a democratic process. "The only political tenet which they could stigmatize with the name of heresy would be that which should attempt to impose an opinion upon their understandings, upon the single principle of authority." It was a defense based upon the First Amendment, such as a lawyer might write, a brief on free speech and free press as fundamental rights in a democracy.

Ironically, John Adams, and not his son, was widely believed to be the author of the Publicola essays, which only led to further criticism of him. John, however, was proud of his son and pleased to observe that his keen intellect and pen had come to the defense of his father. This act might have erased the bad feelings he developed for Jefferson and his journalist friends. Jefferson, however, was embarrassed, and, not knowing how to recover, did nothing for a while. Then he wrote to the president to plead his case that *he had no idea* that his letter would be published and that he had only the *greatest esteem* for John Adams. Perhaps his first letter should have been directed to John Adams, but he only wrote to him after a three-month lapse. "I thought so little of the note," he wrote, meaning the letter that served as the preface to *Rights of Man*, "that I did not even keep a copy of it; nor ever heard a tittle more of it till, the week following I was thunderstruck with seeing it come out at the head of the pamphlet. I had hoped that it would not attract notice."

Jefferson didn't apologize; he explained. "The friendship and confidence which has so long existed between us required this explanation from me," he wrote, "and I know you too well to fear any misconstruction of the motives of it."

"I received your friendly Letter," John responded with heartfelt warmth. "I give full credit to your relation of the manner in which your note was written and prefixed." He attributed the affront to the publisher. He also added, contradicting Jefferson's comment that they had disagreed about politics, "I do not know this. I know not what your Idea is of the best form of Government. You and I have never had a serious conversation together that I can recollect concerning the manner of Government."

There it was—the kind of candid remark that an adversary could not resist. And Jefferson didn't. He wrote back and blamed the entire affair on Publicola. The whole episode would have gone unnoticed, he wrote, if it hadn't been for the publication of the Publicola essays.

John did not respond. After this exchange, the two old friends saw each other infrequently and did not correspond at all for several years. Their friendship had been damaged. Jefferson focused his resistance on Hamilton, and for a few more years he vigorously opposed the economic plans, the military plans, and the foreign policy of the Washington administration. He was as far out of his element in Philadelphia as Hamilton was in, so he resigned, packed his bags, and returned to Monticello, where he dismantled his home and his grounds and began with a new master plan to rebuild the plantation.

PREGNANT AGAIN, NABBY TRAVELED TO PHILADELPHIA WITH her three younger children to visit her parents. This trip was planned as a farewell visit before she embarked with her family for Europe, where William Smith had joined a group selling western lands to European investors. They would be gone for two years.

During Nabby's visit in February 1792, Abigail became very ill with a recurrence of her rheumatism and "intermitting fever." Her symptoms were raging headaches and fever that were so severe that her life was feared for. Nabby nursed her mother for as long as she could before returning to New York, when the job was taken by niece Louisa, Mrs. Briesler, and several friends, who stayed with her around the clock. She was bled three times and twice blistered so badly that her wrists became lame. She later wrote to her sister, "I have scarcly any flesh left." Nabby, once returned to New York, wrote to her father that perhaps the therapy her mother received was too harsh. Could he find another physician? But Abigail refused to see anyone but Dr. Benjamin Rush, John responded. "She is better to-day than she has ever been since her illness began."

The consequence of Abigail's illness was that the Adamses decided that she could no longer live in Philadelphia's climate. She would return to Braintree in April and remain there for the duration of John's tenure as vice president. He would stay in Philadelphia alone for the six months of the year that Congress sat and return home to be with Abigail for the remainder of the year. This arrangement had the added advantage that John would be able to lodge in a single room, as other congressmen did, which would be much more economical. As soon as she could, Abigail began making plans to return home.

Abigail's health returned and so did her interest in politics. She reported about the current clashes in Congress. "The Southern members are determined if possible to Ruin the Secretary of the Treasury," she wrote to Mary, not attempting to hide her exasperation: They will "distroy all his well built systems, if possible and give a Fatal Stab to the funding system." She added: "I firmly believe if I live Ten Years longer, I shall see a devision of the Southern & Northern States, unless more candour & less intrigue, of which I have no hopes, should prevail."

John returned to Philadelphia alone for the remainder of his years as vice president. Washington had reluctantly agreed to run again for the presidency in 1792 and was unanimously elected for a second term. John, too, ran for reelection, and while his electoral vote improved this time, his office was again contested by the same scheming partisanship that had operated during the previous election. Nevertheless, he returned to the position that he considered the most insignificant in man's imagination. His post in Philadelphia was not even graced by the elegance of the renovated Federal Hall in New York, but rather he presided over a modest chamber in Founders Hall from a wooden desk and chair in the front of the room. His living quarters were equally modest at John Francis's boardinghouse where he took his meals along with the other boarders, joining in with their conversations, "conversing amicably with men over whom he had just presided." For the time being, John had made peace with his role.

President Washington's first administration had focused on creating the new government's structure, filling in the offices and establishing precedent for its functioning on the one hand. On the other hand, the overwhelming achievement of this first term had been the establishment of a sound financial system, based on Hamilton's plan that was ferociously debated in Congress. The fierceness of party rancor in these battles would continue into the president's second term, but this time the hostility would turn on the president.

George Washington had been reluctant to run for a second term. He was weary of service; his health was poor and several times in the immediate past his life had been feared for; and he wanted to retire to Mount Vernon. Nevertheless, he was persuaded to run again against his deepest instincts, and he rose once more to the call of duty. His second term was dominated by the impact of European wars upon America, especially the disruption of American commerce and shipping in the Atlantic. Washington dealt with these issues by sending diplomats to negotiate on America's behalf. With Washington no longer immune to criticism as he had been during his first term, his policies led to exacerbated divisions within the country. Adams, in his presidency, would inherit the fallout from his predecessor's foreign policy, one that he supported even though the president excluded him from the inner counsels of policy makers.

Save for Adams, whom he ignored, the president entered his second term with a new set of advisors. Thomas Jefferson had departed first. Next, Hamilton, his work successfully completed, left to resume his private law practice in New York, where he could still retain his position as a leader of the Federalists. General Knox, who suffered too many indignities in office, like Adams taking some of the political fallout from the president's infallibility, fairly danced on his way out of office.

John Adams, as Abigail pointed out, had acquired a new sense of composure and gravitas. He remained calm while the Senate wrangled over the controversial Jay Treaty, which disappointed the Federalists and Anti-Federalists both by securing very little advantage in changing the British incursions on American shipping. He remained calm during the uproar about Citizen Genet, the new French minister, who, when he didn't make progress with the president, appealed directly to the people by traveling about the country making speeches. He even remained calm when twenty thousand western farmers, rebelling against the whiskey tax, began their march to the capital. This time the president himself, accompanied once more by Hamilton as his lieutenant, took the lead as general of a federal army to quell that rebellion. Even Abigail expressed her dismay, as she had during the abortive Shays's Rebellion in her own state years ago, and cheered the president for demonstrating the overall power of the central government.

John had retained his calm for many reasons. One, perhaps the least noted, was that for six months each year he spent his days at home with Abigail. Her health still precarious, she lived more comfortably in the familiar environment of Braintree, among her family and friends. During John's furloughs at home, he tramped over his fields, mended fences, and planned his next expansion of the farm. Following his physical labors, he read and wrote letters. Together they shared the contentment of companionship. During his absence, they lovingly corresponded, keeping each other informed of their quotidian activities. Abigail understood, however, that this tranquility could be short-lived.

John's devotion to his duty in public service aside, another overarching reason for remaining in the vice presidency to perform the most insignificant role ever invented was that he strongly considered himself to be Washington's heir apparent. "I am heir apparent, you know, and a succession is soon to take place," he had written Abigail in January 1796. But for the past six or seven years, he had understood, as he repeatedly told friends whenever the president was seriously ill, that he was but a breath away from the office. At the height of the furious newspaper attacks on the president, when politicians and the press both had turned against him, Washington considered resignation. On several different occasions, John had seen himself close to the precipice. But as it became clear that the president would not again run for office, John knew that he was a primary candidate for the position.

Finally, in September 1796, George Washington announced that he would not run for another term in office. In doing so, he established another precedent that helped set the course for the young democracy. By custom, until the passage of the Twenty-second Amendment to the Constitution in the mid-twentieth century, no president served for more than two terms.

The succession was not a certainty, and many political schemes were hatched by the supporters of possible contenders. Hamilton—now thirty-five years old, referred to by Adams as "his puppyhood"—and, it was rumored, John Jay plotted the candidacy of Charles Cotesworth Pinckney, the South Carolina aristocrat and former military hero. Jefferson privately vowed to Madison, who had retired to his plantation because he hated the Hamiltonian program, that he would defer to Adams: "He has always been my senior," he wrote in a letter that Madison conveniently showed to Adams.

John Adams, still believing it was possible for him to rise above politics, became the forerunner in an election in which no candidate campaigned and no formal political party existed to promote any contender. Factions existed, however, with all the fervor and duplicity of latter-day partisan conflict. In his home state of Massachusetts, the Warrens and Sam Adams could be counted as opponents to his candidacy. Only his old friend Elbridge Gerry remained loyal. Many of the same dynamics existed in this election that had prevailed in John's vice presidential election. But John was still the leading candidate.

In February the electoral votes were counted in the Senate. Ironically, John, as vice president and presiding officer of that body, announced his own victory. He received seventy-one votes; Jefferson would be vice president with sixty-nine, and Pinckney came in third with fifty-nine votes.

A transition from the first to the second presidency was peacefully achieved. While John did not receive the universal acclamation of his predecessor, he did win the majority of the electoral college votes, enough to become president. Hamilton, ineligible for that office because he was foreign-born, had once more attempted to manipulate the outcome in order to maintain his own influence. In the end, he failed.

And Abigail Adams became the second first lady.

Splendid Misery

"YOU ASK ME WHAT I THINK OF COMEING ON IN FEBRY?" ABIGAIL wrote to John Adams from their home in Quincy, Massachusetts, in mid-January 1797. "I answer that I had rather not if I may be excused," she continued politely, giving her health as the reason. The occasion was not ordinary, however. Although neither the formal count of electoral votes nor the official announcement before Congress had been made, it was already clear that John had been elected as the second president of the United States. Now Abigail was negotiating her role as first lady.

She continued that she could not travel to Philadelphia for the March 4 inauguration and to set the stage socially. Nor would she be available to find and furnish accommodations for the president, since, she explained, she thought Congress should appoint a committee for this purpose. "I desire to have nothing to do with it, there are persons who know what is both necessary and proper." She agreed, however, that once the house and furnishings were secured, she would "not be against going to assist in the arrangement of the Household." She offered to help hire and supervise the servants.

One month later, the electoral votes were counted and the results formally announced before a solemn assembly of Congress. "I think you will excuse my attendance at Philadelphia till October," Abigail wrote, postponing her departure for the capital even further. And John agreed: "I believe you should stay till October but if that is the final plan I will be with you in June." He affirmed this plan again, writing to her on the day before his inauguration: "It is best for you not to come till next fall. I will go to you as soon as I can but that is uncertain."

John, meanwhile, struggled with many domestic dilemmas. There was no executive mansion in Philadelphia, and the house that the Washingtons had occupied, appeared too expensive to Adams. Furthermore, the Washingtons had used their own household furnishings, which they planned to take home to Mount Vernon. Not only did Adams wrestle with issues of state in the weeks and months before his inauguration, but he also fretted about domestic arrangements. "The Congress have passed the Law allowing 14,000 d to purchase furniture. The State Legislature have done nothing about their new House; so that I shall take the House the President is in, at £1000 or 2700 dollars rent, nothing better can be done."

He worried, too, about transportation. Should he purchase a coach in Philadelphia or have one constructed in Boston? And horses. Finally, he decided upon

> 1500 dollars for a carriage. 1000 for one Pair of Horses—all the glasses ornaments kitchen furniture the best chairs . . . all the china . . . glass . . . all the Linnen . . . Secretaries, servants, wood . . . the million dittos present such a prospect as is enough to disgust any one—yet not [a] word must we say. We cannot go back—We must stand our ground as long as we can.

Abigail stood her ground in Quincy. Her resistance to traveling to Philadelphia, while genuinely founded on poor health, was determined by other conditions as well. For one thing, she was nervous about her impending position, confessing to John Quincy that "It is the will of providence to place me in a very conspicuous station. . . . I would bear my honour meekly—fully sensible that 'high Stations tumult. but not bliss create None think the Great unhapy but the Great.'"

Lacking control over her great destiny, Abigail established limits where she could. She had remained at home, while John traveled to Philadelphia, in order to establish order in their private lives before embarking upon her new public responsibilities. As she had many times over the years of John's public service, Abigail dealt single-handedly with these difficulties. In his absence, she managed the farm, the farmhands, and the tenants. Her expenses had skyrocketed because of inflation: "Grain, and West India articles are 25 pr cent higher than this time last Year."

Most remarkable, however, though not new to her experience, Abigail was struggling to make ends meet. "Taxes are due—179 dollars and half the Farm tax upon which French & Vinton are to 24 dollars, 16 Burrels." She cursed the representatives: "They will starve their officers." By the middle of March, the debts had compounded. "At present I live on credit," she informed the newly inaugurated president. She could not depend upon him to send her money, as his problems were no less daunting: "My expenses are so enormous," he wrote from his new house in Philadelphia, "that my first Quarter salary will not discharge much more than half of them." Abigail solved her dilemma as she had in the past, by borrowing three hundred dollars from her friend General Lincoln. The Adamses entered the nation's highest offices in debt.

Farming and financial enterprises aside, Abigail was weighed down by family responsibilities as well. John's aging mother, Susanna Hall, was no longer capable of living alone, and provisions had to be made for her. Abigail worried about her children, and especially her daughter, whose wastrel husband had disappeared, leaving Nabby isolated in Upstate New York with her young children. Abigail confided to John that their son-in-law was "a Man wholy devoid of judgment." The news from Europe of John Quincy's engagement was more promising and Abigail warmly welcomed Louisa Catherine Johnson into the fold, requesting her portrait and calling her "daughter." Abigail fretted over Thomas's health and begged him to return home from Europe, where he served as his brother's secretary. Their middle son, Charles, was newly married and a father, but she worried about his work habits.

Besides, Quincy was home. Abigail loved the land, their farm, the climate, her garden, her routine work of domestic management. In addition, their house, called Peacefield by John, had been acquired upon their return from England, and they were in the process of improving and expanding it. It was a project that Abigail and John had entered together with enthusiasm, and it occupied a great deal of their collaborative attention. Her health aside, there were many ties binding Abigail to Quincy. "At my time of Life, the desire or wish to shine in publick Life is wholy extinguished. the retirement to (peacefield, the name which Mr. A has given his farm) is much more eligible to me," she confessed to her old friend Elbridge Gerry.

LESS THAN A MONTH AFTER HIS INAUGURATION, JOHN ADAMS declared to Abigail: "I cannot live without you till October." Four days later he wrote: "From the Situation, where I now am, I see a Scene of Ambition, beyond all my former suspicions and Imaginations. . . . Intrigues all around." He urged her to come to him. Days later he wrote: "I never wanted your Advice & assistance more in my Life." And again, "It is improper We should be in a state of Seperation that I must intreat you to come on. . . . You must hire four Horses in Boston and a Coachman to bring you here, upon as good terms as you can."

In April the pleas became more insistent. "I have written you before, and have only time now to repeat that I pray you to come on," he urged on the first of the month. Two days later, he persisted: "I pray you to come on immediately. I will not live in this State of Seperation. Leave the Place to Jonathan & Polly. to Mears—to my Brother—to any body or nobody. I care nothing about it— But you, I must and will have." He continued to press his message every few days.

> I want your assistance more than [ever]. You must come and leave the Place to the mercy of the Winds. . . . You must come here and see, before you will have an Idea of the continual Application to Business, to which I am called. I should not have believed it possible for my Eyes to have read the Papers which are brought me every day and every hour of the day. . . . You must come, at all Events and leave the Place as you can. . . . I am determined not to be perplexed with Farms.

By the eleventh, his plea was more passionate still: "I must now repeat this with heat and earnestness. I can do nothing without you. . . . I must intreat you to loose not a moments time in preparing to come."

Within days after his inauguration, John Adams's life had changed in ways that he had not anticipated. "The Stilness and Silence astonishes me," he wrote to Abigail. Nothing in his experience had prepared him for his sense of awe and isolation upon assuming the authority of this office. He developed a new appreciation for George Washington, commenting that during the ceremony "he Seemed to me to enjoy a Tryumph over me. Methought I heard him think Ay! I am fairly out and you fairly in! See which of Us will be happiest." And weeks later John observed with new insight: "I wonder not that my Predecessor was weary."

Abigail responded to John's urgent summons with characteristic empathy. "I think you are fastned to a spot which you cannot leave at Will, and I believe you want your Family more than when you was occupied by a daily attendance at Congress. Your mind is . . . so fully employd that you can not think much." She began to make plans to leave Quincy as soon as possible.

It was not so simple to extract herself from domestic responsibilities as John had indicated. "I will do the best I can and come as soon as I can," she confirmed. She described the many "perplexities" with which she was loath to trouble him. "I will surmount those which are to be conquerd, and submit to those which are not." Abigail contended not only with negotiations for tenants in her main house, but rental of their outlying farms, laborers, and oversight of building projects that were in progress. In addition, her niece Polly (Mary) Smith was dying from consumption, and her mother-in-law, now living with her, was ill. "I will make all the dispatch I can, but I find no body to act for me. . . . Mr. Smith has engaged me 4 horses and a Good Driver but He could not get him under two Hundred Dollors to carry me to New York."

In mid-April, a fresh snowstorm delayed Abigail's departure. "The sudden change has confind Your Mother and brought on one of her old Lung complaints," she reported to John.

"My dear and venerable Mother—Alass—I feel for her," John wrote back, himself typically conflicted with the struggle between public life and family. They were no longer an ordinary family, he wrote, and he was no longer an ordinary husband; he was the president. All ordinary responsibilities had to give way to the performance of this new office. In order to function, he wrote over and over again, he needed Abigail. He added, "Provide every thing for my aged and worthy Mother."

By the time he wrote this, however, Mrs. Hall had died, on April 21, just days before the death of Abigail's niece Mary. Abigail grieved while she prepared to depart for Philadelphia. John expressed his sympathy, knowing her lonely burden: "My Mothers Countenance and Conversation was a Source of Enjoyment to me, that is now dried up forever, at Quincy," Looking to the future, he continued grimly, "You and I are now entering on a new Scene, which will be the most difficult, and least agreable of any in our Lives. I hope the burthen will be lighter to both of Us when We come together." By that time, early May, Abigail was en route to Philadelphia.

ABIGAIL'S JOURNEY TO PHILADELPHIA IN THE SPRING OF 1797 ON roads that sometimes were so furrowed by heavy rains and the "constant run of six stages daily" that it "was like a ploughd feild and very dangerous" took under two weeks, including brief visits with Nabby and Charles in New York. She invoked the metaphor of travel to describe the disconnectedness she sensed from her former life. "My Journey was as pleasent as my thoughts upon what was past, and my anticipations of what was to come would permit it to be," she wrote to her sister Mary. She borrowed an ironic biblical phrase—"splendid misery"—to describe the "situation in which I am placed, enviable no doubt in the Eyes of some, but never envy'd or coveted by me."

The phrase was apt, as was Abigail's nervous foreboding of the years ahead. The bedrock upon which her future was grounded was her thirty-year marriage to John Adams. Her public office derived from John's determination to serve the nation. His decision—with her concurrence, because she would always concede to his ideals and ambition—as well as her own historical and religious sense of patriotic duty determined her journey to Philadelphia to assume the role of first lady. This high office, nowhere mentioned in the Constitution, was sanctioned by the marriage contract. John's office automatically prescribed hers. She did it with reluctance but with determination to give it her best spirit, energy, and wisdom.

It is now acknowledged that the greatest test of a new democracy's survival occurs not in its first but in its second administration. The Adamses were aware of this. Not only did they bear the strain of their government's ultimate test, but they did it without a standard blueprint for conduct. That which had worked for the Washingtons was not going to be transferable to the Adamses, because it was based too strongly on the reputation and the style of the first president and lady. Washington's aura had been so personal, so much the effect of his character and reputation, that until the end of his first term, his behavior and his policies went virtually unchallenged by the public and the press.

The issue of succeeding George Washington was one that Abigail frequently though discreetly reiterated to family members in the months before the great man vacated his office. She underscored his advantages to her eldest son, outlining the

> Combination of circumstances which no other man can look for,
> first a unanimous Choice. 2ly personally known to more people by
> having commanded their Armies than any other man 3ly possessed
> of a Large Landed Estate 4ly refusing all emoluments of office both
> in his military and civil capacity.

Abigail, as well as John, had admired rather than resented these attributes of character and circumstances. She concluded: "Take his character all together, and we shall not look upon his like again."

One reason for her complete admiration for the first president was that she fully believed that her husband, for all his contrasting qualities, possessed equal talents for the position. "What is the expected Lot of a Successor? He must be armed as Washington was by integrity, by firmness, by intrepidity. These must be his sheild, and his wall of Brass. and with Religion too. or he will never be able to stand sure and steadfast."

In fact, the Adams administration was caught off guard by the salient issue that would dominate its four-year tenure: the European war. Washington left office warning the nation against entanglements in foreign affairs. Adams's administration was dominated by the politics and diplomacy of maintaining independence and integrity in the face of continual foreign threats to American territory, possessions, trade, and citizens. The playing field of foreign affairs had not been predicted; it would not have been chosen; its terrain and its rules were undesirable for a vulnerable new nation; there existed no expertise or power or even congruence about sides or strategies among its teammates. It was a dangerous contest to be involved in for a young nation. But for all these hazards and complexities, Adams's diplomatic experience served him well. Solitary and supported primarily by his own good judgment—and Abigail's—in diplomacy and statecraft, Adams avoided that which appeared inevitable in his administration, war with a European power.

Too much a New Englander to be moved by only ideals, too great a revolutionary to be a cynic, Adams prided himself as a realist, his pragmatism born of reading history and knowing men. Wary though he was of ambition, understanding its force, he nevertheless was not braced or toughened for the malicious onslaught of factions and opposition parties that developed early in his administration.

Alexander Hamilton was mean. Of this Abigail was certain even in the months before the inauguration. "Beware of that Spair Cassius. has always occured to me when I have seen that cock sparrow," she warned John. "O I have read his Heart in his wicked Eyes many a time. the very devil is in them. they are laciviousness it self. or I have no skill in physiognomy." She added, "Pray burn this Letter. Dead Men tell no tales." While he agreed with her assessment of Hamilton, Adams entered office not naïvely overlooking party and factional opposition but rather believing that like Washington in his early years, he would rise above them.

This would not be the case. Hamilton plotted to control the presidency by using his power over the cabinet members, whom Adams retained from Washington's administration. Adams only learned too late that confidence in his predecessor's advisors was a political blunder. "Pickering and all his colleagues are as much attached to me as I desire," he wrote to his friend Elbridge Gerry, who had become suspicious. "I have no jealousies from that quarter." He meant that he did not fear their disloyalty.

Hamilton, consequently, succeeded with his scheme. The secretary of the treasury, Oliver Wollcot, Jr., and secretary of war, James McHenry, were both beholden to Hamilton for their offices, although neither of them was a notably competent public servant. Nor was Timothy Pickering. the secretary of state, loyal to Adams. Though he came from Massachusetts, he had never been close to Adams politically and colluded against the president's policies, as did Charles Lee, the attorney general, from Virginia. But it would be too long and after too many violations of confidence among his own cabinet members before John would realize that factionalism within his own party was as destructive to his administration as the opposition party. Too late would he begin to clip his secretaries' wings, and by that time the damage had been done.

When Abigail Adams traveled from Quincy to Philadelphia in the spring of 1797, responding to John's urgent summons, she did so reluctantly, with a sense of foreboding, conscious that the next years would be taxing on her health and her spirit. She forced herself to make the journey.

"THE WEATHER WAS SO COLD YESTERDAY THAT WE HAD FIRES in our Rooms," Abigail began conventionally to Mary Cranch in early June 1797, a time remarkable in the nation's capital for more than its unusual cold snap. A diplomatic crisis had developed since John's March inauguration. The Directory, France's governing body, had refused to accept the credentials of the new American minister, Charles Cotesworth Pinckney, who had been appointed by President Washington at the end of his term. This was a grave insult to the United States. But this was not all. The Directory ordered Pinckney out of the country and announced that they would fire upon American ships at sea.

Adams addressed this crisis by calling a meeting of his cabinet to discuss his response to the indignity and the threat to American shipping. He proposed to arm American merchant ships for their protection. Secretaries Wolcott and McHenry immediately informed Hamilton of the president's plan. Hamilton, after thinking about it, concluded that this policy would weaken Adams and agreed with the recommendation. He directed the secretaries to approve the plan. With his cabinet's affirmation, then, and unaware of Hamilton's manipulations behind the scenes, Adams sent his proposal to Congress, where the measure passed, though not without opposition among the Republicans, who still sympathized with France.

Within weeks of becoming president, then, Adams had encountered a massive threat that could portend the outbreak of a war. His primary reaction was to prevent war while protecting American security and dignity. Then, after further consideration, he decided in the interests of maintaining peace to overlook the diplomatic snub by appointing a new delegation of three men to negotiate with the Directory. He reappointed the beleaguered Pinckney and added John Marshall, a brilliant young lawyer from Virginia, and his old friend Francis Dana as emissaries to France. This provoked a different kind of war at home, where the rival Republicans, including Vice President Thomas Jefferson and a dissenting group within his own party, some of them congressmen from his own state of Massachusetts, fought the proposal. These "High Federalists" argued that Adams's approach demonstrated weakness. They preferred a more bellicose response. For Adams this defection within his party was a cruel desertion. He was, furthermore, beset by criticism and even vitriol from the press. Journalists quickly abandoned a honeymoon period after his inauguration to release a barrage of abuse against his proposed policies.

"The appointments of Envoys extraordinary, like every other measure of Government, will be censured by those who make a point of abusing every thing," Abigail wrote to Mary. She was not reporting information about the appointments so much as defending John's policy, which in advance of the envoys' confirmation already experienced opposition. "Mr. Marshall of Virginia is said to be a very fair and Honorable man." She persisted, writing about her husband's opponents, who considered John's appointments a threat to American friendship with the revolutionary regime. She defended John's selection of Francis Dana: "Judge Dana is known to be a decided Character, but not a party Man, nor any other than a true American." Mary was a safe person to confide in.

Abigail actually undertook a more direct role. She wrote an encouraging letter to Mrs. Dana, doubtlessly calculating from her own experience that Dana's wife could prevent his acceptance. She wrote, "to reconcile you to the nomination which was yesterday made by the president to the Senate of your best friend as one of the Envoys extraordinary to the French directory. I do not expect you will give him your thanks for this nomination." Abigail could well sympathize with Mrs. Dana's dismay at the prospect of a prolonged separation.

Dana did, in fact, turn down the appointment, because of his health, and in his stead Adams turned to his old trusted friend and fellow revolutionary Elbridge Gerry, who also was Abigail's friend. Gerry had opposed the adoption of the Constitution and the new government it created. However, he wanted to reassure John that despite his disapproval of the Constitution, he would carry out his mission loyally. He wrote to Abigail as a conduit to the president, knowing that she spoke freely about political issues with John.

Troubles multiplied with the arrival of the American ministers in France. "We have Letters from Mr. Murry," Abigail wrote Mary, referring to William Vans Murray, minister to The Hague, soon after the arrival of the three emissaries. Using the first person plural, she continued: "A few lines from Mr. Marshall to him informs him: that the envoys were not received and he did not believe they would be. They dare not write, knowing that every word would be inspected. They have not been permitted to hold any society or converse with any citizen."

The full story was more complicated still. The French foreign minister,

Charles Talleyrand, had appointed three agents to meet with the American delegation. Adding fuel to the fire of insult, they demanded from the United States a bribe of $250,000 as well as a massive loan of millions of dollars to begin discussions. When this news became known in Congress and was quickly leaked to the press, the reaction was immediate and ferocious. Republicans, still carrying the torch for the French Revolution, found themselves on the defensive, and the country united behind the president, demanding war with France. This further insult to American integrity brought about widespread support for a military response.

Adams, in his report to Congress, referred to the three French agents as X, Y, and Z, which gave a name to the outrage, and the country prepared for war. Congress voted to arm twelve merchant vessels and to support the enlargement of the military to ten thousand soldiers. John Adams, in the first years of his presidency, was entangled in the very scenario that his predecessor had warned against: a dispute with a foreign nation.

While the XYZ affair had rallied support for the country behind the president, it also further polarized the parties and his administration. Republicans lost seats in the congressional elections of 1798, thus diminishing their effectiveness. Jefferson, still their leader within the administration, became more alienated from the president. And Federalists in the cabinet took their marching orders from Hamilton. A quasi war developed between America and France, played out on the high seas, where American ships won most of the battles. A warlike atmosphere prevailed in the now politically divided country

"I fear we shall be driven to War, but to *defend* ourselves is our duty," Abigail wrote to Mary. "War the French have made upon us a long time." At times the rhythm of Abigail's voice echoed her husband's style, the effect of listening to him. One week later she reported: "I cannot say what Congress mean to do. The dispatches are but just decypherd." She referred to Gerry's letter, much of which came in code. "Whether the President will think proper to make any further communications is more than he himself can yet determine," she continued, revealing to Mary that John was still considering his next diplomatic move. By the end of March, the situation had worsened. She wrote:

> In this situation our Country is calld upon to put themselves in a *state of defence*, and to take measures to protect themselves by Sea. This is called a declaration of war on the part of the President, by those who would gladly see their Government prostrate, Religion banishd and I do not know if I should judge too hardly if I said our Country Shared by France.

Now using her own voice, she defended John's policy of strengthening the military, which had been attacked as too aggressive, too costly, and too unfriendly toward France.

From the urgency and depth of her comments, it is clear that Abigail's reflections mirrored conversations in which John had discussed his political and diplomatic dilemmas. Her strong response reflects as well opinions that she undoubtedly expressed to him in return. John talked with Abigail about pressing issues as they developed, because he knew that her comments would be both wise and honest. "Union is what we want," she continued, again mirroring his words, "but that will not be easily obtaind. It is difficult to make the people see their danger, untill it is at their doors, or rouse untill their country is invaded. The Senate are strong. They are much more united in their measures than the House."

And for many long paragraphs Abigail continued to explain the complex and taxing problems that faced the Adams administration. "I shall sigh for my retirement at Piece Feild, before I shall reach it," she wrote on, again sounding like John, who also longed for his hills and his farm.

Abigail clearly possessed current information about the most recent diplomatic developments as well as her husband's state of mind with regard to events. That she wrote about them in letters, albeit to trusted people like her sister Mary, appears tactless if not hazardous. Even she on occasion questioned her lack of self-censorship. But she, too, needed to unburden herself in this time of stress.

In June, Abigail communicated more confidential information to her sister, actually quoting a letter from Murray. "In this Letter he says, 'I learn that France will treat with Mr. Gerry *alone*. The other two will *be orderd* away.' . . . I cannot credit it, yet I know the sin which most easily besets him is obstinacy, and, a mistaken policy." Elbridge Gerry had been seduced into talking with Talleyrand, while the other two envoys returned. She described the reception of this news in her household: "You may easily suppose how distrest the President is at this conduct, and the more so, because he thought Gerry would certainly not go wrong." She added, "This is all between ourselves. You will be particuliarly reserved upon this subject." Abigail wrote highly sensitive information that only John's closest advisors knew about. She was part of his inner circle, because he trusted her intelligence and loyalty.

Foreign affairs became the dominant theme of John's administration, but it was not the exclusive issue. Complicating his life from the onset of his term was the problem of appointments, which were subject to the scrutiny of the ever-critical press. Abigail defended John: "The P[resident] has said he will appoint to office [men of] merit, virtue & Talents, and when Jacobins [she meant Republicans] possess these, they will stand a chance," if, she added, "they are Friends to order and Government." Again, she quoted John's reasoning.

No issue of patronage was more disturbing for the Adamses at this time than John Quincy's appointment as minister to Prussia. In 1794, Washington had selected the then twenty-six-year-old lawyer to become minister at The Hague, an office that he filled stunningly well. Before Washington left office, John showed him a letter that John Quincy had recently written to his mother, in which he had insisted that he receive no further appointments while his father held office. It would be seen as nepotism. He begged his mother to prevail upon the president not to appoint him to any position. John forwarded this letter to Mount Vernon, and Washington responded: "The sentiments do honor to the head and the heart of the writer." He continued:

> If my wishes would be of any avail, [they should go to you in a strong] hope, that you will not withhold merited promotion from Mr. John Quincy Adams because he is your son. . . . Mr. Adams is the most valuable public character we have abroad—and that there remains no doubt in my mind that he will prove himself to be the ablest of our diplomatic corps.

Washington's letter, which clearly swelled the hearts of John Quincy's parents, concluded by saying that it would be a loss to the country if his talents "were to be checked over delicacy on your part."

On the eve of his retirement from office, Washington had shifted the younger Adams to the more important post in Lisbon, and John Quincy prepared for this move. He had recently become engaged to Louisa Catherine Johnson of London, whom he had met years earlier while traveling to his post in The Hague. The Adamses could not have been more surprised than to receive a letter from their eldest son informing them of his engagement. Once recovered, Abigail wrote to her son, reminding him of the seriousness of this step and welcoming Louisa Catherine to the family. Now, while he waited restlessly for final instructions about his move to Portugal, John Quincy closed his household in the Netherlands, sending many items on to Lisbon, contributing a collection of his books to the Harvard Library, and all the while negotiating wedding plans with Louisa Catherine.

Then, abruptly, President John Adams changed this plan. In a move that satisfied almost no one, though it had great merit from his point of view, John reappointed his son to Berlin, where a treaty of neutrality and friendship was about to expire. John wanted this treaty renewed and also possibly treaties of mutual accord with several Scandinavian countries. Who, better than his son, could accomplish this?

To say this caught John Quincy off guard is an understatement. Not only were his plans for Lisbon sabotaged—he already had purchased his (unrefundable) tickets—but the worst crime in his thinking was the appearance of nepotism. He wrote separately to both of his parents in protest. He was humiliated because he would be represented as a "creature of favour," in a station of trust. "I have spoken very freely," he continued, "(perhaps too freely) my sentiments upon this occasion." He accepted the appointment, he stated, because of the "weight of parental authority which I had not calculated at its full force." John Quincy was obedient.

Both parents responded; John rationalized his motives, but upon Abigail fell the burden of a double bind. She understood her son's position, but she needed to defend John. "It has given me real pain to find that the change in your embassy does not meet your ready assent," she confessed. Then, echoing John's reasoning, attempting to soften the parental mandate, she explained the need for trusted as well as skillful diplomats, the importance and sensitivity of the mission to Berlin, and finally that John Quincy would be more useful to his country in Prussia.

John Quincy and Louisa Catherine were soon married, prevailed upon by her father, who planned to return his family to America. The young couple began their married life with the long journey to Berlin.

John Quincy had been prescient. The hostile press quickly seized upon his appointment, as he had predicted they would, charging that this position would improve chances for the Adams dynastic line. From the earliest days of the presidential campaign this topic had provided a subversive motif to undermine John Adams's candidacy. It was argued that because neither Washington nor Jefferson had sons, they presented less a threat to hereditary monarchy than Adams, who had not only three sons but one who had already shown himself to be a shining light in government circles.

Now, any move that gave an appearance of nepotism became journalistic ammunition. One published rumor asserted that the minister's salary had been increased to ten thousand dollars, a sore spot for John Quincy, whose income had actually been reduced by this shift in his orders from the higher rank of the Lisbon post to the minor leagues of Berlin.

Stung by these accusations, Abigail began an offensive to set the record straight. She wrote directly to Benjamin Bache, editor of the opposition newspaper, the *Philadelphia Aurora*, reminding him that he had once been John Quincy's schoolmate and noting that the newspaper attack was a breach of loyalty to a former friend. She would leave Bache "to his own Heart," she piously declared.

She sent her nephew William Cranch, who lived in the newly founded capital city of Washington, information to plant in the newspapers, including letters from her son in which she marked "with inverted commas" the sections he should cite. She sent information to relatives and friends in Massachusetts so that they might plant articles as well.

Abigail initially focused on journalists because they attacked her family: "I expected to be vilified and abused, with my whole Family when I came into this situation," she wrote. At first she dismissed criticism with hauteur, reading it "with a true Phylosiphical contempt," and quoting her husband that "praise for a few weeks mortified him, much more, than all their impudent abuse does."

The press ridiculed her as well. She was called "the Duchess of Braintree." Another time, she and John became "the Happy Old Couple," from an eighteenth-century Yorkshire ballad called Darby and Joan. Abigail snapped back that at least the president had not given his "Children or Grandchildren cause to Blush for any illegitimate ofspring." Her sarcasm targeted Bache's eponymous grandfather. Following Abigail's attendance at a concert, Bache's *Aurora* reported that "the excellent Lady of the Excellent President, was present, and shed Tears of Sensibility upon the occasion. That was a lie," reported Abigail.

Her indignation mounted with time. "Scarcly a day passes but some such scurility appears in Baches paper." Her concern now focused on the effect of the stories on "the common people." She became alarmed that the "lies and falsehoods" that were circulated might endanger the president's personal safety. She remembered the early years, before the Revolution, when radical leaders told exaggerated stories to stir riots. Given the contentious atmosphere in Philadelphia, she wrote, "materials for a Mob might be brought together in 10 minutes."

Abigail's remarks now reflected her husband's growing belief that the press represented a threat to the nation's safety. Private sources had informed him that foreigners were feeding stories to journalists. French agents, it seemed possible, manipulated the media in order to undermine the presidency. Their plan, she pointed out "is to calumniate the President, his family, his administration," so that John would be forced to resign. Then, she continued, "they will Reign triumphant, *headed by the Man of the People*." She referred derisively to Jefferson's support for the French Revolution.

Abigail began to advocate silencing the press. She was not alone. Congress was already considering such a bill. "Nothing will have an Effect untill congress pass a Sedition Bill," she wrote. "The wrath of the public ought to fall upon their devoted Heads." She meant Bache and his fellow journalists, a press that one historian has characterized as "the most violent and vituperative that was to appear in a century and a half of American history."

The issue of a sedition law was a subject she returned to in letters over time. "This would contribute as much to the Peace and harmony of our Country as any measure," she reasoned in May 1798. Impatient by mid-June, she wrote that in other countries the "papers would have been seazd," but here the Congress "are dilly dallying" about passing the legislation to enable the president to seize "suspisious persons, and their papers."

Between mid-June and mid-July 1798, Congress debated and passed four Alien and Sedition Acts, empowering the executive to expel "dangerous" aliens and to punish those found guilty of "printing, writing, or speaking in a scandalous or malicious way against the government of the United States." Abigail triumphantly hailed the acts: "Let the vipers cease to hiss. They will be destroyd with their own poison." She sent her sister a final specimen of the journalism that fueled her wrath. "I inclose to you the dareing outrage which calld for the Arm of Government."

Abigail's personal campaign against the press—waged as best she could on the public front by planting articles and on the private front by venting her anger in correspondence to her sister, her son, anyone she trusted—made sense from her point of view. She was a great reader of newspapers, and she held the press accountable for accurate reporting. More to the point, she was a staunch defender of her husband and her son. When they were abused and the news was distorted, she resented it keenly.

Abigail's observation of events from within the executive orbit transformed her from a tolerant civil libertarian to a conservative on the issue of freedom of the press. "The greater part of the abuse leveld at the Government is from foreigners. Every Jacobin paper in the United States is Edited by a Foreigner," she declared. "What a disgrace to our Country." In the face of this threat, support of the sedition bill appeared patriotic to her.

ABIGAIL DID NOT, HOWEVER, PLAY A ROLE IN THE PASSAGE OF the four pieces of legislation that comprise the Alien and Sedition Acts other than by her constant railing against the press. John did. He signed all four pieces of legislation that were passed through both houses of Congress in July 1798. As result of his presidential signature on these acts, John has taken the historical blame for the passage of these laws that later generations have considered the first breaches of constitutional law by a sitting president. More than any of the achievements of his administration, these acts have contributed to his reputation, not just at the time of their passage but subsequently, for disregard of First Amendment rights of free speech and free press in American history. Abigail's letters of support for the sedition laws tell only part of the story about the climate in which John put his signature on the offending legislation.

Party strife and the general fear among Americans at the time tell the fuller story. Fear of terrorism, as much as any factor, provided the fertile conditions for their passage. The mood in the country, following the XYZ affair, was bellicose. War with France seemed inevitable. As Americans considered the possibility of a French invasion, stories about the bloodbath that followed the French Revolution of 1789 circulated. It had taken some time for these stories to penetrate the consciousness of Americans, who had only recently worn the tricolor cockade in support of the Revolution. Now the same people wore black in support of radical federalism.

Many years later, John described that climate of terror to Jefferson in the famous correspondence that developed between the two elderly ex-presidents, after they resumed their friendship. Pointing his epistolary finger at Jefferson, he wrote: "You never felt the Terrorism of Chaises Rebellion [he meant Shays's Rebellion in Massachusetts]. You never felt the Terrorism of Gallatins Insurrection in Pennsylvania" [he meant the Whiskey rebellion during Washington's administration). "You certainly never felt the Terrorism, excited by Genet, in 1793, when ten thousand People in the Streets of Philadelphia, day after day, threatened to drag Washington out of his House." John continued, setting Jefferson up to read about his own experiences:

> I have no doubt You was fast asleep in philosophical Tranquility, when ten thousand People, and perhaps many more, were parading the Streets of Philadelphia on the Evening of my Fast Day. . . . when Markett Street was as full of Men [as] could stand by one another, and even before my Door; when some of my Domesticks in Phrenzy, determined to sacrifice their Lives in my defence; when all were ready to make a desperate Salley among the multitude, and others were with difficulty and danger dragged back by the others; when I myself judged it prudent and necessary to order Chests and Arms from the War Office to be brought through bye Lane and back Doors; determined to defend my House at the Expence of my Life, and the Lives of the few, very few Domesticks and Friends within it. What think you of Terrorism, Mr. Jefferson? Shall I investigate the Causes, the Motives, the Incentives to these Terrorisms? Shall I remind you of Phillip Freneau, of Loyd? Of Ned

Church? Of Peter Markoe, of Andrew Brown? Of Duane? Of Callender? Of Tom Paine? Of Greenleaf?

John continued to list the names of journalists who had incited the crowds to demonstrate before his presidential home.

"The real terrors of both Parties have always been, and now are, The fear that they shall loose the Elections and consequently the Loaves and Fishes; and that their Antagonists will obtain them." John had worked himself into an eloquent fury. "Both parties," he wrote,

> have excited artificial Terrors and if I were summoned as a Witness to say upon Oath, which Party had excited, Machiavillialy, the most terror, and which had really felt the most, I could not give a more sincere Answer, than in the vulgar Style "Put Them in a bagg and shake them, and then see which comes out first.

John might have exaggerated the size of the crowds that assembled on that April night in front of his house in Philadelphia, and he did not mention that they were rival gangs who either favored war with France or opposed it. What he did capture was the terror that the crowds generated. He recognized that behind the terror in the streets, politicians used the mood of the country in response to a foreign threat to gain support at election time. These same politicians gave journalists the opportunity to print sensational stories, many of them fabricated, for the purpose of maintaining an atmosphere of fear. Both parties were culpable, the elderly Adams wrote to the elderly Jefferson. Terrorism was the handmaiden of politics and politicians.

So in 1798, President John Adams, seething from the journalistic attacks that were a constant irritant, believing, perhaps, along with a majority of his fellow Americans, that immigrants, and especially some of the many thousands of French immigrants who fled to America from the French Revolution, were helping to foment war against the radicals in France, signed the Alien and Sedition Acts. At the foundation of this terror that filled the streets of Philadelphia and other cities was party strife. Together with the climate of militarism that resulted from insult of the XYZ affair, an atmosphere existed that Federalist leaders used to generate terrorism. John Adams did not initiate or support the measures in Congress, but he did sign the laws that greatly blemished his administration in history.

DESPITE HER EXASPERATION WITH THE PRESS, ABIGAIL REGU-larly mailed copies of newspapers, pamphlets, and articles to her closest correspondents. She wrote to John Quincy: "I cannot write you with the freedom I wish. I shall therefore send you some publick papers and some pamphlets and leave you to make your own comments. You will see that an whole Host are rising up in formal array against your country."

John Quincy lacked adequate recent information about what was happening at home. Few people served the function of supplying news to diplomats abroad, and in the absence of formal dispatches, Abigail regularly described events and sent journals to him. This exchange of correspondence, performed as a private family function, actually served a vital national interest, because both Abigail and John Quincy were in public positions, where more formal agencies of communication were inefficient or lacking. Among the Adamses, family business overlapped with the business of the nation. In return, the lengthy dispatches that John Quincy wrote to his father, in addition to those that he sent to the secretary of state, were models of reporting and insight about the full scope of events as they were unfolding in western Europe.

This intersection of family and national interests took many forms during the Adams administration. From the time that his election was confirmed in early 1797, John Adams was besieged by petitions for office. Every mail delivery brought plaintiff pleas from old friends as well as impoverished war veterans. Mostly John had to turn down such requests, even for the deserving. But not everyone sought office with a direct appeal to the president; some hopeful prospects calculated that their interests would be better served by going through Abigail. Charles Storer, who had been in Europe with the Adamses, who had for a time even served as John's secretary, explained that he was "emboldened . . . to presume upon" Abigail to "mention my father to the President and the same time presenting him my best respects." Later that month Thomas Welch of Boston addressed Abigail: "If you think there is no impropriety in it you may if you please communicate to him," and he circumspectly put himself forth for office. But by then, Storer's father had gotten the position.

Some appointments clearly bear witness to Abigail's interference with the president. Her nephew William Smith Shaw upon graduation from Harvard in 1797 became John's secretary, a sensitive office for many reasons, not the least because it required both literacy and loyalty. His mother, Abigail's sister Elizabeth, wrote with gratitude, "I feel myself under particular obligations to the President, & to you my Sister for thinking upon my Son for good." She continued to assure Abigail that William "is not 'loose of Soul' but from a Child considered a Secret as a sacred deposit." Another nephew, William Cranch, benefited from his aunt's largesse in numerous ways, culminating on the eve of John's administration in a judicial appointment, one of the so-called "midnight judges." The ne'er-do-well son-in-law, William Smith, received the bounty of several offices from his father-in-law, who clearly disliked his daughter's husband but indulged him for the sake of his daughter. It makes sense that Abigail's influence was behind these appointments.

In addition to her effect on appointments, Abigail's role as occasional literary critic is evident. She had strong opinions about style. Having read Chief Justice Ellsworth's "charge to the grand jury at New York," she wrote to her husband, judging the man as well as his literary talent! "Did the good gentleman never write before? can it be genuine? the language is stiffer than his person." John's composition did not generally warrant her editorial scrutiny—one historian calls his prose style "the most alive and readable of any written in eighteenth-century America"—but Abigail did intrude to subdue his most impulsive responses. He produced four different versions of an address to the Senate in the fall of 1799 before she was satisfied that he had made his argument calmly and rationally without inciting further animosity among opponents of his programs.

THE SOCIAL OBLIGATIONS OF THEIR PUBLIC ROLE WERE DAUNT-ing for both the president and first lady. John participated in this requirement of high office by attending public events. Abigail managed the operation of their social life with the help of their capable majordomo, whom she always called "Mr. Briesler." Neither of them loved the responsibility of entertaining, but both recognized its symbolic and practical importance to the presidency. Just as George Washington presented the public image of "the president" to his constituencies, so John needed to do so as well. Moreover, much business could be negotiated at social events, if not overtly, then discreetly by providing space for the display of "good behavior" that smoothed political tempers. President and first lady had to entertain grandly, setting a presentable table and serving numerous courses for dinners that conventionally began at three in the afternoon. "To day will be the 5th great dinner I have had," Abigail reported to Mary, "about 36 Gentlemen to day, as many more next week, and I shall have got through the whole of Congress."

More elaborate entertainments followed. "Then comes the 4 July which is a still more tedious day, as we must then have not only all Congress, but all the Gentlemen of the city, the Governour and officers and companies, all of whom the late President used to treat with cake, punch and wine." But Abigail was not just concerned about the magnitude of the party. "I have been informd the day used to cost the late President 500 dollors. More than 200 wt of cake used to be expended, and 2 quarter casks of wine besides spirit. You will not wonder that I dread it." She added, "I hope the day will not be Hot."

The celebration was a success, she later reported: "I got through the 4 July with much more ease than I expected." Guests first visited with the president in a parlor while Abigail received her guests along with the wives of "foreign Ministers & Home Secretaries with a few others." The following year, with the same operation to supervise, Abigail was equally anxious: "The extreem heat of yesterday & the no less prospect of it this day, is beyond any thing I ever experienced in my Life. The Glasses were at 90 in the Shade Yesterday," she complained to Mary. "I must see thousands. I know not how it will be possible to get through."

On one occasion late in the Adams administration, after a dinner attended by many young people, her son Thomas, who had recently returned from Europe, whispered to his mother, "Have you any objection to my having a dance this Evening?" She did not. The tables were removed from their "drawing room" and the candles lit. "At 8 the dancing commenced. At 12 it finished. More pleasure, ease and enjoyment I have rarely witnessd," Abigail recounted to Mary.

The president had retired after an hour, but Abigail, possibly to chaperone the young guests but also because she enjoyed herself, stayed until the end. "Amongst the company," she could not resist gossiping to her sister, was a young lady with manners "perfectly affable, polite and agreeable." However, "I could not but lament, that the uncoverd bosom should display, what ought to have been veild." Fashions had changed since her youth, and Abigail, accustomed to modest dresses, was offended that "the well turnd, and finely proportiond form" was too conspicuous "from the thin drapery which coverd it." She wished that "more had been left to the imagination, and less to the Eye." She added self-consciously, "But wither runs my pen?"

IN THE LATE SPRING AND EARLY SUMMER OF 1798, SOCIAL LIFE took place against the backdrop of preparations for war with France. Congress passed bills to arm American vessels on the sea and raised an army of ten thousand soldiers. John began to explore the issue of military leadership. It was a given that the highest command should go to George Washington for several reasons: first, because it would be impolitic to offer the role to any other general before asking the ex-president, but also because Washington's leadership would insure popular support of the war. Adams sent his secretary of war to visit Mount Vernon to interview the ex-president about his suggestions for the lesser command officers. Once more John was beset by political maneuvering, when the great man insisted on appointing Hamilton as his second in command. The choice of officers should have been left to the president, but in the end, Adams allowed Washington to select his next in command. On one of his lists, however, John had included his son-in-law, but Washington rejected Colonel Smith.

John hoped to avert war, though he was prepared for conflict if the diplomacy would not work. He had many difficult decisions on his mind when Congress adjourned in late July, and the Adamses headed back to Quincy with their retinue of family and servants. They stopped in New York to pick up Nabby and her children, who would spend the summer with them.

A surprise awaited John at home. Ever since their return from France, when they discovered that the "wren's house," as Abigail called it, was too small for their needs, the house had been under reconstruction. John returned to find that in his absence, an entire new wing had been completed that included a large library to serve as his study. He would need it, since even at home, he was still president, and during the months that followed, there was a constant flow of correspondence into and out of his new library.

The pleasure of their homecoming, however, was marred by Abigail's falling ill. For the next several months her disease, accompanied by all her usual symptoms of rheumatism, headaches, and fever, was so severe that her life was feared for. Writing to George Washington in early October about the disposition of army officers, John concluded with good wishes for the health of both Washingtons and added, "Mine is very indifferent, and Mrs. Adams's extremely low. Confined to the bed of sickness for two months, her destiny is still very precarious, and mine in consequence of it."

Despairing over Abigail's health, John delayed his return to the capital city until mid-November, by which time she had somewhat recovered, but not sufficiently to travel or preside over the presidential house. The prospect of another separation was difficult for them both. John's departure just a few weeks before Thanksgiving left Abigail solitary on that holiday. "This is our Thanksgiving day," she wrote to him in an uncommonly bleak mood. "It is usually a day of festivity when the Social Family circle meet together," she complained. "No Husband dignifies my Board, no Children add gladness to it, no Smiling Grandchildren Eyes to sparkle for the plumb pudding," she lamented. "Solitary and alone I behold the day after a sleepless night, without a joyous feeling." She invited her neighbors, Mr. and Mrs. Porter, to join her, as well as Phoebe, "the only surviving parent I have, and thus we shared in the Bounties of providence." Abigail was depressed, and she did not attempt to hide her mood from John. Illness and too many worries took their toll on her.

John's mood was not much better, both because he was lonely and worried about Abigail and because the bellicose mood in Philadelphia alarmed him.

The three emissaries whom he had sent to France had returned, Gerry in disgrace for having met alone with Talleyrand. In correspondence with John and in their meetings during the summer, however, Gerry suggested that Talleyrand might be willing to negotiate. Marshall, upon his return, hinted at the same. There was a glimmer of hope, but the now hawkish leaders in Congress, mostly High Federalists, a term used to describe the most radical wing of the party, were unwilling to risk further insults by sending another mission to Paris. Friends informed Adams that Hamilton had actually come to Philadelphia and maneuvered among his cabinet members to prevent sending a new peace mission to France.

For several reasons John saw things differently than he had in the spring, when he had endorsed military preparedness. In addition to Gerry's report to him, he had received messages from abroad, from both William Vans Murray and John Quincy. Murray, a young lawyer whom John had appointed American minister at The Hague, learned from the French diplomat that Talleyrand would now welcome an American representative in France.

Circumstances had changed; for one thing, Admiral Nelson had defeated the French navy; in addition, there was the prospect of another government coup in France. Murray communicated his information to both the president and his friend John Quincy. Both young ministers advised the president that they believed the time was ripe to attempt another overture to France.

Adams was receptive to these new communications. Other factors influenced him as well. People protested against the taxes that had been levied to support the new army. The Federalist program in Congress was under fire. Because of the Alien and Sedition Acts, support waned for the High Federalists, who advocated war. The states of Virginia and Kentucky passed resolutions against the acts, resolutions that had actually been written by the Republican leadership, including Madison and Jefferson. Moreover, numerous petitions from all states protested the acts. The only strong support for war existed within the ranks of the High Federalists, including Hamilton. Now outside of government, he worked his mischief by exercising influence over politicians on the inside.

However, on his own and in opposition to both his cabinet and the Federalists in Congress, and maybe even the former president, John Adams dropped a bombshell. He had received further assurances from Murray that confirmed the seriousness of the French offer. He sensed that America was not ready for war. Moreover, he had not ever believed that the French intended to invade America, as the hawkish terror peddlers suggested. On February 18 he sent a message to Congress, surprising even the vice president, Thomas Jefferson, who interrupted the business at hand to read it to the astonished Senate. It read: "Always disposed and ready to embrace every plausible appearance of probability of preserving or restoring tranquility, I nominate William Vans Murray, our minister at the Hague, to be minister plenipotentiary of the United States to the French republic."

The reaction, described by Secretary Pickering, was "thunderstruck." News traveled quickly from the Senate to the House, from there to the press, and from the press to the nation. From Quincy, Abigail responded: "There has not been any measure of the Government since you have been placed at the Head of it, which has so universally electrified the public: as the appointment of Mr Murray." She described the political response in Boston: "The whole community were like a flock of frightned pigions; nobody had their story ready: Some call'd it a hasty measure; other condemnd it as an inconsistant one; some swore some curs'd. . . . but what excited the more astonishment, was that the Heads of the departments were not consulted."

In fact, John had consulted his most reliable advisor: Abigail. By spending the past six months in Quincy, he felt both more secure and calm than in the politically charged environment of the capital. At home, he could weigh his options, discuss his ideas, and make a decision based upon the merits of the issues. He was not distracted by worrying whether his enemies would sabotage his ideas. Abigail, always his intelligent, informed, and wise counselor, carried on with him the kind of deliberation that helped him to decide the best course of action. She was the only advisor he trusted to be completely honest with him.

ADAMS HAD CAUGHT EVERYONE OFF GUARD. HIS CABINET MEMbers sputtered and protested, and in the end, he agreed to compromise. They begged him to send two more emissaries to accompany Murray to Paris, so he appointed Chief Justice Oliver Ellsworth and Governor William Davie of North Carolina to the delegation with Murray. And again, he compromised by agreeing to delay their mission until fall. Worn out, his business accomplished for the time being, Adams departed for Quincy in mid-March. He remained there for six months. For as much as Adams has been praised for his bold move to send a minister to France, his decision to remain in Quincy for so long a period during his presidency has puzzled historians. Clearly, many problems troubled him, aside from the business within the government. He needed to walk in his hills, mind his farm, and be close to Abigail. Moreover, he believed there was no compelling reason for him to be in the capital city, when his business could be conducted from Quincy.

In late August, however, he received a missive from the secretary of the navy, Benjamin Stoddert, urging him to return to the seat of government. Adams hesitated until Stoddert sent a second, even more urgent summons a few weeks later. By now the cabal that was against his policy had become alarming. In early October, Adams set off from Quincy to Trenton, where Congress sat while a yellow fever epidemic raged in Philadelphia. Abigail would follow him within weeks, as soon as she could take care of her household business.

Upon his arrival at Trenton, Adams sent Secretary of State Pickering an order to dispatch the emissaries immediately to France. Pickering hesitated but Adams insisted, and the two ministers, Ellsworth and Davie, departed in early November. That Adams could no longer trust his cabinet became even more evident when, within days, Hamilton appeared at his boardinghouse in Trenton to argue against the case for sending the ministers to France.

Adams controlled his temper at the outrageous breach of protocol. This intrusion into government business by a man with no official position made no sense. He listened to Hamilton's arguments with patience, if not contempt for the former secretary's naïveté about the foreign situation. Abigail, who later heard the entire story from John, repeated it to her sister. Hamilton had "been perfectly sanguine" in the belief that before long the French government would collapse and return "Louis the 18th upon the Thone of France." She repeated John's words: "I should as soon expect that the sun, moon & stars will fall from their orbits, as event of that kind take place." He pointed out further: "Have not the Directory Humbled themselves to us more than to any Nation or Power in contest with her?" John was confounded by Hamilton's failure to grasp the situation and, more, at his nerve and his political miscalculation. He summarily dismissed Hamilton, whose hope to lead the American armies in a war against France had been checked.

Adams, furthermore, finally decided to fire his untrustworthy opponents. It had been his plan to fire Pickering first. However, Secretary McHenry received that honor. He had come to discuss an issue of minor importance with the president and happened to mention Hamilton. With this, Adams lost his temper and berated the poor McHenry mercilessly as he perhaps should have done to Hamilton. McHenry, not the most vicious of his enemies, took the brunt of Adams's wrath and offered to resign. Adams apologized for his temper and accepted his resignation. He followed up by demanding Pickering's resignation, which was refused, not once but twice. Adams had no recourse but to remove Pickering from office. Hamilton was now twice refuted. He would need to take other steps to regain his power among the Federalists.

GEORGE WASHINGTON DIED IN DECEMBER, AND THE COUNTRY went into mourning. Adams sent his secretary, William Shaw, to Mount Vernon to carry personally the messages of condolence from himself, Abigail, and Congress. "No Man ever lived, more deservedly beloved and Respected," Abigail wrote to her sister. "History will not produce to us a Parrallel. Heaven has seen fit to take him from us." Thousands of mourners turned out for a memorial service to the former president. The church could only accommodate a small number, but the streets were filled. A few days later, Abigail ironically noted:

> Last frydays drawing Room was the most crowded of any I ever had. The Ladies Grief did not deprive them of taste in ornamenting their white dresses: 2 yds. of Black mode in length, of the narrow kind pleated upon one shoulder, crossd the Back in the form of a Military sash tyed at the side, crosd the peticoat & hung to the bottom of it.

The women had requested that Abigail set the length of the mourning period, but she "declined, and left them to Govern themselves."

The death of Washington brought forth an outpouring of national grief, but no person could have been more upset than Hamilton, who, while he genuinely had cared for his powerful mentor, recognized that his last conduit to political power had departed. As every mode of access closed, he needed to manufacture another route to power, and he did so. The upcoming election was on everyone's mind. Would Adams be reelected? Or had the mood of the country swung in another direction? Once more Hamilton would influence the outcome, this time with his pen. He wrote and circulated a pamphlet in which, because he could not undermine the president's policies, he maligned his character. He amplified Adams's weaknesses by feeding the many spiteful rumors that circulated in the opposition party and press. Adams, the Hamilton story ran, had no control over his temper. He was a madman.

All this time, while foreign policy, politics, social life, and a mean press preoccupied the Adamses, they were distracted by events in their private lives as well. They experienced massive grief over the declining fortunes of two of their children. In 1797, on her initial journey to Philadelphia as first lady, Abigail had stopped in East Chester to visit her daughter. What she discovered could not have surprised her. "My reflections upon prospects there, took from me all appetite to food, and depresst my spirits, before too low," she reported to Mary as soon as she arrived in Philadelphia. Col. Smith, her wastrel son-in-law, who had returned from his European adventures bankrupt, now hoped to recoup his losses with another capricious scheme. "The Col gone a journey, I knew not where, I could not converse with her. I saw her Heart too full." Sensitive to her daughter's plight, Abigail assured her sister, "To her no blame is due. Educated in different Habits, she never enjoyd a life of dissipation."

Again in the fall, Abigail visited her daughter, who was isolated in rural upstate New York with no support: "I want her to take her little Girl & go with us to Philadelphia," she explained. "Her feelings are such as you may suppose on such a proposal. What under different circumstances would have given her great pleasure, she now feels as a soar calimity." Nabby couldn't face the public spectacle of her husband's well-known extravagance and bankruptcy. "I make no reflections but in my own Breast." Abigail couldn't censure her daughter's husband, because like herself, Nabby was committed to her marriage. Unlike her own situation, both the husband and the separation lacked merit. "It is some comfort, to know that she has not been the cause, and that she could not prevent the misfortunes to which she is brought." With this burden of sorrow and anxiety for her daughter, Abigail resumed her journey to Philadelphia. She continued to hope that Abigail Smith would accompany her to the capital city, but the impropriety of her situation—a greatly indebted husband who had disappeared—discouraged her from appearing in public.

Still later Abigail reported to Mary that "Mrs Smith informed me that she had received Letters from the Col.," after many months of silence and that he should be home soon. Abigail no longer trusted him: "I fear that she will be waiting & expecting, expecting & waiting, the rest of the winter, but I cannot advise her not to stay a reasonable time." After more months, Abigail reported that the colonel had returned and "has notified his Credittors to meet him in order to adjust with them his affairs." Abigail's mixed reaction revealed her concerns for Nabby: "I am glad he has returnd. It really seemd to me at times, as if Mrs. Smith would lose herself. She has sometimes written me that existance was a burden to her; and that she was little short of distraction. I have been more distresst for her than I have been ready to own."

Abigail's distress for Nabby, and John's too, would continue through the years of his presidency, contributing to the tensions that they experienced in office. During the illness that would slow her down in the years to come, Nabby and her little daughter, Caroline, stayed with Abigail in Quincy. To assist their daughter, Abigail and John sent their two grandsons to live with Abigail's sister Elizabeth and her husband, just as they had their own sons many years previous. There they could be sure of the boys getting educated in a family environment they approved of.

John, hardly suppressing his anger, attempted to secure a military appointment for his son-in-law, but he delivered a strong tongue lashing as well: "Before you receive this, you will probably receive a letter from the Secretary of

War," he began a letter describing the appointment. "This event has embarrassed me. I know not what to do. I know not whether the Senate will not negative the nomination." The colonel next had to read the following from his father-in-law, who was also the president of the United States:

> Upon this occasion I must be plain with you. Your pride and ostentation, which I myself have seen with inexpressible grief for Many years, have excited among your neighbors so much envy and resentment, that if they have to allege against you any instance of dishonorable and dishonest conduct, as it is pretended they have, you may depend upon it, it will never be forgiven or forgotten. He whose vanity has been indulged and displayed to the humiliation and mortification of others, may depend on meeting their revenge whenever they shall find an opportunity for it. They are now taking vengeance on you with a witness.

Colonel Smith secured a position that was lower in rank than his experience warranted, and he had to serve under men who had previously been in his command. Chastened, he accepted.

Abigail anguished over her daughter's situation. Her letters to her sister Mary invoke religion as well as literature. "This is a very delicate subject," she wrote. "Every soul knows its own bitterness. Shall I receive good and not evil? I will not forget the blessings which sweeten Life," she continued, consoling herself. In the process of writing these words, Abigail worked her way from grief to hope.

But Nabby's miserable marriage was not the only family crisis of the Adamses' presidential years. More heartbreaking still for them both was the struggle of their middle son, Charles, with alcoholism. Mystery surrounds the causes and the course of his disease, reflecting the eighteenth-century shame that it produced. On her early trip to Philadelphia in 1797, Abigail reported to Mary about her visit with Charles and his family in New York: "Charles lives prettily but frugally. He has a Lovely Babe and a discreet woman I think for his wife." She wrote this as if she were relieved that his behavior had changed. Both she and John had vaguely alluded to his previous conduct as improper. Only when she was too sad to contain her words did more of the story spill onto the pages of Abigail's letters.

In October 1799, Abigail described her visit with her young granddaughters, Charles's daughters, in New York: "But I cannot look upon them my dear Sister with that Joy which you do upon yours. They make my Heart ache, and what is worse, I have not any prospect of their being better off." She added: "It is a trial of the worst kind. Any calamity inflicted by the hand of Providence, it would become me in silence to submit to, but when I behold misiry and distress, disgrace and poverty, brought upon a Family by intemperence, my heart bleads at every pore." Abigail did not condemn her son; she suffered because of the misfortune of his family in ruin.

John responded differently. He, too, had stopped to visit his son's family, where he discovered the depth of Charles's illness. At the same time, he carried with him the presidential burdens of preventing a war, defending himself from the scheming tactics of his opposition, and a multitude of decisions to make that affected the national welfare. Into this mix, he experienced the horror of seeing his beloved son, once the child who had bravely crossed the Pyrenees with him in winter; who had become homesick in the Netherlands and returned without a family member on a ship that detoured for three months on the Spanish coast; who had grown into a beautiful man who had some mischievous experiences at Harvard and yet graduated; who became the lawyer his father wished him to be. Yet, when he passed through New York on his way to Trenton, what he discovered was a "calamity." Sally, Charles's wife, had "Opened her Mind to me for the first time. I pitied her, I grieved, I mourned but could do no more." Possessed now with the evidence of the wretched life that Charles lived, John vowed: "I renounce him." These words, written to Abigail, tore at her heart, as did his description of their son as "a mere Rake, Buck, Blood and Beast." John hurt, too.

One year later, Abigail saw Charles for the last time when she traveled the long distance between Quincy and the new capital of Washington, D.C. "Mercy & judgement are the mingled cup allotted me," she wrote, turning once more to the religion that sustained her.

> Shall I receive good and not evil? At N York I found my poor un-
> hapy son, or so I must still call him, laid upon a Bed of sickness,
> destitute of a home. The kindness of a friend afforded him an as-
> sylum. A distressing cough, an affection of the liver and a dropsy
> will soon terminate a Life, which might have been made valuable
> to himself and others. You will easily suppose that this scene was
> too powerfull and distressing to me. Sally was with him, but his
> Physician says, he is past recovery—I shall carry a melancholy
> report to the President, who, pasing through New York without
> stoping, knew not his situation.

Three weeks later Charles was dead. "I know, my much loved Sister," a grief-stricken Abigail wrote:

that you will mingle in my sorrow, and weep with me over the Grave of a poor unhappy child who cannot now add an other pang to those which have peirced my Heart for several years past; Cut off in the midst of his days, his years are numberd and finished; I hope my supplications to heaven for him, that he might find mercy from his maker, may not have been in vain.

AFTER A LENGTHY AND ARDUOUS JOURNEY OVER TREACHER-ous roads, Abigail arrived in the partially built new capital city in the early afternoon of November 16, 1800. John had ridden out to meet her carriage and accompany her into the city. "As I expected to find it a new country, with Houses scatterd over a space of ten miles, and trees & stumps in plenty, with a castle of a House—so I found it," she wrote to Mary. "The Presidents House is in a beautifull situation in front of which is the Potomac with a view of Alexandr[i]a. The country around is romantic but a wilderness at present." She added, "Not one room or chamber is finished of the whole. It is habitable by fires in every part, thirteen of which we are obliged to keep daily, or sleep in wet and damp places." The Capitol, where Congress sat, was nearly two miles from the presidential mansion. "As to roads, we shall make them by the frequent passing." She was "determined to be satisfied and content, to say nothing of inconvenience." Of inconvenience, there was plenty. She dispatched Mr. Briesler to get firewood in Georgetown, which she gave even worse reviews: "It is the very dirtiest hole I ever saw for a place of any trade, or respectability of inhabitants . . . a quagmire after every rain. Here we are obliged to send daily for marketing." Putting her best slant on the unpleasant situation, she told Mary, "This House is built for ages to come."

The Adamses were not alone in their discomfort. Congress was in session, and the members as well as some few wives resided as best they could in boarding situations. The business of government continued, primarily concerned with the immediate issues of building and governing the new city. The delegation of three, John Marshall and Oliver Ellsworth from America and William Vans Murray from the Netherlands, were making their way toward Paris, where they would negotiate with the new ruler Napoléon Bonaparte's ministers about a treaty of amity between the two countries. The primary issue that involved all parties in Congress had to do with the next presidential election; the electors of each state would meet to cast their ballots on December 4. Only slowly did the information trickle into Washington.

While no candidate had overtly campaigned, a campaign had taken place, and an undercurrent of political infighting had ensued for months. The frontrunners, aside from the president, were Thomas Jefferson, whose minions worked the ranks of Republican electors at the state level, and Aaron Burr, the scheming and self-promoting New York lawyer and politician. In the wings was the ubiquitous Alexander Hamilton, determined to take revenge on Adams. His pamphlet, praising Adams as a man of integrity but undermining his character as a vain and temperamental man, was published in October, not long before Adams had set out for the new capital city. It took its toll in a way that Hamilton came to regret, as the one person Hamilton hated more than the president was his rival in New York politics, Aaron Burr.

The early returns in mid-December showed that Adams carried a small majority of the electoral vote, but this, as he well knew, was misleading. Then the "safe" states of Virginia and Massachusetts came in, and Adams still led over Jefferson. Next came South Carolina, giving the lead to Jefferson. Finally came the crushing surprise: Jefferson and Burr had tied, each receiving seventy-three votes, while Adams lagged behind with sixty-five votes. The Adamses received the news of John's defeat for a second term almost simultaneously with the news that Charles had died. If John Adams had a very bad day, which he did, so did Alexander Hamilton.

His administration at an end, John had only to ride out the remainder of his term in office. So did Abigail. About the death of her son, she wrote: "He was no mans Enemy but his own—He was beloved, in spight of his Errors, and all spoke with grief and sorrow for his habits." She loved her son and had deep sorrow for his weakness, for in that era, alcoholism was considered a personal failing, not a disease. And duty claimed her attention. "I would strive to act my part well and Retire with that dignity which is unconscious of doing or wishing ill to any, with a temper disposed to forgive injuries, as I would myself hope to be forgiven, if any I have committed."

The tie in the electoral vote between Thomas Jefferson and Aron Burr caused the election to move into the House of Representatives in February, where on the thirty-sixth ballot, Jefferson received the vote of ten states and became president of the United States. "What a lesson upon Elective Governments have we in our young Republic of 12 years old?" Abigail observed bitterly to her sister. "I have turnd, & turnd, and overturned in my mind at various time the merits & demerits of the two candidates. Long acquaintance, private friendship and the full belief that the private Character of one is much purer than the other, inclines me to him who has certainly from Age, succession and public employment the prior Right," she commented on the virtues of Jefferson. "Yet when I reflect upon the visionary system of Government which will undoubtedly be adopted, the Evils which must result from it to the Country I am sometimes inclined to believe that the more bold, daring and decisive Character would succeed in supporting the Government for a longer time." She meant Burr.

Abigail's outlook was bleak. She had begun to doubt the effectiveness of the electoral process and expressed uncertaintly about the durability of the government. "If ever we saw a day of darkness, I fear this is one." Her disappointment, of course, was personal. Abigail did not take John's defeat for a second term lightly. She felt massive regret for him. From the time he had begun to serve the nation in the early years of the rebellion against Great Britain, she had elided the well-being of the nation with John's service. Now that he had been rejected, she did not separate his programs, his policies, his whole system of belief about the political process and the operation of democratic government from her prognosis for the nation's future. Rejection of John Adams meant only ill for the country. As a consequence, when she departed from Washington, she was relieved to be done with public responsibilities, to return to private life, but she carried grim predictions for the nation's future.

She also dreaded the journey. "It is very formidable to me, not only upon account of the Roads, but the Runs of water which have not any Bridges over them, and must be forded," she complained to Mary. At the same time, she was still the nation's first lady. "To day the Judges and many others with the heads of department & Ladies dine with me for the last time," Abigail wrote to Mary on February 7, 1801. Above all, Abigail was practical, and she carried on her duties with good grace to the end of her term in the White House.

John's response was equally complicated. He put on a brave face as he observed his most formidable rivals conspire to remove him from office. He claimed to feel no enmity toward Thomas Jefferson. He steered through Congress the agreement made by his three agents to France to end that dispute. He appointed the judges that Congress had provided for by statute during his administration, as well as John Marshall to replace the ailing Oliver Ellsworth as chief justice and his nephew William Cranch as an associate judge for the District of Columbia. He secured an appointment of Colonel Smith as a sinecure in New York. He performed these duties as he had always performed his responsibilities of office, with dispatch, but undoubtedly with a different cast of mind. He fulfilled his role but with a heart hurting from the rejection that was greater for the grief he already experienced over the death of his son.

He experienced as well another death, that of his life in public service, a life that had ended before he was ready. He would have continued to serve had he won the election. The choice to retire was not his but that of the electoral college, perhaps the electorate. The system he had spent his productive years constructing had turned on him. More likely, some unscrupulous men had turned on him. To a man of his huge sensibilities, this produced a hurt that went very deep. While he broadly claimed that he would retire with ease to the life of farming—and he would—the choice had not been his. That made all the difference.

His best consolation at this time, as ever it had been during his troubled years in public service, was that Abigail, who always had been his anchor when life became difficult, had gone home to open their house and make it ready for the next chapter in their lives together. Their years of "splendid misery" had ended.

Thirteen

The Adamses Retire

"WELL, MY DEAR SON, SOUTH CAROLINA HAS BEHAVED AS YOUR father always said she would," Abigail wrote to Thomas Boylston Adams in November 1800. "The consequence to us, personally, is that we retire from public life." The operative phrase here is "retire from public life." She continued: "For myself and family I have few regrets. At my age and with my bodily infirmities, I shall be happier at Quincy," but she fretted, "I wish your father's circumstances weren't so limited and circumscribed." She feared that John's disengagement from politics would leave him bereft of activities.

Abigail's sage observation tells a truth that might still resonate. Retirement meant different things to women and men. In a world where the genders had functioned primarily in separate spheres, the lines between the spheres were fixed. Women never retired from their fundamental responsibilities in the domestic life, while men lost much of their basic engagement in the business of living. John acknowledged as much, writing to Abigail's uncle Cotton Tufts shortly before leaving office: "The only question remaining with me is what shall I do with myself? Something I must do, or ennui will rain upon me in buckets." When men retired from public life, they faced a conundrum; the upheaval could be profound and fundamental. Abigail looked forward to the routine that she knew awaited her at Quincy, and soon wrote to a friend that "I have commenced my operation of dairy woman," and that she might be seen "at five o'clock in the morning skimming my milk." She also suspected that John's world had so shifted that the transition would be problematic.

In fact, John took, to retirement more easily than she had predicted by following his own advice to work with his hands. Both Adamses soon reported that early each morning, armed with hoe and shovel, John took to his fields and worked beside his farmhands. His diary entries for the summer months of 1804 describe his farming activities. From early July, he had supervised the haying operations and recorded the regular rhythm of the carts that carried the hay from one place to another. On the third of the month, they had transported "One Load, from the road to the ditch and from the cart path to the pasture Lane." The following day: "Four Loads, over the Way and between the ditch and orchard." And so it continues for weeks until his last entry in August 1804: "The last Week in August We ploughed a ditch and brought the Earth into the Yard and 32 loads of Mud from the Cove." John's best therapy in the months after leaving the presidency had been to engage in the enterprise that had been his lifelong respite. Meanwhile, Abigail, as she knew she would, entered into a familiar world of caring for family and household and socializing. Both Adamses read prodigiously and wrote letters to their far-flung family and friends.

The Adams household at Peacefield, or Manzinilla ("little hill"), as John was wont to call his home in an ironic reference to his presidential successor's plantation, Monticello ("little mountain"), was expansive. Family members came and went. There were constant visits from dignitaries, neighbors, old friends, and the merely curious who dropped by to see the former president. The number of resident members of their household appeared infinitely plastic with the comings and goings of three generations of Adamses. In addition to the permanent fixtures of servants and farm laborers, their children, in-laws, and many grandchildren came regularly and for extended visits.

Peacefield became home for long periods to Sally Adams, the widow of Charles, and her two daughters, Abigail and Susanna. Whenever John Quincy was between posts, he returned to his parents' home, bringing at first his new bride, Louisa Catherine, and their one-year-old child, George Washington Adams. In later years, when John Quincy became the American minister in Saint Petersburg, they left their two older sons under the charge of their grandparents. Thomas came home to practice law in 1803 and lived intermittently with his parents after his marriage to Ann Harrod in 1805. Abigail Smith, her daughter, Caroline, and sometimes her husband, Colonel William Stephens Smith, visited with her parents, staying for a summer when they made the long journey from Upstate New York. The Smith sons, William and John, stayed with their grandparents during their holidays from school in Haverhill, where Abigail's sister Elizabeth resided. Seldom did the Adamses experience silence or neglect in the home that attracted multitudes because of family, social, or political ties. Over all of this commotion, Abigail presided as hostess, sometimes as cook and housekeeper, partly because of her energy, which was too prodigious for her to retire in the face of work that needed to be done. Mostly, however, it conformed to her ethic of hospitality. "To be attentive to our guests is not only true kindness, but true politeness; for if there is a virtue which is its own reward, hospitality is that virtue," she explained to her granddaughter.

For the remainder of her life Abigail was afflicted with recurrent rheumatism and sometimes inflammations of the eyes and skin that defy diagnosis these many years later. John, too, suffered with bouts of the common cold and injuries, such as the time he gashed his leg by tripping over a tree stump while walking after dark. Abigail became more explicitly religious in her letters over the years, invoking blessings and curses, and quoting the prophets. John corresponded about politics and history with his old friends, among them Dr. Benjamin Rush, until the latter's death in 1813.

One exchange of letters in particular survives to illustrate his enduring hurt over the election of 1800—and the resentment, as well, of his correspondent: Mercy Otis Warren. During the many years of their friendship, John had promoted Mercy's literary efforts, reading and commenting on her poetry and plays as well as encouraging their publication. Early in the war, Mercy had considered writing a history of the Revolution, modeling her efforts on her idol, the English historian Catherine Macaulay, and this project, too, both Abigail and John had enthusiastically supported. As time passed, however, the Warrens and the Adamses had grown apart, mostly because of their differing politics, but also because John became prickly when James Warren turned down numerous government positions, while John continued to serve. As result, John worried about Mercy's portrayal of him in her history. "My most profound Respects to Mrs. Warren. I dread her History," he had written to James Warren in early 1780. Later he wrote reminding her to include in her chronicle his important mission to the Netherlands, which had resulted in the large loan that rescued the American economy at a critical time during the war. Mercy published her great *History of the Rise, Progress and Termination of the American Revolution: Interspersed with Biographical, Political and Moral Observations* in 1805.

Given John's anxiety about his place in history and his sensitivity to criticism, Mercy's portrayal of him was devastating. As he had feared, she gave scant attention to his diplomatic achievements and none to his Dutch ministry, while implying that he had become a monarchist and was driven by personal ambition. To say that John was disappointed is a massive understatement. He exploded, and in a flood of letters he discredited himself by attacking her facts, her oversights, her balance, and her interpretation. She, in turn, in a series of responses, distinguished herself by moderation, reason, and patience. He was offended; he was outraged; he was hurt. She, in turn, was rational and defensive. The result was a standoff, except that their correspondence survived and provided more evidence to demean John Adams's lasting legacy. He made the grave mistake of telling her that women should not write history. He wrote in anger, and he clearly did not mean all that he wrote. Had Abigail known at the time he wrote this blast of temperamental rhetoric, she would have doubtlessly tamed his language. It was his private correspondence, and he permitted his emotions to overwhelm his reason. This exchange of letters survived to help paint an enduring image of John Adams as vain, pompous, and a misogynist, which he was not.

But John was not the only person to carry on a secret correspondence during the early years of their retirement. Abigail did as well during a good part of the year 1804. Mary Jefferson Eppes, known as Polly, died in childbirth that year. She had been the little girl that Abigail had cared for in London in 1787, when the child had crossed the ocean to join her father in Paris. During the few weeks that Polly had stayed with Abigail, the lonely mother and the lonely girl had grown to love each other, and both were saddened when Jefferson sent for his daughter. Learning that she had died, Abigail could not restrain herself from writing a condolence letter to Jefferson, despite the breach that had occurred in their friendship in 1801. Adams and Jefferson had ceased to communicate. Abigail, not wishing to revive John's heartache and animosity, wrote without informing him. Jefferson responded to her warmly, but a comment in his letter caused Abigail to reply. As a result, an exchange took place between them over the course of nine months in which each of them attempted to correct the political record of their discord. In the end, they, too, concluded with a standoff, agreeing to disagree about their past. In the end, Abigail showed the whole of their correspondence to John, who left no record of his reaction, other than that he had read through the whole of it. The breach would continue for almost another decade.

This is how the years passed. Abigail and John were surrounded by their family and friends. They no longer traveled, unless it was to Boston or a neighboring village. They engaged in the ordinary activities of daily life; they read and they wrote letters. A new generation of Adamses had entered the ranks of letter writing, as grandchildren grew up and joined in the family sport. Abigail and John lived modestly because their fortunes were small. The failure of a financial speculation in London in 1803 destroyed their security, and now their farm provided the majority of their livelihood. They were content to live frugally and peacefully with each other just as they had longed

Gilbert Stuart failed to complete this portrait of Abigail Adams, begun in 1800, until urged to do so in 1813 by John Quincy Adams. Her dress is preserved at the Adams National Park site in Quincy. Courtesy of the National Gallery of Art.

John Adams was bored when having his portrait painted, but he did enjoy sitting for Gilbert Stuart, who was an excellent conversationalist. This is one of several done by Stuart, completed in 1798. Courtesy of the National Gallery of Art.

to do during the many years of their separations. The tranquility of retirement, however, did not last.

On June 30, 1811, John Quincy Adams, then American minister to the court of Saint Petersburg, wrote to his mother: "The President has informed me of that [letter] which you had written to him, and of which you have *not* [my emphasis] sent me a copy." If this was a rebuke to Abigail, it was as harsh as John Quincy could ever be with his mother. He continued, explaining that "on the 4th day of January last," he had received a recall from his post by the secretary of state, directing him to return to America. One month later, he received a letter from President Madison, explaining the circumstances of the recall and communicating "my official leave to go home."

What had apparently happened was that without informing her son, the diplomat, Abigail had written to President Madison, requesting that her son be recalled from his post in Russia to return home. The president duly complied, and he sweetened the offer by nominating John Quincy to the Supreme Court to fill the position of the late Justice Cushing.

Whatever his private reaction to this situation in which his aged mother had meddled, perhaps too greatly, in his professional life, his response to her was gentle. He explained, quite rationally, that the president's letter had arrived in winter, when the harbor was frozen, and ships weren't sailing until June. By that time it would be inadvisable for them to travel, because—and he coded this reference to a very personal matter—his wife was expecting a baby. Besides, he wrote, he liked Saint Petersburg and they were happy there. And he wrote the words that would be a stab in the heart to any mother: "I have declined the seat on the Bench."

What were Abigail's motives for interfering not only in the professional but also the private affairs of her older son? It was uncharacteristic of her to trespass in the lives of her children—or her husband for that matter. During all the years of the Revolutionary War, when John had served his nation at distant posts, she had tolerated loneliness and adversity without demanding his return. It was not her choice to continue in public service when John became vice president and then president of the United States, yet she had gone along with his ambitions. Nor had she discouraged any of her children in their peregrinations. Only once, when John Quincy served as ambassador to Berlin in 1800, a post to which his father had appointed him, had she urged him to come home. And her justifications to her son at that time were similar to this most recent claim on him.

It was her opinion, she wrote, "that he might render more essential service to his Country at home than he can abroad, but if his Country should not see fit to avail itself of his talents, it is high time for him to think, of making some steady and permanent establishment for himself," and the longer he delayed, the harder it would be to establish himself at home. Diplomats in foreign service, she argued, are soon forgotten, whereas statesmen at home are appreciated. She argued that his children needed him. She noted that his and his wife's health were jeopardized by being abroad rather than in the healthy air of America. But in the end, in both situations, in 1800 and now in 1811, she finally got around to acknowledging her personal motives. "Should the lives of your parents be prolonged a few more years, your presence will prolong and heighten the few remaining pleasures and comforts which remain to advanced Age." Abigail was, in 1811, sixty-seven years old, and John was ten years her senior. She continued, "I will take it for granted that after mature reflection you will resign yourself to the call of your Country and hold the scales of Justice with an honest heart, and a steady hand." She advised him to bring home his "Beds, and linnen, both sheeting and table Linnen, and any other furniture you have suitable for this country." She took for granted that he would return; her letter crossed in the mails with his that informed her of his intention to remain in Saint Petersburg.

That Abigail wanted her son to return in 1800 and again in 1811 had fundamentally to do with conditions in her life and not his. In 1800, John's election defeat was the least of Abigail's trials. At the same time that parties were contesting the presidency, much in the Adamses' personal lives was in disarray. Their beloved middle son, Charles, had died. In addition, Colonel Smith had disappeared into the Northwest Territory and not been heard from in months. Was he dead or had he abandoned the family? They didn't know. Abigail was distraught. Now, in 1811, more than a decade into their "retirement years," more difficult trials awaited her. It was not a good time in the Adams household. If retirement implied ease and repose, a comfortable withdrawal from the complexities of life, this was not the case for the Adamses.

Several months after writing to President Madison suggesting John Quincy's return to America, Abigail wrote to her daughter, then living in upstate New York. "I am very anxious respecting what in your last letter dated January you mentioned to me. I have sent you Dr. Welchs opinion. Dr. Hollbrook concurred in the application of the medicine, but both have agreed you had better be present. that they could judge better & advise to more effect. Let me know particularly concerning the state of it." Then she added, more urgently: "And let me hear from you as soon as possible."

Abigail's oblique references to an illness would soon be confirmed; Nabby had breast cancer. Three months later she was on her way to Quincy to consult with physicians in Boston, Drs. Welch and Hollbrook, who concurred in the diagnosis of what now is considered stage-four cancer. If Abigail Smith was mortified by the prospect of the therapy, her mother was terrified by the prospect of her daughter's demise. In the early nineteenth century, breast cancer—indeed, all cancer—carried a death warrant.

But Nabby's misfortunes were not the only concerns in the Adams household during the spring of 1811. "I have been in great distress for this fortnight for my dear Sister Cranch whose valuable Life has for more than a week been despaired of from a pleurisy fever reduced to the very brink of the Grave." Nor was her sister Mary's tuberculosis the end of the story. Mary's husband, Richard Cranch, too, was afflicted with a mortal disease. These two people were the Adamses' closest relatives—indeed, Richard Cranch had introduced John to Abigail nearly a half century previous, when he courted Mary in the Smith home—but, further, the Cranches were the caretakers of eight grandchildren, some of whom had lived with them since the death of their mother, Elizabeth Cranch Norton. Crisis was heaped upon crisis in the spring of 1811.

Living within the Adams household, furthermore, were Sally Adams, widow of Charles, who died in 1800, and her daughter Susanna. Sally was chronically ill, this time with a "Hectic" and was "puking blood," another grisly symptom that escapes contemporary diagnosis. In addition, Abigail wrote to John Quincy that his brother Thomas had been "confined for 5 weeks from a fall from his

Horse. Which bruised him so much that an absess was formed upon his thigh, which has been opend and we now hope is upon the recovery." Infections could be, in that age before antibiotics, lethal, as everyone well knew.

Abigail's world at this moment in her "retirement" was marked by illness, accidents, and death. John's was, too, but Abigail wrote about it emotionally and at length in letters to her son and other family members, whereas John, who doubtless suffered just as much, did not. Our information about the catastrophes in the Adams household comes from Abigail's legacy of letters.

By the time Abigail again wrote to John Quincy after a very hot summer that everyone complained about, the news was mixed—she wrote of "dirges" but also mercies and judgments," she claimed. "I have past through scenes, my dear son, in this last year, most solumn and impressive. God grant that it may be good for me that I have been afflicted." She regularly called upon her most puritanical religion during these trying times. The Cranches had died within two days of each other, and Abigail wrote on paragraph after paragraph, citing their virtuous and good characters and describing her grief. "Would to heaven my tale of sorrow was closed[;] a more distressing one remains to be told." She broke the news to her daughter-in-law Louisa Catherine Johnson Adams that her mother, Catherine Johnson, had died. "My own Bosom has been so lacerated with repeated stories of woe that I can mingle tear for tear, with the afflicted daughters of my esteemed Friend." And to John Quincy: "Tell them my dear son that I pray for them. That they may be comforted, and that they may find consolation in that religion which teaches us submission and resignation under every dispensation of providence."

But this letter goes on to tell the good news that the operation upon his sister had been performed "in which the whole Breast was taken off," and that Abigail junior was healing rapidly, although she could not yet use her arm. Little is known about the operation in which Mrs. Smith's entire breast was amputated. The precise date of it is unknown, although it probably took place within the first two weeks of October 1811. Nor is there information about the location of the surgery, but again, it probably took place at the Adams home, as was the convention in the eighteenth century. Medical books of the period emphasize that speed was the surgeon's critical skill, since anesthesia did not exist.

There are many reasons for the lack of information about the mastectomy. Abigail's most intimate correspondents, her husband and sisters, lived nearby, and she spoke with them. Then, breast cancer was a forbidden area of discourse, into the late twentieth century. A recent author has written that cancer "is felt to be obscene—in the original meaning of the word: ill-omened, abominable, repugnant to the senses."

Among the ordeals that afflicted the Adamses in 1811, Nabby's apparent recovery was a blessing. Abigail also acknowledged gratefully the birth of John
Quincy and Louisa Catherine's daughter. She admitted to her son that "your
Father and I are quite satisfied with your declining the seat upon the Bench as
you could not return in season . . . but I am not satisfied with your other arguments. I think your samples not well founded. But you must think and judge for
yourself." Abigail did not give up easily.

Nabby and her daughter, Caroline, remained at Quincy through that winter,
and in the spring returned to their home in upstate New York after a confirmation of a complete recovery by her Boston surgeons. Abigail was thrilled. Only
in April there was again cause to grieve in the Adams household, this time announced to John Quincy by his father, who wrote that he had "been called
lately to weep . . . over the remains of a beautiful Babe of your Brother's, less
than a year old." John mourned: "Why have I been preserved more than three
quarters of a Century, and why was that fair flower wasted so soon: are questions that we are not permitted to ask." John, too, practiced Christian submission and resignation. Only a few months later, in Saint Petersburg, John Quincy's
newborn daughter also died.

Nabby's reprieve was not long-lasting. The following winter she was afflicted with what everyone called "rheumatism," although this probably repre-
sents a classic case of denial. By the spring of 1813 it was clear that the cancer
had returned in the other breast and had, in fact, metastasized throughout her
body. Abigail despaired that she was too infirm to travel to New York: "My heart
bleeds," she wrote to John Quincy. "I cannot get to her. Nor she to me. I am too
infirm myself to undertake such a journey." Despite her condition, in a desperate
effort of will and accompanied by her daughter, Caroline, and son John, Nabby
made the arduous journey to be with her parents. She rode the rough three-
hundred-mile highway for fifteen days by stagecoach and cart to die in her parents' home. "She is indeed a very sick woman. Spasms draw her up. Cannot take
food. Everything oppresses her," Abigail wrote to her niece. Three weeks later
Nabby died. She was forty-nine years old.

It has been observed that the English language, while it has a word for children who lose parents and spouses who lose spouses, has no word for the parent
who suffers the loss of a child. It is so unnatural, so grotesque, perhaps, that no
word exists to describe the condition. This was Abigail Adams's response to the
death of her daughter. Her grief poured out in letter after letter to whomever
she could think to write. She described her daughter's virtues, her suffering, her
courage, and she described her own changed state: "Years of affliction have

made such depredations upon your parents, more particularly upon your mother," she wrote to John Quincy, "that should she live to see you again, you will find her so changed in person, that you will hardly know her." For months, indeed for two years at least, the Adams household had been a scene not of tranquil retirement but rather of sickness and death, fear and grief.

Something else was going on during this period, however, that has much more grabbed the attention of historians than the problems within the Adams household. This was the two-year period when very tentatively John Adams initiated the resumption of contact with Thomas Jefferson after a hiatus of more than ten years. After Jefferson responded to Adams, the two Founding Fathers found a way to mend a breach that had separated them since Thomas Jefferson became president in 1801.

The story is familiar. In 1801, a defeated and wounded John Adams departed from the capital—crept out of town, the story goes—in the early hours before Jefferson's inaugural, seething with anger and envy, hurt beyond words by his electoral defeat for reasons that had less to do with the merits of his tenure as president than it did with pernicious and secretive political subversion by his enemies in both parties. More than anyone else, John focused his distress on Jefferson for his political chicanery and disloyalty. Thereafter, but for a few perfunctory business notes in 1801, the two former close friends did not communicate. Both remained fixed in their hostility, even after the nine-month period in 1804, when Abigail briefly corresponded with Jefferson following the death of his daughter Polly.

The story continues that after another long passage of time, in 1811, Dr. Benjamin Rush, who had for several years attempted to mend the breach between his two friends, succeeded in bringing them together. More specifically, during the summer of 1811, John Adams received as a visitor Edward Coles, then secretary to President Madison. In the course of conversation, Coles mentioned Jefferson, which set Adams off in a typical tirade, recalling all of the abuse he had suffered at Jefferson's hand. After rehearsing his grievances, John paused and then exclaimed, "I always loved Jefferson and love him still." Coles, the story continues, lost no time in insuring that John's words of affection got back to Jefferson. Jefferson, not one to act peremptorily in a personal matter, forwarded the information to Benjamin Rush, who in turn once more wrote to John that Jefferson would be receptive to contact. Significantly, John wrote to Jefferson on January 1, 1812, and the process of reconciliation was begun. This is how historians know the story.

No doubt that there is truth in this explanation of the reformation of the

Adams-Jefferson breach and the restoration of their epistolary friendship. But this political reconciliation can be explained differently, by shifting the historic lens to events within the Adams domestic world.

John's letter to Jefferson, actually only a note to accompany the gift of a pamphlet by John Quincy, was addressed January 1, 1812, perhaps not so coincidentally, a few months after his daughter's mastectomy and the whole string of catastrophes in the Adams household that was only beginning when Edward Coles visited in the summer of 1811. The connections between all these events begin to fall into place.

John Adams reached out to Jefferson, offered an olive branch in the winter of 1812, not just because Coles's visit had given him an opportunity to send a message to his erstwhile friend and now adversary, not only because Rush had been working behind the scenes to repair the relationship between the Founding Fathers, not only because political men maneuvered and engineered this reunion, but because of family circumstances. The events of 1811 had so "lacerated" John's bosom that he, like Abigail, constructed an avenue of hope as a coping mechanism to allay the fear and pain that encompassed their lives.

While Abigail attached her fantasy to the prospect of John Quincy Adams's return home "to the bosom of his parents," John also discovered a bold means to protect himself from circumstances as they were. It was a radical move that had the effect of drawing his attention away from the scenes of illness and death that pervaded his household. And just as Abigail announced that she had changed and was possibly unrecognizable from the person she had been, John, too, was experiencing an upheaval in his world.

Possibly he, too, now placed greater importance on contact with old friends as more gratifying than living with conflict. While Abigail wrote about her grief and her changed demeanor in her letters, John found a way to palliate his suffering by taking the measure of his commitments and finding that caring for people was less hurtful to him than fighting with them.

And clearly the same dynamic was at work when John Adams broke with Jefferson and sneaked out of the capital on the morning of March 4, 1801. Certainly he was wounded by the loss of the presidency, certainly he was angry with Jefferson and the whole gang of Federalists who had maneuvered the rejection of his presidency, but he also was suffering what he called "the greatest grief of my life," over the death of his beloved and charming son Charles. Battered by complex and compounded emotions, his world shattered, he hadn't the strength or the taste to face a public ceremony to celebrate his defeat.

The rest is history. After 1812, Adams and Jefferson corresponded until the time of their miraculous simultaneous deaths on July 4, 1826. John Quincy Ad-

ams did return to the bosom of his parents, triumphantly in 1815, having negotiated the peace that ended the War of 1812. This time his mother's heart was
inflated, and she preened: "Just think," she wrote to her sister Elizabeth, John
Quincy was now chosen to repeat the triumph of his father in writing a peace
treaty to end the belligerence with England that would establish, finally, American independence.

When Abigail worried to Thomas Boylston Adams in 1800 that John would
face difficulty in his retirement, she had miscalculated on several fronts. John
did what was for him, probably, the healthiest occupation; he farmed, and if
physical activity did not eliminate his sorrows, it at least diminished their impact
on his conscious world. It did not, however, remove his grief. Ten years later, in
the midst of another set of crises that perhaps recalled the earlier torments, he
once more took action that sheltered him from events. The fact is that personal
issues, factors from the private family sphere, had moved John Adams to take
action in the familiar sphere of his lifelong activities, in politics. His behavior,
consequently, has been misunderstood; events in the private life of his family
were manifest in his reaction to events in his public life. Historians have noted
primarily the public activity as motivated by character and personality without
taking account of primary sources of the entire complex of enterprises that
framed his life.

And just as John's behavior in the public sphere resonated to impulses in his
private life, so too were Abigail's activities marked not only by her passive
reading, thinking, and talking about events in the world of politics. Abigail
ventured to influence public life when she wrote to President Madison to request that her son be recalled from his ministerial duties in Saint Petersburg.
Whereas her plea to John Quincy to return in 1800 had been made within the
confines of family exchanges, this time, in 1811, she was a first lady in retirement, and she was emboldened to take another route to accomplish her ends.
This time she wrote directly to the president and used her personal influence to
get his attention, knowing that he would respect her as a former public figure.

The domestic and the public spheres are permeable. What happens in the one
affects what happens in the other. This might not be news, but hitherto our sights
have mostly been fixed on the influence of the public world on the domestic
world. The path of influence, however, runs in two directions, as has been
clearly seen in this story about retirement in the Adams household.

There are many further observations to make about retirement. We note
that old age is not for the faint-hearted. Abigail observed as much when she
wrote to John Quincy that grief and suffering had been reserved to her later
years, belying the myth of leisure and easy repose. Like John, however, she

kept up her spirits greatly by staying alert to the public events of her time, lecturing her sister Elizabeth, for instance, about the conduct of the War of 1812. "Until you know what goes into decision making at the highest level," she wrote, "you do not have sufficient information to criticize the president's policies." She disliked Napoléon and cheered his defeat, though she worried that he might be exiled to America. She heaped praise upon Admiral Perry for his conquest on Lake Erie and in the end got to exult in her son's appointment as a delegate to negotiate the peace in 1815. Perhaps, in some measure, this compensated for John Quincy's continued absence and his decline of a seat on the Supreme Court.

Fourteen

Time and Silence

"I HAVE BEEN READING A NOVEL CALLED THE WILD IRISH GIRL," Abigail wrote to her granddaughter Caroline, and explained the novel's plot about a young woman, who, after a devastating war, lived with her reclusive father in an "ancient barony" and, besides playing the harp, learned history and became a botanist. Abigail's storytelling to grandchildren generally included a lesson, in this case the importance of female education, especially in the disciplines that had traditionally been privileged to men only. Her many grandchildren received the same bounty of lectures that many years ago her own children had read. She wrote: "Always remember that you are accountable to that being who brought you into existence, for your time and talents," reminding Caroline of her religious obligations, and

> that you were not born for yourself, but to fill every hour with some useful employment, as says the song:
>
> > Man was created for useful employ,
> > From earth's first creation till now;
> > And 'tis good for his health, his comfort and joy,
> > To live by the sweat of his brow.

John, too, in the years remaining to him wrote letters to his far-flung family, keeping intact the firm connections between the generations. His messages to them were affectionate, whimsical, and reflective, but served the same purpose

as Abigail's, to bind the Adams family line by a set of values that included service and vocation in the tradition of their forebears. He wrote to his granddaughter to congratulate her on the birth of a baby girl, telling her that she
should imitate her mothers and grandmothers from the seventh and eighth generation. "Such a race of mothers has rarely existed in this world, I believe." To
his young grandsons, when they left for England to join their parents, he suggested "they should always carry a pencil in their pockets and be prepared
to make notes on any unusual or extraordinary thing they saw or heard." The
family habit of maintaining a diary or journal was "indispensable."

As they lived through the last years of their lives, Abigail and John both
were increasingly afflicted with physical infirmities that curtailed their activities. Both of them knew that their days were limited, a perception that persisted,
actually, for many years. Almost a decade before she died, Abigail wrote to
Caroline that "old age with its infirmities assail me. I have reason to be thankful
that my senses are so much in action, that my hearing is not at all impaired, but
my memory and recollection are not what they once were." She echoed the familiar observations about old age, fear of losing the capacity to function independently. She continued, however: "My heart is still warm, and my affections
fervent towards my dear children and friends." She expressed her gratitude for
her intact emotions: "When they cease to beat for their welfare and happiness,
nature itself will expire, and the cold hand of death close the eyes of your affectionate grandmother."

Similarly, John enjoyed the bounty of his grandchildren, though he missed
his eldest son. "You know not the grief that your long absence of almost five
years has given me!" he wrote to John Quincy. But John Quincy, now serving
in his father's former post as American minister in London, and Louisa Catherine had left their sons with Abigail and John for their education. Charles
(named for his uncle) was his grandfather's "little jewel," George his "friend
and companion," and John "the most high-spirited of the three."

Two years after his daughter's terrible death, John wrote to John Quincy
that "the last Fourteen years have been the happiest of my life." What he meant,
clearly, was that he felt more at peace with himself. No small part of this transformation in his temperament had to do with Abigail. For fourteen uninterrupted years they had lived together, sharing adversity and grief, circumstances
that he now accepted were beyond his capacity to control. John Adams no longer carried the burden of shaping himself and his world to conform to remote
standards.

Abigail, had she written about John's changed outlook, would have attributed it directly to adversity and grief. She had coped by submitting to her para-

doxical religious belief that good was always embedded in a terrible experience, and further, that there cannot be good without evil. Her providential acceptance of circumstances informed her that human suffering was preordained for some good reason beyond human understanding. While she suffered, she also assumed that she would be reunited with her loved ones in the afterlife.

John merely mellowed. He stopped fighting with the world; he permitted himself to heal old wounds and tolerate people and events as they were. John, too, was religious, and he spent a good deal of ink thrashing out his religious beliefs with his friend Jefferson during the course of their renewed correspondence. Jefferson spent his ink explaining to Adams the many ways in which his religious faith had been misinterpreted. In the end, the two old statesmen agreed that they were not too far apart in their beliefs, that both believed in a force greater than man and in an afterlife. Their primary religious concern had to do with morality, a topic that launched the two founders on their exploration of human behavior.

But Abigail and John were both correct in their assessment of John's different demeanor. For the first time since their wedding, they had a conventional marriage, and if anything, they grew closer. They were loving, compassionate, and expressive with each other. When their granddaughter Caroline invited them to visit her in New York, Abigail declined, because while she was willing to make the arduous trip, John was not, and she would not leave him alone, even for a few weeks. Both of them suffered infirmities, Abigail more so than John. Each time they said good-bye to a relative or friend, they thought they were seeing them for the last time. Believing the end of life to be near, they treasured their companionship with more tender consideration and care for each other.

But adversity had also made its claim on John's temperament. It was after the deaths of their daughter, the Cranches, and many others that John renewed his friendship with Jefferson. His vast correspondence with family and friends took on a different tone. He no longer expressed anger for slights; he forgot the old enmities; he praised his children and grandchildren, overlooking their flaws and extolling their virtues. He relished the luxury of freedom to read in his vast library and his discussions with his many visitors, some of them young college men who arrived to test their learning against the old scholar. He devoted himself to his grandchildren, who lived with him, perhaps as a compensation for having missed the youth of his own children.

Among their afflictions, as they aged, their declining eyesight counted as a major problem. Both complained about the difficulty of writing and reading. Likely, they both had cataracts or another ocular impediment that impaired vision. As a result, their handwriting became more difficult to read, though John's palsy also caused his hands to tremble too badly to write. Often Louisa Smith, Abigail's niece who had lived with them since her father had died in 1783, read to them. Sometimes it was Susanna Adams Clark, Charles's daughter, who had married young, been widowed, and returned with her child to live with them. Nor does it appear that they despaired when their son Thomas failed in his law practice, possibly because he, like his older brother, had become alcoholic. Thomas with his wife and six children came to live in their ever-flexible household. Thomas's children, too, became readers for their grandparents.

Longtime close friends among the revolutionary generation began to pass on, among them James Warren, Benjamin Rush, and Elbridge Gerry. In 1815, Abigail's younger sister Elizabeth, who had cared for all of the Adams children and some of their grandchildren, breathed her last, and Abigail cried "till her eyes were red." And when Mercy Otis Warren died, Abigail wrote: "Take her all in all, we shall not look upon her like again." Old antagonisms were forgotten. "To me she was a friend of more than fifty summers ripening." Colonel Smith's death evoked yet another painful recollection of a life that had become dearer after the Adamses became reconciled to his foolish but well-meaning character. Each time Abigail wept and grieved, and each time, along with John, she found solace in the belief that they would meet their loved ones hereafter.

"Yesterday completed half a century since I entered the married state, then just your age," Abigail wrote to Caroline. Summarizing those years, she continued: "I have great cause of thankfulness that I have lived so long, and enjoyed so large a portion of happiness as has been my lot." Like John, Abigail in her old age looked back over her life with gratitude. "The greatest source of unhappiness I have known in that period, has arisen from the long and cruel separations which I was called in a time of war, and with a young family around me, to submit to." Separation from John Adams had been her "great unhappiness." She wrote the same to Secretary of State James Monroe: "Early instructed to relinquish personal considerations and enjoyment to the call of my country, Surrounded with a young family, I submitted to many years of seperation during the revolution from my protecter, the friend of my youth, my companion and husband of my choice." In each case, she emphasized the sacrifice of companionship with her husband as her greatest regret but also her response to the call of duty in wartime.

At the end of her life, Abigail reflected to her sister Elizabeth that: "After half a century, I can say, my choice would be the same if I again had youth. And the opportunity to make it." She affirmed that she did not regret marrying John Adams, this most momentous choice in her life. She had cursed the circumstances that separated them, but not the man to whom she had contracted to submit her destiny. She admitted, however, that marriage had not been without conflict: "I have sometimes insisted upon my own way. And my opinion and sometimes yealded silently." She satisfied herself that she had made choices about their lives together as well as acquiescing to John's choices. Her last thoughts ranged over the span of her dynamic years without regret about her choice of partner, but she confessed that marriage had involved compromises on both their parts.

IN THE FALL OF 1818, ABIGAIL CONTRACTED HER FINAL ILLNESS, typhus, which lingered for weeks of terrible fevers and infirmity. She was surrounded by family members who cared for her. As he sat by her bedside during her last days, John lamented: "I wish I could lie down beside her and die, too." Death came to her on October 28, 1818.

John Quincy, then secretary of state, had come from Washington in late August with Louisa Catherine, but to his bitter disappointment, he departed before her death. Bereft, he wrote: "Had she lived to the age of the Patriarchs, every day of her life would have been filled with clouds of goodness and love. There is not a virtue that can abide in the female heart but it was the ornament of hers. Never have I known another human being the perpetual object of whose life was so unremittingly to do good." He concluded with Solomon: "Her price indeed was above rubies."

John Adams received sympathetic letters from many people, none more moving to him than one from Thomas Jefferson, who wrote: "I know well, and feel what you have lost, what you have suffered, are suffering, and have yet to endure. The same trials have taught me that, for ills so immeasurable, time and silence are the only medicines." John Adams memorialized Abigail simply as "the dear Partner of my Life for fifty four Years as a Wife and for many years more as a Lover."

For the eight years that remained of his life, he reminisced again about Abigail, and like her, his memory focused on the difficult years of the Revolution. He recalled in a letter to his granddaughter Caroline that more than forty years earlier he had purchased for his wife a copy of "the life and letters of Lady Russell." The year was 1775, and he had "sent it to your grandmother, with an express intent and desire, that she should consider it a mirror in which to contemplate herself." John had chosen biography, a life based on letters, he explained, to forecast a possible scenario about their situation and to carry a message about her prospects. "I thought it extremely probable, from the daring and dangerous career I was determined to run, that she would one day find herself in the situation of Lady Russell, her husband without a head."

John continued his reverie about Abigail: "This Lady was more beautiful than Lady Russell, had a brighter genius, more information, a more refined taste, and, at least, her equal in the virtues of the heart; equal fortitude and firmness of character, equal resignation to the will of Heaven, equal in all the virtues and graces of the christian life." He then shifted from character to behavior: "She never by word or look discouraged me from running all hazards for the salvation of my country's liberties; she was willing to share with me, and that her children should share with us both, in all the dangerous consequences we had to hazard." She had been, he told his granddaughter, above all and quintessential within their revolutionary generation, a patriotic wife and mother.

John's survival amazed him and those around him. His family was concerned about how he would manage without Abigail. He always had thought, he wrote, that because she was ten years younger, he would predecease her. Since that had not been the case, he carried on with as bright an outlook as he could muster. "The bitterness of death is past," he wrote to John Quincy. "The grim Specter so terrible to human Nature has no sting left for me." He did have many consolations. His house was full of children, and he loved that. John Quincy's three sons as well as Thomas's six children and Susan's little daughter graced his homestead. Louisa Smith took over management of the household and, together with others, cared for John. He rarely wrote any longer but sometimes dictated letters that others penned for him.

To his great satisfaction, John Quincy had been summoned home to become secretary of state in the Monroe administration. Not only did that mean that John could see his accomplished son on occasion, but John also began to suspect that, as it had been for Monroe and his predecessors, the office might be a stepping stone to the presidency. And equal to all the pleasures of John Quincy's return was the relationship that developed between the ancient father-in-law and the delightful young daughter-in-law. Louisa Catherine possessed all the attributes that John appreciated in a woman: warmth, charm, beauty, and above all, erudition. Knowing John's great loneliness, she wrote to him regularly, telling him about social life in Washington, describing the books she read, poetry, music she listened to. Louisa filled a great gap in his "desolation and solitude." When she began to send him her translations of Plato, he was overjoyed. He was "astonished."

He was given his due in honors as well. A corps of cadets from West Point— two hundred strong—traveled down from Boston to entertain him with a parade past his house, flags flying and band playing. He saluted them from his porch and served them refreshments. One year later the town of Quincy honored him by electing him as their delegate to revise the state constitution that he himself had written forty years earlier. After giving it consideration, he decided to accept and attended the convention in Boston, though the cost was an illness that laid him low for several weeks afterward.

At John Quincy's behest, he agreed to sit for another portrait, this one by the aging artist Gilbert Stuart. The result is a classic, perhaps the best painting of Adams, perhaps one of the best paintings ever of an elderly man. The body is clearly that of an old person, the shoulders slumped, the face sagging. But the spirit in the portrait sparkles with good humor, intelligence, and the satisfaction of a life well lived. It was a fitting tribute to Adams.

John died on the fiftieth anniversary of the signing of the Declaration of Independence, within hours of his colleague in independence and his friend during his adult lifetime, Thomas Jefferson. The miraculous simultaneous passing on July 4, 1826, was acknowledged immediately as prophetic of their enduring contribution to America's history. It was a remarkable coincidence that even John Adams did not expect when he uttered his last words: "Jefferson survives."

In death John and Abigail Adams lie next to each other in the foyer of the First Unitarian Church of Quincy. For almost two centuries they have rested together, commemorating a marriage of enduring love and loyalty and duty to the nation.

Acknowledgments

In 1807, Abigail Adams wrote to Mercy Otis Warren, her friend of nearly four decades, that "if we were to count our years by the revolutions we have witnessed, we might number them with the anti-diluvians." She meant that she was awed by the changes they had experienced in their lifetimes. She was left, she said, gazing at what she "could neither fathom nor comprehend."

Life is like that; we are dazzled by the attempt to make sense of our own pasts. Every year that I continue to write about history, the credits mount. This double biography, for instance, is the result not only of several intense years of work but of a lifetime of reading and writing and teaching. I owe my love of history to my father and to my brothers, Henry, Walter, and David, who also inherited discerning curiosity from both our parents, Yentha and Louis Gelles, and to my teachers at Cornell and Yale and especially at the University of California, Irvine, who inspired me with their excitement about the Puritans, the founders, and American history. I owe a debt to Herodotus, Gibbon, Beard, Perry Miller, and everyone in between and since for writing the narratives that have inspired me. More specifically, this work is indebted to the authors listed in the bibliography, some of whom I know personally, others through their books.

I have been blessed to come of age as a historian during the awakening of scholars to the lives of women and to the many women whose pioneering work made it possible for me to become a feminist historian. I am grateful for students who challenged and asked questions. I have attended myriads of conferences and seminars where ideas surfaced that changed mine. Like Abigail's, my mind, "though fleet in its progress, has been outstripped by them."

At the Massachusetts Historical Society, James Taylor, editor in chief, and Margaret Hogan, managing editor, of the Adams Papers, have been generous with time and information, as have Greg Lint, Conrad Wright, Elaine Grublin, and Peter Drummy for many years. I cannot say enough about my colleagues and friends at the Adams National Historic Site. Caroline Keinath, deputy superintendent, has given life to the Adamses' domestic world, and I thank her for always being available with time and information.

To those who have read and critiqued with great and gentle insight, my gratitude: Joanna Gillespie, Diane Feldman, Pamela Herr, Susan Groag Bell, Nan Blackledge, Judith Schwartz, Lauren Cetlin, Sheila Cole, Sally Hufbauer, my brother David Gelles and sister-in-law Pamela Gelles, and my sons, Noah and Adam, for help untangling the mysteries of my iMac. My friends at Stanford have been interested and interesting and always stimulating; I miss Jay Fliegelman, that unique, wry, wise, and brilliant man. What would I do without Bart Bernstein as a pal and critic! It's been a pleasure to discuss my John and Abigail with Jack Rakove as he completed his latest great opus on the founders. And Caroline Winterer, my expert on topics classical. My erudite friend John Ferling has provided advice, information, and encouragement for years. Lots of people have answered my calls for special help, especially Bob Middlekauff, Richard Buel, David Konig, Laurel Thatcher Ulrich, Barbara Oberg, Bill Pencak, Dick Beckman, Mary Felstiner, and Marty Greenstein. Elaine Forman Crane, Sheila Skemp, and Rosemarie Zagarri have been colleagues, dear friends, and indispensable models for writing about our early-American women. So, too, have the incomparable Mary Beth Norton and Linda Kerber. I have been blessed, to use Abigail's term, with friendship and dialogue with Susan Faludi for many years.

Without comrades life would be dull. Sheila Cole is my Mercy Otis Warren, a lifelong friend with whom I discuss work and life. So, too, are Phyllis Koestenbaum, Pam Herr, Sally Hufbauer, and Gerre McKenna. So, too, my sisters-in-law, the Carols. So, too, Janet and Abbas Orumchian and Shirley D'Andrea and Rob Roy McGregor. Readers, many unknown, engage with me in my projects. For a number of years, a teacher at a college in Texas assigned my *Portia: The World of Abigail Adams* to his classes with the additional assignment that they had to interview me. Every spring for many years I received fifteen or so letters that requested my biography, and for many years I tried to write original responses to each letter until I wore down and began to send boilerplate scripts. The letters have stopped coming.

For twenty-five years I have been a scholar at Stanford's Center for Research on Women (now called the Michelle R. Clayman Institute for Gender Research). Many scholars have come and gone over the years, but the six senior scholars have been enduring colleagues and critics: I am grateful to Marilyn Yalom for my title and much else; to Karen Offen for all the years that we discussed "republican motherhood" and much else; to Susan Groag Bell for telling me to read "Three Guineas" and much else; to Betsy Roden for almost letting me play the role of Dorothea in her play of that name. Phyllis Koestenbaum introduced me to the world of the poet, and sometimes I think about the rhythm and meter of her work when I write.

Jill Marsal, my agent, has been encouraging and delightful and oh so helpful. My fine editor, David Highfill, has style and has made this a better book.

No credit would be complete without mention of my coaches and playmates on the Rinconada Masters Swim Team. Thanks to all for being there on the coldest, wettest mornings as well as on sunny days: Aldo, Bobbi, Carol, Cindy, Ken, Luba, Nan, Patsy, Eloise, Paul, Suki, Oleg, Lindsay, Sylvia, Shawn, Sue, Tom, Chris, David, and everyone else.

My sons have warmed my heart by becoming doctors, albeit of computer science and physics. They warm my heart, mainly, by being who they are: loving, wise, and funny. I cannot imagine life without Adam and Noah at the center. Or Esther, who has become a daughter. Or Michael, to whom I have dedicated past books and who deserves this one as well but has been preempted by little Leila in hopes that she will continue to have amazing adventures—and perhaps also, when she is done with her princess phase, like history.

Abbreviations

Adams-Jefferson	Lester Cappon, ed. *The Adams-Jefferson Letters: The Complete Correspondence Between Thomas Jefferson and Abigail and John Adams.* 2 vols. Chapel Hill: University of North Carolina Press, 1959.
AFC	L. H. Butterfield et al., eds. *Adams Family Correspondence.* 8 vol. in print, 1 vol. in press. *The Adams Papers.* Cambridge, Mass.: Harvard University Press, 1963–.
A P	Adams Papers. Microfilm ed. 608 reels. Massachusetts Historical Society.
Birthplaces	Laurel A. Racine. *The Birthplaces of Presidents John Adams and John Quincy Adams: Adams National Historical Park. Vol. 1: Historical Data.* Quincy, Mass.: National Park Service, 2001.
CFA	Charles Francis Adams, ed. *Letters of Mrs. Adams, the Wife of John Adams.* 4th ed. Boston: Charles C. Little & James Brown, 1848.
DA	L. H. Butterfield et al., eds. *Diary and Autobiography of John Adams.* 4 vols. *The Adams Papers.* Cambridge, Mass.: Harvard University Press, 1961.
DeWindt	Caroline DeWindt, ed. *Journal and Correspondence of Miss Adams, Daughter of John Adams.* New York: Wiley & Putnam, 1841.
DJQA	David Grayson Allen, ed. *Diary of John Quincy Adams, 1779–1788.* 2 vols. Cambridge, Mass.: Harvard University Press, 1981.
EDJA	Butterfield, L. H., Wendell D. Garrett, and Marc Friedlaender, eds. *The Earliest Diary of John Adams.* The Adams Papers. Cambridge, Mass.: Harvard University Press, 1966.
NL	Stewart Mitchell, ed. *New Letters of Abigail Adams, 1788–1801.* Westport, Conn.: Greenwood Press, 1947.
Papers	Robert J. Taylor, Mary-Jo Kline, and Gregg Lint, eds. *Papers of John Adams.* 13 vols. in print, 1 vol. forthcoming. *The Adams Papers.* Cambridge, Mass.: Harvard University Press, 1977–.
Portraits	Andrew Oliver. *Portraits of John and Abigail Adams.* Cambridge, Mass.: Harvard University Press, 1967.
Shaw Papers	Shaw Papers. Microfilm ed. 4 reels. Library of Congress, Manuscript Division.
Smith Diaries	"Diaries of Rev. William Smith and Dr. Cotton Tufts, 1738–1784," Massachusetts Historical Society, *Proceedings*, 3rd series, 2 (1908–1909), 444–70.
Three Episodes	Charles Francis Adams, Jr., *Three Episodes of Massachusetts History:*

	The Settlement of Boston Bay; The Antinomian Controversy; A Study of Church and Town Government. 3rd ed., 2 vols. Boston: Houghton Mifflin, 1892.
Warren-Adams	*Warren-Adams Letters. Being Chiefly a Correspondence Among John Adams, Samuel Adams, and James Warren.* 2 Vols. 72–73. Boston: Massachusetts Historical Society, 1917–1925.
Works	Charles Francis Adams, ed. *The Works of John Adams, Second President of the United States: With a Life of the Author, Notes and Illustrations, by His Grandson Charles Francis Adams.* 10 vols. Boston: Books for Libraries Press, 1851–1856.

Notes

I: THE STEEL AND THE MAGNET

2   *"For John came":* Adams, "Memoir of Mrs. Adams," xiv–xv.

3   *Perfection was just too hard: Smith Diaries,* 449.

3   *Puritan pedigree:* Adams, "Memoir of Mrs. Adams," xiv–xv.

4   *We know these stories: Three Episodes,* vol. 1, 1–343; vol. 2, 681–88.

5   *Just up the coast: DA,* vol. 3, 253–54.

6   *John's observance:* Ibid., 225.

7   *Her great-uncle:* Ibid., 256.

7   *"I spent my time":* Ibid., 257.

7   *"I wont have": DA,* vol. 1, 65–66.

8   *Abigail's other grandmother:* Rebora, *John Singleton Copley,* 253–57.

8   *"I shall never forget":* DeWindt, 216.

8   *"To Mr. Gay": Smith Diaries,* 449.

9   *"Sweet, and harmonious": AFC,* vol. 1, 3.

9   *"It was whispered": DA,* vol. 3, 257–63.

9   *"The school": Papers,* vol. 1, xix, 2, Sept. 2, 1755.

9   *"I find": DA,* vol. 1, 13–14.

11   *"cruel Reproaches":* Ibid., 64.

11   *"Now I feel":* Ibid., 63.

11   *"An early marriage":* Ibid., 55–56.

11   *"Polly and Nabby are wits":* Ibid., 108.

12   *"apparently frank":* Ibid., 68.

12   *"What am I doing":* Ibid., 73.

12   *"Sewal and Esther":* Ibid., 87.

12   *"Accidents":* Ibid.

12   *"Good nature":* Ibid., 108.

13   *"Believe me": CFA,* vol. 1, 3–6.

13   *"Here we are": AFC,* vol. 1, 1.

14   *"I presume":* Ibid., 2.

14   *"I have taken":* Ibid.

14   *"Dr. Tufts": DA,* vol. 1, 231–32.

15   *"Before 20 years":* Ibid., 209–10, Apr. 1761.

15   *"The Character of Aunt Nell":* Ibid., 234, Feb. 1763.

15   *John inherited: DA,* vol. 3, 277.

15   *campaign opposing taverns: DA*, vol. 1, 128–29.

15   *"These fue Lins cums": Papers*, vol. 1.

15   *"Cruel for detaining": AFC*, vol. 1, 3.

17   *"I could not help laughing"*: Ibid., 10, n. 3.

18   *catalog of her "faults"*: Ibid., 44–45.

18   *a "critick" of her writing*: Ibid., 32.

18   *"I assure you"*: Ibid., 34.

18   *"heigh day"*: Ibid., 38.

18   *"Oh my dear"*: Ibid., 49.

18   *"confind extremely weak"*: Ibid., 51.

18   *"The cart you mentioned"*: Ibid., 50.

19   *"a tye more binding"*: Ibid., 6.

2: A TYE MORE BINDING

22   *"my Squemish Wife": AFC*, vol. 1, 52, June 29, 1766.

22   *"My Good Man"*: Ibid., 56, Oct. 6, 1766.

22   *"On the 14 day of July": DA*, vol. 3, 284.

23   *"The adventurers": Works*, 448–64.

23   *"this little production": DA*, vol. 3, 284.

23   *"Your Diana become": AFC*, vol. 1, 51.

24   *"I could behold"*: Ibid., 60–61.

24   *"Alass": DA*, vol. 1, 90.

24   *"a private Association"*: Ibid., 2551, Jan. 24, 1765.

24   *"The Year 1765"*: Ibid., 263.

25   *"Otis is extreamly"*: Ibid., 84.

25   *"he had the most habitual"*: Ibid., 271, Dec. 23, 1765.

25   *"I have had upon a visit": AFC*, vol. 1, 54, July 15, 1766.

26   *"The People": DA*, vol. 1, 263, Dec. 18, 1765.

27   *"At home"*: Ibid., 273–85, Dec. 1765–Jan. 1766.

27   *"Since the Stamp Act": AFC*, vol. 1, 52, June 29, 1766.

28   *"You ask me"*: Ibid., 54, July 15, 1766.

28   *"the most elegant": DA*, vol. 1, 318–19, Aug. 6, 1766.

28   *Benjamin Blyth's: Portraits*, 5–13.

30   *Only in her old age*: AP, reel 415, Jan. 30, 1813.

30   *"first battle"*: Zobel, *Boston Massacre*, 194.

30   *"spirit stirring drum": DA*, vol. 3, 290.

30   *evening of March 5*: Zobel, *Boston Massacre*, 192–201.

31   *At home with her servants: DA*, vol. 3, 291.

31   *Before long*: Ibid., 291–92.

32   *"tears streaming"*: Ibid., 293.

32   *"most exhausting"*: Ibid., 293.

33   *"At this time"*: Ibid., 294.

33   *"That excellent Lady"*: Ibid., 296.

33   *"Obligation to speak"*: Ibid.

34   *"keep off my Neighbours": DA,* vol. 2, 41, June 25, 1771.
34   *"not from the Noisy": AFC,* vol. 1, 76, Apr. 20, 1771.
36   *"I have a great desire":* Ibid., 77, Feb. 20, 1771.
36   *"with public Affairs": DA,* vol. 2, 63, Sept. 22, 1772.
36   *"What an Atom":* Ibid., 64, Oct. 19, 1772.
37   *"Righteousness, Temperance":* Ibid., 72.
37   *"My Country":* Ibid., 75, Dec. 31, 1772.
37   *"mean and a merciless Administration":* Ibid., 76.
37   *"The young Ladies":* Ibid., 85, Aug. 30, 1773.
37   *"The kind reception": AFC,* vol. 1, 84, July 16, 1773.
39   *"The Tea that bainfull weed":* Ibid., 88, Dec. 5, 1773.
40   *"Last Night": DA,* vol. 2, 86, Dec. 17, 1773.
41   *"My Fancy": AFC,* vol. 1, 111, June 29, 1774.
41   *"I am so idle":* Ibid., 124.
41   *"I cant be easy":* Ibid.
41   *"I write you":* Ibid., 119.
41   *"I will not lie":* Ibid.
41   *"I believe it is Time":* Ibid., 129.
41   *"Let us therefore":* Ibid., 114.
42   *John had purchased: DA,* vol. 2, 87.
42   *"mowing and": AFC,* vol. 1, 129.
42   *"I must intreat you":* Ibid., 119, July 1, 1774.
42   *Abigail had been: DA,* vol. 2, 95.
42   *"Thus you see": AFC,* vol. 1, 135, July 9, 1774.
43   *"I wander alone": DA,* vol. 2, 97, June 25, 1774.
43   *"You cannot be": AFC,* vol. 1, 172, Oct. 16, 1774.
43   *"I think it will":* Ibid., 129, July 6, 1774.

3: SEPARATION AND THE NEW COVENANT

44   *"Oh that I was": AFC,* vol. 1, 207, May 29, 1775.
44   *halls of Congress:* Ibid., 347, Feb. 13, 1776.
44   *"My Health":* Ibid., 213, June 10, 1775.
44   *"The Difficulty":* Ibid., 255–56, July 24, 1775.
46   *"the Remainder of my Days": DA,* vol. 2, 64.
46   *"taken a very great": AFC,* vol. 1, 142–43, Aug. 19, 1774.
47   *"I hope they will:":* Ibid., 139, Aug. 9, 1774.
47   *"As We came": DA,* vol. 2, 100, Aug. 16, 1774.
47   *"Dish of Coffee":* Ibid., 97–112, Aug. 10–23, 1774.
48   *"the Moment I get": AFC,* vol. 1, 151, Sept. 14, 1774.
48   *his list went on:* Ibid., 164, Oct. 7, 1774.
48   *"There is in the Congress":* Ibid., 150, Sept. 8, 1774.
48   *"The first of September":* Ibid., 143, Aug. 19, 1774.
48   *"I want much":* Ibid., 142–43, Sept. 19, 1774.
48   *"I am very impatient":* Ibid., 146, Sept. 2, 1774.

49   *"Five weeks":* Ibid., 151, Sept. 14, 1774.

49   *"It really":* Ibid., 152, Sept. 16, 1774.

49   *"You will burn":* Ibid., 154.

49   *"Coll. Washington made":* DA, vol. 2, 117.

49   *"This Assembly":* AFC, vol. 1, 166, Sept. 9, 1774.

49   *"a little clashing of parties":* Ibid., 152, Sept. 16, 1774.

50   *"We are burnt":* Ibid., 140, Aug. 15, 1774.

50   *"The drought":* Ibid., 147–48.

50   *"Shall I own":* Ibid., 138, Aug. 9, 1774.

50   *"we shall never":* Ibid., 181, Jan. 28, 1775.

51   *"Took our Departure":* DA, vol. 2, 157, Oct. 28, 1774.

51   *"I dare not":* AFC, vol. 1, 172, Oct. 16, 1774.

51   *"My Birthday":* DA, vol. 1, 158, Oct. 30, 1774.

52   *"Should I attempt":* AFC, vol. 1, 177.

53   *"Is it not better":* Ibid., 180, Jan. 25, 1775.

53   *"Those who have":* Ibid., 184.

53   *"If you please":* Ibid., 187, Feb. 25, 1775.

54   *They lived unhappily:* Forbes, *Paul Revere*, 96; Fischer, *Paul Revere's Ride*, 97, 387.

54   *"Artillery, Arms, Cloathing":* DA, vol. 3, 314.

54   *"a great Number":* Ibid.

55   *"The Congress":* AFC, vol. 1, 207, May 29, 1775.

55   *"Congress have made":* Ibid., 215.

56   *"piddling genious":* Ibid., 256, n. 1

56   *"We now expect":* Ibid., 217, June [16], 1775.

56   *"The year 1775":* To Joseph Sturge, Mar. 1846, cited in ibid., 223, n. 3.

56   *"The constant roar":* AFC, vol. 1, 222–23, June 18, 1775.

57   *"Courage of an Aria":* Ibid., 182, Jan. 28, 1775.

57   *"God Almightys":* Ibid., June 23, 1775.

58   *Fearing an invasion:* Ibid., June 22, 1775.

58   *"Your good Mother":* Ibid., 231, June 25, 1775.

58   *"I would not":* Ibid., 240, July 4, 1775.

58   *"Our Consolation":* Ibid., 241–42.

59   *"I have met":* Ibid., 243–45, July 12, 1775.

59   *"suffocating Heats":* Ibid., 251–52, July 17, 1775.

59   *"All the Letters":* Ibid., 247, July 16, 1775.

60   *"It is now":* Ibid., 255, July 24, 1775.

60   *"There is a degree":* Ibid., 239, July 5, 1775.

60   *"Dr. Franklin":* Ibid., 253, July 23, 1775.

60   *"Your Brother":* Ibid., 72.

61   *This Congress:* DA, vol. 2, 162, n. 1.

61   *He dashed:* DA, vol. 3, 325, Aug. 75.

61   *"Since you left":* AFC, vol. 1, 276–78.

62   *"Tis now two days":* Ibid., 277, Sept. 10, 1775.

63   *"Nelson is":* DA, vol. 2, 172–72, Sept. 15–19, 1775.

63   *The reason:* AFC, vol. 1, 287, Sept. 27, 1775.

63   *"I feel"*: Ibid., 289.
63   *"I set myself down"*: Ibid., 278–79, Sept. 16, 1775.
64   *"I set down with a heavy Heart"*: Ibid., 284, July 25, 1775.
64   *"Have pitty"*: Ibid., 288–89, Oct. 1, 1775.
64   *"I should have"*: Ibid., 291, Oct. 2, 1775.
65   *"One great Distress"*: Ibid., 292, Oct. 4, 1775.
65   *"From my earliest Entrance"*: Ibid., 295–96, Oct. 7, 1775.
65   *"You and I"*: Ibid., 301, Oct. 13, 1775.
66   *the cruel stroke:* Ibid., 297–98, Oct. 9, 1775.
67   *They debated: DA,* vol. 2, 179–83.
67   *"20,000 Negroes"*: Ibid.
67   *He carefully recorded:* Ibid., 220–22.
67   *It was the reticent: DA,* vol. 3, 336.
67   *"Your letters"*: *AFC,* vol. 1, 319.
68   *"The most agreeable Time"*: Ibid., 331.
68   *"No less"*: Ibid., 312–13, Oct. 25, 1775.
68   *"I think" however:* Ibid., 321, Nov. 5, 1775.
68   *"We have done Evil"*: Ibid., 313, Oct. 25, 1775.
68   *"cruel Pestilence"*: Ibid., 312, Oct. 23, 1775.
68   *"You know"*: Ibid., 327, Nov. 18, 1775.
68   *"a true patriot"*: Ibid., 321, Nov. 5, 1775.
68   *foundation of morality:* Ibid., 327, Nov. 18, 1775.

4: A NEW CODE OF LAWS

70   *"Jaundice, Rhumatism"*: *AFC,* vol. 1, 329.
71   *"I am more"*: Ibid., 329–30, Nov. 27, 1775.
73   *"Washington"*: *DA,* vol. 2, 227, Jan. 24, 1776.
73   *"Our Country"*: *AFC,* vol. 1, 422.
74   *propagandists for generations:* Maier, *American Scripture;* Middlekauff, *Glorious Cause.*
75   *"will soon make"*: *AFC,* vol. 1, 348, Feb. 18, 1776.
75   *"His Arguments"*: *DA,* vol. 3, 330–31.
75   *"I felt" myself:* Ibid., 334.
75   *"I had read"*: Ibid., 358–59.
75   *"Tis highly prized here"*: Ibid., 350, Feb. 21, 1776.
76   *"I suppose"*: *AFC,* vol. 1, 336–37, Dec. 10, 1775.
76   *"I have sometimes"*: Ibid., 369, Mar. 31, 1776.
77   *sin of slavery:* Ibid., 313, Oct. 25, 1775.
77   *"not a Slave"*: Ibid., 162, Sept. 22, 1774.
77   *It was that simple:* Smith's will freed Phoebe with a settlement of $100 a year. For Smith's will, see *AFC,* vol. 5, 303.
77   *"I long to hear"*: *AFC,* vol. 1, 370.
78   *"On Man's Lust for Power"*: John quoted Daniel Defoe. *Papers,* vol. 1, 81–83.
78   *"My pen"*: *AFC,* vol. 1, 310.
79   *"Why then"*: Ibid., 370.

79   *most progressive female advocates:* For instance, Mary Wollstonecraft.
80   *"As to your extraordinary":* AFC, vol. 1, 282–83.
81   *"But as our weak":* Ibid., 92, Jan. 19, 1774.
81   *"But we have":* Ibid., Jan. 28, 1775.
81   *"I am sure":* Ibid., 382–83, Apr. 14, 1776.
82   *"He is very sausy":* Ibid., 396, Apr. 27, 1776.
82   *"I can not say":* Ibid., 402, May 7, 1776.
83   *"They look":* Ibid., 358, Mar. 17, 1776.
83   *"I shall suffer":* Ibid., 361.
83   *"Is there no Way":* Ibid., Apr. 28, 1776.
84   *a declaration:* See Maier, *American Scripture;* Middlekauff, *Glorious Cause;* and Ferling, *Almost a Miracle.*
84   *Jefferson had objected:* DA, vol. 3, 335.
85   *but still formidable:* Maier, *American Scripture,* 103.
85   *"This was the first":* DA, vol. 3, 397.
85   *delegates to the Congress:* Maier, *American Scripture,* 149–53.
86   *General Washington:* Middlekauff, *Glorious Cause,* 347–48.

5: WAR AND THE WAY OF DUTY

87   *"de facto Secretary":* Ferling, *John Adams,* 160.
87   *"The Education":* AFC, vol. 1, 145, Aug. 28, 1774.
87   *"Make them consider":* Ibid., 383–84, Apr. 15, 1776.
89   *"Education makes a greater":* Ibid., 317, Oct. 29, 1775.
89   *"I feel a gaieti de Coar":* Ibid., 370, Mar. 31, 1776.
89   *Washington eventually decided:* Middlekauff, *Glorious Cause,* 530–34.
89   *"Our Misfortunes in Canada":* AFC, vol. 2, 23–24, June 26, 1776.
90   *"In a Letter":* Ibid., 50.
91   *"I have really":* Ibid., 45–46, July 13–14, 1776.
91   *"The Air":* Ibid., 52.
91   *"It makes me happy":* Ibid., 63, July 27, 1776.
91   *a guinea for the inoculation:* Ibid., 37, July 7, 1776.
91   *"Now I fear":* Ibid., 67, July 29, 1776.
92   *"The common Practice":* Ibid., 72, Aug. 1, 1776.
92   *"Nabby has enough":* Ibid., 86–87.
92   *"I have possession":* Ibid., 112, Aug. 29, 1776.
93   *"Geography is a Branch":* Ibid., 90–91, Aug. 13, 1776.
93   *"the deficiency of Education":* Ibid., 93–94, July 14, 1776.
94   *"Your Sentiments":* Ibid., 109–10, Aug. 25, 1776.
94   *"Girls knew quite enough":* Tupper and Brown, *Grandmother Tyler's Book,* 7, 9, 13–14, cited in ibid., 95, n. 5.
95   *"6 or 7 hundred boils":* AFC, vol. 2, 94, Aug. 14, 1776.
95   *"Give my love":* Ibid., 115, Aug. 30, 1776.
95   *"This is a Beautifull Morning":* Ibid., 115–16, Aug. 31, 1776; Sept. 2, 1776.
96   *certain disaster:* Middlekauff, *Glorious Cause,* 346–55.

96   *"In the Course":* AFC, vol. 2, 117, Sept. 4, 1776; 122, Sept. 7, 1776.

96   *For this reason:* Ferling, *Leap in the Dark,* 186–90.

97   *"I shall wait here":* AFC, vol. 2, 117, Sept. 4, 1776.

97   *"The Report of your being dead":* Ibid., 122, Sept. 7, 1776.

97   *John, in turn:* Ibid., 124, Sept. 14, 1776.

97   *"At Brunswick":* DA, vol. 3, 418.

98   *"for some hours":* Ibid., 419.

98   *"I cannot consent":* AFC, vol. 2, 128–29, Sept. 20, 1776.

98   *"There are paerticuliar times":* Ibid., 133–34, Sept. 23, 1776.

99   *"I have not":* Ibid.

99   *the loss of New York:* Ibid., 131–32, Oct. 1, 1776.

99   *especially those in Congress:* Higginbotham, *War of American Independence,* 162–71; Middlekauff, *Glorious Cause,* 363–69, 390–93.

100 *taxes must be raised:* AFC, vol. 2, 154, Feb. 7, 1777.

100 *"Many circumstances conspire":* Ibid., 150.

100 *"It [is] now a Month":* Ibid., 159, Feb. 10, 1777.

101 *"You make some inquiries":* Ibid., 173, Mar. 9, 1777.

101 *"His Most Gracious Majesty":* Ibid., 187, Mar. 26; 194, April 2, 1777.

101 *"I see by the news paper":* Ibid., 174, Mar. 10, 1777.

101 *"placed a chair before me":* AFC, vol. 1, 335.

101 *"confined, but otherwise" AFC,* vol. 2, 196, Apr. 2, 1777.

102 *"Was anyone Blessed":* Shaw Papers, reel 1, Feb. 8, 1771.

102 *"highly favored among Women":* AFC, vol. 1, 168.

102 *"I cannot do your Message":* AFC, vol. 2, 173, Mar. 9, 1777.

102 *"plunged [her] in the Gall":* AFC, vol. 1, 105, Mar. 7, 1774.

103 *"An Idea of 30 years":* AFC, vol. 2, 173.

103 *"Mrs. Howard":* Ibid., 212, Apr. 17, 1777.

103 *"I will quit":* Ibid.

103 *"Tis four Months":* Ibid., 231, May 6, 1777.

103 *"I cannot say":* Ibid., 232, May 9, 1777.

104 *salt rheum:* Ibid., n. 3.

104 *"A most Horrid plot":* Ibid., 232, May 9, 1777.

104 *John was furious:* Ibid., 248, May 27, 1777.

104 *"loose my rest a nights":* Ibid., 250–51, June 1, 1777.

104 *"I sit down to write":* Ibid., 277, July 9, 1777.

105 *A "prize" had arrived:* Ibid., 278–79, July 10, 1777.

105 *"Join with me my dearest Friend":* Ibid., 282–83, July 16, 1777. The infant had probably been strangled by the umbilical cord.

106 *"Never in my whole life":* Ibid., 292, July 28, 1777.

106 *"I have . . . Health":* Ibid., 287.

106 *"Never was [a] Wretch":* Ibid., 298.

106 *"The troops loved":* Middlekauff, *Glorious Cause,* 390.

107 *The case:* AFC, vol. 2, 370, n. 2.

108 *"Your Letters arrived":* Ibid., 370–71, Dec. 15, 1777.

109 *"The old Lady":* DA, vol. 4, 6–7.

109 *"five O Clock"*: Ibid.
109 *"And now cannot you imagine me"*: *AFC*, vol. 2, 390, Feb. 15, 1778.

6: REPUBLICAN FATHER

110 *"Patience, Fortitude"*: *AFC*, vol. 2, 142, Oct. 15, 1776.
110 *"Portia stands alone"*: *AFC*, vol. 5, 37, Nov. 13, 1782.
110 *"I have sacrificed"*: *AFC*, vol. 2, 395, Feb. 24, 1778; 397, ca. Mar. 1, 1778.
110 *"a Bottle"*: *DA*, vol. 2, 274–75, Feb. 18, 1778.
111 *"It would be fruitless"*: Ibid., 274–75.
111 *"It is a great Satisfaction"*: 276.
111 *"200 Miles in 24 Hours"*: Ibid., 283.
111 the snow-capped mountains: Ibid., 289–90.
112 *"Europe thou"*: Ibid., 292.
112 *"We passed the Bridge"*: Ibid., 296.
112 *"It is in vain"*: Ibid., 297.
112 *"Dined at Monsr. Brillon's"*: Ibid., 298.
113 *"politely received"*: Ibid., 298–99.
113 *"very Well"*: *AFC*, vol. 3, 16, Apr. 20, 1778.
114 *"You cannot wonder"*: *AFC*, vol. 2, 396, Mar. 1, 1778.
114 *"Call me not a Savage"*: *AFC*, vol. 3, 1.
114 *"so often troubling"*: Ibid., 41.
115 *"Amiable tho"*: Ibid., 43, June 13, 1778.
115 *"I know not"*: Ibid., 48.
115 *"The Delights"*: Ibid., 9, Apr. 12, 1778.
116 *"To tell you the truth"*: Ibid., 17, Apr. 25, 1778.
116 *"beautiful and accomplished"*: *DA*, vol. 4, 119.
116 women bussed his cheek: *Schiff, Great Improvisation*.
116 take neither side: *DA*, vol. 2, 304–5.
117 spying on John himself: *DA*, vol. 4, 120.
117 *"Your Son"*: *AFC*, vol. 3, 125, Dec. 2, 1778.
117 *"How dear"*: Ibid., 108–9, Oct. 21, 1778.
117 *"3 very short Letters"*: Ibid.
117 his letters must have: Ibid., 118, Nov. 12, 1778.
117 *"so many of our letters"*: Ibid., 114, Nov. 6, 1778.
117 *"You must not expect"*: Ibid., 128, Dec. 3, 1778.
118 *"the famous Adams"*: *DA*, vol. 2, 351, Feb. 11, 1779.
118 *"drudging"*: *Warren-Adams*, vol. 2, 105, June 13, 1776.
118 more elaborate language: Ibid., 114, July 29, 1778.
119 *"The House"*: *AFC*, vol. 3, 7, Apr. 9, 1778.
119 *"The Farm remains"*: Ibid., 7.
119 *"Brothers newly married"*: Ibid., 61, July 15, 1778.
119 *"lately sit up"*: Ibid., 136, Dec. 13, 1778.
119 Her requests: *AFC*, vol. 4, 316, Apr. 25, 1782; 347, Aug. 18, 1782.
120 Mercy Warren: Ibid., 42, Dec. 21, 1780.

120 *"Yesterday two Cases"*: Ibid., 81–82, Feb. 27, 1781.

120 *"I propose"*: *AFC*, vol. 2, 251, June 1, 1777.

121 *"28 acres"*: *AFC*, vol. 1, 415, Mar. 27, 1776.

122 *"This is a cruel Disappointment"*: *DA*, vol. 2, 359.

122 *"my Eye"*: Ibid., 362–63.

122 *"He has the most"*: Ibid., 367.

122 *"The Chevalier"*: Ibid.

122 *"my Son correcting"*: Ibid., 385.

123 *"tended to the honor"*: Page Smith, *John Adams*, 441–43.

124 *loyal to Benjamin Franklin:* Bemis, *Diplomacy of the American Revolution;* Dull, *Diplomatic History;* Hutson, *John Adams.*

125 *"My habitation"*: *AFC*, vol. 3, 233–34, Nov. 14, 1779.

125 *"Charles is much pleased"*: Ibid., 234.

126 *"was an old Frigate"*: *DA*, vol. 4, 191–93.

126 *"Don Quixots"*: *AFC*, vol. 3, Dec. 15, 1779.

126 *"We entered into"*: *DA*, vol. 2, 416.

127 *"but I never"*: Ibid., 426–27.

127 *"Our present situation"*: *AFC*, vol. 3, 371, July 5, 1780.

128 *"I dare venture to say"*: Ibid., 249, Dec. 13, 1779.

128 *"You will see"*: Ibid., 256.

129 *"How do you do"*: Ibid., 257, Jan. 13, 1780.

129 *"I must I will"*: Ibid., 273.

130 *"What a figure"*: Ibid., 273–74, Feb. 13, 1780.

130 *He would not be chastened:* For understanding Sterne, I thank the James Joyce scholar Richard Beckman.

130 *"Mr. Dana and my self"*: *Works*, vol. 7, 121–22.

131 *"shirtsleeve diplomacy"*: Bemis, *Diplomacy of the American Revolution*, 49.

131 *exasperating and crude:* Ibid; Dull, *Diplomatic History;* Hutson, *John Adams.*

132 *The militia fled:* Ferling, *Almost a Miracle*, 409–29.

7: DIPLOMACY AT HOME AND ABROAD

134 *Soon after arriving:* Dull, *Diplomatic History;* Hutson, *John Adams;* Morris, *Peacemakers.*

135 *"La Desobeissance"*: *AFC*, vol. 4, 11–12, Nov. 10, 1780. "The Disobedience and Impertinence of your eldest Son, who does his best to corrupt his kind Brother, has become intolerable, since he seeks through his brutality (rudeness), to bring forth the punishment he deserves, in Hope of leaving the School.

So I ask you Sir to have the goodness to withdraw him from here, rather than to see public Discipline ridiculed, since I will in the end be forced to treat him as of the Laws of our School.

I am honored to be your Very Humble Servant

H. Verheyk Recotr Gymn. Publ." Trans. Guilhem Rerolle

135 *"This morning"*: *DJQA*, vol. 1, 40, 47, Aug. 5, 1780.

135 *"Delft and Rotterdam"*: Ibid., Aug. 8, 1780.

135 *"It is perhaps":* AFC, vol. 4, 35, Dec. 18, 1780.

135 *"One of these Boys":* AFC, vol. 3, 425, Sept. 25, 1780.

135 *"How long":* AFC, vol. 4, 12, Nov. 13, 1780.

135 *"As you are separated":* AFC, vol. 3, 293, Mar. 2, 1780.

136 *"O My dear children":* AFC, vol. 4, 136, May 26, 1781.

136 *"Praise is a Dangerous Sweet":* Ibid., 135.

136 *"I hope my dear":* Ibid.

136 *"Those who Envy him":* AFC, vol. 3, 288–89, Feb. 28, 1780.

137 *"The Quarterly tax":* Ibid., 371, July 5, 1780.

137 *"I have been trying":* Ibid., 321, Apr. 15, 1780.

137 *she mentioned this property:* Ibid., 335, May 1, 1780. There is no record of this farm as part of the Adamses' property in the Adams National Historic Site's "Topographical Notes on John Adams' Farm at Penn's Hill." Typescript. Adams National Historical Park, n.d.

137 *"that had belonged":* AFC, vol. 5, 153, May 7, 1783.

137 *"Your Purchase":* Ibid., 222, Aug. 14, 1783.

138 *"I have a desire":* AFC, vol. 4, 106, Apr. 23, 1781.

138 *she could not possess:* Ibid., 345, July 18, 1782.

138 *"Don't meddle":* AFC, vol. 5, 15, Oct. 12, 1782.

138 *"God willing":* Works, vol. 9, 513, June 17, 1782.

138 *"I am afraid":* AFC, vol. 5, 125, Apr. 16, 1783.

138 *shipments and invoices:* AFC, vol. 4, 134–35, May 25, 1781.

139 *"I am not":* Morris, *Peacemakers,* 205.

140 *The young man:* AFC, vol. 4, 171, n. 3.

140 *"My dear" Charles:* Ibid., 170, July 11, 1781.

140 *"My second son":* Ibid., n. 2.

140 *"Ah! How great":* Ibid., 256, Dec. 9, 1781.

141 *Charles sailed:* Ibid., 272, Jan. 4, 1782.

141 *"I have been Sick":* Ibid., 273, Jan. 8, 1782.

141 *"the safe arrival":* Ibid., 284–85, Feb. 3, 1782.

141 *she complained:* Ibid., 220, Sept. 29, 1781.

141 *"You flatter me":* Ibid., 230, Oct. 21, 1781.

141 *"Two years":* Ibid., 257.

142 *"Soon after my Return:* Ibid., 224, Oct. 9, 1781.

142 *"Blessing":* AFC, IV, 225, n. 3.

142 *"constant anxiety":* Ibid., 293, Mar. 17, 1782.

143 *While John suspected:* Ibid., 265, Dec. 18, 1781.

143 *"Your humble Servant":* Ibid., 300, Mar. 22, 1782.

143 *"A Child":* Ibid., 323, May 14, 1782.

143 *"I want you":* Ibid., May 13, 1782.

144 *"Sweeden":* AFC, vol. 5, 214–17, July 23, 1783. See also *DJQA,* vol. 1, 153–75.

144 *"My Son":* AFC, vol. 5, 218, July 26, 1783.

144 *"I cannot say":* AFC, vol. 4, 306–7, Apr. 10, 1782.

145 *"The Letter":* Ibid., 337–39, July 1, 1782.

146 *"the sweetest of all praise":* Ibid., 358, Aug. 5, 1782.

147 *"He wished"*: Ibid.

147 *Nabby, left behind: AFC*, vol. 3, 137, Dec. 15, 1778.

147 *"Our daughter": AFC*, vol. 4, 373, Sept. 3, 1782.

147 *"What think you"*: Ibid., 344, July 17, 1782.

147 *John's note:* Ibid., 383, Oct. 26, 1782.

147 *traveled to Paris from Spain:* Bemis, *Diplomacy of the American Revolution;* Morris, *Peacemakers.*

148 *Vergennes was: DA*, vol. 3, 49.

149 *There were other issues:* See Morris, *Peacemakers,* 462–64.

149 *"We all went out": DA*, vol. 3, 82.

149 *"How did my heart dilate": AFC*, vol. 5, 278–79, Dec. 15, 1783.

150 *"Went to Versailles": DA*, vol. 3, 107.

150 *"If my dear friend": AFC*, vol. 5, Dec. 27, 1783.

150 *"If it were only:* Ibid., 89, Feb. 4, 1783.

150 *"Permit me"*: Ibid., 5, Oct. 8, 1782.

150 *"Who is there left"*: Ibid., 37, Nov. 13, 1782.

150 *"I cannot bear"*: Ibid., 211, July 21, 1783.

151 *"Come to me"*: Ibid., 89, Feb. 4, 1783.

151 *"I am determined"*: Ibid., 96, Feb. 28, 1783.

151 *"Here I am"*: Ibid., 167, May 30, 1783.

151 *"You know your Man"*: Ibid., 218, July 26, 1783.

151 *"nor to please his daughter"*: Ibid., 203, July 17, 1783.

151 *"If Congress"*: Ibid., 259, Oct. 19, 1783.

151 *"My life is Sweetened"*: Ibid., 264, Nov. 8, 1783.

151 *"I know not"*: Ibid., 277, Dec. 7, 1783.

151 *"I think if you"*: Ibid., 280, Dec. 15, 1783.

152 *"We have"*: Ibid., 55, Dec. 23, 1782.

152 *"I dont like the Subject"*: Ibid., 74–75, Jan. 22, 1783.

153 *"pretty patrimony"*: Ibid., 55, Dec. 28, 1782.

153 *"Indeed my dear"*: Ibid., 7, Oct. 8, 1782.

154 *Tyler was:* Shipton, *Sibley's Harvard Graduates*, vol. 11, 313–18; Tanselle, *Royall Tyler;* Tupper and Brown, *Grandmother Tyler's Book.*

154 *Abigail reported: AFC*, vol. 5, 143, Feb. 28, 1783; 151, May 7, 1783.

154 *When young Abigail returned:* Ibid., 259–60, Oct. 19, 1783.

154 *Tyler, meanwhile:* Ibid., 286, Dec. 27, 1783.

154 *"I wish"*: Ibid., 260, Oct. 19, 1783.

154 *"In consequence"*: Ibid., 291, Jan. 3, 1784.

155 *"Forgive me"*: Ibid., 291–93; 118, Apr. 7, 1783.

155 *"to whom my Father"*: Ibid., 303, Feb. 11, 1784.

155 *she might marry her daughter:* Ibid., 301, Jan. 25, 1783.

155 *Tyler, meanwhile:* Ibid., 297–98, Jan. 13, 1784.

155 *"I derive"*: Ibid., 331, May 25, 1784.

156 *"And now I have adjusted"*: Ibid., 318, Apr. 12, 1784.

156 *More sadly for Royall Tyler:* Ibid., 316–17, Apr. 3, 1784.

8: IN THE MIDST OF THE WORLD
IN SOLITUDE

157 *"In hopes of having"*: AP, reel 363, June 19, 1784.

157 *"to sail tomorrow"*: AP, reel 363, June 19, 1784.

157 *"the Capt."*: Ibid., 155.

157 *"The decency"*: AFC, vol. 5, 358–59, July 6, 1784.

158 *"conceive any inducement"*: Abigail Adams, "Diary of Her Voyage from Boston to Dial, 20 June–20 July, 1784," in *DA*, vol. 3, 157.

158 *"A fine wind"*: DA, vol. 3, 161, July 2, 1784.

158 *"Very little attention"*: Ibid., 157.

158 *"If our cook"*: AFC, vol. 5, 364, July 10, 1784.

158 *"I think the price"*: DA, vol. 3, 158.

158 *one hundred miles each day*: AFC, vol. 5, 364, July 8, 1784.

158 *"I went last evening"*: Ibid.

159 *"You will hardly"*: Ibid., 367–69, July 20, 22, 1784.

159 *"A well dressed hostess"*: Ibid., 370.

160 *"A robbery"*: Ibid., 371.

160 *"the ladies"*: AP, reel 363, June 6, 1784.

160 *"not to wait any longer"*: AFC, vol. 5, 341, June 6, 1784.

160 *"determined on tarrying"*: Ibid., 382, July 30, 1784.

161 *"I will not attempt to describe"*: Ibid., 412.

161 *"My dearest Friend"*: Ibid., 416, Aug. 1, 1784.

161 *"Purchase Johnsons Lives of the Poets"*: Ibid.

161 *"Everything around"*: DeWindt, viii.

161 *"Arrived at the Adelphi Buildings"*: DA, vol. 3, 170, Aug. 7, 1784; *AFC*, vol. 5, 455, Sept. 5, 1784.

161 *"I think myself"*: AFC, vol. 5, 455, 5, 1784.

161 *"You inquire"*: Ibid., 436.

162 *"in the midst of the world"*: Ibid., 452, n. 11.

163 *At times John had negotiated*: AP, reel 364, Jan. 3, 1784.

163 *"Upon occasion"*: AFC, vol. 5, 439–40.

163 *"with twenty thousand livres"*: AFC, vol. 6, 74.

163 *"the stairs"*: AFC, vol. 5, 440.

164 *"It is customary"*: Ibid., 448.

164 *"I took my dictionary"*: AFC, vol. 6, 7–8.

164 *In time she reported*: AFC, vol. 5, 446.

164 *"Conversation"*: AFC, vol. 6, 121–22.

164 *"with so much amazement"*: Ibid., 48.

164 *"entered the room"*: Ibid., 436–37.

165 *"one of the choice"*: Ibid., 119.

165 *He had arrived*: Rice, *Thomas Jefferson's Paris*, 37.

166 *"I dined"*: AFC, vol. 6, 80.

166 *"She is a very agreeable lady"*: Ibid., 15–16.

166 *"If the man"*: DeWindt, 68.

166 *"He lives"*: *AFC*, vol. 6, 142.

167 *"I have become"*: *AFC*, vol. 5, 442–43.

167 *"penny wise"*: Ibid., 442.

168 *"not quite so early"*: *AFC*, vol. 6, 46–47.

168 *"profeses himself so much"*: Ibid., 29.

169 *"Mr. A"*: Ibid., 18.

169 *"I have pleasures"*: Ibid., 46.

169 *"there are some"*: Ibid., 48.

169 *"What Idea"*: *AFC*, vol. 5, 447.

170 *"We have no days"*: Ibid.

170 *"The first dance"*: *AFC*, vol. 6, 67.

172 *"Were I now"*: *DJQA*, vol. 1, 256.

173 *"I am convinced"*: *AFC*, vol. 6, 20.

173 *"You can hardly"*: Ibid., 187.

174 *"This day was"*: Ibid., 151.

174 *"I have seen"*: Ibid., 67.

9: AT THE COURT OF ST. JAMES'S

175 *"too public"*: *AFC*, vol. 6, 186.

175 *"Why whom"*: Ibid., 118–19.

176 *"His Lordship"*: *Works*, vol. 8, 251–52.

176 *"When we arrived"*: Ibid., 256–59, June 1, 1785.

178 *"under £50"*: *AFC*, vol. 6, 187.

178 *"about five houses"*: Ibid., 213.

178 *"The wages"*: Ibid.

179 *without going into debt:* Ibid., 180.

179 *"Though a guinea"*: Ibid., 330.

179 *"what renders it"*: Ibid., 188–89.

180 *"We were placed"*: Ibid., 190.

180 *"I know I am"*: Ibid., 392.

181 *"When I reflect"*: *AFC*, vol. 7, 178–79.

181 *"In Europe"*: *AFC*, vol. 6, 332.

181 *"The foolish idea"*: *AFC*, vol. 7, 178.

181 *He first sensed:* *DA*, vol. 3, 182, n. 2.

181 *he presented:* *Works*, vol. 8, 268–72, June 17, 1785.

182 *"Although I have been"*: Ibid., 274, June 26, 1785.

182 *"as Abigail acknowledged"*: *AFC*, vol. 6, 200–1, June 30, 1785.

182 *John learned:* *Works*, vol. 8, 274–76, June 26, 1785.

182 *"The popular pulse"*: Ibid., 282, July 19, 1785.

182 *These tactics:* Bemis, *Diplomacy of the American Revolution.*

183 *The king turned his back:* *Works*, vol. 1, 420; Malone, *Thomas Jefferson and Rights of Man*, 55.

183 *"the two friends":* Malone, *Thomas Jefferson and Rights of Man,* 56.
184 *"Mr Smith":* AFC, vol. 6, 169–71, June 6, 1785.
184 *What transpired:* See Marshall, *Peabody Sisters,* 28–32.
185 *"strickt honour":* AFC, vol. 7, 237.
185 *The family at home:* AFC, vol. 6, 261–62, 285, 500–1; vol. 7, 57.
185 *"My dear neice":* AFC, vol. 6, 440.
185 *"Such* neglect*":* Ibid., 453.
185 *"showed about":* Ibid., 454–55, 504.
185 *He wrote to Abigail:* Ibid., 416–17, 427–31.
185 *in favor of her niece:* Tupper and Brown, *Grandmother Tyler's Book,* 76–80.
186 *"We live":* AFC, vol. 7, 342–43, Sept. 24, 1786.
186 *"overwhelmd":* AFC, vol. 6, 407, Oct. 5, 1786.
186 *"I congratulate you":* Ibid., 463, Nov. 20, 1786.
186 *Whether the two former soldiers:* Ibid., 267, n. 1.
187 *Even Abigail:* AFC, vol. 7, 217–220.
187 *"Some evil":* Ibid., 220.
187 *"I wish the Gentleman":* Ibid., 188.
187 *"I do not wonder":* AP, reel 368, July 19, 1786.
188 *"partner and fellow-travellor":* AFC, vol. 7, 333.
188 *"O that":* Ibid., 319–20, Sept. 15, 1786.
188 *"Such a storm":* Ibid., 329, 331, Sept. 3, 24, 1786.
188 *"Of civility":* Works, vol. 1, 425.
188 *"This is such":* AFC, vol. 6, 381.
189 *"Do you get out":* AFC, vol. 7, 34.
189 *"A very tasty picture":* AFC, vol. 6, 216.
189 *"my whole frame":* AFC, vol. 7, 16–17.
189 *Titian's* Death of Actaeon*:* AFC, vol. 6, 380.
189 *"laying aside all etiquette":* Works, vol. 4, 9, "Preface" (1819), Novanglus.
190 *"When Mr. Adams":* Berkin, *Jonathan Sewall,* 142.
190 *caused by a broken heart:* Ibid., 143.
190 *"rough as a little sailor":* AFC, vol. 8, 94, June 27, 1787.
190 *"If I had thought":* Ibid., 107–8, July 6, 1787.
191 *"that your goodness":* Ibid., 112, July 10, 1787.
191 *"such a flutter of joy":* AP, reel 370, Oct. 4, 1787.
191 *"I am a* Grandmamma*!":* AFC, vol. 8, 24, Apr. 26, 1787.
192 *"washes the little master":* Ibid., 28, Apr. 28, 1787.
192 *"so novel":* Warren-Adams, vol. 2, 272–73, Apr. 30, 1786.
192 *"It is easier":* Ibid.
193 *"I now write":* Works, vol. 4, 421–25, Jan. 24, 25, 1787.

IO: LOOKING HOMEWARD

194 *"Your Father":* AFC, vol. 7, 395–96.
195 *"Ignorant, wrestless":* Ibid., 455, Jan. 29, 1787.
195 *"The Massachusetts Assembly":* Adams-Jefferson, 156, Nov. 30, 1786.

195 *"I like a little rebellion": AFC,* vol. 7, 468, Feb. 22, 1787.

196 *John's primary arguments:* This section is informed by *Works,* vol. 4, "The Defence," 271–588; Elkins and McKitrick, *Age of Federalism,* 529–92; Shaw, *Character of John Adams,* 207–23: Howe, *Changing Political Thought,* 156–92; Wood, *Creation,* 576–82.

196 *Some theorists still:* Wood, *Creation,* 568.

196 *"I have read": Adams-Jefferson,* 174, Feb. 23, 1787.

196 *"natural aristocracy": Works,* vol. 4, 291–92.

197 *"it forms a body of men":* Ibid., 397.

197 *James Madison:* Wood, *Creation,* 582.

198 *John declined: AFC,* vol. 7, 442, Jan. 17, 1787.

199 *"not only for the infirm": CFA,* 314–15.

199 *"having visited Bath": AFC,* vol. 7, 414, Dec. 30, 1786.

199 *"Dont be solicitous":* Ibid., 412, Dec. 25, 1786.

199 *she and John set out:* AP, reel 370, July 18, 1787.

200 *"Can it be wondered": CFA,* 330.

200 *"oil-cloth cap":* Ibid.; *AFC,* vol. 9 (forthcoming), 155.

200 *"like a garden":* AP, reel 370, Oct. 10, 1787.

201 *"He Was well": AFC,* vol. 7, 464, Feb. 9, 1787; 253, July 14, 1786.

201 *"I loved her":* AP, reel 368, Aug. 1, 1786.

201 *Most distressing:* Ibid.

201 *William Smith was described:* AP, reel 365, Aug. 12, 1785; reel 366, Oct. 26, 1785.

201 *"The same air":* AP, reel 370, Nov. 17, 1787.

201 *"I give you":* Ibid., July 18, 1787.

201 *"deluded farmers": AFC,* vol. 7, 381, Oct. 22, 1786; 423–24, Feb. 2, 1787.

202 *"You will consider":* AP, reel 365, Aug. 10, 1785.

202 *"Excuse my being":* Ibid.

202 *"Begone Politicks!": AFC,* vol. 7, 68, Feb. 16, 1786.

202 *"Mr A would":* Ibid., 73, Feb. 21, 1786.

202 *"I long my dear":* AP, reel 370, May 14, 1787.

202 *"You never can:"* Ibid., June 29, 1787.

202 *"to come with Capt. Callahan":* AP, reel 371, Jan. 1, 1788.

202 *"I could wish":* AP, reel 370, Oct. 10, 1787.

202 *"He has asked":* AP, reel 371, Feb. 20, 1788.

202 *"This delay":* Ibid., Mar. 11, 1788.

203 *"Remember":* Ibid.

203 *"I rejoice":* Ibid.

203 *"My dear friend".* Ibid., Mar. 23, 1788.

11: THE MOST INSIGNIFICANT OFFICE

204 *"after a very tedious passage": AFC,* vol. 8, 278, July 7, 1788; 284, Aug. 6, 1788.

205 *"Mr Wibird":* Ibid., 285, Aug. 6, 1788.

205 *"There is not":* Ibid., 279, July 16, 1788.

206 *"Mrs. Clinton":* Ibid., 274, June 15, 1788.

207 *"You may be anxious":* Ibid., 279, July 16, 1788.

207 *"party cabals":* Ibid., 289, Aug. 13, 1788; 281, July 7, 1788.

208 *"the subject of Federal":* Ibid., 292, Aug. 20, 1788.

208 *"The happiness":* Ibid., 299, Sept. 28, 1788; 302, Oct. 5, 1788.

208 *"If you can":* Ibid., 302, Oct. 5, 1788.

209 *"I think every Seperation":* Ibid., 313, Dec. 3, 1788.

209 *"I am with the tenderest":* Ibid., 312; 324, Jan. 12, 1789; 341, May 1, 1789.

209 *"This place is":* Ibid., 316, Dec. 13, 1788.

209 *Smith reported:* Ibid., 319, Dec. 15, 1788.

210 *"he was sure":* Ibid., 318.

210 *By April:* Page Smith, *John Adams,* 740; Ferling, *John Adams,* 300–2.

211 *Happily arrived:* AFC, vol. 8, 332–33, Apr. 19, 1789.

211 *The renovations:* Torres, "Federal Hall Revisited."

211 *New York was:* Rothschild, *New York City Neighborhoods;* Blackmar, *Manhattan for Rent.*

212 *He acknowledged:* For John's address, see Maclay, *Sketches of Debate,* 2–4.

213 *"The eyes":* "For we must consider that we shall be a city upon a hill. The eyes of all people are upon us," *A Model of Christian Charity,* sermon spoken on board the *Arabella* in 1630.

213 *"Mr. Adams":* Maclay, *Sketches of Debate,* 5.

214 *"His Rotundity":* Fer Ling, *John Adams,* 304.

214 *"A solemn silence":* Ibid., 10.

214 *"the most insignificant office":* AFC, vol. 9 (forthcoming), Dec. 19, 1793.

215 *"President was conducted":* *Works of Fisher Ames,* vol. 1, 34, quoted in Maclay, *Sketches of Debate,* 17 n.

215 *"I have taken":* AFC, vol. 8, 341, May 1, 1789; 351, May 13, 1789.

216 *"If you think it best":* Ibid., 353, May 14, 1789.

216 *"Col Smith":* Ibid., 368, June 6, 1789.

217 *"I have a favour":* Ibid., 388.

218 *"Mrs. Washington":* Ibid., 388–89.

218 *"I could say":* Ibid., 332, Apr. 12, 1789.

218 *"Tho' you love":* Ibid., 335, Apr. 25, 1789.

218 *John answered: Works,* vol. 8, 495–96.

218 *"Gen Warren has":* Warren-Adams, vol. 2, 310–12, May 7, 1789.

218 *"You, my Dear":* Ibid.

219 *"There was no necessity":* Ibid., 313–14, May 29, 1789.

220 *"advice and consent":* Maclay, *Sketches of Debate,* 24–26.

220 "gracious": Ibid., 20, 22.

222 *"I have never before":* AFC, vol. 8, 397–98, Aug. 9, 1789.

222 *"respectfully curtsied":* Ibid., 397.

223 *"in the first place":* Ibid., 399, Aug. 9, 1789.

223 *"The News writers":* Ibid., 400, Aug. 8, 1789; 401, n. 4.

223 *"I have reason":* NL, 22–23.

224 *"I feel":* AFC, vol. 9, Oct. 3, 1790.

225 *Abigail did try:* Ibid., Aug. 14, 1790.

226 *asked John:* Ibid., Oct. 21, 1791.

226 *"There remains neither bush":* Ibid., Jan. 9, 1791.

227 *"I have run":* cited in Shaw, *Character of John Adams,* 231; AP, reel 115, June 4–14, 1790.

227 *"passion for":* Shaw, *Character of John Adams,* 233.

227 *She stopped: AFC,* vol. 9, May 12, 1791.

227 *"I have been":* Ibid., June 25, 1791.

228 *"I have always":* McCullough, *John Adams,* 430.

229 *"I thought so little": Adams-Jefferson,* 246, July 17, 1791.

229 *"I received":* Ibid., 247, July 29, 1791.

229 *The whole episode:* Ibid., 251, Aug. 30, 1791.

230 *"intermitting fever": AFC,* vol. 9, Mar. 20, 1792.

230 *"I have scarcly":* Ibid.

230 *"She is better":* Ibid., Mar. 10, 1792.

230 *"The Southern members":* Ibid., Apr. 20, 1792.

231 *"conversing amicably":* Twining, *Travels in America,* 37–39, cited in McCullough, *John Adams,* 455.

232 *"I am heir":* AP, transcript, Jan. 20, 1796. [Uncorrected transcripts of Adams Family letters that exist for the period Jan. 1794 to June 1797.]

232 *The succession:* Ferling, *John Adams,* 329–33; Page Smith, *John Adams,* 907–15.

12: SPLENDID MISERY

234 *"You ask me":* AP, reel 383, Jan. 14, 1797.

234 *"Quincy":* In 1792, the north precinct of Braintree was renamed Quincy after Abigail's grandfather.

234 *"I think":* AP, reel 383, Feb. 13, 1797.

234 *"I believe":* Ibid., Feb. 20, 1797.

234 *"It is best":* Ibid., Mar. 3, 1797.

235 *"The Congress":* Ibid., Feb. 2, 1797. The vice presidential salary was $25,000. See Ferling, *John Adams,* 334.

235 *"It is the will":* The lines are from Edward Young, *The Love of Fame,* satire 1, line 238, in AP, reel 383, Feb. 5, 1797. Earlier she wrote to John Quincy, "Joy dwells in these dear silent shades at Quincy and domestic pleasure in peace and tranquility; if I should be calld to qwit thee, with what regret shall I part from thee." AP, reel 382, Nov. 8, 1796.

235 *"Grain, and West India":* AP, reel 383, Jan. 30, 1797.

235 *"Taxes are due":* Ibid., Feb. 13, 1797.

236 *"At present":* Ibid., Mar. 18, 1797.

236 *"My expenses":* Ibid., Mar. 27 and 29, 1797.

236 *Susanna Hall:* Ibid., Feb. 19 and Mar. 25, 1797. Little is known about John Adams's mother, whose second husband, Lieutenant John Hall, is also a historical enigma. Abigail always wrote fondly of her mother-in-law. See *AFC,* vol. 1, 23, 60.

236 *"a Man wholy":* AP, reel 383, Jan. 28, 1797.

236 *"daughter":* AP, reel 382, Nov. 25, 1796.

236 *Their middle son, Charles:* "Charles *seems to be* very busy" (my italics): AP, reel 383, Jan. 5, 1797. Knowing that Charles would die of alcoholism less than four years later, it is tempting to read these references to him as enigmatic, as if there was a private family code that signified some secret about Charles to those who knew him well.

236 *"At my time":* AP, reel 382, Dec. 28, 1797.

236 *"I cannot live":* Ibid., Mar. 17, 22, and 27, 1797.

237 *"I have written":* AP, reel 384, Apr. 1, 3, 7, and 11, 1797.

237 *"The Stilness":* AP, reel 383, Mar. 9 and 5, 1797; reel 384, Apr. 7, 1797.

237 *"I think you":* AP, reel 383, Mar. 31, Apr. 6 and 12, 1797.

238 *"The sudden change":* AP, reel 383, Apr. 17, 1797.

238 *"My dear":* Ibid., Apr. 24, 1797.

238 *Mrs. Hall had died:* Polly (Mary) Smith was the daughter of Abigail's brother, William, and sister of Louisa, who lived with the Adamses and accompanied Abigail to Philadelphia.

238 *"My Mothers":* AP, reel 383, May 4, 1797. Abigail wrote to John of his mother's death on April 23, 1797 (AP, reel 383) and perhaps also in lost letters on April 21 and 22, to which John Adams's letter of May 4 refers.

238 *"constant run":* Abigail attributed the phrase to her aunt. "Mrs. [Cotton] Tufts once stiled my situation, splendid misery. She was not far from the Truth." *NL,* 89–90, May 16, 1797; 87, April 30, 1797.

239 *"Combination of circumstances":* AP, reel 382, paraphrasing *Hamlet,* act 1, scene 2, lines 187–88.

239 *"What is the expected":* AP, reel 382, Nov. 8, 1796.

239 *the Adams administration:* Elkins and McKitrick, *Age of Federalism,* 529; Kurtz, *Presidency of John Adams,* 340.

240 *"Beware of":* AP, reel 383, Jan. 28, 1797. John Adams's comments were even spicier. He called Hamilton the "bastard brat of a Scotch peddler." See Malone, *Ordeal of Liberty,* 330.

240 *"Pickering and all his colleagues":* *Works,* vol. 8, 523.

241 *"The weather":* AP, reel 385, June 3, 1797.

242 *"The appointments":* Ibid.

242 *"to reconcile you":* Ibid., July 3, 1797.

242 *"We have Letters":* *NL,* 125, Jan. 20, 1798.

243 *"I fear":* *NL,* 140–43, Mar. 5, 1798.

243 *Gerry's letter:* *Works,* vol. 9, 156, Mar. 5, 1798.

243 *"Whether the President":* *NL,* 143, Mar. 13, 1798.

243 *"In this situation":* *NL,* 148, Mar. 27, 1798.

244 *"In this Letter":* *NL,* 192, June 13, 1798, Oct. 1, 1800, 206, n. 4. John Adams's policy had succeeded.

244 *"The P[resident]":* *NL,* 127, Feb. 1–5, 1798.

245 *"The sentiments":* *Works,* vol. 8, 529–30.

245 *John Quincy prepared:* See AP, reel 384, passim.

246 *"creature of favour":* AP, reel 385, July 22, 1797.

246 *"It has given me":* AP, reel 386, Nov. 3, 1797.

246 *It was argued:* AP, reel 382, Nov. 8, 1796. Also see Page Smith, *John Adams,* 1034–35.

247 *"to his own Heart"*: Abigail Adams to Benjamin Bache, Mar. 17, 1798, Bache Papers, Castle Collection, American Philosophical Society, cited in Faÿ, *Two Franklins*, 339.

247 *"with inverted commas"*: AP, reel 386, Nov. 19, 1797.

247 *"I expected to be vilified"*: NL, 97, June 8, 1797.

247 *"praise for a few weeks"*: NL, 94, June 3, 1797.

247 *"Children or Grandchildren"*: NL, 116, Dec. 12, 1797; 118–19, Dec. 12, 1797; 120, Dec. 26, 1797.

247 *"Scarcly a day"*: NL, 112, Nov. 15, 1797; 116, Dec. 12, 1797; 154, Apr. 7, 1798.

247 *"is to calumniate"*: NL, 146–47, Mar. 20, 1798.

247 *"Nothing will have an Effect"*: NL, 164–66, Apr. 26, 1798.

248 *"the most violent"*: Page Smith, *John Adams*, 977.

248 *"This would contribute"*: NL, 172, May 10, 1798; 193, June 19, 1798; 196, June 23, 1798.

248 *Alien and Sedition Acts:* For the controversy over the Alien and Sedition Acts, see Bailyn and Hench, *Press and the American Revolution;* Levy, *Emergence of a Free Press and Jefferson and Civil Liberties;* John Miller, *Crisis in Freedom;* and James Morton Smith, *Freedom's Fetters.*

248 *"Let the vipers"*: NL, 200–1, July 9, 1798.

248 *"The greater part"*: NL, 216, Nov. 26, 1799.

249 *"You never felt"*: Adams-Jefferson, 346–47, June 30, 1813.

251 *"I cannot write you"*: AP, reel 385, July 6 and 14, 1797.

251 *"emboldened"*: Ibid., July 15, 1797.

251 *"If you think"*: NL, 185.

251 *"I feel myself"*: AP, reel 385, July 29, 1797.

251 *"midnight judges"*: NL, 232–34, Feb. 12 and 27, 1800.

252 *"charge to the grand jury"*: NL, 181, May 26, 1798. For John's address, see *Works*, vol. 9, 189.

252 *"the most alive"*: Bailyn, *Faces of Revolution*, 9.

252 *"To day will be"*: NL, 98–99, June 23, 1797.

253 *"I got through"*: NL, 199, July 3, 1798.

253 *"foreign Ministers"*: NL, 98, June 23, 100, July 6, 1797.

253 *"Have you any objection"*: NL, 247–48, Apr. 26, 1800.

254 *"Mine is very indifferent"*: Works, vol. 8, 601, Oct. 9, 1798.

254 *"This is our"*: AP, reel 392, Nov. 29, 1798.

255 *The three emissaries:* Elkins and McKitrick, *Age of Federalism*, 610–18.

256 *"Always disposed"*: Cited in Ibid., 618.

256 *"There has not been"*: AP, reel 393, Mar. 3, 1799.

257 *"been perfectly"*: NL, 224, Dec. 30, 1799.

258 *"No Man"*: NL, 222, Dec. 22, 1799.

258 *"Last frydays drawing Room"*: NL, 225, Dec. 30, 1799.

258 *"My reflections"*: NL, 89, May 16, 1797.

259 *"I want her"*: NL, 109, Oct. 22, 1797; 111, Nov. 15, 1797.

259 *"Mrs Smith informed"*: NL, 113, Nov. 28, 1797; 130–31, Feb. 6, 1797.

259 *"Before you receive this"*: Works, vol. 8, 617–18, Dec. 19, 1798.

260 *"This is a very"*: NL, 252–53, May 26, 1800.

260 *"Charles lives prettily": NL*, 89, May 16, 1797.
260 *"But I cannot": NL*, 89, May 16, 1797; 211, Oct. 31, 1799.
261 *"Opened her Mind": AP*, reel 396, Oct. 12, 1799.
261 *"Mercy & judgement": NL*, 255, Nov. 10, 1800.
261 *"I know," my much: NL*, 263, Jan. 15, 1801.
262 *"As I expected": NL*, 256–59, Nov. 21, 1800.
263 *"He was no mans Enemy": NL*, 262, Dec. 8, 1800.
263 *"What a lesson": NL*, 264–66, Feb. 7, 1801.
264 *"It is very formidable": NL*, 266.

13: THE ADAMSES RETIRE

266 *"Well, my dear": CFA*, vol. 2, 237, Nov. 13, 1800.
266 *Retirement meant:* The literature about women's sphere in early America is now vast. For a selection, see some classics: Norton, *Liberty's Daughters;* Cott, *Bonds of Womanhood;* Ulrich, *Good Wives.*
266 *"The only question": AP*, reel 399, Dec. 26, 1800.
266 *"I have commenced": AP*, reel 400, May 3, 1801.
267 *"One Load": DA*, vol. 3, 249–50.
268 *"To be attentive":* DeWindt, vol. 2, 213, Aug. 30, 1808.
268 *"My most profound Respects": Warren-Adams*, vol. 2, 155, Dec. 9, 1780.
269 *He was offended:* Ibid.
269 *he was hurt:* Zagarri, *Woman's Dilemma*, 150–55; Gelles, *Abigail Adams*, 55–60.
270 *"The President": AP*, reel 411, June 30, 1811.
271 *"I have declined":* Ibid.
271 *"that he might": AP*, reel 328, Aug. 20, 1800.
271 *"Should the lives": AP*, reel 411, Mar. 4, 1811.
272 *"I am very anxious":* Ibid.
272 *death warrant: Portia*, 150–72.
272 *"I have been": AP*, reel 411, June 21, 1811.
272 *"Hectic": AP*, reel 412, Sept. 24, 1811.
272 *"confined for 5 weeks": AP*, reel 411, June 21, 1800.
273 *"I have past": AP*, reel 412, Nov. 17, 1811.
273 *"is felt to be":* Sontag, *Illness as Metaphor*, 9.
274 *She admitted: AP*, reel 412, Nov. 26, 1811.
274 *"been called lately": AP*, reel 413, Apr. 7, 1812.
274 *"I cannot get": AP*, reel 416, July 1, 1813.
274 *"Years of affliction":* Ibid., Nov. 8, 1813.
275 *The story:* For instance, see Ellis, *American Sphinx*, 239; McCullough, *John Adams*, 600; Peterson, *Thomas Jefferson and the New Nation*, 853–54; Page Smith, *John Adams*, 1103–5; Shaw, *Character of John Adams*, 311.
275 *"I always loved": Adams-Jefferson*, vol. 2, 283–89.
276 *John's letter:* Ibid., 290.
276 *beloved and charming son Charles:* Ibid., 264, Mar. 24, 1801.
277 *"Just think":* Shaw Papers, reel 1, Feb. 26, 1815.

277 *The domestic and the public:* Elshtain, *Public Man;* Habermas, *Structural Transformation;* Okin, *Justice, Gender.*

278 *"Until you know":* Shaw Papers, reel 1, May 12, 1814, Feb. 26, 1815; AP, reel 416, Oct. 22, 1813.

14: TIME AND SILENCE

279 *"I have been reading":* DeWindt, 214, Aug. 30, 1808.

279 *"Always remember":* Ibid., 215, Feb. 2, 1809.

280 *"Such a race of mothers":* AP, reel 426, Nov. 12, 1815; Page Smith, *John Adams,* 1124.

280 *"they should always carry":* AP, reel 423, May 3, 1815; Page Smith, *John Adams,* 1117.

280 *"old age":* DeWindt, 220–21, Dec. 9, 1809.

280 *"You know not":* AP, reel 426, Aug. 27, 1815; Page Smith, *John Adams,* 1117.

281 *"his religious beliefs":* Adams-Jefferson, 318–92.

282 *"Take her":* DeWindt, 229, Oct. 23, 1814.

282 *"Yesterday completed":* Ibid.

282 *"Early instructed":* AP, reel 415, Apr. 20, 1813.

283 *"I have sometimes":* Shaw Papers, reel 1, Apr. 29, 1813.

283 *"I wish I could lie":* AP, reel 445, Nov. 1818; McCullough, *John Adams,* 623.

283 *"Had she lived":* John Quincy Adams, *Memoirs,* vol. 4, 157–58, 202, cited in Bemis, *John Quincy Adams,* 177.

283 *"I know well":* Adams-Jefferson, 529, Nov. 13, 1818.

283 *"the dear Partner":* Ibid., Oct. 20, 1818.

283 *"the life and letters":* DeWindt, 246, July 12, 1820.

284 *"The bitterness":* Page Smith, *John Adams,* 1122.

285 *"though the cost":* Ibid., 1129–30.

Bibliography

PRIMARY SOURCES

Abigail Adams Papers. American Antiquarian Society.

Adams Papers. Microfilm ed. 608 reels. Massachusetts Historical Society.

Cranch Papers. Microfilm ed. 2 reels. Library of Congress, Manuscripts Division.

Shaw Papers. Microfilm ed. 4 reels. Library of Congress, Manuscripts Division.

Adams, Charles Francis, ed. "Memoir of Mrs. Adams." In *Letters of Mrs. Adams, the Wife of John Adams*. 4th ed. Boston: Charles C. Little & James Brown, 1848.

———. *Correspondence Between John Adams and Mercy Warren*. New York: Arno Press, 1972.

———. *The Familiar Letters of John Adams and His Wife Abigail Adams During the Revolution*. Boston: Hurd & Houghton, 1876.

———. *Letters of Mrs. Adams, the Wife of John Adams*. 4th ed. Boston: Charles C. Little & James Brown, 1848.

———. *The Works of John Adams, Second President of the United States: With a Life of the Author, Notes and Illustrations, by His Grandson Charles Francis Adams*. 10 vols. Boston: Books for Libraries Press, 1851–1856.

Allen, David Grayson, ed. *The Diary of John Quincy Adams, 1788–1788*. 2 vols. Cambridge, Mass.: Harvard University Press, 1981.

Betts, Edwin M., and James Adam Bear, Jr., eds. *The Family Letters of Thomas Jefferson*. Charlottesville: University Press of Virginia, 1986.

Butterfield, L. H., et al., eds. *Adams Family Correspondence*. 8 vols. in print, 1 vol. forthcoming. *The Adams Papers:* Cambridge, Mass.: Harvard University Press, 1963–.

———. *Diary and Autobiography of John Adams*. 4 vols. *The Adams Papers.* Cambridge, Mass.: Harvard University, 1961.

———. *The Book of Abigail and John: Selected Letters of the Adams Family 1762–1784*. Cambridge, Mass.: Harvard University Press, 1975.

Butterfield, L. H., Wendell D. Garrett, and Marc Friedlaender. *The Earliest Diary of John Adams*. Cambridge, Mass.: Harvard University Press, 1966.

Butterfield, L. H., ed. *Letters of Benjamin Rush*. 2 vols. Princeton, N.J.: American Philosophical Society, 1951.

Cappon, Lester, ed. *The Adams-Jefferson Letters: The Complete Correspondence Between Thomas Jefferson and Abigail and John Adams*. 2 vols. Chapel Hill: University of North Carolina Press, 1959.

DeWindt, Caroline Smith, ed. *The Journal and Correspondence of Miss Adams, Daughter of John Adams*. New York: Wiley & Putnam, 1841.

"Diaries of Rev. William Smith and Dr. Cotton Tufts, 1738–1784." Massachusetts Historical Society, *Proceedings*, 3rd series, 2 (1908–1909): 444–70.

Fields, Joseph E., edr. *"Worthy Partner": The Papers of Martha Washington*. Westport, Conn.: Greenwood Press, 1994.

Ford, Worthington Chauncey, ed. *Writings of John Quincey Adams*. 7 vols. New York: Macmillan, 1913–1917.

Hogan, Margaret A., and C. James Taylor, eds. *My Dearest Friend: Letters of John and Abigail Adams*. Cambridge, Mass.: Harvard University Press, 2007.

Mitchell, Stewart, ed. *New Letters of Abigail Adams, 1788–1801*. Westport, Conn.: Greenwood Press, 1947.

Paltsits, Victor H., ed. "Berlin and the Prussian Court in 1798: Journal of Thomas B. Adams," *Bulletin of the New York Public Library* 19 (1915): 803–43.

Schutz, John A., and Douglass Adair, eds. *The Spur of Fame: Dialogues of John Adams and Benjamin Rush, 1805–1813*. San Marino, Calif.: Huntington Library, 1966.

Taylor, Robert J., Mary-Jo Kline, and Gregg Lint, eds. *Papers of John Adams*. 13 vols. in print, 1 vol. forthcoming. *The Adams Papers*. Cambridge, Mass.: Harvard University Press, 1977–.

Tupper, Frederick, and Helen Tyler Brown, eds. *Grandmother Tyler's Book: The Recollections of Mary Palmer Tyler, 1775–1866*. New York: G. P. Putnam's, 1925.

Warren, Mercy Otis. *History of the Rise, Progress, and Termination of the American Revolution*. 3 vols. 1805. Reprint, New York: AMS Press, 1970.

Warren-Adams Letters: Being Chiefly a Correspondence Among John Adams, Samuel Adams, and James Warren. 2 vols. 72–73. Boston: Massachusetts Historical Society, 1917–1925.

Washburn, Charles G., ed. "Letters of Thomas B. Adams to William Smith Shaw, 1799–1823." *Proceedings of the American Antiquarian Society*, new series, 27 (1917): 83–126.

SECONDARY SOURCES

Adams, Charles Francis, Jr. *Three Episodes of Massachusetts History: The Settlement of Boston Bay; The Antinomian Controversy; A Study of Church and Town Government*. 2 vols. 3rd edn. Boston: Houghton Mifflin, 1892.

Adams, William Howard. *The Paris Years of Thomas Jefferson*. New Haven, Conn.: Yale University Press, 1997.

Akers, Charles W. *Abigail Adams: An American Woman*. Boston: Little, Brown, 1980.

Allgor, Catherine. *A Perfect Union: Dolly Madison and the Creation of the American Nation*. New York: Henry Holt, 2006.

———. *Parlor Politics*. Charlottesville: University of Virginia Press, 2000.

Anderson, Howard, Philip B. Daghlian, and Irvin Ehrenpreis, eds. *The Familiar Letter in the Eighteenth Century*. Lawrence: University of Kansas. Press, 1966.

Anthony, Carl Sferrazza. *First Ladies: The Saga of the Presidents' Wives and Their Power, 1789–1961*. New York: William Morrow, 1990.

Appleby, Joyce. *Inheriting the Revolution: The First Generation of Americans*. Cambridge, Mass.: Harvard University Press, 2000.

Bailyn, Bernard. "Butterfield's Adams: Notes for a Sketch," *William and Mary Quarterly* 19 (Apr. 1962): 249–50.

———. *Education in the Formation of American Society: Needs and Opportunities for Study*. New York: W. W. Norton, 1960.

———. *Faces of Revolution: Personalities and Themes in the Struggle for American Independence*. New York: Alfred A. Knopf, 1990.

———. *The Ideological Origins of the American Revolution*. Cambridge, Mass.: Harvard University Press, 1967.

———. *The Ordeal of Thomas Hutchinson*. Cambridge, Mass.: Harvard University Press, 1974.

———. *To Begin the World Anew: The Genius and Ambiguities of the American Founders*. New York: Vintage, 2003.

———, and John B. Hench, eds. *The Press and the American Revolution*. Worcester, Mass.: American Antiquarian Society, 1980.

Bemis, Samuel Flagg. *The Diplomacy of the American Revolution*. New York: A. Appleton-Century, 1935.

———. *A Diplomatic History of the United States*. 3rd ed. New York: Henry Holt, 1950.

———. *John Quincy Adams and the Foundations of American Foreign Policy*. New York: W. W. Norton, 1949.

Berkin, Carol. *A Brilliant Solution: Inventing the American Constitution*. Orlando, Fla.: Harcourt, 2002.

———. *First Generations: Women in Colonial America*. New York: Hill and Wang, 1996.

———. *Jonathan Sewall: Odyssey of an American Loyalist*. New York: Columbia University Press, 1974.

———. *Revolutionary Mothers: Women in the Struggle for America's Independence*. New York: Alfred A. Knopf, 2005.

Blackmar, Elizabeth. *Manhattan for Rent, 1785–1850*. Ithaca, N.Y.: Cornell University Press, 1989.

Bloch, Ruth H. "American Feminine Ideals in Transition: The Rise of the Moral Mother, 1785–1815." *Feminist Studies* 4 (1978): 101–26.

———. "The Gendered Meanings of Virtue in Revolutionary America." *Signs: Journal of Women in Culture and Society* 13 (1987): 37–58.

Bonomi, Patricia U. *Under the Cope of Heaven: Religion, Society and Politics in Colonial America*. New York: Oxford University Press, 1987.

Boydston, Jeanne. *Home and Work: Housework, Wages, and the Ideology of Labor in the Early Republic*. New York: Oxford University Press, 1990.

Brewer, Holly. *By Birth or Consent: Children, Law, and the Anglo-American Revolution in Authority*. Chapel Hill: University of North Carolina Press, 2005.

Bridenbaugh, Carl. *Cities in Revolt: Urban Life in America, 1733–1776*. New York: Alfred A. Knopf, 1955.

Brodie, Fawn. *Thomas Jefferson: An Intimate History*. New York: W. W. Norton, 1974.

Brookhiser, Richard. *Alexander Hamilton*. New York: Free Press, 1999.

———. *Alexander Hamilton, American*. New York: Simon & Schuster, 1999.

————. *Founding Father: Rediscovering George Washington.* New York: Free Press, 1996.

Brown, Ralph Adams *The Presidency of John Adams.* Lawrence: University Press of Kansas, 1975.

Brown, Richard D. *Revolutionary Politics in Massachusetts: The Boston Committee of Correspondence and the Towns, 1772–1774.* New York: W. W. Norton, 1970.

Brown, Walt. *John Adams and the American Press.* Jefferson, N.C.: McFarland, 1995.

Buel, Joy Day, and Richard Buel, Jr. *The Way of Duty: A Woman and Her Family in Revolutionary America.* New York: W. W. Norton, 1984.

Burrows, Edwin G., and Mike Wallace. *A History of New York City to 1898.* New York: Oxford University Press, 1999.

Burstein, Andrew. *Jefferson's Secrets: Death and Desire at Monticello.* New York: Basic Books, 2005.

————. *The Inner Jefferson: Portrait of a Grieving Optimist.* Charlottesville: University of Virginia Press, 1995.

Butterfield, L. H. "The Papers of the Adams Family: Some Account of Their History." Massachusetts Historical Society, *Proceedings* 71 (1959): 328–56.

Caroli, Betty Boyd. *First Ladies.* New York: Oxford University Press, 1995.

Cash, Philip, Eric H. Christianson, and J. Worth Estes, eds. *Medicine in Colonial Massachusetts, 1620–1820.* Boston: Colonial Society of Massachusetts, 1980.

Casper, Scott E. *Constructing American Lives.* Chapel Hill: University of North Carolina Press, 1999.

Chernow, Ron. *Alexander Hamilton.* New York: Penguin Books, 2004.

Chodorow, Nancy. *The Reproduction of Mothering: Psychoanalysis and the Sociology of Gender.* Berkeley and Los Angeles: University of California Press, 1978.

Cohen, Lester H. "Explaining the Revolution: Ideology and Ethics in Mercy Otis Warren's Historical Theory." *William and Mary Quarterly* 37 (1980): 200–18.

————. "Mercy Otis Warren: The Politics of Language and the Aesthetics of Self." *American Quarterly* 35 (1983): 481–98.

Coontz, Stephanie. *Marriage, A History: From Obedience to Intimacy or How Love Conquered Marriage.* New York: Viking, 2005.

Cornell, Saul. *The Other Founders: Anti-Federalism and the Dissenting Tradition in America, 1788–1828.* Chapel Hill: University of North Carolina Press, 1999.

Cott, Nancy F. *The Bonds of Womanhood: "Woman's Sphere" in New England, 1780–1835.* New Haven, Conn.: Yale University Press, 1977.

Crane, Elaine Forman. *Ebb Tide in New England: Women, Seaports, and Social Change, 1630–1800.* Boston: Northeastern University Press, 1998.

————. *The Diary of Elizabeth Drinker: The Life Cycle of an Eighteenth-Century Woman.* Boston: Northeastern University Press, 1994.

————. *Killed Strangely: The Death of Laura Cornell.* Ithaca, N.Y.: Cornell University Press, 2003.

Craven, Wayne. *Colonial American Portraiture: The Economic, Religious, Social, Cultural, Philosophical, Scientific, and Aesthetic Foundations.* Cambridge: Cambridge University Press, 1986.

Cunliffe, Marcus. *George Washington: Man and Monument.* New York: New American Library, 1959.

Davies, Kate. *Catherine Macaulay and Mercy Otis Warren: The Revolutionary Atlantic and the Politics of Gender*. Oxford: Oxford University Press, 2005.

Day, Robert Adams. *Told in Letters: Epistolary Fiction Before Richardson*. Ann Arbor: University of Michigan Press, 1966.

Dayton, Cornelia Hughes. *Women Before the Bar: Gender, Law, and Society in Connecticut, 1639–1789*. Chapel Hill: University of North Carolina Press, 1995.

DePauw, Linda Grant. "The American Revolution and the Rights of Women: The Feminist Theory of Abigail Adams." In *The Legacy of the American Revolution*, edited by Larry R. Gerlach et al. Logan: Utah State University Press, 1978.

———. *Founding Mothers: Women of America in the Revolutionary Era*. Boston: Houghton Mifflin, 1975.

Diggins, John Patrick. *John Adams*. New York: Henry Holt, 2003.

Dull, Jonathan. *A Diplomatic History of the American Revolution*. New Haven, Conn.: Yale University Press, 1985.

East, Robert A. *John Quincy Adams: The Critical Years, 1785–1794*. New York: Bookman, 1962.

Elkins, Stanley, and Eric McKitrick. *The Age of Federalism: The Early American Republic, 1788–1800*. New York: Oxford University Press, 1993.

Ellis, Joseph J. *After the Revolution*. New York: W. W. Norton, 1979.

———. *American Sphinx: The Character of Thomas Jefferson*. New York: Alfred A. Knopf, 1997.

———. *Founding Brothers: The Revolutionary Generation*. New York: Alfred A. Knopf, 2001.

———. *His Excellency: George Washington*. New York: Alfred A. Knopf, 2004.

———. *Passionate Sage: The Character and Legacy of John Adams*. New York: W. W. Norton, 1993.

Elshtain, Jean Bethke. *Public Man, Private Woman: Women in Social and Political Thought*. Princeton, N.J.: Princeton University Press 1981.

Faÿ, Bernard. *The Two Franklins: Fathers of American Democracy*. New York: AMS Press, 1969.

Felstiner, Mary Lowenthal. *Out of Joint: A Private and Public Story of Arthritis*. Lincoln: University of Nebraska Press, 2005.

Fenn, Elizabeth A. *Pox Americana: The Great Smallpox Epidemic of 1775–82*. New York: Hill & Wang, 2001.

Ferling, John. *Adams vs. Jefferson: The Tumultuous Election of 1800*. New York: Oxford University Press, 2004.

———. *Almost a Miracle: The American Victory in the War of Independence*. New York: Oxford University Press, 2007.

———. *The First of Men: A Life of George Washington*. Knoxville: University of Tennessee Press, 1988.

———. *John Adams: A Life*. Knoxville: University of Tennessee Press, 1992.

———. *A Leap in the Dark: The Struggle to Create the American Republic*. New York: Oxford University Press, 2003.

———. *Setting the World Ablaze: Washington, Adams, Jefferson, and the American Revolution*. New York: Oxford University Press, 2000.

Fischer, David Hackett. *Albion's Seed: Four British Folkways in America*. New York: Oxford University Press, 1989.

————. *Growing Old in America*. Ithaca, N.Y.: Cornell University Press, 1977.

————. *Paul Revere's Ride*. New York: Oxford University Press, 1994.

————. *Washington's Crossing*. New York: Oxford University Press, 2004.

Flexner, James Thomas. *George Washington*. 4 vols. Boston: Little, Brown, 1965–1972.

————. *Washington: The Indispensable Man*. Boston: Little, Brown, 1974.

————. *Young Hamilton: A Biography*. Boston: Little, Brown, 1978.

Fliegelman, Jay. *Declaring Independence: Jefferson, Natural Language, and the Culture of Performance*. Stanford, Calif.: Stanford University Press, 1993.

————. *Prodigals and Pilgrims: The American Revolution Against Patriarchal Authority, 1750–1800*. New York: Cambridge University Press, 1982.

Foote, Henry Wilder. "Benjamin Blyth: Eighteenth-Century Artist." Massachusetts Historical Society, *Proceedings* 71 (1959): 64–65.

Forbes, Allyn B. "Abigail Adams, Commentator." Massachusetts Historical Society, *Proceedings* 66 (1966).

Forbes, Esther. *Paul Revere and the World He Lived In*. Boston: Houghton Mifflin, 1942.

Freeman, Joanne B. *Affairs of Honor: National Politics in the New Republic*. New Haven, Conn.: Yale University Press, 2001.

Gelles, Edith B. *"First Thoughts": Life and Letters of Abigail Adams*. New York: Twayne, 1998. Reprinted as *Abigail Adams: A Writing Life*. New York: Routledge, 2002.

————. *Portia: The World of Abigail Adams*. Bloomington: Indiana University Press, 1992.

Gillespie, Joanna Bowen. *The Life and Times of Martha Laurens Ramsay, 1559–1811*. Columbia: University of South Carolina Press, 2001.

Gilligan, Carol. *In a Different Voice: Psychological Theory and Women's Development*. Cambridge, Mass.: Harvard University Press, 1982.

Goldsmith, Elizabeth C., ed. *Writing the Female Voice: Essays on Epistolary Literature*. Boston: Northeastern University Press, 1989.

Greven, Philip J., Jr. *The Protestant Temperament: Patterns in Child Rearing, Religious Experience, and the Self in Early America*. New York: Alfred A. Knopf, 1977.

Habermas, Jurgen. *The Structural Transformation of the Public Sphere*. Cambridge, Mass.: Harvard University Press, 1989.

Hall, David D. *Worlds of Wonder, Days of Judgment: Popular Religious Belief in Early New England*. Cambridge, Mass.: Harvard University Press, 1990.

Harris, Wilhelmina S. *Adams National Historic Site*. Washington, D.C.: U.S. Government Printing Office, 1983.

Higginbotham, Don. *George Washington: Uniting a Nation*. Lanham, Md.: Rowman & Littlefield, 2002.

————. *The War of American Independence: Military Attitudes, Policies, and Practice, 1763–1789*. New York: Macmillan, 1971.

Hoffman, Ronald, and Peter J. Albert, eds. *Women in the Age of the American Revolution*. Charlottesville: University of Virginia Press, 1989.

Hoff-Wilson, Joan. "The Illusion of Change: Women and the American Revolution." In *The American Revolution: Explorations in the History of American Radicalism*. Edited by Alfred A. Young. DeKalb: Northern Illinois University Press, 1976.

Howe, John R., Jr. *The Changing Political Thought of John Adams*. Princeton, N.J.: Princeton University Press, 1966.

Hutson, James H. *John Adams and the Diplomacy of the American Revolution*. Lexington: University Press of Kentucky, 1980.

Illick, Joseph E. "John Quincy Adams: The Maternal Influence." *Journal of Psychohistory* 4 (1976): 185–95.

Isenberg, Nancy. *Fallen Founder: The Life of Aaron Burr*. New York: Viking, 2007.

Juster, Susan. *Disorderly Women: Sexual Politics and Evangelicalism in Revolutionary New England*. Ithaca, N.Y.: Cornell University Press, 1994.

Keller, Rosemary. *Patriotism and the Female Sex: Abigail Adams and the American Revolution*. New York: Carlson, 1994.

Kerber, Linda K. "The Republican Mother: Women and the Enlightenment—An American Perspective." *American Quarterly* 28 (1976): 187–205.

———. "Separate Spheres, Female Worlds, Women's Place: The Rhetoric of Women's History." *Journal of American History* 75 (1988): 9–39.

———. *Women of the Republic: Intellect and Ideology in Revolutionary America*. Chapel Hill: University of North Carolina Press, 1980.

Kitch, Sally L. *This Strange Society of Women: Reading the Letters and Lives of the Woman's Commonwealth*. Columbus: Ohio Star University Press, 1994.

Koehler, Lyle. *A Search for Power: The "Weaker Sex" in Seventeenth-Century New England*. Urbana: University of Illinois Press, 1980.

Kurtz, Stephen G. *The Presidency of John Adams: The Collapse of Federalism, 1795–1800*. Philadelphia: University of Pennsylvania Press, 1957.

Levin, Phyllis Lee. *Abigail Adams*. New York: St. Martin's, 1987.

Levy, Leonard W. *Emergence of a Free Press*. New York: Oxford University Press, 1985.

———. *Jefferson and Civil Liberties: The Darker Side*. Cambridge, Mass.: Harvard University Press, 1963.

Longmore, Paul K. *The Invention of George Washington*. Berkeley and Los Angeles: University of California Press, 1988.

Lovell, Margaretta M. *Art in a Season of Revolution: Painters, Artisans, and Patrons in Early America*. Philadelphia: University of Pennsylvania Press, 2005.

Maclay, William. *Sketches of Debate in the First Senate of the United States in 1789–90–92*. Edited by George W. Harris. Harrisburg, Penn.: Lane S. Hart, 1880.

Maier, Pauline. *American Scripture: Making the Declaration of Independence*. New York: Alfred A. Knopf, 1997.

———. *From Resistance to Revolution. Colonial Radicals and the Development of American Opposition to Britain, 1765–1776*. London: Routledge & Kegan Paul, 1973.

———. *The Old Revolutionaries: Political Lives in the Age of Samuel Adams*. New York: Alfred A. Knopf, 1980.

Main, Gloria L. "Gender, Work, and Wages in Colonial New England." *William and Mary Quarterly* 51 (1994): 39–66.

Malone, Dumas. *Jefferson and the Ordeal of Liberty*. Boston: Little, Brown, 1962.

———. *Thomas Jefferson and the Rights of Man*. Boston: Little, Brown, 1951.

Marshall, Megan. *The Peabody Sisters: Three Women Who Ignited American Romanticism*. Boston: Houghton Mifflin, 2005.

McCullough, David. *John Adams*. New York: Simon & Schuster, 2001.

———. *1776*. New York: Simon & Schuster, 2005.

Middlekauff, Robert. *Ancients and Axioms: Secondary Education in Eighteenth-Century New England*. New Haven, Conn.: Yale University Press, 1963.

———. *Benjamin Franklin and His Enemies*. Berkeley: University of California Press, 1996.

———. *The Glorious Cause: The American Revolution, 1763–1789*. New York: Oxford University Press, 1982.

———. *The Mathers: Three Generations of Puritan Intellectuals 1596–1728*. New York: Oxford University Press, 1971.

Miller, John C. *Crisis in Freedom: The Alien and Sedition Acts*. Boston: Little, Brown, 1951.

———. *The Federalist Era, 1789–1801*. New York: Harper & Row, 1960.

———. *Sam Adams: Pioneer in Propaganda*. Stanford, Calif.: Stanford University Press, 1960.

Miller, Perry. *Errand into the Wilderness*. New York: Harper & Brothers, 1956.

———. *The New England Mind: From Colony to Province*. Boston: Beacon, 1961.

———. *The New England Mind: The Seventeenth Century*. Boston: Beacon, 1961.

Morgan, Edmund S. *Benjamin Franklin*. New Haven, Conn.: Yale University Press, 2002.

———. *The Birth of the Republic 1763–1789*. Chicago: University of Chicago Press, 1956.

———. *The Genius of George Washington*. New York: W. W. Norton, 1977.

———. *The Meaning of Independence*. New York: W. W. Norton, 1976.

———. *The Puritan Family: Religion and Domestic Relations in Seventeenth-Century New England*. New York: Harper & Row, 1966.

———, and Helen M. Morgan. *The Stamp Act Crisis: Prologue to Revolution*. New York: Collier, 1962.

Morris, Richard B. *The Peacemakers: The Great Powers and American Independence*. New York: Harper & Row, 1965.

———. "Women's Rights in Early American Law." In *Studies in the History of American Law*. New York: Columbia University Press, 1964.

Musto, David F. "The Adams Family." Massachusetts Historical Society, *Proceedings* 93 (1981): 40–58.

———. "The Youth of John Quincy Adams." American Philosophical Society, *Proceedings* 113 (1969): 269–82.

Nagel, Paul C. *The Adams Women: Abigail and Louisa Adams, Their Sisters and Daughters*. New York: Oxford University Press, 1987.

———. *Descent from Glory: Four Generations of the John Adams Family*. New York: Oxford University Press, 1983.

———. *John Quincy Adams: A Public Life, a Private Life*. New York: Alfred A. Knopf, 1997.

Nash, Gary B. *The Urban Crucible: Social Change, Political Consciousness, and the Origins of the American Revolution*. Cambridge: Harvard University Press, 1979.

Nordholt, J. W. Schulte. *The Dutch Republic and American Independence*. Chapel Hill: University of North Carolina Press, 1982.

Norton, Mary Beth. "The Constitutional Status of Women in 1787." *Law and Inequality: A Journal of Theory and Practice* 6 (1988): 7–15.

———. "The Evolution of White Women's Experience in Early America." *American Historical Review* 89 (1984): 593–619.

———. *Founding Mothers and Fathers: Gendered Power and the Forming of American Society*. New York: Alfred A. Knopf, 1996.

———. *Liberty's Daughters: The Revolutionary Experience of American Women, 1750–1800*. Boston: Little, Brown, 1980.

Oberg, Barbara, and Doron Ben-Atar, eds. *Federalists Reconsidered*. Charlottesville: University of Virginia Press, 1998.

Offen, Karen. "Defining Feminism: A Comparative Historical Perspective." *Signs: Journal of Women in Culture and Society* 14 (1988): 119–57.

Okin, Susan. *Justice, Gender and the Family*. New York: Basic Books, 1989.

Oliver, Andrew. *Portraits of Abigail and John Adams*. Cambridge, Mass.: Harvard University Press, 1967.

Pasley, Jeffrey L., Andres W. Robertson, and David Waldstreicher. *Beyond the Founders: New Approaches to the Political History of the Early American Republic*. Chapel Hill: University of North Carolina Press, 2004.

Pateman, Carole. *The Sexual Contract*. Stanford, Calif.: Stanford University Press, 1988.

Pennebaker, James W. "Confession, Inhibition, and Disease," *Advances in Experimental Social Psychology* 22 (1989): 211–44.

———. *Opening Up: The Healing Power of Confiding in Others*. New York: William Morrow, 1990.

Perkins, Bradford. *The First Rapprochement: England and the United States, 1795–2005*. Berkeley: University of California Press, 1955.

Peterson, Merrill D. *Adams and Jefferson: A Revolutionary Dialogue*. Oxford: Oxford University Press, 1976.

———. *Thomas Jefferson and the New Nation*. New York: Oxford University Press, 1970.

Pocock, J. G. A. *Virtue, Commerce and History: Essays on Political Thought and History, Chiefly in the Eighteenth Century*. New York: Cambridge University Press, 1985.

Racine, Laurel A. *The Birthplaces of Presidents John Adams and John Quincy Adams: Adams National Historical Park*. Vol. 1. *Historical Data*. Quincy, Mass.: National Park Service, 2001.

Rakove, Jack N. *The Beginnings of National Politics: An Interpretive History of the Continental Congress*. New York: Alfred A. Knopf, 1979.

———. *James Madison and the Creation of the American Republic*. 2d ed. New York: Longman, 2002.

———. *Original Meanings: Politics and Ideas in the Making of the Constitution*. New York: Alfred A. Knopf, 1996.

Raphael, Ray. *A People's History of the American Revolution: How Common People Shaped the Fight for Independence*. New York: Perrenial, 2002.

Rebora, Carrie, et al. *John Singleton Copley in America*. New York: Abrams, 1995.

Renier, Jacqueline. *From Virtue to Character: American Childhood, 1775–1850*. New York: Twayne, 1996.

Rice, Howard C., Jr. *The Adams Family in Auteuil 1784–1785: As Told Through the Letters of Abigail Adams*. Boston: Massachusetts Historical Society, 1956.

————. *Thomas Jefferson's Paris*. Princeton, N.J. Princeton University Press, 1976.

Rich, Adrienne. *Of Woman Born: Motherhood as Experience and Institution*. New York: W. W. Norton, 1986.

Richards, Jeffrey. *Mercy Otis Warren*. New York: Twayne, 1995.

Richards, Leonard L. *The Life and Times of Congressman John Quincy Adams*. New York: Oxford University Press, 1986.

Roof, Katharine Metcalf. *Colonel William Smith and Lady*. Boston: Houghton Mifflin, 1929.

Rothman, Ellen K. *Hands and Hearts: A History of Courtship in America*. New York: Basic Books, 1984.

Rothschild, Nan A. *New York City Neighborhoods: The Eighteenth Century*. San Diego: Academic Press, 1990.

Ruddick, Sara. *Maternal Thinking: Toward a Politics of Peace*. Boston: Beacon, 1989.

Salmon, Marylynn. *Women and the Law of Property in Early America*. Chapel Hill: University of North Carolina Press, 1986.

Schiff, Stacy. *A Great Improvisation: Franklin, France, and the Birth of America*. New York: Henry Holt, 2005.

Schochet, Gorden. *Patriarchalism in Political Thought*. Oxford: Basil Blackwell, 1975.

Scholten, Catherine M. *Childbearing in American Society: 1650–1850*. New York: New York University Press, 1985.

Shammas, Carole, Marylynn Salmon, and Michael Dahlin. *Inheritance in America: From Colonial Times to the Present*. New Brunswick, N.J.: Rutgers University Press, 1987.

Shaw, Peter: *The Character of John Adams*. Chapel Hill: University of North Carolina Press, 1976.

Shepard, Jack. *Cannibals of the Heart: A Personal Biography of Louisa Catherine and John Quincy Adams*. New York: McGraw-Hill, 1980.

Shipton, Clifford K. *New England Life in the Eighteenth Century*. Cambridge, Mass.: Harvard University Press, 1995.

————, et al. *Sibley's Harvard Graduates*. Boston: Massachusetts Historical Society, 1873–.

Shryock, Richard Harrison. *Medicine and Society in America, 1660–1860*. New York: New York University Press, 1960.

Shy, John. *A People Numerous and Armed: Reflections on the Military Struggle for American Independence*. Ann Arbor: University of Michigan Press, 1990.

Silverman, Kenneth. *The Life and Times of Cotton Mather*. New York: Harper & Row, 1984.

Skemp, Sheila L. *Benjamin and William Franklin: Father and Son, Patriot and Loyalist*. New York: St. Martin's, 1994.

————. *William Franklin: Son of a Patriot, Servant of a King*. New York: Oxford University Press, 1990.

Smith, Billy. *Life in Early Philadelphia*. University Park: Pennsylvania State University, 1995.

Smith, James Morton. *Freedom's Fetters: The Alien and Sedition Laws and American Civil Liberties*. Ithaca, N.Y.: Cornell University Press, 1956.

Smith, Page. *Daughters of the Promised Land: Women in American History*. Boston: Little, Brown, 1970.

————. *John Adams*. 2 vols. New York: Doubleday, 1962.

Sontag, Susan. *Illness as Metaphor*. New York: Farrar, Straus, and Giroux 1977.

Sprague, Waldo Chamberlain. *The President John Adams and President John Quincy Adams Birthplaces*. Quincy, Mass.: Quincy Historical Society, 1959.

Stannard, David E. *The Puritan Way of Death*. New York: Oxford University Press, 1977.

Stinchcombe, William C. *The American Revolution and the French Alliance*. Syracuse, N.Y. Syracuse University Press, 1969.

————. *The XYZ Affair*. Westport, Conn.: Greenwood Press, 1980.

Strasser, Susan. *Never Done: A History of American Housework*. New York: Pantheon, 1982.

Tanselle, G. Thomas. *Royall Tyler*. Cambridge, Mass.: Harvard University Press, 1967.

Thompson, C. Bradley. *John Adams and the Spirit of Liberty*. Lawrence: University Press of Kansas, 1998.

Thorne, Barrie, ed., with Marilyn Yalom. *Rethinking the Family*. New York: Longman, 1982.

Torres, Louis. "Federal Hall Revisited." *Journal of the Society of Architectural Historians* 29 (1970): 327–38.

Twining, Thomas. *Travels in America a Hundred Years Ago*. New York: Harper Bros., 1894.

Ulrich, Laurel Thatcher. *The Age of Homespun: Objects and Stories in the Creation of an American Myth*. New York: Vintage, 2001.

————. *Good Wives: Images and Reality in the Lives of Women in Northern New England, 1650–1750*. New York: Oxford University Press, 1980.

————. *A Midwife's Tale: The Life of Martha Ballard, Based on Her Diary, 1785–1812*. New York: Alfred A. Knopf, 1990.

————. "Wheels, Looms, and the Gender Division of Labor in Eighteenth-Century New England." *William and Mary Quarterly* 55 (1998): 3–38.

Waldstreicher, David. *In the Midst of Perpetual Fetes: The Making of American Nationalism, 1776–1820*. Chapel Hill: University of North Carolina Press, 1997.

————. *Runaway America: Benjamin Franklin, Slavery, and the American Revolution*. New York: Hill & Wang, 2004.

Waters, John J., Jr. *The Otis Family in Provincial and Revolutionary Massachusetts*. Chapel Hill: University of North Carolina Press, 1968.

Wiencek, Henry. *An Imperfect God: George Washington, His Slaves, and the Creation of America*. New York: Farrar, Straus, and Giroux, 2003.

Will, George. *Inventing America: Jefferson's Declaration of Independence*. New York: Doubleday, 1978.

Wilson, Daniel M. *Colonel John Quincy of Mt. Wollaston, 1689–1767, Public Character of New England's Provincial Period*. Boston: George Ellis, 1909.

Winterer, Caroline. *The Culture of Classicism: Ancient Greece and Rome in American Intellectual Life, 1780–1910*. Baltimore: Johns Hopkins University Press, 2002.

————. *The Mirror of Antiquity: American Women and the Classical Tradition, 1750–1900.* Ithaca, N.Y. Cornell University Press, 2007.

Withey, Lynne. *Dearest Friend: A Life of Abigail Adams.* New York: Free Press, 1981.

Wood, Gordon S. *The Americanization of Benjamin Franklin.* New York: Penguin 2004.

————. *The American Revolution: A History.* New York: Modern Library, 2002.

————. *The Creation of the American Republic, 1776–1787.* Chapel Hill: University of North Carolina Press, 1969.

————. *The Radicalism of the American Revolution.* New York: Alfred A. Knopf, 1992.

Wright, Esmund. *Franklin of Philadelphia.* Cambridge, Mass.: Harvard University Press, 1986.

Young, Alfred F. *The Shoemaker and the Tea Party: Memory and the American Revolution.* Boston: Beacon, 1999.

Zagarri, Rosemarie. *Revolutionary Backlash: Women and Politics in the Early American Republic.* Philadelphia: University of Pennsylvania Press, 2007.

————. *A Woman's Dilemma: Mercy Otis Warren and the American Revolution.* Wheeling, Ill.: Harlan Davidson, 1995.

Zobel, Hiller B. *The Boston Massacre.* New York: W. W. Norton, 1970.

Index

Note: Page numbers in *italics* refer to illustrations.